CELEBRITY DEATH CERTIFICATES 3

ALSO BY M. F. STEEN

Celebrity Death Certificates
(McFarland, 2003)

Celebrity Death Certificates 2
(McFarland, 2005)

CELEBRITY DEATH CERTIFICATES 3

M. F. Steen

McFarland & Company, Inc., Publishers
Jefferson, North Carolina, and London

Acknowledgments: The success of *Celebrity Death Certificates* and *Celebrity Death Certificates 2* was not one person's effort. I would like to acknowledge the work, support and encouragement of the following: Bill Schneid, Judi Adams, Steve Goldstein, Bernard Johnson, David Lotz, Karen McHale, Scott Michaels, R. Bart Mruz, Erick Tilton, Ron McConnell, and Socorro Gutierrez.

LIBRARY OF CONGRESS CATALOGUING-IN-PUBLICATION DATA

Celebrity death certificates 3 / [compiled by] M. F. Steen.
p. cm.
Includes bibliographical references.

ISBN 978-0-7864-5935-3
softcover : 50# alkaline paper ∞

1. Actors—United States—Death. 2. Celebrities—United States—Death. 3. Death certificates—United States.
I. Steen, M. F. (Michael F.), 1946– II. Title.
PN2285.C3433 2010 791.092′273—dc22 2010018797

British Library cataloguing data are available

©2010 M. F. Steen. All rights reserved

No part of this book may be reproduced or transmitted in any form or by any means, electronic or mechanical, including photocopying or recording, or by any information storage and retrieval system, without permission in writing from the publisher.

Cover images: lily ©2010 Shutterstock;
border ©2010 EclectiCollections Publishing Ltd.

Manufactured in the United States of America

McFarland & Company, Inc., Publishers
Box 611, Jefferson, North Carolina 28640
www.mcfarlandpub.com

To the people who love and support me every day:
Bill, Marian, Judi and Judi
Also to my Friday Letter Club:
Sharon Parker, Glen Payne, Bertrina DeRouen,
Winifred Kulhanek, Marian Shoenwether,
Pastor Davie Pellitier and the Meierhenry Family;
Howard (age 102), Linda and Roger

Table of Contents

Preface 1

Edie Adams 4
Stella Adler 5
Renée Adorée 6
Eddie Albert 7
Edward Albert 8
Peter Allen 9
Steve Allen 10–11
Robert Altman 12
Dana Andrews 13
Pier Angeli 14–15
Robert Armstrong 16
Edward Arnold 17
Bea Arthur 18
Agnes Ayres 19
Raymond Bailey 20
Suzan Ball 21
Gene Barry 22
Judith Barsi 23
Warner Baxter 24
Wallace Beery 25
Ralf Belmont 26
Bea Benaderet 27
Joey Bishop 28
Erma Bombeck 29
Frank Brill 30
Sorrell Brooke 31
Roscoe Lee Brown 32
Katherine Browne 33
Lenny Bruce 34
Smiley Burnette 35
Judy Canova 36
Kathryn Card 37
Ron Carey 38
George Carlin 39
Karen Carpenter 40–41

Allan Carr 42
Charles Chaplin, Jr. 43
Virginia Christine 44
Andy Clyde 45
Lee J. Cobb 46
Nicholas Colasanto 47
Chester Conklin 48
Darlene Conley 49
Chuck Connors 50
Richard Conte 51
Bert Convy 52
Merian C. Cooper 53
Wendell Corey 54
Aneta Corsault 55
Joseph Cotten 56
Mary Jane Croft 57
Pauline Curley 58
Esther Dale 59
Royal Dano 60
Richard Deacon 61
Yvonne DeCarlo 62
Sandra Dee 63
Don DeFore 64
Dom DeLuise 65
John Derek 66
Joe Derita 67
Jenny Dolly and Yansci Dolly 68
Ann Doran 69
Mignon G. Eberhart 70
Herb or Herbert Edelman 71
Ross Elliott 72
Muriel Evans 73
Farrah Fawcett 74
Peter Finch 75
Larry Fine 76
George Fitzmaurice 77

Paul Fix 78
Wayland Flowers 79
Nina Foch 80
Glenn Ford 81
Michael Fox 82
Mary Frann 83–84
Friz Freleng 85
Bobby Fuller 86
Marvin Gaye 87
Will Geer 88
George Gershwin 89
Estelle Getty 90
Alice Ghostley 91
Jerry Giesley 92
Samuel Goldwyn 93
Thomas Gomez 94
Gerald Gordon 95
Leo Gordon 96
Sandra Gould 97
Robert Goulet 98
Sid Grauman 99
Sydney Greenstreet 100
Jane Greer 101
Merv Griffin 102
David Groh 103
William Haines 104
Conrad L. Hall 105
Carrie Hamilton 106
Neil Hamilton 107
Oliver Hardy 108
Vinton Hayworth 109
Ted Healy 110
Emmette Evan Heflin 111
Leona Helmsley 112
Margaux Hemingway 113–114
Shirley Hemphill 115–116

Charlton Heston   117
Dana Hill   118
Jonathan Hole   119
Fred Holliday   120
John Holmes   121
Edward Everett Horton   122
Betty Hutton   123
Michael Jackson   124–125
Brion James   126
Dennis James   127
Michael Jeter   128–129
Henry Jones   130
Spike Jones   131
Janis Joplin   132–133
Stanley Kamel   134
Andy Kaufman   135
Buster Keaton   136
DeForest Kelley   137
Edgar Kennedy   138
Eartha Kitt   139
Ted Knight   140
Harvey Korman   141
Elsa Lanchester   142
Carole Landis   143
Charles Lane   144
Harry Langdon   145
Charles Laughton   146
Stan Laurel   147
Anthony Lee   148–149
Philip Leeds   150
Queenie Leonard   151
Terry Lester   152
Oscar Levant   153
Peter Lorre   154
Allen Ludden   155
James Luisi   156
Charles Macaulay   157
Karl Malden   158
Louis Malle   159
Frederic March   160
Hal March   161
Herbert Marshall   162

Dick Martin   163
Roddy McDowall   164
Cameron Mitchell   165
Vic Mizzy   166
Ricardo Montalban   167
Elizabeth Montgomery   168
Harry Monty   169
Frank Morgan   170
Gary Morton   171
Richard Mulligan   172
Gene Nelson   173
Evelyn Nesbit   174
Paul Newman   175
Mabel Normand   176
Paul Novak   177
Merle Oberon   178
Dennis O'Keefe   179
Dick O'Neill   180
Bette Page   181
Jack Palance   182
Larry Parks   183
Robert Pastorelli   184–185
Anthony Perkins   186
Jean Peters   187
Charles Pierce   188
Suzanne Pleshette   189
Don Porter   190
Tom Poston   191
Richard Powell   192
Richard Pryor   193
Anne Ramsey   194
David Rappaport   195
Virginia Rappe   196
Gene Raymond   197
Steve Reeves   198
Charles Nelson Reilly   199
Duncan Renaldo   200
Brad Renfro   201–202
Stafford Repp   203
Marjorie Reynolds   204
Minnie Riperton   205
Theodore Roberts   206

Rochester   207
Charles Buddy Rogers   208
Roxie Roker   209
Gilbert Roland   210
Ruth Roman   211
Ruth Rose   212
Isabel Sanford   213
Ernest Schoedsack   214
Del Shannon *see* Charles
   Weedon Westover
Sidney Sheldon   215
Jack Soo   216
Kenneth Steadman   217
Jess Stearn   218
McLean Stevenson   219
Anita Mary Stewart   220
Lewis Stone   221
Barry Sullivan   222
Patrick Swayze   223–224
Carl Switzer   225
William Taylor   226
Jess Kenneth Tobey   227
William Tuttle   228
Lee Van Cleef   229
Harry von Zell   230
Kim Anne Walker   231
Michael Wayne   232
Lawrence Welk   233
Charles Weedon Westover
   (Del Shannon)   234
Richard Widmark   235
Dick Wilson   236
Arthur Wilson   237
Joy Windsor   238
Stanley Winston   239
Thelma Wolpa   240
Jane Wyatt Ward   241
Ed Wynn   242

Biographical Notes   243

Preface

A death certificate is an intriguing document. On one page, a person's life is encapsulated. It's all there! Where a person was born and to whom, in the case of adoption by whom; amount of education and length of career, place of residence; whether the person was married at the time of death, and, if so, to whom; what caused the death; and finally what happened to the "remains."

A death certificate is a state-originated document. The information required on the certificate may vary from year to year and state to state.

Each state views a death certificate in a different way. California and Connecticut think of them as public documents, available to anyone. California is now issuing two different types of death certificates. One is a standard full certificate without any reservations. The other is one which indicates it is "For information only, not for identification."

Other states, such as Texas, New York, and Arizona do not consider death certificates public documents. In those states, death certificates are officially available only to family members and others showing a direct need for a copy. Satisfying curiosity is not considered a need.

Florida will offer a death certificate to anyone, but the cause of death is not disclosed for 50 years.

This book contains death certificate of Hollywood's famous and infamous. You will find examples from the Silent Era; some from Hollywood's Golden Era; and some from recent times. You will find people who worked behind the scenes, or who became famous on the small screen, in song, or by the written word.

Many famous people, whose certificates would have been interesting to include, died in New York. The restrictions mentioned above prevented their inclusion.

The certificates are presented in alphabetical order by familiar name. Otherwise, people like Peter Allen (whose certificate lists his name as

Peter Richard Woolnough) and Beatrice Arthur (Bernice Saks) would be difficult to find.

In the case of *Celebrity Death Certificates* and *Celebrity Death Certificates 2*, selection was a pick and choose effort. It was more a collaborative effort. Friends and relatives all gave me input as to whom should be included. Plus, I selected some of my favorites.

For *Celebrity Death Certificates 3*, the selection took on a different form.

This book includes the balance of my collection as well as all of the people who had died since *Celebrity Death Certificates 2*.

Collecting death certificates is a bit unusual for a hobby. A little imagination could lead one to collect the death certificates of celebrities, sports figures, authors, or presidents of the United Sates, to mention just a few of the many options.

I started my collection in July 1991. I had seen a book of death certificates of celebrities and presidents. I had a hard time finding the relevance of the two subjects.

My collection began with Marilyn Monroe and nine other of my favorite celebrities. I had worked at Westwood Memorial Park and Mortuary since 1974. I had assisted her fans on a daily basis. I knew how important she was to them. Many of them were not even born when she died, so clearly her legacy continues.

Death certificates are available from the county health department in the state where the death occurred. The fees range from $5.00 to nearly $30.00 per copy. They change from time to time, so one needs to check before ordering. Many states offer applications for death certificates online.

The state health department is another place to order death certificates. In many instances, getting them from the state takes a lot longer than ordering from the county health department. Currently if one orders a death certificate from the state of California, the wait time is between nine months and one year. Hardly what I would call a "timely manner."

The county or state often will not search for a certificate if the information provided is incorrect or incomplete. This can cause a guessing game, particularly where women are concerned. Was the certificate filed under the birth name, professional name, or married name? Sometimes several attempts may be necessary to get it right.

If you order certificates from the same place over a period of time, you may develop a relationship with the person filling your order. This can be beneficial if a problem or question should arise.

Online www.imdb.com (Internet Movie Database) is a good place to start your research. Many times, the birth name is provided as well as the name of his or her spouse(s).

When you have the possible names, then check Social Security death records. Normally, what Social Security shows for the name is how the individual's death certificate was filed.

California has changed the way death certificates are created and filed. They are all done electronically which eliminates the difference in handwriting for the cause of death, as well as the physician's signature and the embalmer's signature.

THE DEATH CERTIFICATES

STATE OF CALIFORNIA
CERTIFICATION OF VITAL RECORD
COUNTY OF LOS ANGELES DEPARTMENT OF PUBLIC HEALTH

CERTIFICATE OF DEATH — STATE OF CALIFORNIA

STATE FILE NUMBER: 3200819042964

DECEDENT'S PERSONAL DATA
- 1. NAME OF DECEDENT — FIRST: EDIE
- 3. LAST: ADAMS
- 4. DATE OF BIRTH: 04/16/1927
- 5. AGE: 81
- 6. SEX: F
- 9. BIRTH STATE/FOREIGN COUNTRY: PA
- 10. SOCIAL SECURITY NUMBER: 102-22-7556
- 11. EVER IN U.S. ARMED FORCES?: NO
- 12. MARITAL STATUS: DIVORCED
- 7. DATE OF DEATH: 10/15/2008
- 8. HOUR: 0245
- 13. EDUCATION: BACHELOR
- 16. DECEDENT'S RACE: WHITE
- 17. USUAL OCCUPATION: ACTRESS
- 18. KIND OF BUSINESS OR INDUSTRY: ENTERTAINMENT
- 19. YEARS IN OCCUPATION: 58

USUAL RESIDENCE
- 20. DECEDENT'S RESIDENCE: 8040 OKEAN TERRACE
- 21. CITY: LOS ANGELES
- 22. COUNTY: LOS ANGELES
- 23. ZIP CODE: 90046
- 24. YEARS IN COUNTY: 55
- 25. STATE: CA

INFORMANT
- 26. INFORMANT'S NAME, RELATIONSHIP: JOSHUA D. MILLS, SON
- 27. MAILING ADDRESS: 1201 N. CRESCENT HEIGHTS BLVD #203, LOS ANGELES, CA 90046

SPOUSE AND PARENT INFORMATION
- 31. NAME OF FATHER — FIRST: SHELDON
- 32. MIDDLE: ALONZO
- 33. LAST: ENKE
- 34. BIRTH STATE: PA
- 35. NAME OF MOTHER — FIRST: ADA
- 37. LAST (Maiden): ADAMS
- 38. BIRTH STATE: PA

FUNERAL DIRECTOR / LOCAL REGISTRAR
- 39. DISPOSITION DATE: 10/23/2008
- 40. PLACE OF FINAL DISPOSITION: FOREST LAWN MEMORIAL PARK, 6300 FOREST LAWN DRIVE, LOS ANGELES, CA 90068
- 41. TYPE OF DISPOSITION: BU
- 42. SIGNATURE OF EMBALMER: SCOTT FOW
- 43. LICENSE NUMBER: 8257
- 44. NAME OF FUNERAL ESTABLISHMENT: FOREST LAWN MEMR PRKS & MTYS
- 45. LICENSE NUMBER: FD 904
- 46. SIGNATURE OF LOCAL REGISTRAR: JONATHAN FIELDING, MD
- 47. DATE: 10/21/2008

PLACE OF DEATH
- 101. PLACE OF DEATH: WEST HILLS HOSPITAL & MEDICAL CENTER
- 102: IP
- 104. COUNTY: LOS ANGELES
- 105. FACILITY ADDRESS: 7300 MEDICAL CENTER DRIVE
- 106. CITY: WEST HILLS

CAUSE OF DEATH
- 107. CAUSE OF DEATH:
  - (A) IMMEDIATE CAUSE: CARDIOPULMONARY ARREST — MINS
  - (B) RESPIRATORY FAILURE — DAYS
  - (C) ADENOCARCINOMA OF THE COLON WITH METASTASIS — WKS
- 108. DEATH REPORTED TO CORONER: NO
- 109. BIOPSY PERFORMED?: NO
- 110. AUTOPSY PERFORMED?: NO
- 112. OTHER SIGNIFICANT CONDITIONS: NONE
- 113. WAS OPERATION PERFORMED: NO
- 113A. IF FEMALE, PREGNANT IN LAST YEAR?: NO

PHYSICIAN'S CERTIFICATION
- 114. CERTIFY DEATH OCCURRED AT HOUR, DATE, PLACE STATED
- 115. SIGNATURE AND TITLE OF CERTIFIER: GEORGE J DANIAL, DO
- 116. LICENSE NUMBER: 20A4720
- 117. DATE: 10/20/2008
- (A) Decedent Attended Since: 10/11/2008
- (B) Decedent Last Seen Alive: 10/14/2008
- 118. TYPE ATTENDING PHYSICIAN'S NAME, MAILING ADDRESS: GEORGE J DANIAL, DO, 4621 RUBIO AVE, ENCINO, CA 91436

CORONER'S USE ONLY
- 119. MANNER OF DEATH: (blank)

INFORMATIONAL, NOT A VALID DOCUMENT TO ESTABLISH IDENTITY

State Registrar certification: *012008000914294* *HD1427234*

This is a true certified copy of the record filed in the County of Los Angeles Department of Public Health if it bears the Registrar's signature in purple ink.

Jonathan E Fielding MD
Director of Public Health and Registrar

DATE ISSUED: DEC 10 2008

This copy not valid unless prepared on engraved border displaying seal and signature of Registrar.

ANY ALTERATION OR ERASURE VOIDS THIS CERTIFICATE

CERTIFICATION OF VITAL RECORD

COUNTY OF LOS ANGELES • REGISTRAR-RECORDER/COUNTY CLERK

CERTIFICATE OF DEATH
STATE OF CALIFORNIA
USE BLACK INK ONLY

State File Number: 39219054155

DECEDENT PERSONAL DATA

- 1A. Name of Decedent—First (Given): STELLA
- 1C. Last (Family): ADLER
- 2A. Date of Death—Mo, Day, Yr: DECEMBER 21, 1992
- 2B. Hour: 0600
- 3. Sex: F
- 4. Race: CAUCASIAN
- 5. Hispanic—Specify: No (X)
- 6. Date of Birth—Mo, Day, Yr: FEBRUARY 10, 1901
- 7. Age in Years: 91
- 8. State of Birth: NY
- 9. Citizen of What Country: U.S.A.
- 10A. Full Name of Father: JACOB ADLER
- 10B. State of Birth: RUSSIA
- 11A. Full Maiden Name of Mother: SARA LEVITZKY
- 11B. State of Birth: RUSSIA
- 12. Military Service: 19__ to 19__ (X) None
- 13. Social Security No.: 563-22-9174
- 14. Marital Status: WIDOWED
- 15. Name of Surviving Spouse: NONE
- 16A. Usual Occupation: TEACHER/ACTRESS
- 16B. Usual Kind of Business or Industry: THEATRE
- 16C. Usual Employer: SELF-EMPLOYED
- 16D. Years in Occupation: 70
- 17. Education—Years Completed: 12

USUAL RESIDENCE

- 18A. Residence—Street and Number or Location: 8936 THRASHER AVE.
- 18B. City: LOS ANGELES
- 18C. Zip Code: 90069
- 18D. County: LOS ANGELES
- 18E. Number of Years in This County: 20
- 18F. State or Foreign Country: CALIFORNIA
- 20. Name, Relationship, Mailing Address and Zip Code of Informant: ELLEN ADLER – DAUGHTER, 1016 5th AVENUE, NEW YORK, NY 10028

PLACE OF DEATH

- 19A. Place of Death: RESIDENCE
- 19C. County: LOS ANGELES
- 19D. Street Address—Street and Number or Location: 8936 THRASHER AVE.
- 19E. City: LOS ANGELES
- 22. Was Death Reported to Coroner: No (X)

CAUSE OF DEATH

- 21. Death was caused by:
  - (A) Immediate Cause: CEREBROVASCULAR HEMORRHAGE — 2 HOURS
  - (B) Due to: ATHEROSCLEROSIS — 3 YEARS
- 23. Was Biopsy Performed: No (X)
- 24A. Was Autopsy Performed: No (X)
- 24B. Was it Used in Determining Cause of Death:
- 25. Other Significant Conditions Contributing to Death But Not Related to Cause Given in 21: NONE
- 26. Was Operation Performed for Any Condition in Item 21 or 25: NO

PHYSICIAN'S CERTIFICATION

- 27A. Decedent Attended Since: 6/18/1983
- Decedent Last Seen Alive: 12/15/1992
- 27B. Signature and Title of Certifier: (signed)
- Type Attending Physician's Name and Address: ROBERT KARNS, M.D., 8920 WILSHIRE BLVD., BEVERLY HILLS, CA 90210
- 27C. Certifier's License Number: G7277
- 27D. Date Signed: 12-21-92

FUNERAL DIRECTOR AND LOCAL REGISTRAR

- 34A. Disposition(s): TR/BU
- 34B. Place of Final Disposition: MT. CARMEL CEMETERY, QUEENS, NY (QUEENS COUNTY)
- 34C. Date, Mo, Day, Yr: 12-24-92
- 35A. Signature of Embalmer: Bruce C. Broyelton
- 35B. License No.: 6345
- 36A. Name of Funeral Director: MALINOW & SILVERMAN MORTUARY
- 36B. License No.: FD-487
- 37. Signature of Local Registrar: (signed) Robert C. Stutz
- 38. Registration Date: DEC 22 1992

431 01-9-1-700E

This is to certify that this document is a true copy of the official record filed with the Registrar-Recorder/County Clerk.

NOV 14 1995
19-055598

This copy not valid unless prepared on engraved border displaying the Seal of the Registrar-Recorder/County Clerk.

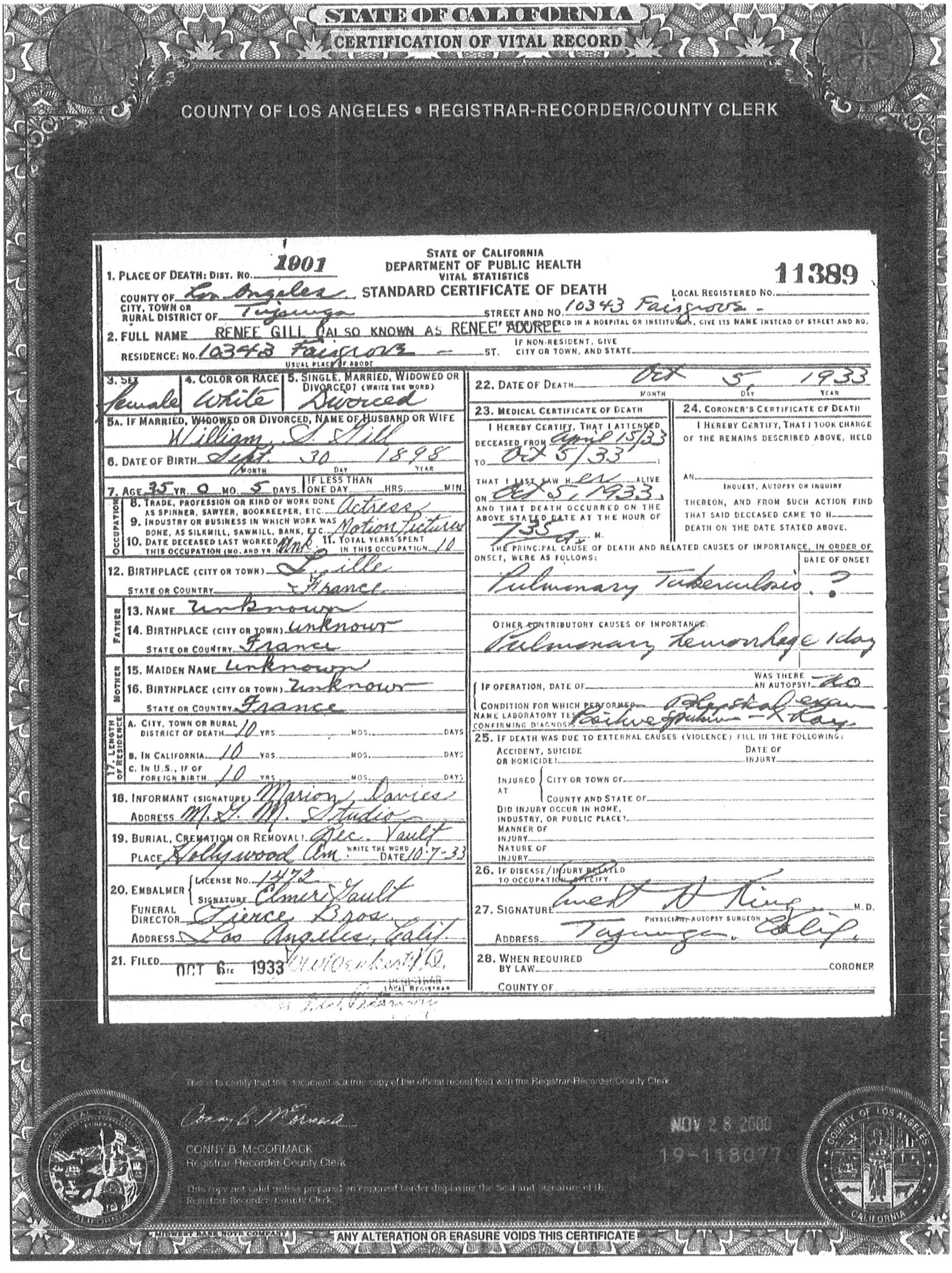

COUNTY OF LOS ANGELES
DEPARTMENT OF HEALTH SERVICES

CERTIFICATE OF DEATH

- 1. NAME OF DECEDENT — FIRST (Given): EDDIE
- 2. MIDDLE: —
- 3. LAST (Family): ALBERT
- 4. DATE OF BIRTH: 04/22/1906
- 5. AGE Yrs.: 99
- 6. SEX: M
- 9. BIRTH STATE/FOREIGN COUNTRY: IL
- 10. SOCIAL SECURITY NUMBER: 062-05-5121
- 11. EVER IN U.S. ARMED FORCES?: YES
- 12. MARITAL STATUS: WIDOWED
- 7. DATE OF DEATH: 05/26/2005
- 8. HOUR: 2010
- 13. EDUCATION: SOME COLLEGE
- 14/15. HISPANIC/LATINO: NO
- 16. DECEDENT'S RACE: WHITE
- 17. USUAL OCCUPATION: ACTOR
- 18. KIND OF BUSINESS OR INDUSTRY: THEATER/MOTION PICTURES/TELEVISION
- 19. YEARS IN OCCUPATION: 60
- 20. DECEDENT'S RESIDENCE: 719 ALMAFI DR
- 21. CITY: PACIFIC PALISADES
- 22. COUNTY/PROVINCE: LOS ANGELES
- 23. ZIP CODE: 90272
- 24. YEARS IN COUNTY: 60
- 25. STATE/FOREIGN COUNTRY: CA
- 26. INFORMANT'S NAME, RELATIONSHIP: EARLE ZUCHT - SON-IN-LAW
- 27. INFORMANT'S MAILING ADDRESS: 1 CENTAURUS IRVINE CA 92603
- 28. NAME OF SURVIVING SPOUSE — FIRST: —
- 31. NAME OF FATHER — FIRST: FRANK
- 33. LAST: HEIMBERGER
- 34. BIRTH STATE: MN
- 35. NAME OF MOTHER — FIRST: JULIA
- 37. LAST (Maiden): JONES
- 38. BIRTH STATE: WS
- 39. DISPOSITION DATE: 06/01/2005
- 40. PLACE OF FINAL DISPOSITION: WESTWOOD VILLAGE MEMORIAL PARK 1218 GLENDON AVE LOS ANGELES CA 90024
- 41. TYPE OF DISPOSITION(S): CR/BU
- 42. SIGNATURE OF EMBALMER: NOT EMBALMED
- 44. NAME OF FUNERAL ESTABLISHMENT: PIERCE BROS WESTWOOD
- 45. LICENSE NUMBER: FD-951
- 47. DATE: 05/31/2005

- 101. PLACE OF DEATH: OWN RESIDENCE
- 103. IF OTHER THAN HOSPITAL: Decedent's Home
- 104. COUNTY: LOS ANGELES
- 105. FACILITY ADDRESS: 719 ALMAFI DR
- 106. CITY: PACIFIC PALISADES
- 107. CAUSE OF DEATH:
  - (A) IMMEDIATE CAUSE: PNEUMONIA — DAYS
  - (B) ALZHEIMERS DEMENTIA — 10YRS
- 108. DEATH REPORTED TO CORONER?: NO
- 109. BIOPSY PERFORMED?: NO
- 110. AUTOPSY PERFORMED?: NO
- 111. USED IN DETERMINING CAUSE?: —
- 112. OTHER SIGNIFICANT CONDITIONS: ATRIAL FIBRILLATION
- 113. WAS OPERATION PERFORMED: NO
- 114. Decedent Attended Since: 02/18/2003; Last Seen Alive: 05/13/2005
- 116. LICENSE NUMBER: G48952
- 117. DATE: 05/30/2005
- 118. ATTENDING PHYSICIAN: BRIAN L. FLYER MD 1125 S BEVERLY DR LOS ANGELES CA 90035

INFORMATIONAL, NOT A VALID DOCUMENT TO ESTABLISH IDENTITY

This is a true certified copy of the record filed in the County of Los Angeles Department of Health Services if it bears the Registrar's signature in purple ink.

215 DATE ISSUED: JUN 2 0 2005

Director of Health Services and Registrar

This copy not valid unless prepared on engraved border displaying seal and signature of Registrar.

910114718

STATE OF CALIFORNIA — CERTIFICATION OF VITAL RECORD

COUNTY OF LOS ANGELES • REGISTRAR-RECORDER/COUNTY CLERK

CERTIFICATE OF DEATH

State File Number: 3 2006 19 040083

Decedent's Personal Data
- Name: Edward Laurence Albert
- Date of Birth: 02/20/1951
- Age: 55
- Sex: M
- Birth State: CA
- Social Security Number: 567-68-5789
- Ever in U.S. Armed Forces: No
- Marital Status: Married
- Date of Death: 09/22/2006
- Hour: 0345
- Education: Bachelor's
- Hispanic: No
- Race: White
- Usual Occupation: Actor
- Kind of Business/Industry: Movie Industry
- Years in Occupation: 44

Usual Residence
- 27322 Winding Way
- City: Malibu
- County: Los Angeles
- Zip: 90265
- Years in County: 55
- State: CA

Informant
- Kate Albert, WIFE
- PO Box 6613 Malibu CA 90269

Spouse and Parent Information
- Surviving Spouse: Kate Woodville
- Father: Eddie Albert — Birth State: MN
- Mother: Margo Bolado — Birth State: MEX

Funeral Director / Local Registrar
- Disposition Date: 09/29/2006
- Place of Final Disposition: RES: Kate Albert 27322 Winding Way Malibu CA 90265
- Type of Disposition: CR/RES
- Not Embalmed
- Funeral Establishment: AARON Cremation & Burial Ser / Mark B Shaw Chapel
- License Number: FD 406
- Signature of Local Registrar: Jonathan E Fielding
- Date: 09/27/2006

Place of Death
- Residence
- County: Los Angeles
- Facility Address: 27322 Winding Way
- City: Malibu
- Decedent's Home

Cause of Death
- Immediate Cause: Metastatic Lung Cancer
- Other Significant Conditions: NONE
- Operation Performed: NO
- Death Reported to Coroner: No
- Biopsy Performed: No
- Autopsy Performed: No
- Used in Determining Cause: No

Physician's Certification
- Decedent Attended Since: 09/01/2004
- Decedent Last Seen Alive: 09/21/2006
- Signature: Jesse Hanley MD
- Attending Physician: Jesse Hanley MD, 27560 E Winding Way Malibu CA 90265
- License Number: G48328
- Date: 9/27/06

FAX AUTH #: 545-5922

This is to certify that this document is a true copy of the official record filed with the Registrar-Recorder/County Clerk.

SEP 16 2009

Dean C. Logan
Registrar-Recorder/County Clerk

000002374

INFORMATIONAL, NOT A VALID DOCUMENT TO ESTABLISH IDENTITY

STATE OF CALIFORNIA
CERTIFICATION OF VITAL RECORD

COUNTY OF SAN DIEGO
GREGORY J. SMITH
ASSESSOR/RECORDER/COUNTY CLERK

CERTIFICATE OF DEATH — STATE OF CALIFORNIA

Local Registration District and Certificate Number: 39237008518

1A. Name of Decedent — First (Given)	Peter
1B. Middle	Richard
1C. Last (Family)	Woolnough
2A. Date of Death	June 18, 1992
2B. Hour	1245
3. Sex	Male
4. Race	White
5. Hispanic	No
6. Date of Birth	February 10, 1944
7. Age in Years	48
8. State of Birth	Australia
9. Citizen of What Country	Australian
10A. Full Name of Father	Richard Woolnough
10B. State of Birth	Australia
11A. Full Maiden Name of Mother	Marion Davison
11B. State of Birth	Australia
12. Military Service?	None
13. Social Security No.	118-40-4135
14. Marital Status	Divorced
15. Name of Surviving Spouse	None
16A. Usual Occupation	Entertainer
16B. Usual Kind of Business or Industry	Music
16C. Usual Employer	Self-Employed
16D. Years in Occupation	33
17. Education — Years Completed	12
18A. Residence	1550 Neptune Avenue
18B. City	Leucadia
18C. Zip Code	92024
18D. County	San Diego
18E. Number of Years in This County	15
18F. State or Foreign Country	California
20. Name, Relationship, Mailing Address and Zip Code of Informant	Bruce Cudd, Friend, 164 Jupiter Street, Encinitas, CA. 92024
19A. Place of Death	Mercy Hosp. and Medical Center
19B. If Hospital, Specify	IP
19C. County	San Diego
19D. Street Address	4077 Fifth Avenue
19E. City	San Diego

21. Death Was Caused By:
- Immediate Cause (A): Respiratory Failure — days
- Due to (B): Kaposi's Sarcoma — 1 or 2 months
- Due to (C): AIDS — years

22. Was Death Reported to Coroner? Yes — 6-244

23. Was Biopsy Performed? No
24A. Was Autopsy Performed? No
24B. Was it Used in Determining Cause of Death? No

25. Other Significant Conditions Contributing to Death But Not Related to Cause Given in 21: Tuberculosis

26. Was Operation Performed for Any Condition in Item 21 or 25? No

Physician's Certification:
- 27B. Signature: Julian Lichter MD
- 27C. Certifier's License Number: A033711
- 27D. Date Signed: 6/19/92
- 27A. Decedent Attended Since: 5/21/91; Decedent Last Seen Alive: 6/18/92
- 27E. Type Attending Physician's Name and Address: Julian P. Lichter, MD, 4033 3rd Ave. Suite 300, San Diego, CA. 92103

Funeral Director and Local Registrar:
- 34A. Disposition(s): CR/RES
- 34B. Place of Final Disposition: Bruce Cudd: 164 Jupiter Street, Encinitas, CA. 92024
- 34C. Date: 6/22/92
- 35A. Signature of Embalmer: Not Embalmed
- 36A. Name of Funeral Director: Encinitas Mortuary
- 36B. License No.: FD 857
- 38. Registration Date: JUN 22 1992

663435

This is a true and exact reproduction of the document officially registered and placed on file in the office of the San Diego County Recorder/Clerk

October 19, 2001

Gregory J. Smith
Assessor/Recorder/County Clerk

This copy is not valid unless prepared on an engraved border displaying date, seal and signature of the Recorder/County Clerk

CERTIFICATE OF DEATH
STATE OF CALIFORNIA
COUNTY OF LOS ANGELES • REGISTRAR-RECORDER/COUNTY CLERK

State File Number: 3 2000 19 048387

Decedent Personal Data
- **1. Name (First):** STEPHEN
- **2. Middle:** VALENTINE
- **3. Last:** ALLEN
- **4. Date of Birth:** 12/26/1921
- **5. Age:** 78
- **6. Sex:** M
- **7. Date of Death:** 10/30/2000
- **8. Hour:** 2100
- **9. State of Birth:** NY
- **10. Social Security No:** 350-18-0537
- **11. Military Service:** Yes
- **12. Marital Status:** MARRIED
- **13. Education:** 14
- **14. Race:** CAUCASIAN
- **15. Hispanic:** No
- **16. Usual Employer:** MEADOW LANE ENTERPRISES, INC.
- **17. Occupation:** ENTERTAINER
- **18. Kind of Business:** ENTERTAINMENT
- **19. Years in Occupation:** 60

Usual Residence
- **20. Residence:** 16185 WOODVALE RD
- **21. City:** ENCINO
- **22. County:** LOS ANGELES
- **23. Zip Code:** 91436
- **24. Yrs in County:** 40
- **25. State:** CA

Informant
- **26. Name, Relationship:** WILLIAM C ALLEN, SON
- **27. Mailing Address:** 15201 BURBANK BL., VAN NUYS, CA 91411

Spouse and Parent Information
- **28. Surviving Spouse (First):** JAYNE
- **29. Middle:** MEADOWS
- **30. Last (Maiden):** COTTER
- **31. Father (First):** CARROLL
- **32. Middle:** WILLIAM
- **33. Last:** ALLEN
- **34. Birth State:** PA
- **35. Mother (First):** ISABELLE
- **36. Middle:** CORETTA
- **37. Last (Maiden):** DONAHUE
- **38. Birth State:** IL

Disposition
- **39. Date:** 11/13/2000
- **40. Place of Final Disposition:** FOREST LAWN MEMORIAL PARK, LOS ANGELES, CA 90068
- **41. Type of Disposition:** CR/BU
- **42. Signature of Embalmer:** NOT EMBALMED
- **44. Name of Funeral Director:** FOREST LAWN HOLLYWOOD HILLS
- **45. License No:** FD 904
- **47. Date:** 11/11/2000

Place of Death
- **101. Place of Death:** ENCINO-TARZANA REG. MED. CTR.
- **102.** ER/OP
- **104. County:** LOS ANGELES
- **105. Street Address:** 16237 VENTURA BLVD.
- **106. City:** ENCINO

Cause of Death
- **107. Immediate Cause (A):** DEFERRED
- **108. Death Reported to Coroner:** YES — Referral Number 2000-07891
- **109. Biopsy Performed:**
- **110. Autopsy Performed:** YES

Coroner's Use Only
- **119. Manner of Death:** PENDING INVESTIGATION
- **126. Signature of Coroner:** Mary T. Macias
- **127. Date:** 11/09/2000
- **128. Typed Name:** MARY T. MACIAS, DEPUTY CORONER

This is to certify that this document is a true copy of the official record filed with the Registrar-Recorder/County Clerk.

CONNY B. McCORMACK
Registrar-Recorder/County Clerk

FEB 7 2001
19-232278

STATE OF CALIFORNIA
CERTIFICATION OF VITAL RECORD
COUNTY OF LOS ANGELES • REGISTRAR-RECORDER/COUNTY CLERK

AMENDMENT OF MEDICAL AND HEALTH DATA—DEATH

00-013674
3 2000 19 048387

PART I — INFORMATION TO LOCATE RECORD

1. NAME—FIRST (GIVEN)	2. MIDDLE	3. LAST (FAMILY)	4. SEX
STEPHEN	VALENTINE	ALLEN	M

5. DATE OF EVENT—MM/DD/CCYY	6. CITY OF OCCURRENCE	7. COUNTY OF OCCURRENCE
10/30/2000	ENCINO	LOS ANGELES

2 OF 2

PART II — INFORMATION AS IT APPEARS ON RECORD

107. DEATH WAS CAUSED BY:
- IMMEDIATE CAUSE (A) Deferred
- (B)
- (C)
- DUE TO (D)

108. DEATH REPORTED TO CORONER: YES ☒
REFERRAL NUMBER: 2000-07891
109. BIOPSY PERFORMED
110. AUTOPSY PERFORMED: YES ☒
111. USED IN DETERMINING CAUSE

112. OTHER SIGNIFICANT CONDITIONS CONTRIBUTING TO DEATH BUT NOT RELATED TO CAUSE GIVEN IN 107:

113. WAS OPERATION PERFORMED FOR ANY CONDITION IN ITEM 107 or 112?

119. MANNER OF DEATH: PENDING INVESTIGATION ☒

PART III — INFORMATION AS IT SHOULD APPEAR

107. DEATH WAS CAUSED BY:
- IMMEDIATE CAUSE (A) Hemopericardium Due To Myocardial Rupture — Mins.
- (B) Myocardial Infarction — Days
- (C) Occlusive Coronary Artery Atherosclerosis — Years
- DUE TO (D)

108. DEATH REPORTED TO CORONER: YES ☒
REFERRAL NUMBER: 2000-07891
109. BIOPSY PERFORMED: NO ☒
110. AUTOPSY PERFORMED: YES ☒
111. USED IN DETERMINING CAUSE: YES ☒

112. OTHER SIGNIFICANT CONDITIONS CONTRIBUTING TO DEATH BUT NOT RELATED TO CAUSE GIVEN IN 107:
Effects Of Motor Vehicle Accident; Hypertension, History Of Colon Cancer

113. WAS OPERATION PERFORMED: Local Resection Of Colon Cancer — Unknown

119. MANNER OF DEATH: ACCIDENT ☒
120. INJURY AT WORK: NO ☒
121. INJURY DATE: 10/30/2000
122. HOUR: 1945
123. PLACE OF INJURY: In Vehicle
124. DESCRIBE HOW INJURY OCCURRED: Effects Of Auto Vs. Auto (Driver)

125. LOCATION: 16000 Block Of Valley Vista Blvd., Encino 91436

DECLARATION OF CERTIFYING PHYSICIAN OR CORONER

8. SIGNATURE	9. DATE SIGNED	10. TYPED OR PRINTED NAME AND DEGREE/TITLE OF CERTIFIER
L. Scheinin, MD	12/27/2000	Lisa Scheinin, M.D. DME

11. ADDRESS	12. CITY	13. STATE	14. ZIP CODE
1104 N. Mission Road	Los Angeles	CA	90033

15. OFFICE OF STATE REGISTRAR OR SIGNATURE OF LOCAL REGISTRAR
16. DATE ACCEPTED FOR REGISTRATION: 12/29/2000

This is to certify that this document is a true copy of the official record filed with the Registrar-Recorder/County Clerk.

CONNY B. McCORMACK
Registrar-Recorder/County Clerk

FEB 7 2001
19-232277

ANY ALTERATION OR ERASURE VOIDS THIS CERTIFICATE

STATE OF CALIFORNIA

CERTIFICATION OF VITAL RECORD

COUNTY OF LOS ANGELES • REGISTRAR-RECORDER/COUNTY CLERK

CERTIFICATE OF DEATH
STATE OF CALIFORNIA
USE BLACK INK ONLY / NO ERASURES, WHITEOUTS OR ALTERATIONS
VS-11 (REV 3/06)

STATE FILE NUMBER

3 200619048682
LOCAL REGISTRATION NUMBER

DECEDENT'S PERSONAL DATA

1. NAME OF DECEDENT—FIRST (Given): ROBERT	2. MIDDLE: BERNARD	3. LAST (Family): ALTMAN
AKA. ALSO KNOWN AS—Include full AKA (FIRST, MIDDLE, LAST): –	4. DATE OF BIRTH mm/dd/ccyy: 02/20/1925	5. AGE Yrs: 81
IF UNDER ONE YEAR (Months / Days)	IF UNDER 24 HOURS (Hours / Minutes)	6. SEX: M
9. BIRTH STATE/FOREIGN COUNTRY: MISSOURI	10. SOCIAL SECURITY NUMBER: 488-22-1898	11. EVER IN U.S. ARMED FORCES? ☐ YES ☒ NO ☐ UNK
12. MARITAL STATUS/SRDP* (at Time of Death): MARRIED	7. DATE OF DEATH mm/dd/ccyy: 11/20/2006	8. HOUR (24 Hours): 2100
13. EDUCATION—Highest Level/Degree (see worksheet on back): SOME COLLEGE	14/15. WAS DECEDENT HISPANIC/LATINO(A)/SPANISH? (If yes, see worksheet on back): ☐ YES ☒ NO	16. DECEDENT'S RACE—Up to 3 races may be listed (see worksheet on back): CAUCASIAN
17. USUAL OCCUPATION—Type of work for most of life. DO NOT USE RETIRED: FILM DIRECTOR	18. KIND OF BUSINESS OR INDUSTRY (e.g. grocery store, road construction, employment agency, etc.): FILM INDUSTRIES	19. YEARS IN OCCUPATION: 28

USUAL RESIDENCE

20. DECEDENT'S RESIDENCE (Street and number, or location): 25124 MALIBU RD				
21. CITY: MALIBU	22. COUNTY/PROVINCE: LOS ANGELES	23. ZIP CODE: 90265	24. YEARS IN COUNTY: 50	25. STATE/FOREIGN COUNTRY: CALIFORNIA

INFORMANT

26. INFORMANT'S NAME, RELATIONSHIP: KATHRYN ALTMAN – WIFE	27. INFORMANT'S MAILING ADDRESS (Street and number, or rural route number, city or town, state and zip): 25124 MALIBU RD, MALIBU, CA 90265

SPOUSE/SRDP AND PARENT INFORMATION

28. NAME OF SURVIVING SPOUSE/SRDP*—FIRST: KATHRYN	29. MIDDLE: –	30. LAST (BIRTH NAME): REED	
31. NAME OF FATHER/PARENT—FIRST: BERNARD	32. MIDDLE: C.	33. LAST: ALTMAN	34. BIRTH STATE: MISSOURI
35. NAME OF MOTHER/PARENT—FIRST: HELEN	36. MIDDLE: –	37. LAST (BIRTH NAME): MATTHEWS	38. BIRTH STATE: MISSOURI

FUNERAL DIRECTOR / LOCAL REGISTRAR

39. DISPOSITION DATE mm/dd/ccyy: 12/05/2006	40. PLACE OF FINAL DISPOSITION: RES: KATHRYN ALTMAN, 25124 MALIBU RD, MALIBU, CA 90265		
41. TYPE OF DISPOSITION(S): CR/RES	42. SIGNATURE OF EMBALMER: NOT EMBLAMED		43. LICENSE NUMBER: –
44. NAME OF FUNERAL ESTABLISHMENT: FUNERARIA DEL ANGEL PIERCE BROTHERS MORTUARY	45. LICENSE NUMBER: FD-8	46. SIGNATURE OF LOCAL REGISTRAR: Jonathan E. Fielding MD	47. DATE mm/dd/ccyy: 11/30/2006

PLACE OF DEATH

101. PLACE OF DEATH: CEDARS SINAI HOSPITAL	102. IF HOSPITAL, SPECIFY ONE: ☒ IP ☐ ER/OP ☐ DOA	103. IF OTHER THAN HOSPITAL, SPECIFY ONE: ☐ Hospice ☐ Nursing Home/LTC ☐ Decedent's Home ☐ Other
104. COUNTY: LOS ANGELES	105. FACILITY ADDRESS OR LOCATION WHERE FOUND (Street and number, or location): 8700 BEVERLY BLVD.	106. CITY: LOS ANGELES

CAUSE OF DEATH

107. CAUSE OF DEATH — Enter the chain of events—diseases, injuries, or complications—that directly caused death. DO NOT enter terminal events such as cardiac arrest, respiratory arrest, or ventricular fibrillation without showing the etiology. DO NOT ABBREVIATE.

		Time Interval Between Onset and Death	
IMMEDIATE CAUSE (Final disease or condition resulting in death) (A)	METASTATATIC RENAL CANCER	(AT) 18 MONTHS	108. DEATH REPORTED TO CORONER? ☐ YES ☒ NO; REFERRAL NUMBER
Sequentially, list conditions, if any, leading to cause on Line A. Enter UNDERLYING CAUSE (disease or injury that initiated the events resulting in death) LAST (B)		(BT)	109. BIOPSY PERFORMED? ☒ YES ☐ NO
(C)		(CT)	110. AUTOPSY PERFORMED? ☐ YES ☒ NO
(D)		(DT)	111. USED IN DETERMINING CAUSE? ☐ YES ☐ NO

112. OTHER SIGNIFICANT CONDITIONS CONTRIBUTING TO DEATH BUT NOT RESULTING IN THE UNDERLYING CAUSE GIVEN IN 107: HEART TRANSPLANT DUE TO CARDIOMYOPATHY

113. WAS OPERATION PERFORMED FOR ANY CONDITION IN ITEM 107 OR 112? (If yes, list type of operation and date.): HEART TRANSPLANT 12/05/1993, LEFT EMPHRECTOMY 02/02/2004

113A. IF FEMALE, PREGNANT IN LAST YEAR? ☐ YES ☐ NO ☐ UNK

PHYSICIAN'S CERTIFICATION

114. I CERTIFY THAT TO THE BEST OF MY KNOWLEDGE DEATH OCCURRED AT THE HOUR, DATE, AND PLACE STATED FROM THE CAUSES STATED. Decedent Attended Since (A) mm/dd/ccyy: 04/29/2001; Decedent Last Seen Alive (B) mm/dd/ccyy: 11/20/2006	115. SIGNATURE AND TITLE OF CERTIFIER: FR Rosenfelt	116. LICENSE NUMBER: C32656	117. DATE mm/dd/ccyy: 11/29/2006
118. TYPE ATTENDING PHYSICIAN'S NAME, MAILING ADDRESS, ZIP CODE: FRED ROSENFELT, M.D. 9090 WILSHIRE BLVD. BEVERLY HILLS, CA 90211			

CORONER'S USE ONLY

21

119. I CERTIFY THAT IN MY OPINION DEATH OCCURRED AT THE HOUR, DATE, AND PLACE STATED FROM THE CAUSES STATED. MANNER OF DEATH ☐ Natural ☐ Accident ☐ Homicide ☐ Suicide ☐ Pending Investigation ☐ Could not be determined	120. INJURED AT WORK? ☐ YES ☐ NO ☐ UNK	121. INJURY DATE mm/dd/ccyy	122. HOUR (24 Hours)
123. PLACE OF INJURY (e.g., home, construction site, wooded area, etc.)			
124. DESCRIBE HOW INJURY OCCURRED (Events which resulted in injury)			
125. LOCATION OF INJURY (Street and number, or location, and city, and zip)			
126. SIGNATURE OF CORONER / DEPUTY CORONER	127. DATE mm/dd/ccyy	128. TYPE NAME, TITLE OF CORONER / DEPUTY CORONER	

564

STATE REGISTRAR	A	B	C	D	E	FAX AUTH.#	CENSUS TRACT

INFORMATIONAL, NOT A VALID DOCUMENT TO ESTABLISH IDENTITY

This is to certify that this document is a true copy of the official record filed with the Registrar-Recorder/County Clerk. SEP 16 2009

Dean C. Logan
DEAN C. LOGAN
Registrar-Recorder/County Clerk

000002373

This copy not valid unless prepared on engraved border displaying the Seal and Signature of the Registrar-Recorder/County Clerk.

FBNCO (Rev) 07/09

THE GREAT SEAL OF THE STATE OF CALIFORNIA — EUREKA

REGISTRAR-RECORDER/COUNTY CLERK — COUNTY OF LOS ANGELES, CALIFORNIA

ANY ALTERATION OR ERASURE VOIDS THIS CERTIFICATE

STATE OF CALIFORNIA
CERTIFICATION OF VITAL RECORD

COUNTY OF ORANGE
SANTA ANA, CALIFORNIA

CERTIFICATE OF DEATH — 3-92-30-014359
STATE OF CALIFORNIA — USE BLACK INK ONLY

DECEDENT PERSONAL DATA

- 1A. NAME OF DECEDENT—FIRST (GIVEN): CARVER
- 1B. MIDDLE: DANA
- 1C. LAST (FAMILY): ANDREWS
- 2A. DATE OF DEATH—MO, DAY, YR: DECEMBER 17, 1992
- 2B. HOUR: 0105
- 3. SEX: MALE
- 4. RACE: CAUCASIAN
- 5. HISPANIC—SPECIFY: No
- 6. DATE OF BIRTH—MO, DAY, YR: JANUARY 1, 1909
- 7. AGE IN YEARS: 83
- 8. STATE OF BIRTH: MS
- 9. CITIZEN OF WHAT COUNTRY: USA
- 10A. FULL NAME OF FATHER: CHARLES F. ANDREWS
- 10B. STATE OF BIRTH: FLORIDA
- 11A. FULL MAIDEN NAME OF MOTHER: ANNIS SPEED
- 11B. STATE OF BIRTH: MS
- 12. MILITARY SERVICE?: None
- 13. SOCIAL SECURITY NO.: 551-10-0419
- 14. MARITAL STATUS: MARRIED
- 15. NAME OF SURVIVING SPOUSE: MARY OLIVE TODD
- 16A. USUAL OCCUPATION: ACTOR
- 16B. USUAL KIND OF BUSINESS OR INDUSTRY: ENTERTAINMENT
- 16C. USUAL EMPLOYER: SELF EMPLOYED
- 16D. YEARS IN OCCUPATION: 50
- 17. EDUCATION—YEARS COMPLETED: 15

USUAL RESIDENCE

- 18A. RESIDENCE—STREET AND NUMBER OR LOCATION: 4828 LENNOX AVE.
- 18B. CITY: SHERMAN OAKS
- 18C. ZIP CODE: 91423
- 18D. COUNTY: LOS ANGELES
- 18E. NUMBER OF YEARS IN THIS COUNTY: 62
- 18F. STATE OR FOREIGN COUNTRY: CALIFORNIA
- 20. NAME, RELATIONSHIP, MAILING ADDRESS AND ZIP CODE OF INFORMANT: MARY ANDREWS (WIFE), 4828 LENNOX AVE., SHERMAN OAKS, CA 91423

PLACE OF DEATH

- 19A. PLACE OF DEATH: LOS ALAMITOS MEDICAL CTR.
- 19B. IF HOSPITAL, SPECIFY: IP
- 19C. COUNTY: ORANGE
- 18D. STREET ADDRESS: 3751 KATELLA
- 19E. CITY: LOS ALAMITOS

CAUSE OF DEATH

- 21. DEATH WAS CAUSED BY:
  - IMMEDIATE CAUSE (A): Cardiopulmonary Arrest — seconds
  - DUE TO (B): Atherosclerotic Heart Disease — years
  - DUE TO (C):
- TIME INTERVAL BETWEEN ONSET AND DEATH
- 22. WAS DEATH REPORTED TO CORONER?: No
- 23. WAS BIOPSY PERFORMED?: No
- 24A. WAS AUTOPSY PERFORMED?: No
- 24B. WAS IT USED IN DETERMINING CAUSE OF DEATH?:
- 25. OTHER SIGNIFICANT CONDITIONS CONTRIBUTING TO DEATH BUT NOT RELATED TO CAUSE GIVEN IN 21: None
- 26. WAS OPERATION PERFORMED FOR ANY CONDITION IN ITEM 21 OR 25?: No

PHYSICIAN'S CERTIFICATION

- 27A. DECEDENT ATTENDED SINCE: 2/25/92
- DECEDENT LAST SEEN ALIVE: 12/16/92
- 27B. SIGNATURE AND DEGREE OR TITLE OF CERTIFIER: P. Narain MD
- 27C. CERTIFIER'S LICENSE NUMBER: A 40903
- 27D. DATE SIGNED: 12/17/92
- 27E. TYPE ATTENDING PHYSICIAN'S NAME AND ADDRESS: PRAKASH NARAIN, M.D., 1661 GOLDEN RAIN, SEAL BEACH, CA 90740

FUNERAL DIRECTOR AND LOCAL REGISTRAR

- 34A. DISPOSITION(S): CR/RES
- 34B. PLACE OF FINAL DISPOSITION—NAME AND ADDRESS: RES: 4828 LENNOX AVE., SHERMAN OAKS, CA 91423
- 34C. DATE: 12/22/92
- 35A. SIGNATURE OF EMBALMER: NOT EMBALMED
- 35B. LICENSE NUMBER: NONE
- 36A. NAME OF FUNERAL DIRECTOR: PIERCE BROS. WESTWOOD VILLAGE
- 36B. LICENSE NO.: F-951
- 38. REGISTRATION DATE: DEC 21 1992

859703

CERTIFIED COPY OF VITAL RECORDS

STATE OF CALIFORNIA } ss
COUNTY OF ORANGE

DATE ISSUED: OCT 18 2001

GARY L. GRANVILLE, Clerk-Recorder
ORANGE COUNTY, CALIFORNIA

This is a true and exact reproduction of the document officially registered and placed on file in the office of the Orange County Clerk-Recorder.

This copy not valid unless prepared on engraved border displaying seal and signature of Clerk-Recorder.

ANY ALTERATION OR ERASURE VOIDS THIS CERTIFICATE

CERTIFICATE OF DEATH — STATE OF CALIFORNIA, DEPARTMENT OF PUBLIC HEALTH

State File Number: 7097-045255
Local Registration District and Certificate Number: (as above)

Decedent Personal Data
- **1A. Name of Deceased — First Name:** Anna
- **1B. Middle Name:** Maria
- **1C. Last Name:** Pierangeli
- **2A. Date of Death:** Sept 10, 1971
- **2B. Hours:** 12:20 PM
- **3. Sex:** Female
- **4. Color or Race:** Cauc
- **5. Birthplace:** Italy
- **6. Date of Birth:** June 19, 1932
- **7. Age:** 39 Yrs
- **8. Name and Birthplace of Father:** Luigi Pierangeli — Italy
- **9. Maiden Name and Birthplace of Mother:** Enrica Romiti — Italy
- **10. Citizen of What Country:** Italy
- **11. Social Security Number:** 566-42-5889
- **12. Married, Never Married, Widowed, Divorced:** Divorced
- **13. Name of Surviving Spouse:** —
- **14. Last Occupation:** Actress
- **15. Number of Years in This Occupation:** 21 Yrs
- **16. Name of Last Employing Company or Firm:** Metro Goldwyn Mayer
- **17. Kind of Industry or Business:** Movie Industry

Place of Death
- **18A. Place of Death:**
- **18B. Street Address:** 355 S McCarty Dr
- **18C. Inside City Corporate Limits:** Yes
- **18D. City or Town:** Beverly Hills
- **18E. County:** Los Angeles
- **18F. Length of Stay in County of Death:** 9 months
- **18G. Length of Stay in California:** 9 months

Usual Residence
- **19A. Usual Residence — Street Address:** 355 S McCarty Dr
- **19B. Inside City Corporate Limits:** Yes
- **19C. City or Town:** Beverly Hills
- **19D. County:** Los Angeles
- **19E. State:** California
- **20. Name and Mailing Address of Informant:** Enrica Pierangeli, 5 Ave Delille, Rueil-Malmaison 92-France

Physician's or Coroner's Certification
- **21A. Coroner:** Investigation
- **21C.** Thomas T. Noguchi, M.D., Coroner — Hall of Justice, Los Angeles
- **21D. Date Signed:** 9-13-71

Funeral Director and Local Registrar
- **22A. Specify Burial, Entombment or Cremation:** Burial
- **22B. Date:** 9-15-71 Ships
- **23. Name of Cemetery or Crematory:** Rueil Malmaison, France
- **24. Embalmer Signature / License Number:** Paul K. Shefsfield 5848
- **25. Name of Funeral Director:** PIERCE BROTHERS — BEVERLY HILLS
- **27. Local Registrar:** (signed) MD
- **28. Date Accepted:** SEP 13 1971

Cause of Death
- **29. Part I. Death was Caused by:** Deferred
- **30. Part II. Other Significant Conditions:** —
- **31. Was Operation or Biopsy Performed:** No
- **32. Autopsy:** Yes

Injury Information
- (blank)

APR 10 2000
19-565612

CONNY B. McCORMACK
Registrar-Recorder/County Clerk

STATE OF CALIFORNIA
CERTIFICATION OF VITAL RECORD

COUNTY OF LOS ANGELES • REGISTRAR-RECORDER/COUNTY CLERK

No. 718267

AMENDMENT OF MEDICAL AND HEALTH SECTION DATA—DEATH

State Certificate Number: 7097-045255

IDENTIFICATION OF THE RECORD

- 1a. FIRST NAME: Anna
- 1b. MIDDLE NAME: Maria
- 1c. LAST NAME: Pierangeli
- 2. PLACE OF OCCURRENCE—CITY OR COUNTY: Beverly Hills
- 3. DATE OF EVENT: Sept. 10, 1971
- 4. DATE ORIGINAL FILED: 9-13-71

ORIGINALLY REPORTED INFORMATION

29. PART I. DEATH WAS CAUSED BY:
 - (A) IMMEDIATE CAUSE: Deferred
 - (B) DUE TO, OR AS A CONSEQUENCE OF:
 - (C) DUE TO, OR AS A CONSEQUENCE OF:

31. WAS OPERATION OR BIOPSY PERFORMED: No
32A. AUTOPSY: Yes

INFORMATION AS IT SHOULD BE STATED ON THE ORIGINALLY REGISTERED CERTIFICATE

29. PART I. DEATH WAS CAUSED BY:
 - (A) IMMEDIATE CAUSE: ACUTE CARDIAC INSUFFICIENCY
 - (B) DUE TO, OR AS A CONSEQUENCE OF: NONSPECIFIC FOCAL AND DIFFUSE MYOCARDITIS
 - (C) DUE TO, OR AS A CONSEQUENCE OF:

31. WAS OPERATION OR BIOPSY PERFORMED: No
32A. AUTOPSY: Yes
32B. IF YES, WERE FINDINGS CONSIDERED IN DETERMINING CAUSE OF DEATH: Yes

33. SPECIFY ACCIDENT, SUICIDE OR HOMICIDE: Natural

38. WERE LABORATORY TESTS DONE FOR DRUGS OR TOXIC CHEMICALS: Yes
39. WERE LABORATORY TESTS DONE FOR ALCOHOL: Yes

DECLARATION OF CERTIFYING PHYSICIAN OR CORONER

6A. SIGNATURE OF PHYSICIAN OR CORONER: [signature]
6B. DATE SIGNED: 10-29-71
7A. NAME OF PHYSICIAN OR CORONER: BY: E. B. Weissburd, DEPUTY
7C. ADDRESS: HALL OF JUSTICE, LOS ANGELES, CALIFORNIA

REGISTRAR'S OFFICE

8A. OFFICE OF STATE OR LOCAL REGISTRAR: Ga. Heidbreder M.D.
8B. DATE ACCEPTED: NOV 3 1971

STATE OF CALIFORNIA, DEPARTMENT OF PUBLIC HEALTH, BUREAU OF VITAL STATISTICS (REV. 1-1-69) FORM VS-24B

This is to certify that this document is a true copy of the official record filed with the Registrar-Recorder/County Clerk.

CONNY B. McCORMACK
Registrar-Recorder/County Clerk

APR 10 2000
19-567588

STATE OF CALIFORNIA
CERTIFICATION OF VITAL RECORD

COUNTY OF LOS ANGELES • REGISTRAR-RECORDER/COUNTY CLERK

CERTIFICATE OF DEATH — 7097-019320

STATE OF CALIFORNIA—DEPARTMENT OF PUBLIC HEALTH

DECEDENT PERSONAL DATA

- 1A. Name of Deceased—First Name: Robert
- 1B. Middle Name: William
- 1C. Last Name: Armstrong
- 2A. Date of Death: April 20, 1973
- 2B. Hour: 1830
- 3. Sex: male
- 4. Color or Race: cauc
- 5. Birthplace: Michigan
- 6. Date of Birth: Nov. 20 1890
- 7. Age: 82 years
- 8. Name and Birthplace of Father: William N Armstrong – Mich
- 9. Maiden Name and Birthplace of Mother: Mina Lehman – New York
- 10. Citizen of What Country: U.S.A.
- 11. Social Security Number: 565 12 3903
- 12. Married, Never Married, Widowed, Divorced: married
- 13. Name of Surviving Spouse: Claire Louise
- 14. Last Occupation: Actor
- 15. Number of Years in This Occupation: 50
- 17. Kind of Industry or Business: Motion Pictures

PLACE OF DEATH

- 18A. Place of Death: St Johns Hospital
- 18B. Street Address: 1328 22nd St.
- 18C. Inside City Corporate Limits: YES
- 18D. City or Town: Santa Monica
- 18E. County: Los Angeles
- 18F. Length of Stay in County of Death: 45 years
- 18G. Length of Stay in California: 45 years

USUAL RESIDENCE

- 19A. Street Address: 1088 Villa Grove Dr.
- 19B. Inside City Corporate Limits: yes
- 19C. City or Town: Pacific Palisades
- 19D. County: Los Angeles
- 19E. State: Calif
- 20. Name and Mailing Address of Informant: Claire Louise Armstrong — same

PHYSICIAN'S OR CORONER'S CERTIFICATION

- 21A. From 4-14-73 To 4-20-73, 4-20-73
- 21D. Address: 2021 Santa Monica Bld
- 21E. License Number: A-05525
- 21G. Date Signed: 4/23/73

FUNERAL DIRECTOR AND LOCAL REGISTRAR

- 22. Burial: Cremation
- 22B. Date: 4-24-73
- 23. Name of Cemetery or Crematory: Westwood Memorial Park
- 24. Embalmer: Not embalmed
- 25. Name of Funeral Director: Westwood Village Mortuary
- 28. Date Accepted for Registration: APR 24 1973

CAUSE OF DEATH

- 29. Part I. Death was caused by:
  - (A) Immediate Cause: Cardiac Arrest (Old MI) — 10 min
  - (B) Due to: Blood loss – Primary Anemia – P.O. bleeding

INJURY INFORMATION

(blank)

This is to certify that this document is a true copy of the official record filed with the Registrar-Recorder/County Clerk.

Conny B. McCormack
Registrar-Recorder/County Clerk

APR 14 2003

190884374

This copy not valid unless prepared on engraved border displaying the Seal and Signature of the Registrar-Recorder/County Clerk.

ANY ALTERATION OR ERASURE VOIDS THIS CERTIFICATE

STATE OF CALIFORNIA
CERTIFICATION OF VITAL RECORD
COUNTY OF LOS ANGELES • REGISTRAR-RECORDER/COUNTY CLERK

CERTIFICATE OF DEATH
STATE OF CALIFORNIA—DEPARTMENT OF PUBLIC HEALTH

REGISTRATION DISTRICT NO. 7053 — REGISTRAR'S NUMBER 840

DECEDENT PERSONAL DATA

- 1a. Name of Deceased—First Name: Edward
- 1c. Last Name: Arnold
- 2a. Date of Death: 4/26/56
- 2b. Hour: 2:20 A.M.
- 3. Sex: Male
- 4. Color or Race: Cauc.
- 5. Married
- 6. Date of Birth: February 18, 1890
- 7. Age (Last Birthday): 66 years
- 8a. Usual Occupation: Actor
- 8b. Kind of Business or Industry: Motion Pictures
- 9. Birthplace: New York
- 10. Citizen of What Country: United States
- 11. Name and Birthplace of Father: John Schneider, Germany
- 12. Maiden Name and Birthplace of Mother: Elizabeth Ohse, Germany
- 13. Name of Present Spouse: Cleo Arnold
- 14. Was Deceased Ever in U.S. Armed Forces: No
- 15. Social Security Number: 548-05-9591
- 16. Informant: Cleo Arnold

PLACE OF DEATH

- 17a. County: Los Angeles
- 17b. City or Town: Los Angeles (Encino)
- 17c. Length of Stay in This City or Town: 24 years
- 17d. Full Name of Hospital or Institution: Home
- 17e. Address: 17349 Rancho St.

LAST USUAL RESIDENCE

- 18a. State: California
- 18b. County: Los Angeles
- 18c. City or Town: Encino
- 18d. Street or Rural Address: 17349 Rancho St.

PHYSICIAN'S OR CORONER'S CERTIFICATION

- 19a. Physician certified death occurred from 4-23-56 to 4-26-56, last saw deceased alive 4-26-56
- 19c. Signature: E.H. Tyson M.D.
- 19d. Address: 4811 Coldwater Cyn, Van Nuys
- 19e. Date Signed: 4-26-56

FUNERAL DIRECTOR AND REGISTRAR

- 20a. Specify Burial, Cremation: Burial
- 20b. Date: 4/28/56
- 20c. Cemetery or Crematory: San Fernando Mission
- 22. Funeral Director: J.T. Oswald Mortuary
- 23. Date Received by Local Registrar: APR 27 1956

CAUSE OF DEATH

- 25. Disease or Condition Directly Leading to Death: (a) Medullary Failure — 3 hrs
- Due to: (b) Massive Cerebral Hemorrhage — 3 hrs
- Due to: (c) Arteriosclerosis
- 26. Other Significant Conditions: Arteriosclerotic Heart Disease
- 28. Autopsy: No

Conny B. McCormack
Registrar-Recorder/County Clerk

NOV 28 2000
19-118078

STATE OF CALIFORNIA
CERTIFICATION OF VITAL RECORD

COUNTY OF LOS ANGELES • REGISTRAR-RECORDER/COUNTY CLERK

CERTIFICATE OF DEATH

State File Number: 3200919017207

1. Name of Decedent — First	BERNICE
3. Last (Family)	SAKS
AKA Also Known As	BEATRICE ARTHUR
4. Date of Birth	05/13/1922
5. Age	86 Yrs
6. Sex	F
9. Birth State/Foreign Country	NY
10. Social Security Number	215-20-4418
11. Ever in U.S. Armed Forces?	YES
12. Marital Status	DIVORCED
7. Date of Death	04/25/2009
8. Hour (24 Hours)	0215
13. Education	HS GRADUATE
14/15. Was Decedent Hispanic/Latino	NO
16. Decedent's Race	WHITE
17. Usual Occupation	ACTRESS
18. Kind of Business or Industry	ENTERTAINMENT
19. Years in Occupation	65
20. Decedent's Residence	2000 OLD RANCH ROAD
21. City	LOS ANGELES
22. County/Province	LOS ANGELES
23. Zip Code	90049
24. Years in County	37
25. State/Foreign Country	CA
26. Informant's Name / Relationship	MATTHEW PHILLIP SAKS, SON
27. Informant's Mailing Address	990 S. CARMELINA AVENUE, LOS ANGELES, CA 90049
31. Name of Father — First	PHILLIP
33. Last	FRANKEL
34. Birth State	UNKNOWN
35. Name of Mother — First	REBECCA
37. Last (Maiden)	PRESSNER
38. Birth State	UNKNOWN
39. Disposition Date	04/29/2009
40. Place of Final Disposition	RESIDENCE: MATTHEW PHILLIP SAKS, 990 S. CARMELINA AVENUE, LOS ANGELES, CA 90049
41. Type of Disposition(s)	CR/RES
42. Signature of Embalmer	NOT EMBALMED
44. Name of Funeral Establishment	GATES, KINGSLEY & GATES MOELLER
45. License Number	FD451
46. Signature of Local Registrar	JONATHAN FIELDING, MD
47. Date	04/28/2009
101. Place of Death	RESIDENCE
103. If Other Than Hospital	Decedent's Home
104. County	LOS ANGELES
105. Facility Address	2000 OLD RANCH ROAD
106. City	LOS ANGELES
107. Cause of Death (Immediate)	(A) METASTATIC NON-SMALL CELL LUNG CANCER
Time Interval	7 YRS
108. Death Reported to Coroner	YES
Referral Number	2009-53043
109. Biopsy Performed?	NO
110. Autopsy Performed?	NO
111. Used in Determining Cause?	—
112. Other Significant Conditions	NONE
113. Was Operation Performed	NO
113A. If Female Pregnant in Last Year	NO
Decedent Attended Since	05/16/2002
Decedent Last Seen Alive	04/03/2009
115. Signature and Title of Certifier	BARRY EUGENE ROSENBLOOM M.D.
116. License Number	G22745
117. Date	04/27/2009
118. Attending Physician's Mailing Address	9090 WILSHIRE BLVD STE 200, BEVERLY HILLS, CA 90211

Barcode: *010001001207677*

This is to certify that this document is a true copy of the official record filed with the Registrar-Recorder/County Clerk.

Dean C. Logan
Registrar-Recorder/County Clerk

JAN 0 4 2010

000179253

This copy not valid unless prepared on engraved border displaying the Seal and Signature of the Registrar-Recorder/County Clerk.

INFORMATIONAL, NOT A VALID DOCUMENT TO ESTABLISH IDENTITY

ANY ALTERATION OR ERASURE VOIDS THIS CERTIFICATE

STATE OF CALIFORNIA
CERTIFICATION OF VITAL RECORD
COUNTY OF LOS ANGELES • REGISTRAR-RECORDER/COUNTY CLERK

District No. 1901 Registrar's No. 17217

1. **FULL NAME:** AGNES AYRES
2. **PLACE OF DEATH:**
   - (A) County: LOS ANGELES
   - (B) City or Town: LOS ANGELES
   - (C) Name of Hospital or Institution: ST. VINCENTS HOSPITAL
   - (D) Length of Stay: In Hospital or Institution: 2 DAYS; In this Community: 20 YRS.; In California: 20 YRS.
   - (E) If foreign born, how long in U.S.A.: —
3. **USUAL RESIDENCE OF DECEASED:**
   - (A) State: CALIFORNIA
   - (B) County: LOS ANGELES
   - (C) City or Town: LOS ANGELES
   - (D) Street No.: 834 No. ALFRED ST., L.A.

20. **DATE OF DEATH:** Month: DECEMBER Day: 25 Year: 1940 Hour: 3 Minute: 15 A.M.

3. (A) **If Veteran, Name of War:** No
   (B) **Social Security No.:** 568-03-0227
4. **Sex:** FEMALE
5. **Color or Race:** CAUC.
6. (A) **Single, Married, Widowed or Divorced:** DIVORCED
   (B) **Name of Husband or Wife:** MANUEL REACHI
   (C) **Age of Husband or Wife if Alive:** Unk YEARS
7. **Birthdate of Deceased:** APRIL 4 1898
8. **Age:** 42 Yrs. 8 Mos. 21 Days
9. **Birthplace:** CARBONDALE, ILLINOIS
10. **Usual Occupation:** ACTRESS
11. **Industry or Business:** MOTION PICTURE
12. **Father's Name:** SOLON AGUSTUS HENKEL
13. **Birthplace:** NEW MARKET, VIRGINIA
14. **Mother's Maiden Name:** EMMA S. AYRES
15. **Birthplace:** UNKNOWN
16. (A) **Informant:** MRS. ROLLINSON
    (B) **Address:** 1759 N. SIERRA BONITA
17. (A) **Burial, Cremation or Removal:** CREMATION (B) **Date:** DEC. 27, 1940
    (C) **Place:** HOLLYWOOD CREMATORY
18. (A) **Embalmer's Signature:** Norman W. Miller License No. 2233
    (B) **Funeral Director:** PIERCE BROS. HOLLYWOOD
    Address: 5959 SANTA MONICA BLVD.
    By: Milton W. Russom

19. **Date Filed:** DEC 27 1940
    Registrar's Signature: George Parrish M.D.

21. **MEDICAL CERTIFICATE:** I hereby certify that I attended the deceased from Feb 1 1939 to Dec 25 1940. That I last saw h-- alive on Dec 24 1940, and that death occurred on the date and hour stated above.
    Immediate Cause of Death: Cerebral Hemorrhage — 36 hrs
    Due to: Hypertension — 4 yrs.

24. **Physician's Signature:** Francis L. Browne M.D.
    Address: 1930 Wilshire
    Date: 12 27 40

CERTIFICATE OF DEATH

STATE OF CALIFORNIA — DEPARTMENT OF PUBLIC HEALTH
U.S. DEPT. OF COMMERCE — BUREAU OF THE CENSUS

Conny B. McCormack, Registrar-Recorder/County Clerk
DEC 07 2000
19-147104

STATE OF CALIFORNIA
CERTIFICATION OF VITAL RECORD

COUNTY OF ORANGE
SANTA ANA, CALIFORNIA

BK 238 | Pg 832

CERTIFICATE OF DEATH
STATE OF CALIFORNIA

3000 03238

DECEDENT PERSONAL DATA
- 1A. Name of Decedent—First: RAYMOND
- 1B. Middle: THOMAS
- 1C. Last: BAILEY
- 2A. Date of Death: April 15, 1980
- 2B. Hour: 1400
- 3. Sex: Male
- 4. Race: Caucasian
- 6. Date of Birth: May 6, 1904
- 7. Age: 75
- 8. Birthplace: CA
- 9. Name and Birthplace of Father: NFI Bailey/NFI
- 10. Birth Name and Birthplace of Mother: Alice O'Brien/NFI
- 11. Citizen of What Country: United States
- 12. Social Security Number: 565-14-1925
- 13. Marital Status: Married
- 14. Name of Surviving Spouse: Gaby George
- 15. Primary Occupation: Actor
- 16. Number of Years: 50
- 17. Employer: Filmways Productions
- 18. Kind of Industry or Business: Film Making

USUAL RESIDENCE
- 19A. Street Address: 5622 Highgate
- 19C. City or Town: Irvine
- 19D. County: Orange
- 19E. State: California
- 20. Name and Address of Informant—Relationship: Gaby Bailey - wife, 5622 Highgate, Irvine, CA. 92715

PLACE OF DEATH
- 21A. Place of Death: Residence
- 21B. County: Orange
- 21C. Street Address: 5622 Highgate
- 21D. City or Town: Irvine

CAUSE OF DEATH
- 22. Death was caused by:
  - (A) Intracerebral hemorrhage, right
  - (B) Cerebral arteriosclerosis, severe
- 24. Was Death Reported to Coroner: 80-1359-F
- 25. Was Biopsy Performed: no
- 26. Was Autopsy Performed: yes
- 27. Was Operation Performed: No

CORONER'S USE ONLY
- 35A. Investigation
- RAY GATES, SHERIFF-CORONER By: [signature]
- 35C. Date Signed: 4-17-80

- 36. Disposition: Cremation
- 37. Date: Apr. 18, 1980
- 38. Name and Address of Cemetery or Crematory: HARBOR LAWN CREMATORY, 1625 Gisler, Costa Mesa, Ca.
- 39. Embalmer: not embalmed
- 40. Name of Funeral Director: THE NEPTUNE SOCIETY
- 42. Date Accepted by Local Registrar: APR 17 1980

859541

CERTIFIED COPY OF VITAL RECORDS
STATE OF CALIFORNIA
COUNTY OF ORANGE } SS
DATE ISSUED OCT 18 2001

GARY L. GRANVILLE, Clerk-Recorder
ORANGE COUNTY, CALIFORNIA

This is a true and exact reproduction of the document officially registered and placed on file in the office of the Orange County Clerk-Recorder.

This copy not valid unless prepared on engraved border displaying seal and signature of Clerk-Recorder.

ANY ALTERATION OR ERASURE VOIDS THIS CERTIFICATE

CERTIFICATE OF DEATH

STATE OF CALIFORNIA — DEPARTMENT OF PUBLIC HEALTH

State File No: 55-063968
Registration District No: 7013
Registrar's Number: 10670

Decedent Personal Data

- **1a. Name of Deceased:** SUZAN BALL
- **1c. Last Name:** LONG
- **2a. Date of Death:** August 5, 1955
- **2b. Hour:** 4:10 P
- **3. Sex:** Female
- **4. Color or Race:** Caucasian
- **5. Marital Status:** Married
- **6. Date of Birth:** February 3, 1934
- **7. Age:** 21 Years
- **8a. Usual Occupation:** Actress
- **8b. Kind of Business or Industry:** Motion Pictures
- **9. Birthplace:** New York
- **10. Citizen of What Country:** U.S.A.
- **11. Name and Birthplace of Father:** Howard Dale Ball – Michigan
- **12. Maiden Name and Birthplace of Mother:** Marleah Francis O'Leary – New York
- **13. Name of Present Spouse:** Richard M. Long
- **14. Was Deceased Ever in U.S. Armed Forces?:** No
- **15. Social Security Number:** 557-40-5240
- **16. Informant:** Richard M. Long

Place of Death

- **17a. County:** Los Angeles
- **17b. City or Town:** Beverly Hills
- **17c. Length of Stay in This City or Town:** 8 Years
- **17d. Full Name of Hospital or Institution:** (None)
- **17e. Address:** 624 North Roxbury Drive

Last Usual Residence

- **18a. State:** California
- **18b. County:** Los Angeles
- **18c. City or Town:** Beverly Hills
- **18e. Street or Rural Address:** 624 North Roxbury Drive

Physician's Certification

- **19. Physician:** Attended deceased from 10-28-53 to 8-5-55; last saw deceased alive on 8-5-55
- **19. Signature:** Francis C. Guglielmo M.D.
- **19. Address:** 6317 Wilshire, L.A. 48
- **19. Date Signed:** 8-5-55

Funeral Director and Registrar

- **20a. Burial**
- **20b. Date:** Aug. 9, 1955
- **20c. Cemetery or Crematory:** Forest Lawn Memorial Park
- **22. Funeral Director:** Forest Lawn Memorial Park Ass'n, Inc., Glendale, California
- **23. Date Received by Local Registrar:** Aug 9 1955

Cause of Death

- **25. Disease or Condition Directly Leading to Death:** METASTATIC FIBROSARCOMA
- EXTENSIVE LUNG METASTASES
- CAUSING PNEUMONIA
- **Antecedent Causes — Due to (b):** FIBROSARCOMA RIGHT FEMUR
- MIDTHIGH AMPUTATION 1-12-54
- **Interval Between Onset and Death:** 2½ yrs

Operation

- **27a. Date of Operation:** 1-12-54
- **27b. Major Findings of Operation:** MIDTHIGH AMPUTATION RIGHT FEMUR
- **28. Autopsy:** No

STATE OF CALIFORNIA

CERTIFICATION OF VITAL RECORD

COUNTY OF LOS ANGELES • REGISTRAR-RECORDER/COUNTY CLERK

INFORMATIONAL, NOT A VALID DOCUMENT TO ESTABLISH IDENTITY

CERTIFICATE OF DEATH

STATE OF CALIFORNIA
USE BLACK INK ONLY / NO ERASURES, WHITEOUTS OR ALTERATIONS
VS-11 (REV 1/04)

STATE FILE NUMBER

LOCAL REGISTRATION NUMBER: 3200919050593

DECEDENT'S PERSONAL DATA

1. NAME OF DECEDENT — FIRST (Given): GENE
2. MIDDLE: -
3. LAST (Family): BARRY

AKA. ALSO KNOWN AS — Include full AKA (FIRST, MIDDLE, LAST):

4. DATE OF BIRTH mm/dd/ccyy: 06/14/1919
5. AGE Yrs: 90
IF UNDER ONE YEAR: Months / Days
IF UNDER 24 HOURS: Hours / Minutes
6. SEX: M

9. BIRTH STATE/FOREIGN COUNTRY: NEW YORK
10. SOCIAL SECURITY NUMBER: 055-12-7517
11. EVER IN U.S. ARMED FORCES? [ ] YES [X] NO [ ] UNK
12. MARITAL STATUS (at Time of Death): WIDOWED
7. DATE OF DEATH mm/dd/ccyy: 12/09/2009
8. HOUR (24 Hours): 1206

13. EDUCATION — Highest Level/Degree (see worksheet on back): SOME COLLEGE
14/15. WAS DECEDENT HISPANIC/LATINO(A)/SPANISH? (If yes, see worksheet on back) [ ] YES [X] NO
16. DECEDENT'S RACE — Up to 3 races may be listed (see worksheet on back): WHITE

17. USUAL OCCUPATION — Type of work for most of life. DO NOT USE RETIRED: ACTOR
18. KIND OF BUSINESS OR INDUSTRY (e.g. grocery store, road construction, employment agency, etc.): ENTERTAINMENT
19. YEARS IN OCCUPATION: 70

USUAL RESIDENCE

20. DECEDENT'S RESIDENCE (Street and number or location): 622 N MAPLE DRIVE
21. CITY: BEVERLYHILLS
22. COUNTY/PROVINCE: LOS ANGELES
23. ZIP CODE: 90210
24. YEARS IN COUNTY: 58
25. STATE/FOREIGN COUNTRY: CALIFORNIA

INFORMANT

26. INFORMANT'S NAME, RELATIONSHIP: FREDRIC BARRY, SON
27. INFORMANT'S MAILING ADDRESS (Street and number or rural route number, city or town, state, ZIP): 21140 BRUNNELL COURT, TOPANGA, CA 90290

SPOUSE AND PARENT INFORMATION

28. NAME OF SURVIVING SPOUSE — FIRST: -
29. MIDDLE: -
30. LAST (Maiden Name): -

31. NAME OF FATHER — FIRST: MARTIN
32. MIDDLE: -
33. LAST: KLASS
34. BIRTH STATE: RUSSIA

35. NAME OF MOTHER — FIRST: EVA
36. MIDDLE: -
37. LAST (Maiden): COHN
38. BIRTH STATE: PA

FUNERAL DIRECTOR/LOCAL REGISTRAR

39. DISPOSITION DATE mm/dd/ccyy: 12/18/2009
40. PLACE OF FINAL DISPOSITION: HILLSIDE MEMORIAL PARK, 6001 CENTINELA AVENUE, LOS ANGELES, CA 90045

41. TYPE OF DISPOSITION(S): BU
42. SIGNATURE OF EMBALMER: NOT EMBALMED
43. LICENSE NUMBER: -

44. NAME OF FUNERAL ESTABLISHMENT: HILLSIDE MEMORIAL PARK MORTUARY
45. LICENSE NUMBER: FD1358
46. SIGNATURE OF LOCAL REGISTRAR: JONATHAN FIELDING, MD
47. DATE mm/dd/ccyy: 12/18/2009

PLACE OF DEATH

101. PLACE OF DEATH: SUNRISE ASSISTED LIVING
102. IF HOSPITAL, SPECIFY ONE: [ ] IP [ ] ER/OP [ ] DOA
103. IF OTHER THAN HOSPITAL, SPECIFY ONE: [ ] Hospice [ ] Nursing Home/LTC [ ] Decedent's Home [X] Other
104. COUNTY: LOS ANGELES
105. FACILITY ADDRESS OR LOCATION WHERE FOUND (Street and number or location): 20461 VENTURA BOULEVARD
106. CITY: WOODLAND HILLS

CAUSE OF DEATH

107. CAUSE OF DEATH — Enter the chain of events — diseases, injuries, or complications — that directly caused death. DO NOT enter terminal events such as cardiac arrest, respiratory arrest, or ventricular fibrillation without showing the etiology. DO NOT ABBREVIATE.

IMMEDIATE CAUSE (Final disease or condition resulting in death)
(A) ISCHEMIC HEART DISEASE — Time Interval Between Onset and Death (AT): YRS

Sequentially, list conditions, if any, leading to cause on Line A. Enter UNDERLYING CAUSE (disease or injury that initiated the events resulting in death) LAST
(B) ATHEROSCLEROTIC CARDIOVASCULAR DISEASE — (BT): YRS
(C) — (CT)
(D) — (DT)

108. DEATH REPORTED TO CORONER? [X] YES [ ] NO — REFERRAL NUMBER: 2009-08444
109. BIOPSY PERFORMED? [ ] YES [X] NO
110. AUTOPSY PERFORMED? [X] YES [ ] NO
111. USED IN DETERMINING CAUSE? [X] YES [ ] NO

112. OTHER SIGNIFICANT CONDITIONS CONTRIBUTING TO DEATH BUT NOT RESULTING IN THE UNDERLYING CAUSE GIVEN IN 107: INTRACRANIAL HEMORRHAGE, BLUNT FORCE HEAD AND LEG TRAUMA

113. WAS OPERATION PERFORMED FOR ANY CONDITION IN ITEM 107 OR 112? (If yes, list type of operation and date.): NO
113A. IF FEMALE, PREGNANT IN LAST YEAR? [ ] YES [ ] NO [ ] UNK

PHYSICIAN'S CERTIFICATION

114. I CERTIFY THAT TO THE BEST OF MY KNOWLEDGE DEATH OCCURRED AT THE HOUR, DATE, AND PLACE STATED FROM THE CAUSES STATED. Decedent Attended Since (A) mm/dd/ccyy — Decedent Last Seen Alive (B) mm/dd/ccyy
115. SIGNATURE AND TITLE OF CERTIFIER
116. LICENSE NUMBER
117. DATE mm/dd/ccyy
118. TYPE ATTENDING PHYSICIAN'S NAME, MAILING ADDRESS, ZIP CODE

CORONER'S USE ONLY

119. I CERTIFY THAT IN MY OPINION DEATH OCCURRED AT THE HOUR, DATE, AND PLACE STATED FROM THE CAUSES STATED. MANNER OF DEATH [ ] Natural [X] Accident [ ] Homicide [ ] Suicide [ ] Pending Investigation [ ] Could not be determined
120. INJURED AT WORK? [ ] YES [X] NO [ ] UNK
121. INJURY DATE mm/dd/ccyy: 12/05/2009
122. HOUR (24 Hours): UNK

123. PLACE OF INJURY (e.g., home, construction site, wooded area, etc.): NURSING HOME
124. DESCRIBE HOW INJURY OCCURRED (Events which resulted in injury): FALL IN NURSING HOME
125. LOCATION OF INJURY (Street and number, or location, and city, and ZIP): 20461 VENTURA BLVD, WOODLAND HILLS, CA 91364

126. SIGNATURE OF CORONER / DEPUTY CORONER: REGINA M AUGUSTINE
127. DATE mm/dd/ccyy: 12/18/2009
128. TYPE NAME, TITLE OF CORONER / DEPUTY CORONER: REGINA M AUGUSTINE, DEPUTY CORONER

STATE REGISTRAR: A B C D E — *010001001375913* — FAX AUTH. # — CENSUS TRACT

This is to certify that this document is a true copy of the official record filed with the Registrar-Recorder/County Clerk. JAN 04 2010

DEAN C. LOGAN
Registrar-Recorder/County Clerk

000190063

This copy not valid unless prepared on engraved border displaying the Seal and Signature of the Registrar-Recorder/County Clerk.

PBNCO (Rev) 07/09

ANY ALTERATION OR ERASURE VOIDS THIS CERTIFICATE

STATE OF CALIFORNIA
CERTIFICATION OF VITAL RECORD
COUNTY OF LOS ANGELES • REGISTRAR-RECORDER/COUNTY CLERK

CERTIFICATE OF DEATH — STATE OF CALIFORNIA — 3881 9035187

1A. Name — First	JUDITH
1B. Middle	EVA
1C. Last	BARSI
2A. Date of Death	July 27, 1988 (Found)
2B. Hour	0900
3. Sex	Female
4. Race/Ethnicity	White /Hungarian
5. Spanish/Hispanic	NO
6. Date of Birth	June 6, 1978
7. Age	10 Years
8. Birthplace of Decedent	Burbank
9. Name and Birthplace of Father	Joseph Barsi — Hungary
10. Birth Name and Birthplace of Mother	Maria Benko — Hungary
11A. Citizen of What Country	USA
11B. Military Service	19 -- TO 19 --
12. Social Security Number	563-53-8073
13. Marital Status	Never Married
15. Primary Occupation	Actress
16. Number of Years	8
17. Employer	Self-Employed
18. Kind of Industry or Business	Entertainment
19A. Usual Residence — Street Address	22100 Michale Street
19C. City or Town	Canoga Park
19D. County	Los Angeles
19E. State	California
20. Informant	E. Broom-Public Administrator, Hall Of Records, 9th Floor, 320 W. Temple Street, Los Angeles, California 90012
21A. Place of Death	Home
21B. County	Los Angeles
21C. Street Address	22100 Michale St
21D. City or Town	Canoga Park
22. Death Was Caused By (A)	GUNSHOT WOUND TO HEAD
24. Was Death Reported to Coroner?	88-7461
25. Was Biopsy Performed?	No
26. Was Autopsy Performed?	No
27. Was Operation Performed	No
29. Accident, Suicide, etc.	Homicide
30. Place of Injury	Home
31. Injury at Work	No
32A. Date of Injury	Unknown
32B. Hour	Unk.
33. Location	22100 Michale St - Canoga Park
34. Describe How Injury Occurred	Shot
35B. Coroner	Deputy Coroner
35C. Date Signed	8-4-88
36. Disposition	Burial
37. Date	August 9, 1988
38. Cemetery	Forest Lawn Memorial Park, 6300 Forest Lawn Drive, Los Angeles, CA
39. Embalmer	Not Embalmed
40A. Funeral Director	Forest Lawn Hollywood Hills Mty
40B. License No.	F-904
42. Date Accepted by Local Registrar	AUG 8 1988

1 of 2

This is to certify that this document is a true copy of the official record filed with the Registrar-Recorder/County Clerk.

CONNY B. McCORMACK
Registrar-Recorder/County Clerk

This copy not valid unless prepared on engraved border displaying the Seal and Signature of the Registrar-Recorder/County Clerk.

OCT 0 4 2001
19-673796

CERTIFICATION OF VITAL RECORD

COUNTY OF LOS ANGELES • REGISTRAR-RECORDER/COUNTY CLERK

FILED MAY 18 1949 MAME B. BEATTY, COUNTY RECORDER

CERTIFICATE OF DEATH

- REGISTRATION DISTRICT NO.: 1916
- REGISTRAR'S NUMBER: 43
- STATE FILE NO.: 5867

Decedent Personal Data
- 1A. Name (First): Wallace
- 1B. Middle Name: (blank)
- 1C. Last Name: Beery
- 2A. Date of Death: April 15, 1949
- 2B. Hour: 10:05pm
- 3. Sex: Male
- 4. Color or Race: Cauc
- 5. Married/Divorced: Divorced
- 6. Date of Birth: April 1 1885
- 7. Age: 64 years
- 8A. Usual Occupation: Actor
- 8B. Kind of Business or Industry: Motion Pictures
- 9. Birthplace: Missouri
- 10. Citizen of What Country: USA
- 11. Name of Father: Noah W Beery
- 12. Maiden Name of Mother: Margaret Fitzgerald
- 13. Name of Spouse: (blank)
- 14. Was Deceased Ever in U.S. Armed Forces: No
- 15. Social Security Number: 569-18-8820
- 16. Informant: Jack Nerdrum, 1115 Charm Acres Pl

Place of Death
- 17A. Place of Death: Beverly Hills
- 17B. Length of Stay: 25yr
- 17C. County: Los Angeles
- 17D. Full Name and Address of Hospital: 816 No Alpine Dr

Usual Residence
- 18A. Street Address: 816 No Alpine Dr
- 18B. City or Town: Beverly Hills
- 18C. County: Los Angeles
- 18D. State: Calif

Cause of Death
- 19-IA. Disease or Condition Directly Leading to Death: Aortic Stenosis — 20yr
- 19-IB. Due to: Rheumatic heart disease — 20yr

Operations / Autopsy
- 21. Autopsy: YES

Physician's or Coroner's Certification
- Attended deceased from 4-15-49, last saw alive 4-15-49
- 23C. Signature: Eliot Corday MD
- 23D. Address: Beverly Hills Calif
- 23E. Date Signed: 4-18-49

Funeral Director and Registrar
- 24B. Date: 4-19-49
- 24C. Cemetery or Crematory: Forest Lawn Cemetery
- 25. Signature of Embalmer: H H Houston — License Number 1674
- 27. Date Received by Local Registrar: 4-20-49
- 28. Signature of Local Registrar: B J Firminger
- 26. Signature of Funeral Director: Forest Lawn Meml Pk Assn, R E McElfresh, Glendale

STATE OF CALIFORNIA — DEPARTMENT OF PUBLIC HEALTH

This is to certify that this document is a true copy of the official record filed with the Registrar-Recorder/County Clerk.

Beatriz Valdez
BEATRIZ VALDEZ
Registrar-Recorder/County Clerk

This copy not valid unless prepared on engraved border displaying the Seal and Signature of the Registrar-Recorder/County Clerk.

AUG 25 1995
19-000051

ANY ALTERATION OR ERASURE VOIDS THIS CERTIFICATE

STATE OF CALIFORNIA
CERTIFICATION OF VITAL RECORD

COUNTY OF LOS ANGELES • REGISTRAR-RECORDER/COUNTY CLERK

CERTIFICATE OF DEATH
STATE OF CALIFORNIA—DEPARTMENT OF PUBLIC HEALTH

LOCAL REGISTRATION DISTRICT AND CERTIFICATE NUMBER: 7053   19682

DECEDENT PERSONAL DATA
- 1A. NAME OF DECEASED—FIRST NAME: RALF
- 1C. LAST NAME: BELMONT
- 2A. DATE OF DEATH: September 21, 1964
- 2B. HOUR: 9:34 P.M.
- 3. SEX: Male
- 4. COLOR OR RACE: Caucasian
- 5. BIRTHPLACE: Italy
- 6. DATE OF BIRTH: April 9, 1882
- 7. AGE: 82 YEARS
- 8. NAME AND BIRTHPLACE OF FATHER: Nicholas Romeo – Italy
- 9. MAIDEN NAME AND BIRTHPLACE OF MOTHER: Unknown Unknown – Unknown
- 10. CITIZEN OF WHAT COUNTRY: U.S.A.
- 11. SOCIAL SECURITY NUMBER: 569-50-6872
- 12. LAST OCCUPATION: Actor and Writer
- 13. NUMBER OF YEARS IN THIS OCCUPATION: Unknown
- 14. NAME OF LAST EMPLOYING COMPANY OR FIRM: Self-employed
- 15. KIND OF INDUSTRY OR BUSINESS: Entertainment
- 16. IF DECEASED WAS EVER IN U.S. ARMED FORCES, GIVE WAR OR DATES OF SERVICE: No
- 17. SPECIFY MARRIED, NEVER MARRIED, WIDOWED, DIVORCED: Widowed

PLACE OF DEATH
- 19A. PLACE OF DEATH—NAME OF HOSPITAL: Hollywood Receiving Hospital
- 19C. STREET ADDRESS: 1350 North Wilcox Avenue (Inside City Corporate Limits)
- 19D. CITY OR TOWN: Los Angeles
- 19E. COUNTY: Los Angeles
- 19F. LENGTH OF STAY IN COUNTY OF DEATH: 51 YEARS
- 19G. LENGTH OF STAY IN CALIFORNIA: 51 YEARS

LAST USUAL RESIDENCE
- 20A. STREET ADDRESS: 1830 North Cherokee Avenue
- 20B. INSIDE CITY CORPORATE LIMITS: X
- 20D. CITY OR TOWN: Los Angeles
- 20E. COUNTY: Los Angeles
- 20F. STATE: California
- 21A. NAME OF INFORMANT: Ken Rogers
- 21B. ADDRESS OF INFORMANT: Hollywood and Cahuenga, Hollywood, Calif.

PHYSICIAN'S OR CORONER'S CERTIFICATION
- 22C. CORONER: autopsy
- 22B. Theo. J. Curphey, M.D., Chief Medical Examiner-Coroner
- 22D. ADDRESS: Hall of Justice, Los Angeles
- 22E. DATE SIGNED: 10-1-64

FUNERAL DIRECTOR AND LOCAL REGISTRAR
- 23. DISPOSAL: Entombment
- 24. DATE: 9-29-64
- 25. NAME OF CEMETERY OR CREMATORY: Mausoleum Forest Lawn Memorial-Park
- 27. NAME OF FUNERAL DIRECTOR: Forest Lawn Memorial-Park Assn., Glendale, California
- 28. DATE ACCEPTED: OCT - 5 1964

CAUSE OF DEATH
- PART I. IMMEDIATE CAUSE (A): CRUSH INJURY OF CHEST AND ABDOMEN WITH LUNG CONTUSION, INTERNAL HEMORRHAGE, AND FRACTURE OF SPINE WITH SPINAL CORD COMPRESSION

INJURY INFORMATION
- 34A. SPECIFY ACCIDENT, SUICIDE OR HOMICIDE: Accident
- 34B. DESCRIBE HOW INJURY OCCURRED: Pedestrian Struck by auto
- 35A. TIME OF INJURY: 9:10 P.M. 9 21 64
- 35B. INJURY OCCURRED NOT WHILE AT WORK
- 35C. PLACE OF INJURY: street
- 35D. CITY, TOWN, OR LOCATION: Los Angeles, L.A., Calif.

Filed OCT 30 1964   RAY E. LEE, COUNTY RECORDER

This is to certify that this document is a true copy of the official record filed with the Registrar-Recorder/County Clerk.

Conny B. McCormack
CONNY B. McCORMACK
Registrar-Recorder/County Clerk

APR 23 2002
19-210626

This copy not valid unless prepared on engraved border displaying the Seal and Signature of the Registrar-Recorder/County Clerk.

ANY ALTERATION OR ERASURE VOIDS THIS CERTIFICATE

COUNTY OF ORANGE
HEALTH CARE AGENCY
1200 N. MAIN STREET, SUITE 100-A
SANTA ANA, CA 92701

STATE OF CALIFORNIA — CERTIFICATION OF VITAL RECORD

CERTIFICATE OF DEATH — 3200730013519

- **1. Name of Decedent — First:** JOEY
- **2. Middle:** -
- **3. Last:** BISHOP
- **AKA:** JOSEPH ABRAHAM GOTTLIEB
- **4. Date of Birth:** 02/03/1918
- **5. Age:** 89
- **6. Sex:** M
- **7. Date of Death:** 10/17/2007
- **8. Hour:** 2005
- **9. Birth State/Foreign Country:** NY
- **10. Social Security Number:** 179-07-9280
- **11. Ever in U.S. Armed Forces:** YES
- **12. Marital Status:** WIDOWED
- **13. Education:** 12ND
- **14/15. Hispanic:** NO
- **16. Race:** CAUCASIAN
- **17. Usual Occupation:** COMEDIAN
- **18. Kind of Business/Industry:** ENTERTAINMENT
- **19. Years in Occupation:** 80
- **20. Decedent's Residence:** 534 VIA LIDO NORD
- **21. City:** NEWPORT BEACH
- **22. County:** ORANGE
- **23. Zip:** 92663
- **24. Years in County:** 36
- **25. State:** CA
- **26. Informant's Name, Relationship:** NORA A GARIBOTTI, FRIEND
- **27. Informant's Mailing Address:** 534 VIA LIDO NORD, NEWPORT BEACH, CA 92663
- **31. Name of Father — First:** JACOB
- **33. Last:** GOTTLIEB
- **34. Birth State:** AUSTRIA
- **35. Name of Mother — First:** ANNA
- **37. Last (Maiden):** SIEGEL
- **38. Birth State:** ROMANIA
- **39. Disposition Date:** 10/22/2007
- **40. Place of Final Disposition:** AT SEA OFF THE COAST OF ORANGE COUNTY
- **41. Type of Disposition:** CR/SEA
- **42. Signature of Embalmer:** NOT EMBALMED
- **44. Name of Funeral Establishment:** PACIFIC VIEW MORTUARY
- **45. License Number:** FD 1176
- **46. Signature of Local Registrar:** ERIC G. HANDLER, M.D.
- **47. Date:** 10/19/2007
- **101. Place of Death:** RESIDENCE
- **104. County:** ORANGE
- **105. Facility Address:** 534 VIA LIDO NORD
- **106. City:** NEWPORT BEACH
- **107. Cause of Death:**
  - Immediate Cause (A): ASPIRATION PNEUMONIA — 1 MOS
  - (B): LUNG CANCER — YRS
- **112. Other Significant Conditions:** LUNG CANCER
- **113. Was Operation Performed:** NO
- **115. Signature and Title of Certifier:** RICHARD JOSEPH HASKELL M.D.
- **116. License Number:** G41879
- **117. Date:** 10/18/2007
- **Decedent Attended Since:** 12/02/1997
- **Decedent Last Seen Alive:** 10/11/2007
- **118. Attending Physician's Name/Address:** RICHARD JOSEPH HASKELL M.D., 415 OLD NEWPORT BLVD STE 200, NEWPORT BEACH, CA 92663
- **108. Death Reported to Coroner:** YES
- **Coroner Number:** 07-05853-OS
- **109. Biopsy Performed:** NO
- **110. Autopsy Performed:** NO

012007000631218

CERTIFIED COPY OF VITAL RECORDS

STATE OF CALIFORNIA } SS
COUNTY OF ORANGE

DATE ISSUED: JAN 0 3 2008

This is a true and exact reproduction of the document officially registered and placed on file in the office of the VITAL RECORDS SECTION, ORANGE COUNTY HEALTH CARE AGENCY.

ERIC G. HANDLER, M.D.
HEALTH OFFICER
ORANGE COUNTY, CALIFORNIA

This copy not valid unless prepared on engraved border displaying seal and signature of Registrar.

002246055

INFORMATIONAL, NOT A VALID DOCUMENT TO ESTABLISH IDENTITY

ANY ALTERATION OR ERASURE VOIDS THIS CERTIFICATE

STATE OF CALIFORNIA — CERTIFICATE OF DEATH

DECEDENT PERSONAL DATA

- 1. Name of Decedent—First (Given): Erma
- 2. Middle: L
- 3. Last (Family): Bombeck
- 4. Date of Birth: 02/21/1927
- 5. Age Yrs.: 69
- 6. Sex: F
- 7. Date of Death: 04/22/1996
- 8. Hour: 0330
- 9. State of Birth: Ohio
- 10. Social Security No.: 284-20-7303
- 11. Military Service: None
- 12. Marital Status: Married
- 13. Education—Years Completed: 16
- 14. Race: Caucasian
- 15. Hispanic: No
- 16. Usual Employer: Self
- 17. Occupation: Writer
- 18. Kind of Business: Author / Columnist
- 19. Years in Occupation: 40

USUAL RESIDENCE

- 20. Residence—Street and Number or Location: 4632 E Foothill Drive
- 21. City: Paradise Valley
- 22. County: Maricopa
- 23. Zip Code: 85253
- 24. Yrs in County: 25
- 25. State or Foreign Country: Arizona

INFORMANT

- 26. Name, Relationship: William L. Bombeck
- 27. Mailing Address: 4632 E Foothill Dr., Paradise Valley, AZ 85253

SPOUSE AND PARENT INFORMATION

- 28. Name of Surviving Spouse—First: William
- 29. Middle: L.
- 30. Last (Maiden Name): Bombeck
- 31. Name of Father—First: Casius
- 33. Last: Fiste
- 34. Birth State: Ohio
- 35. Name of Mother—First: Erma
- 37. Last (Maiden): Haines
- 38. Birth State: Ohio

DISPOSITION(S) / FUNERAL DIRECTOR AND LOCAL REGISTRAR

- 39. Date: 04/29/1996
- 40. Place of Final Disposition: St Francis Cemetery, Phoenix, AZ
- 41. Type of Disposition(s): TR / BU
- 43. License No.: 5757
- 44. Name of Funeral Director: McAvoy O'Hara Company
- 45. License No.: FD 523
- 47. Date: 04/24/1996

PLACE OF DEATH

- 101. Place of Death: UCSF Medical Center
- 102. If Hospital, Specify One: IP
- 104. County: San Francisco
- 105. Street Address: 505 Parnassus Avenue
- 106. City: San Francisco

CAUSE OF DEATH

- 107. Death was caused by:
  - (A) Immediate Cause: Cardiac Arrest — Mins
  - (B) Due to: End Stage Renal Failure — Years
- 108. Death Reported to Coroner: No
- 109. Biopsy Performed: Yes
- 110. Autopsy Performed: No
- 112. Other Significant Conditions: Thrombrocytopenia, Cholangitis, GI Bleeding, Acute Tubular Necrosis
- 113. Was Operation Performed: Cadaveric Renal Transplant 04/03/1996

PHYSICIAN'S CERTIFICATION

- 114. Decedent Attended Since: 04/02/1996; Decedent Last Seen Alive: 04/22/1996
- 115. Signature and Title of Certifier: Peter Bretan
- 116. License No.: G 046251
- 117. Date: 04/22/1996
- 118. Type Attending Physician's Name, Mailing Address: Peter Bretan, MD. 505 Parnassus Ave., SF, CA 94143

This is to certify that, if bearing the embossed seal of the San Francisco Department of Public Health, this is a true copy of the document on file in the Bureau of Records and Statistics as of this date.

Sandra R. Hernández, M.D., Health Officer & Local Registrar — 06/06/1996

CERTIFICATE OF DEATH
STATE OF CALIFORNIA
COUNTY OF LOS ANGELES DEPARTMENT OF PUBLIC HEALTH

STATE FILE NUMBER: 3052009204500
LOCAL REGISTRATION NUMBER: 3200919050291

DECEDENT'S PERSONAL DATA
- 1. NAME OF DECEDENT — FIRST: FRANK
- 2. MIDDLE: —
- 3. LAST (Family): BRILL
- AKA, ALSO KNOWN AS: FRANK - FEINSTEIN
- 4. DATE OF BIRTH: 10/31/1918
- 5. AGE: 91
- 6. SEX: M
- 9. BIRTH STATE/FOREIGN COUNTRY: NEW YORK
- 10. SOCIAL SECURITY NUMBER: 054-01-4878
- 11. EVER IN U.S. ARMED FORCES?: YES
- 12. MARITAL STATUS: DIVORCED
- 7. DATE OF DEATH: 12/15/2009
- 8. HOUR: 2135
- 13. EDUCATION: HS GRADUATE
- 14/15. HISPANIC/LATINO: NO
- 16. DECEDENT'S RACE: WHITE
- 17. USUAL OCCUPATION: PRODUCER
- 18. KIND OF BUSINESS OR INDUSTRY: MOTION PICTURE AND TELEVISION
- 19. YEARS IN OCCUPATION: 60

USUAL RESIDENCE
- 20. DECEDENT'S RESIDENCE: 9649 CEDARBROOK DR.
- 21. CITY: BEVERLY HILLS
- 22. COUNTY/PROVINCE: LOS ANGELES
- 23. ZIP CODE: 90210
- 24. YEARS IN COUNTY: 50
- 25. STATE/FOREIGN COUNTRY: CALIFORNIA

INFORMANT
- 26. INFORMANT'S NAME; RELATIONSHIP: ROBERT A. FINKELSTEIN, DPOA
- 27. INFORMANT'S MAILING ADDRESS: 8573 W. OLYMPIC BL., LOS ANGELES, CA 90035

SPOUSE AND PARENT INFORMATION
- 28-30. NAME OF SURVIVING SPOUSE: —
- 31. NAME OF FATHER — FIRST: UNKNOWN
- 32. MIDDLE: UNKNOWN
- 33. LAST: FEINSTEIN
- 34. BIRTH STATE: UNKNOWN
- 35. NAME OF MOTHER — FIRST: UNKNOWN
- 36. MIDDLE: UNKNOWN
- 37. LAST (Maiden): UNKNOWN
- 38. BIRTH STATE: UNKNOWN

FUNERAL DIRECTOR / LOCAL REGISTRAR
- 39. DISPOSITION DATE: 12/18/2009
- 40. PLACE OF FINAL DISPOSITION: BRILL RESIDENCE, 9649 CEDARBROOK DR., BEVERLY HILLS, CA 90210
- 41. TYPE OF DISPOSITION(S): CR/RES
- 42. SIGNATURE OF EMBALMER: NOT EMBALMED
- 44. NAME OF FUNERAL ESTABLISHMENT: MALINOW & SILVERMAN MORTUARY
- 45. LICENSE NUMBER: FD-487
- 46. SIGNATURE OF LOCAL REGISTRAR: JONATHAN FIELDING, MD
- 47. DATE: 12/17/2009

PLACE OF DEATH
- 101. PLACE OF DEATH: RESIDENCE
- 103. IF OTHER THAN HOSPITAL: Decedent's Home
- 104. COUNTY: LOS ANGELES
- 105. FACILITY ADDRESS: 9649 CEDARBROOK DR.
- 106. CITY: BEVERLY HILLS

CAUSE OF DEATH
- 107. IMMEDIATE CAUSE (A): ALZHEIMER'S DISEASE — YEARS
- 108. DEATH REPORTED TO CORONER?: NO
- 109. BIOPSY PERFORMED?: NO
- 110. AUTOPSY PERFORMED?: NO
- 112. OTHER SIGNIFICANT CONDITIONS: NONE
- 113. WAS OPERATION PERFORMED: NO

PHYSICIAN'S CERTIFICATION
- 114. (A) Decedent Attended Since: 11/24/2009 (B) Decedent Last Seen Alive: 12/15/2009
- 115. SIGNATURE AND TITLE OF CERTIFIER: ISAAC HERNANDEZ VIELMA M.D.
- 116. LICENSE NUMBER: A90584
- 117. DATE: 12/17/2009
- 112. TYPE ATTENDING PHYSICIAN'S NAME, MAILING ADDRESS, ZIP CODE: ISAAC HERNANDEZ VIELMA M.D., 16600 SHERMAN WAY STE 266, VAN NUYS, CA 91406

This is a true certified copy of the record filed in the County of Los Angeles Department of Public Health if it bears the Registrar's signature in purple ink.

Jonathan E. Fielding MD
Director of Public Health and Registrar

DATE ISSUED: DEC 28 2009

HD2064815

This copy not valid unless prepared on engraved border displaying seal and signature of Registrar.

INFORMATIONAL, NOT A VALID DOCUMENT TO ESTABLISH IDENTITY

STATE OF CALIFORNIA
CERTIFICATION OF VITAL RECORD

COUNTY OF LOS ANGELES • REGISTRAR-RECORDER/COUNTY CLERK

CERTIFICATE OF DEATH — State File Number: 3200719015523

1. Name of Decedent – First	ROSCOE
2. Middle	LEE
3. Last (Family)	BROWNE
4. Date of Birth	05/02/1922
5. Age	84
6. Sex	M
7. Date of Death	04/11/2007
8. Hour (24 Hours)	0030
9. Birth State/Foreign Country	NEW JERSEY
10. Social Security Number	140-12-3735
11. Ever in U.S. Armed Forces?	YES
12. Marital Status	NEVER MARRIED
13. Education	BACHELOR'S
14/15. Hispanic/Latino?	NO
16. Decedent's Race	AFRICAN AMERICAN
17. Usual Occupation	ACTOR/POET
18. Kind of Business or Industry	ENTERTAINMENT
19. Years in Occupation	51
20. Decedent's Residence	3535 WONDERVIEW DR.
21. City	LOS ANGELES
22. County/Province	LOS ANGELES
23. Zip Code	90068
24. Years in County	35
25. State/Foreign Country	CA
26. Informant's Name, Relationship	LAURENCE FISHBURNE, III, DPOA
27. Informant's Mailing Address	5750 WILSHIRE BLVD. STE 580, LOS ANGELES CA 90036
31. Name of Father/Parent – First	SYLVANUS
32. Middle	SILAS
33. Last	BROWNE
34. Birth State	KY
35. Name of Mother/Parent – First	LOVIE
36. Middle	LEE
37. Last (Birth Name)	USHER
38. Birth State	TX
39. Disposition Date	04/18/2007
40. Place of Final Disposition	5/10 RES: LAURENCE FISHBURNE III, 5750 WILSHIRE BLVD STE 580, LOS ANGELES, CA 90036
41. Type of Disposition	CR/RES
42. Signature of Embalmer	NOT EMBALMED
44. Name of Funeral Establishment	FOREST LAWN HOLLYWOOD HILLS MTY.
45. License Number	FD904
47. Date	04/16/2007
101. Place of Death	CEDARS SINAI MED CTR
102. If Hospital	IP
104. County	LOS ANGELES
105. Facility Address	8700 BEVERLY BLVD
106. City	LOS ANGELES
107. Cause of Death – Immediate Cause (A)	LIVER FAILURE — 2 WKS
(B)	METASTATIC LUNG CANCER — 3 WK
108. Death Reported to Coroner?	NO
109. Biopsy Performed?	YES
110. Autopsy Performed?	NO
111. Used in Determining Cause?	NO
112. Other Significant Conditions	NONE
113. Was Operation Performed	NO
116. License Number	G40178
117. Date	04/12/2007
(A) Decedent Attended Since	03/21/2007
(B) Decedent Last Seen Alive	04/11/2007
118. Attending Physician	LELAND M GREEN, MD 9090 WILSHIRE BLVD, BEVERLY HILLS, CA 90211

Date certified: JAN 2 2 2008

INFORMATIONAL, NOT A VALID DOCUMENT TO ESTABLISH IDENTITY

019042564

COUNTY OF LOS ANGELES
DEPARTMENT OF HEALTH SERVICES

CERTIFICATE OF DEATH
STATE OF CALIFORNIA

1. NAME OF DECEDENT — FIRST (Given)	KATHERINE
2. MIDDLE	JACQUELINE
3. LAST (Family)	BROWNE – MCGAVIN
4. DATE OF BIRTH	09/19/1930
5. AGE Yrs.	72
6. SEX	FEM
7. DATE OF DEATH	04/08/2003
8. HOUR (24 Hours)	0616
9. BIRTH STATE/FOREIGN COUNTRY	CA
10. SOCIAL SECURITY NUMBER	571-30-3029
11. EVER IN U.S. ARMED FORCES?	NO
12. MARITAL STATUS	MARRIED
13. EDUCATION	BACHELOR'S
14/15. HISPANIC/LATINO?	NO
16. DECEDENT'S RACE	WHITE
17. USUAL OCCUPATION	ACTRESS
18. KIND OF BUSINESS OR INDUSTRY	ENTERTAINMENT
19. YEARS IN OCCUPATION	45
20. DECEDENT'S RESIDENCE	1129 BENEDICT CANYON
21. CITY	BEVERLY HILLS
22. COUNTY/PROVINCE	LOS ANGELES
23. ZIP CODE	90210
24. YEARS IN COUNTY	50
25. STATE/FOREIGN COUNTRY	CA
26. INFORMANT'S NAME, RELATIONSHIP	LEONARD GRAINGER – FRIEND
27. INFORMANT'S MAILING ADDRESS	9903 KIP DR., BEVERLY HILLS, CA 90210
28. NAME OF SURVIVING SPOUSE — FIRST	DARREN
30. LAST (Maiden Name)	MCGAVIN
31. NAME OF FATHER — FIRST	UNK
33. LAST	UNK
34. BIRTH STATE	UNK
35. NAME OF MOTHER — FIRST	UNK
37. LAST (Maiden)	UNK
38. BIRTH STATE	UNK
39. DISPOSITION DATE	04/19/2003
40. PLACE OF FINAL DISPOSITION	FOREST LAWN MEMORIAL PARK 6300 FOREST LAWN DRIVE LOS ANGELES CA 90068
41. TYPE OF DISPOSITION(S)	BU
42. SIGNATURE OF EMBALMER	Michael Atock
43. LICENSE NUMBER	8155
44. NAME OF FUNERAL ESTABLISHMENT	FOREST LAWN HOLLYWOOD HILLS
45. LICENSE NUMBER	FD 904
46. SIGNATURE OF LOCAL REGISTRAR	Thomas L. Garthwaite MD
47. DATE	04/17/2003
101. PLACE OF DEATH	CEDAR SINAI MED CTR
102. IF HOSPITAL	ER/OP
104. COUNTY	LOS ANGELES
105. FACILITY ADDRESS	8700 BEVERLY BLVD
106. CITY	LOS ANGELES
107. CAUSE OF DEATH — IMMEDIATE CAUSE (A)	Arteriosclerotic Cardiovascular Disease
Time Interval	Unk
108. DEATH REPORTED TO CORONER?	YES — REFERRAL 2003-02789
109. BIOPSY PERFORMED?	NO
110. AUTOPSY PERFORMED?	NO
111. USED IN DETERMINING CAUSE?	NO
112. OTHER SIGNIFICANT CONDITIONS	NONE
113. WAS OPERATION PERFORMED	NO
113A. IF FEMALE, PREGNANT IN LAST YEAR?	NO
119. MANNER OF DEATH	Natural
126. SIGNATURE OF CORONER	Lisa Branson
127. DATE	04/16/2003
128. TYPE NAME, TITLE OF CORONER	Lisa Branson, Deputy Coroner
FAX AUTH. #	273/258

090615396

This is a true certified copy of the record filed in the County of Los Angeles Department of Health Services if it bears the Registrar's signature in purple ink.

Thomas L. Garthwaite
Director of Health Services and Registrar

ISSUED 234 APR 29 2003

This copy not valid unless prepared on engraved border displaying seal and signature of Registrar.

ANY ALTERATION OR ERASURE VOIDS THIS CERTIFICATE

CERTIFICATION OF VITAL RECORD

COUNTY OF LOS ANGELES • REGISTRAR-RECORDER/COUNTY CLERK

CERTIFICATE OF DEATH
STATE OF CALIFORNIA—DEPARTMENT OF PUBLIC HEALTH

Local Registration District and Certificate Number: 7097-034362

DECEDENT PERSONAL DATA
- Name of Deceased: Leonard Alfred Schneider AKA Lenny Bruce
- Date of Death: August 3, 1966, 6:55 PM
- Sex: Male
- Color or Race: Caucasian
- Birthplace: New York
- Date of Birth: October 13, 1925
- Age: 40 years
- Name and Birthplace of Father: Myron Schneider, England
- Maiden Name and Birthplace of Mother: Sadie Kitchenberg, New York
- Citizen of What Country: U.S.A.
- Social Security Number: 567-48-8307
- Last Occupation: Entertainer
- Number of Years in This Occupation: 20
- Name of Last Employing Company or Firm: Self Employed
- Kind of Industry or Business: Entertainment
- Armed Forces: World War #2
- Marital Status: Divorced

PLACE OF DEATH
- Street Address: 8825 Hollywood Blvd.
- City or Town: Los Angeles
- County: Los Angeles
- Length of Stay in County of Death: 13 years
- Length of Stay in California: 13 years

LAST USUAL RESIDENCE
- Street Address: 8825 Hollywood Blvd.
- City or Town: Los Angeles (1942)
- County: Los Angeles
- State: California
- Name of Informant: Sadie Kitchenberg
- Address of Informant: 8825 Hollywood Blvd., L.A.

PHYSICIAN'S OR CORONER'S CERTIFICATION
- Autopsy
- Physician or Coroner Signature: Theo J. Curphey, M.D., Chief Medical Examiner-Coroner
- Address: Hall of Justice, Los Angeles
- Date Signed: 8-12-66

FUNERAL DIRECTOR AND LOCAL REGISTRAR
- Burial
- Date: August 5, 1966
- Name of Cemetery: Eden Memorial Park
- Embalmer Signature: John E. Conely, License Number 3317
- Name of Funeral Director: Willen-Glasband Hollywood
- Date Accepted for Registration: AUG 19 1966

CAUSE OF DEATH
- Immediate Cause (A): ACUTE MORPHINE POISONING
- Due to (B): INJECTION OF OVERDOSE

INJURY INFORMATION
- Accident, prior to
- Describe How Injury Occurred: AS ABOVE
- Time of Injury: 6:55 P, 8-3-66
- Injury Occurred: Not While At Work
- Place of Injury: HOME
- City, Town, or Location: LOS ANGELES
- County: LA
- State: CALIF

CHARLES WEISSBURD
Registrar-Recorder/County Clerk

19-314771

This copy not valid unless prepared on engraved border displaying the Seal and Signature of the Registrar-Recorder/County Clerk.

ANY ALTERATION OR ERASURE VOIDS THIS CERTIFICATE

SMILEY BURNETTE

CERTIFICATION OF VITAL RECORD
COUNTY OF LOS ANGELES • REGISTRAR-RECORDER/COUNTY CLERK

CERTIFICATE OF DEATH
STATE OF CALIFORNIA—DEPARTMENT OF PUBLIC HEALTH

LOCAL REGISTRATION DISTRICT AND CERTIFICATE NUMBER: 7097-006507

DECEDENT PERSONAL DATA
- 1A. Name of Deceased—First Name: LESTER
- 1B. Middle Name: ALVIN
- 1C. Last Name: BURNETTE (BURNETTE AKA ALVIN)
- 2A. Date of Death: 2-16-67
- 2B. Hour: 9:25 P.M.
- 3. Sex: Male
- 4. Color or Race: Caucasian
- 5. Birthplace: Illinois
- 6. Date of Birth: March 18, 1911
- 7. Age: 55 Years
- 8. Name and Birthplace of Father: George Washington Burnette — Illinois
- 9. Maiden Name and Birthplace of Mother: Almira Heslip — Kansas
- 10. Citizen of What Country: U.S.A
- 11. Social Security Number: 561-01-3520
- 12. Last Occupation: Actor
- 13. Number of Years in This Occupation: 36
- 14. Name of Last Employing Company or Firm: Filmways
- 15. Kind of Industry or Business: Television Industry
- 16. If Deceased Was Ever in U.S. Armed Forces: None
- 17. Married/Widowed/Divorced/Never Married: Married
- 18A. Name of Present Spouse: Dallas Burnette
- 18B. Present or Last Occupation of Spouse: Housewife

PLACE OF DEATH
- 19A. Place of Death—Name of Hospital: West Valley Baptist Hospital
- 19B. Street Address: 5333 Balboa Blvd.
- 19C. City or Town: Encino (Los Angeles)
- 19D. County: Los Angeles
- 19E. Length of Stay in County of Death: 36 Years
- 19F. Length of Stay in California: 36 Years

LAST USUAL RESIDENCE
- 20A. Last Usual Residence—Street Address: 4557 Coldwater Canyon
- 20C. City or Town: North Hollywood
- 20D. County: Los Angeles
- 20E. State: California
- 21A. Name of Informant: Mr. Stephen S. Burnette (son)
- 21B. Address of Informant: 7560 Woodman Place, Van Nuys 91405, California

PHYSICIAN'S OR CORONER'S CERTIFICATION
- 22A. Physician: 2/16/67
- 22C. Physician or Coroner—Signature: James A. Bilkin, MD
- 22D. Address: 6221 Wilshire Blvd, Los Angeles
- 22E. Date Signed: 2/18/67

FUNERAL DIRECTOR AND LOCAL REGISTRAR
- 23. Specify Burial or Cremation: Burial
- 24. Date: Feb. 20, 1967
- 25. Name of Cemetery or Crematory: Forest Lawn Hollywood Hills, 6300 Forest Lawn Dr., Los Angeles 28, Calif.
- 26. Embalmer—Signature: W.R. Glidewell — License Number 2953
- 27. Name of Funeral Director: Forest Lawn Hollywood Hills, 6300 Forest Lawn Dr., Los Angeles 28, Calif.
- 28. Date Accepted for Registration by Local Registrar: FEB 20 1967

CAUSE OF DEATH
- 30. Cause of Death — Immediate Cause (A): Acute Leukemia — Approximate Interval Between Onset and Death: 2 months

OPERATION AND AUTOPSY
- 31. Operation: No Operation Performed
- 33. Autopsy: No

FILED MAR 10 1967 / RAY E LEE COUNTY RECORDER

OCT 4 1996
19-387365

CONNY B. McCORMACK
Registrar-Recorder/County Clerk

Judy Canova

STATE OF CALIFORNIA
CERTIFICATION OF VITAL RECORD
COUNTY OF ORANGE
SANTA ANA, CALIFORNIA

BOOK 101 **PAGE** 246

CERTIFICATE OF DEATH
STATE OF CALIFORNIA—DEPARTMENT OF PUBLIC HEALTH

LOCAL REGISTRATION DISTRICT AND CERTIFICATE NUMBER: 3000-969

DECEDENT PERSONAL DATA
- 1A. Name of Deceased—First Name: Kathryn
- 1B. Middle Name: Card
- 1C. Last Name: Carman
- 2A. Date of Death: March 1, 1964
- 2B. Hour: 9:30 P.M.
- 3. Sex: Female
- 4. Color or Race: Cauc.
- 5. Birthplace: Montana
- 6. Date of Birth: October 4, 1892
- 7. Age (Last Birthday): 71 Years
- 8. Name and Birthplace of Father: Michael Sheehan, N.Y.
- 9. Maiden Name and Birthplace of Mother: Ester McCurdy, Mass.
- 10. Citizen of What Country: U.S.A.
- 11. Social Security Number: 475-05-0880
- 12. Last Occupation: Actress
- 13. Number of Years in this Occupation: 40 Yrs.
- 14. Name of Last Employing Company or Firm: M.G.M.
- 15. Kind of Industry or Business: Entertainment
- 16. If Deceased was Ever in U.S. Armed Forces: No
- 17. Specify Married, Never Married, Widowed, Divorced: Widowed

PLACE OF DEATH
- 19A. Place of Death—Name of Hospital: a residence
- 19B. Street Address: 2060 Newport Blvd.
- 19C. City or Town: Costa Mesa
- 19D. County: Orange
- 19E. Length of Stay in County of Death: 2 Years
- 19F. Length of Stay in California: 20 Years

LAST USUAL RESIDENCE
- 20A. Last Usual Residence—Street Address: P.O. Box 103 Hot Springs Canyon Rd.
- 20C. City or Town: San Juan Capistrano
- 20D. County: Orange
- 20E. State: Calif.
- 21A. Name of Informant: Ann Espeland
- 21B. Address of Informant: 2060 Newport Blvd, Costa Mesa

PHYSICIAN'S OR CORONER'S CERTIFICATION
- 22F. Date Signed: 3-2-64

FUNERAL DIRECTOR AND LOCAL REGISTRAR
- 23. Burial
- 24. Date: 3-4-64
- 25. Name of Cemetery or Crematory: Harbor Rest Memorial Park, Santa Ana, Calif.
- 27. Name of Funeral Director: Ronold Bros. Mortuary, Garden Grove, Calif.
- 28. Date Accepted for Registration: 3-4-64

CAUSE OF DEATH
- 30. Part I. Death was Caused by:
  - Immediate Cause (A): Coronary thrombosis
  - Due to (B): Hypertension with angina
  - Due to (C): Arterio sclerotic heart disease
- Approximate Interval Between Onset and Death: 7 years

- 34A. Specify Accident, Suicide or Homicide: no
- 34B. Describe How Injury Occurred: no

DC22

691976

CERTIFIED COPY OF VITAL RECORDS
STATE OF CALIFORNIA } SS
COUNTY OF ORANGE
DATE ISSUED: JAN 11 2001

GARY L. GRANVILLE, Clerk-Recorder
ORANGE COUNTY, CALIFORNIA

This is a true and exact reproduction of the document officially registered and placed on file in the office of the Orange County Clerk-Recorder.

This copy not valid unless prepared on engraved border displaying seal and signature of Clerk-Recorder.

ANY ALTERATION OR ERASURE VOIDS THIS CERTIFICATE

STATE OF CALIFORNIA

CERTIFICATION OF VITAL RECORD

COUNTY OF LOS ANGELES • REGISTRAR-RECORDER/COUNTY CLERK

CERTIFICATE OF DEATH

STATE OF CALIFORNIA

USE BLACK INK ONLY / NO ERASURES, WHITEOUTS OR ALTERATIONS

VS-11 (REV 1/04)

STATE FILE NUMBER

3200819027124

LOCAL REGISTRATION NUMBER

INFORMATIONAL, NOT A VALID DOCUMENT TO ESTABLISH IDENTITY

DECEDENT'S PERSONAL DATA

1 NAME OF DECEDENT — FIRST (Given): GEORGE

2 MIDDLE: DENIS

3 LAST (Family): CARLIN

AKA, ALSO KNOWN AS — Include full AKA (FIRST, MIDDLE, LAST)

4 DATE OF BIRTH mm/dd/ccyy: 05/12/1937

5 AGE Yrs: 71

IF UNDER ONE YEAR: Months / Days

IF UNDER 24 HOURS: Hours / Minutes

6 SEX: M

9 BIRTH STATE/FOREIGN COUNTRY: NY

10 SOCIAL SECURITY NUMBER: 095-26-8013

11 EVER IN U.S. ARMED FORCES? [X] YES [ ] NO [ ] UNK

12 MARITAL STATUS (at Time of Death): WIDOWED

7 DATE OF DEATH mm/dd/ccyy: 06/22/2008

8 HOUR (24 Hours): 1855

13 EDUCATION — Highest Level/Degree (see worksheet on back): 09

14/15 WAS DECEDENT HISPANIC/LATINO(A)/SPANISH? (If yes, see worksheet on back) [ ] YES [X] NO

16 DECEDENT'S RACE — Up to 3 races may be listed (see worksheet on back): CAUCASIAN

17 USUAL OCCUPATION — Type of work for most of life. DO NOT USE RETIRED: COMEDIAN

18 KIND OF BUSINESS OR INDUSTRY (e.g. grocery store, road construction, employment agency, etc.): ENTERTAINMENT

19 YEARS IN OCCUPATION: 51

USUAL RESIDENCE

20 DECEDENT'S RESIDENCE (Street and number, or location): 3111 BEL AIR DRIVE 24D

21 CITY: LAS VEGAS

22 COUNTY/PROVINCE: CLARK

23 ZIP CODE: 89109

24 YEARS IN COUNTY: 10

25 STATE/FOREIGN COUNTRY: NV

INFORMANT

26 INFORMANT'S NAME, RELATIONSHIP: KELLY M. MCCALL, DAUGHTER

27 INFORMANT'S MAILING ADDRESS (Street and number or rural route number, city or town, state, ZIP): 7918 NAYLOR AVE., LOS ANGELES, CA 90045

SPOUSE AND PARENT INFORMATION

28 NAME OF SURVIVING SPOUSE — FIRST: -

29 MIDDLE: -

30 LAST (Maiden Name): -

31 NAME OF FATHER — FIRST: JOHN

32 MIDDLE: PATRICK

33 LAST: CARLIN

34 BIRTH STATE: IRELAND

35 NAME OF MOTHER — FIRST: MARY

36 MIDDLE: FRANCES

37 LAST (Maiden): BEAREY

38 BIRTH STATE: NY

FUNERAL DIRECTOR/LOCAL REGISTRAR

39 DISPOSITION DATE mm/dd/ccyy: 06/30/2008

40 PLACE OF FINAL DISPOSITION: RESIDENCE OF KELLY M. MCCALL, 7918 NAYLOR AVE., LOS ANGELES, CA 90045

41 TYPE OF DISPOSITION(S): CR/RES

42 SIGNATURE OF EMBALMER: ▸ CARLOS SOLORZANO

43 LICENSE NUMBER: EMB8704

44 NAME OF FUNERAL ESTABLISHMENT: GATES, KINGSLEY & GATES MOELLER

45 LICENSE NUMBER: FD451

46 SIGNATURE OF LOCAL REGISTRAR: ▸ JONATHAN FIELDING, MD

47 DATE mm/dd/ccyy: 06/26/2008

PLACE OF DEATH

101 PLACE OF DEATH: ST. JOHN HEALTH CENTER

102 IF HOSPITAL, SPECIFY ONE: [ ] IP [X] ER/OP [ ] DOA

103 IF OTHER THAN HOSPITAL, SPECIFY ONE: [ ] Hospice [ ] Nursing Home/LTC [ ] Decedent's Home [ ] Other

104 COUNTY: LOS ANGELES

105 FACILITY ADDRESS OR LOCATION WHERE FOUND (Street and number, or location): 1328 22ND STREET

106 CITY: SANTA MONICA

CAUSE OF DEATH

107 CAUSE OF DEATH — Enter the chain of events — diseases, injuries, or complications — that directly caused death. DO NOT enter terminal events such as cardiac arrest, respiratory arrest, or ventricular fibrillation without showing the etiology. DO NOT ABBREVIATE

	Cause	Time Interval Between Onset and Death
IMMEDIATE CAUSE (Final disease or condition resulting in death) (A)	ASYSTOLE	(AT) 5 MIN
Sequentially, list conditions, if any, leading to cause on Line A. Enter UNDERLYING CAUSE (disease or injury that initiated the events resulting in death) LAST (B)	PULMONARY EDEMA	(BT) 1 HR
(C)	MYOCARDIAL INFARCTION	(CT) 4 HRS
(D)	CORONARY ARTERY DISEASE	(DT) YRS

108 DEATH REPORTED TO CORONER? [ ] YES [X] NO — REFERRAL NUMBER

109 BIOPSY PERFORMED? [ ] YES [X] NO

110 AUTOPSY PERFORMED? [X] YES [ ] NO

111 USED IN DETERMINING CAUSE? [X] YES [ ] NO

112 OTHER SIGNIFICANT CONDITIONS CONTRIBUTING TO DEATH BUT NOT RESULTING IN THE UNDERLYING CAUSE GIVEN IN 107: CARDIOMYOPATHY

113 WAS OPERATION PERFORMED FOR ANY CONDITION IN ITEM 107 OR 112? (If yes, list type of operation and date.): CORONARY STENT 12/29/2005

113A IF FEMALE, PREGNANT IN LAST YEAR? [ ] YES [ ] NO [ ] UNK

PHYSICIAN'S CERTIFICATION

114 I CERTIFY THAT TO THE BEST OF MY KNOWLEDGE DEATH OCCURRED AT THE HOUR, DATE, AND PLACE STATED FROM THE CAUSES STATED. Decedent Attended Since (A) mm/dd/ccyy: 06/22/2008 — Decedent Last Seen Alive (B) mm/dd/ccyy: 06/22/2008

115 SIGNATURE AND TITLE OF CERTIFIER: ▸ PETER PELIKAN M.D.

116 LICENSE NUMBER: G43904

117 DATE mm/dd/ccyy: 06/25/2008

118 TYPE ATTENDING PHYSICIAN'S NAME, MAILING ADDRESS, ZIP CODE: PETER PELIKAN M.D., 2001 SANTA MONICA BLVD, SANTA MONICA, CA 90404

CORONER'S USE ONLY

119 I CERTIFY THAT IN MY OPINION DEATH OCCURRED AT THE HOUR, DATE, AND PLACE STATED FROM THE CAUSES STATED. MANNER OF DEATH [ ] Natural [ ] Accident [ ] Homicide [ ] Suicide [ ] Pending Investigation [ ] Could not be determined

120 INJURED AT WORK? [ ] YES [ ] NO [ ] UNK

121 INJURY DATE mm/dd/ccyy

122 HOUR (24 Hours)

123 PLACE OF INJURY (e.g. home, construction site, wooded area, etc.)

124 DESCRIBE HOW INJURY OCCURRED (Events which resulted in injury)

125 LOCATION OF INJURY (Street and number, or location, and city, and ZIP)

126 SIGNATURE OF CORONER / DEPUTY CORONER ▸

127 DATE mm/dd/ccyy

128 TYPE NAME, TITLE OF CORONER / DEPUTY CORONER

STATE REGISTRAR A B C D E

012008000847023

FAX AUTH # CENSUS TRACT

This is to certify that this document is a true copy of the official record filed with the Registrar-Recorder/County Clerk.

SEP 16 2009

Dean C Logan

DEAN C. LOGAN
Registrar-Recorder/County Clerk

000002375

This copy not valid unless prepared on engraved border displaying the Seal and Signature of the Registrar-Recorder/County Clerk.

FBNCO (Rev) 07/09

THE GREAT SEAL OF THE STATE OF CALIFORNIA — EUREKA

REGISTRAR-RECORDER/COUNTY CLERK — COUNTY OF LOS ANGELES • CALIFORNIA

ANY ALTERATION OR ERASURE VOIDS THIS CERTIFICATE

CERTIFICATE OF DEATH
STATE OF CALIFORNIA

STATE FILE NUMBER: 0190-012181

COUNTY OF LOS ANGELES • REGISTRAR-RECORDER/COUNTY CLERK

1A. Name of Decedent—First	Karen
1B. Middle	Anne
1C. Last	Carpenter
2A. Date of Death	February 4, 1983
2B. Hour	0951
3. Sex	Female
4. Race	White
5. Ethnicity	American
6. Date of Birth	March 2, 1950
7. Age	32
8. Birthplace of Decedent	Connecticut
9. Name and Birthplace of Father	Harold B. Carpenter — China
10. Birth Name and Birthplace of Mother	Agnes R. Tatum — Maryland
11. Citizen of What Country	U.S.A.
12. Social Security Number	564-82-9174
13. Marital Status	Married
14. Name of Surviving Spouse	Thomas J. Burris
15. Primary Occupation	Recording Artist
16. Number of Years This Occupation	12
17. Employer	Self-employed
18. Kind of Industry or Business	Music
19A. Usual Residence—Street Address	2222 Avenue of The Stars
19C. City or Town	Los Angeles
19D. County	Los Angeles
19E. State	California
20. Name and Address of Informant—Relationship	Richard L. Carpenter — Brother, 8341 Lubec Street, Downey, California 90240
21A. Place of Death	Downey Community Hospital
21B. County	Los Angeles
21C. Street Address	11500 Brookshire
21D. City or Town	Downey

AMENDED 1 OF 2

22. Death was Caused By: Immediate Cause (A): DEFERRED

24. Was Death Reported to Coroner? 83-1611
25. Was Biopsy Performed? No
26. Was Autopsy Performed? Yes
27. Was Operation Performed: No

35B. Coroner—Signature: S. Everson, Deputy Coroner
35C. Date Signed: 2-5-83

36. Disposition: Entombment
37. Date: Feb 8, 1983
38. Name and Address of Cemetery or Crematory: Forest Lawn Cypress — 4471 Lincoln Ave., Cypress, California
39. Embalmer's License Number and Signature: Edward E. Hayes, 6985
40. Name of Funeral Director: Utter-McKinley Downey, 9830 Lakewood Blvd., #1081
42. Date Accepted Local Registrar: FEB 7 1983

9315

01-9-4-0243

This is to certify that this document is a true copy of the official record filed with the Registrar-Recorder/County Clerk.

CONNY B. McCORMACK
Registrar-Recorder/County Clerk

APR 0 7 2000

19-555698

STATE OF CALIFORNIA
CERTIFICATION OF VITAL RECORD
COUNTY OF LOS ANGELES • REGISTRAR-RECORDER/COUNTY CLERK

THIS FORM MUST BE COMPLETED IN BLACK INK
AMENDMENT OF MEDICAL AND HEALTH SECTION DATA-DEATH

STATE CERTIFICATE NUMBER: 0190-012181
LOCAL REGISTRATION DISTRICT AND CERTIFICATE NUMBER: 833227

IDENTIFICATION OF THE RECORD
- 1A FIRST NAME: Karen
- 1B MIDDLE NAME: Anne
- 1C LAST NAME: Carpenter
- 2 PLACE OF OCCURRENCE—CITY OR COUNTY: Downey
- 3 DATE OF EVENT: February 4, 1983
- 4 DATE ORIGINAL FILED: Feb 7, 1983

ORIGINALLY REPORTED INFORMATION
- 22. DEATH WAS CAUSED BY:
  - (A) IMMEDIATE CAUSE: Deferred
  - (B) DUE TO:
  - (C) DUE TO:
- 24. WAS DEATH REPORTED TO CORONER: 83-1611
- 25. WAS BIOPSY PERFORMED: No
- 26. WAS AUTOPSY PERFORMED: Yes
- 27. WAS OPERATION PERFORMED: No

INFORMATION AS IT SHOULD BE STATED ON THE ORIGINALLY REGISTERED CERTIFICATE
- 22. DEATH WAS CAUSED BY:
  - (A) IMMEDIATE CAUSE: EMETINE CARDIOTOXICITY
  - (B) DUE TO: ANOREXIA NERVOSA
  - (C) DUE TO:
- 24. WAS DEATH REPORTED TO CORONER: 83-1611
- 25. WAS BIOPSY PERFORMED: No
- 26. WAS AUTOPSY PERFORMED: Yes
- 27. WAS OPERATION PERFORMED: No

DECLARATION OF CERTIFYING PHYSICIAN OR CORONER
- 6A SIGNATURE OF PHYSICIAN OR CORONER: [signed]
- 6B DATE SIGNED: 3-15-83
- 7A NAME OF PHYSICIAN OR CORONER: Ronald Kornblum, M.D.
- 7B DEGREE OR TITLE: Acting Chief Medical Examiner-Coroner

REGISTRAR'S OFFICE
- 8. OFFICE OF STATE REGISTRAR: [signed]
- MAR 21 1983

STATE OF CALIFORNIA, DEPARTMENT OF HEALTH SERVICES, OFFICE OF THE STATE REGISTRAR OF VITAL STATISTICS — FORM VS 24A (REV 10-78)

This is to certify that this document is a true copy of the official record filed with the Registrar-Recorder/County Clerk.

Conny B. McCormack
CONNY B. McCORMACK
Registrar-Recorder/County Clerk

APR 0 7 2000
19-555697

This copy not valid unless prepared on engraved border displaying the Seal and Signature of the Registrar-Recorder/County Clerk.

ANY ALTERATION OR ERASURE VOIDS THIS CERTIFICATE

COUNTY OF LOS ANGELES
DEPARTMENT OF HEALTH SERVICES
CERTIFICATE OF DEATH
STATE OF CALIFORNIA

1. Name of Decedent—First (Given)	ALLAN
2. Middle	-
3. Last (Family)	CARR
4. Date of Birth	05/27/1937
5. Age Yrs.	62
6. Sex	MALE
7. Date of Death	06/29/1999
8. Hour	1410
9. State of Birth	IL
10. Social Security No.	350-28-7154
11. Military Service	No
12. Marital Status	NEVER MARRIED
13. Education—Years Completed	16
14. Race	CAUCASIAN
15. Hispanic	No
16. Usual Employer	SELF-EMPLOYED
17. Occupation	PRODUCER
18. Kind of Business	ENTERTAINMENT
19. Years in Occupation	40
20. Residence	1220 BENEDICT CANYON DRIVE
21. City	BEVERLY HILLS
22. County	LOS ANGELES
23. Zip Code	90210
24. Yrs in County	28
25. State or Foreign Country	CALIFORNIA
26. Name, Relationship	CHARLES KIVOWITZ - DPOA
27. Mailing Address	435 N. ROXBURY, #300, BEVERLY HILLS, CA 90210
31. Name of Father—First	ALBERT
32. Middle	LEE
33. Last	SOLOMON
34. Birth State	IL
35. Name of Mother—First	ANN
37. Last (Maiden)	NIEMIEC
38. Birth State	IL
39. Date	07/09/1999
40. Place of Final Disposition	RES: CHARLES KIVOWITZ, 435 N.ROXBURY,#300 BEVERLY HILLS, CA 90210
41. Type of Disposition(s)	CR/RES
42. Signature of Embalmer	NOT EMBALMED
44. Name of Funeral Director	Pierce Bros. Westwood Village
45. License No.	FD 951
47. Date	07/07/1999
101. Place of Death	RESIDENCE
103. Facility Other than Hospital	OTHER
104. County	LOS ANGELES
105. Street Address	1220 BENEDICT CANYON DRIVE
106. City	BEVERLY HILLS
107A. Immediate Cause	HEPATO-RENAL SYNDROME — 3 DAYS
107B. Due to	METASTATIC UNDIFFERENTIATED LIVER AND BONE CARCINOMA — MONTHS
108. Death Reported to Coroner	No
109. Biopsy Performed	Yes
110. Autopsy Performed	No
112. Other Significant Conditions	NONE
113. Operation Performed	NO
114. Decedent Attended Since	04/01/1971
Decedent Last Seen Alive	06/28/1999
116. License No.	G 16910
117. Date	07/06/1999
118. Attending Physician	CHARLES F. KIVOWITZ, MD, 435 N.ROXBURY DRIVE, #300, BEVERLY HILLS, CA 90210

Date Issued: JUL 14 1999

VIRGINIA CHRISTINE

CERTIFICATE OF DEATH
STATE OF CALIFORNIA

State File Number: 3961903I753

DECEDENT PERSONAL DATA
- 1. Name (First): VIRGINIA
- 2. Middle: -
- 3. Last (Family): FELD
- 4. Date of Birth: 03/05/1920
- 5. Age: 76
- 6. Sex: FEMALE
- 7. Date of Death: 07/24/1996
- 8. Hour: 0830
- 9. State of Birth: IOWA
- 10. Social Security No.: 553-28-0229
- 11. Military Service: None
- 12. Marital Status: WIDOWED
- 13. Education: 14
- 14. Race: WHITE
- 15. Hispanic: No
- 16. Usual Employer: SELF EMPLOYED
- 17. Occupation: ACTRESS
- 18. Kind of Business: ENTERTAINMENT
- 19. Years in Occupation: 45

USUAL RESIDENCE
- 20. Residence: 12348 ROCHEDALE LANE
- 21. City: LOS ANGELES
- 22. County: LOS ANGELES
- 23. Zip: 90049
- 24. Yrs in County: 60
- 25. State: CALIFORNIA

INFORMANT
- 26. Name, Relationship: DANNY FELD - SON
- 27. Mailing Address: 4441 DON FELIPE DRIVE, LOS ANGELES, CA 90008

SPOUSE AND PARENT INFORMATION
- 31. Father: GEORGE RICKETTS — Birth State: USA-UNK
- 35. Mother: HELGA OSSIAN — Birth State: IOWA

DISPOSITION
- 39. Date: 07/30/1996
- 40. Place: MOUNT SINAI MEMORIAL PARK 5950 FOREST LAWN DRIVE, L.A., CA 90068
- 41. Type: CR/BU
- 42. Signature of Embalmer: NOT EMBALMED
- 44. Funeral Director: MOUNT SINAI MORTUARY
- 45. License No.: FD-1010
- 47. Date: 07/29/1996

PLACE OF DEATH
- 101. Place of Death: RESIDENCE
- 104. County: LOS ANGELES
- 105. Street Address: 12348 ROCHEDALE LANE
- 106. City: LOS ANGELES

CAUSE OF DEATH
- 107(A) Immediate Cause: RUPTURED THORACIC AORTIC ANEURYSM — MINUTES
- 107(B) Due to: SEVERE ATHEROSCLEROTIC CARDIOVASCULAR DISEASE — YEARS
- 108. Death Reported to Coroner: No
- 109. Biopsy Performed: No
- 110. Autopsy Performed: No
- 112. Other Significant Conditions: HYPERTENSION, HYPERCHOLESTEROLEMIA
- 113. Operation Performed: NONE

PHYSICIAN'S CERTIFICATION
- 116. License No.: G35140
- 117. Date: 07/24/1996
- Decedent Attended Since: 05/17/1988
- Last Seen Alive: 07/21/1996
- 118. Physician: EARL GORDON, M.D. 11860 WILSHIRE BLVD. #305 L.A., CA 90025

Fax Auth. #: 195/11148

CERTIFICATE OF DEATH
STATE OF CALIFORNIA—DEPARTMENT OF PUBLIC HEALTH

Local Registration District and Certificate Number: 7097-020473

Decedent Personal Data

- **1a. Name of Deceased—First Name:** Andrew
- **1b. Middle Name:** Allen
- **1c. Last Name:** Clyde
- **2a. Date of Death:** May 18, 1967
- **2b. Hour:** approx. 2AM
- **3. Sex:** Male
- **4. Color or Race:** Cauc
- **5. Birthplace:** Scotland
- **6. Date of Birth:** March 25, 1892
- **7. Age:** 75
- **8. Name and Birthplace of Father:** John Clyde—Scotland
- **9. Maiden Name and Birthplace of Mother:** Mary Allen—Scotland
- **10. Citizen of What Country:** U.S.A.
- **11. Social Security Number:** 568-05-5724
- **12. Last Occupation:** Actor
- **13. Number of Years in this Occupation:** 62
- **14. Name of Last Employing Company or Firm:** Desilu Studios
- **15. Kind of Industry or Business:** Motion Pictures
- **16. If Deceased was ever in U.S. Armed Forces:** no
- **17. Specify Married, Never Married, Widowed, Divorced:** Married
- **18a. Name of Present Spouse:** Elsie Clyde
- **18b. Present or Last Occupation of Spouse:** Housewife

Place of Death

- **19a. Place of Death—Name of Hospital:** 1843
- **19b. Street Address:** 2166 Canyon Drive
- **19c. City or Town:** Los Angeles
- **19d. County:** Los Angeles
- **19e. Length of Stay in County of Death:** 50 years
- **19f. Length of Stay in California:** 50 years

Last Usual Residence

- **20a. Last Usual Residence—Street Address:** 2166 Canyon Drive
- **20c. City or Town:** Los Angeles
- **20d. County:** Los Angeles
- **20e. State:** California
- **21a. Name of Informant:** Elsie Clyde
- **21b. Address of Informant:** SAME

Physician's or Coroner's Certification

- **22c. Physician or Coroner—Signature:** Frederic Wachsfelder M.D.
- **22d. Address:** 6153 Hollywood Blvd, Los Angeles
- **22e. Date Signed:** 5-18-67

Funeral Director and Local Registrar

- **23. Specify Burial, Entombment or Cremation:** Burial
- **24. Date:** 5-20-67
- **25. Name of Cemetery or Crematory:** Forest Lawn Glendale
- **26. Embalmer—Signature / License Number:** Walter R. Rainey 5373
- **27. Name of Funeral Director or Person Acting as Such:** Pierce Bros. Hollywood
- **28. Date Accepted for Registration by Local Registrar:** MAY 19 1967
- **29. Local Registrar—Signature:** [signed]

Cause of Death

- **30. Part I. Death was caused by:**
  - (A) Immediate Cause: Congestive cardiac failure — ca 2 mth
  - (B) Due to: arteriosclerosis — ca 10 yrs
- **Part II. Other Significant Conditions:** Emphysema

Operation and Autopsy

- **31. Operation:** No operation performed
- **33. Autopsy:** No autopsy performed

This is to certify that this document is a true copy of the official record filed with the Registrar-Recorder/County Clerk.

Conny B. McCormack
CONNY B. McCORMACK
Registrar-Recorder/County Clerk

OCT 4 1996
19-387364

This copy not valid unless prepared on engraved border displaying the Seal and Signature of the Registrar-Recorder/County Clerk.

CERTIFICATE OF DEATH — STATE OF CALIFORNIA

COUNTY OF LOS ANGELES • REGISTRAR-RECORDER/COUNTY CLERK

State File Number: 3851901060

Decedent Personal Data
- 1A. Name (First): NICHOLAS
- 1C. Last: COLASANTO
- 2A. Date of Death: FEBRUARY 12, 1985 (Found)
- 2B. Hour: 1430
- 3. Sex: Male
- 4. Race/Ethnicity: White/American
- 5. Spanish/Hispanic: NO
- 6. Date of Birth: JANUARY 19, 1924
- 7. Age: 61 years
- 8. Birthplace of Decedent: Rhode Island
- 9. Name and Birthplace of Father: Joseph Colasanto – Rhode Island
- 10. Birth Name and Birthplace of Mother: Maria Gelfoni – Italy
- 11. Citizen of What Country: United States
- 12. Social Security Number: 039-09-6143
- 13. Marital Status: Divorced
- 14. Name of Surviving Spouse: N/A
- 15. Primary Occupation: Actor
- 16. Number of Years This Occupation: 30
- 17. Employer: Charles, Barrows, Charles
- 18. Kind of Industry or Business: Entertainment

Usual Residence
- 19A. Street Address: 12354 Sarah Street
- 19C. City or Town: Studio City
- 19D. County: Los Angeles
- 19E. State: California
- 20. Name and Address of Informant — Relationship: Bridget B. Colleary – Executrix, 10537 Valley Spring Lane, Toluca Lake, CA 91602

Place of Death
- 21A. Place of Death: Residence
- 21B. County: Los Angeles
- 21C. Street Address: 12354 Sarah Street
- 21D. City or Town: Studio City

Cause of Death
- 22. Death was caused by:
  - (a) Immediate Cause: Cardiomyopathy
  - (b) Congestive Heart Failure
  - (c) Ventricular Arrhythmia
- 23. Other Significant Conditions: Recent Gastro-Intestinal Bleeding
- 24. Was Death Reported to Coroner: YES 85-2278
- 25. Was Biopsy Performed: No
- 26. Was Autopsy Performed: No
- 27. Was Operation Performed: No

Physician's Certification
- 28A. Attended Decedent Since: 12/22/1967; Last Saw Decedent Alive: 1/15/1985
- 28B. Physician Signature: Elsie Giorgi MD
- 28C. Date Signed: 2/13/1985
- 28D. Physician's License Number: G6692
- 28E. Physician's Name and Address: Elsie Giorgi, M.D., 153 S. Lasky Dr., Beverly Hills, CA

Disposition
- 36. Disposition: Burial
- 37. Date: Feb. 16, 1985
- 38. Name and Address of Cemetery: St. Ann's Cemetery, Cranston, Rhode Island
- 39. Embalmer: Not Embalmed
- 40A. Name of Funeral Director: J. T. OSWALD MORTUARY, N.H.
- 40B. License No.: 1047
- 41. Local Registrar Signature: Robert Mate — FEB 13 1985

State Registrar: 4254 / 01-9-1-7005

This is to certify that this document is a true copy of the official record filed with the Registrar-Recorder/County Clerk.

CONNY B. McCORMACK, Registrar-Recorder/County Clerk

NOV 28 2000
19-116319

STATE OF CALIFORNIA
CERTIFICATION OF VITAL RECORD
COUNTY OF LOS ANGELES • REGISTRAR-RECORDER/COUNTY CLERK

CERTIFICATE OF DEATH — 7097-043292

DECEDENT PERSONAL DATA
- 1a. Name (First): Chester
- 1b. Middle: Cooper
- 1c. Last: Conklin
- 2a. Date of Death: October 11, 1971
- 2b. Hour: 12:10 A.M.
- 3. Sex: Male
- 4. Color or Race: Cauc
- 5. Birthplace: Iowa
- 6. Date of Birth: January 11, 1886
- 7. Age: 85 years
- 8. Father: Thilemon Conklin — Iowa
- 9. Mother: Alice Cooper — Virginia
- 10. Citizen of: U.S.A.
- 11. Social Security Number: 565-14-6310
- 12. Married
- 13. Surviving Spouse: June Ayres
- 14. Last Occupation: Actor
- 15. Number of Years: 68
- 16. Last Employing Company: Warner Brothers
- 17. Industry: Motion Pictures

PLACE OF DEATH
- 18a. Motion Picture & Television Hospital
- 18b. 23388 Mulholland Drive
- 18c. Inside City Corporate Limits: No
- 18d. City: Woodland Hills
- 18e. County: Los Angeles
- 18f. Length of stay in county: 66 years
- 18g. Length of stay in California: 66 years

USUAL RESIDENCE
- 19a. 4201 Topanga Canyon
- 19b. Woodland Hills
- 19c. Los Angeles
- 19d. California
- 20. Informant: June Conklin, 4201 Topanga Canyon, Woodland Hills, California

PHYSICIAN'S OR CORONER'S CERTIFICATION
- From 9/30/71 to 10/11/71; Last seen alive 10/10/71
- 21e. Address: 23388 Mulholland Drive, W.H.
- 21d. Date Signed: 10/11/71
- 21f. License Number: C 30949

FUNERAL DIRECTOR AND LOCAL REGISTRAR
- 22a. Cremation
- 22b. Date: 10-16-71
- 23. Chapel of the Pines
- 24. Embalmer: John J. Aylward — License 3853
- 25. Funeral Director: Pierce Bros. Valhalla
- 26. Reported to Coroner: No
- 28. Date Accepted: OCT 13 1971

CAUSE OF DEATH
- 29. Part I
  - (A) Immediate cause: EMPHYSEMA — 4 YRS
  - (B) Due to: PULMONARY HEART DISEASE — 4 YRS
- 30. Part II: METASTATIC CARCINOMA – PROSTATE
- 31. Operation: No
- 32a. Autopsy: No

Conny B. McCormack
Registrar-Recorder/County Clerk
NOV 28 2000
19-113449

DARLENE CONLEY

STATE OF CALIFORNIA
CERTIFICATION OF VITAL RECORD

COUNTY OF LOS ANGELES • REGISTRAR-RECORDER/COUNTY CLERK

CERTIFICATE OF DEATH
STATE OF CALIFORNIA

LOCAL REGISTRATION NUMBER: 3200719002794

1. NAME OF DECEDENT- FIRST (Given)	DARLENE
2. MIDDLE	ANN
3. LAST (Family)	CONLEY
AKA ALSO KNOWN AS	—
4. DATE OF BIRTH	07/18/1934
5. AGE Yrs	72
6. SEX	FEMALE
9. BIRTH STATE/FOREIGN COUNTRY	ILLINOIS
10. SOCIAL SECURITY NUMBER	346-26-7967
11. EVER IN U.S ARMED FORCES?	NO
12. MARITAL STATUS	DIVORCED
7. DATE OF DEATH	01/14/2007
8. HOUR	1920
13. EDUCATION	HS GRADUATE
14/15. WAS DECEDENT HISPANIC/LATINO?	NO
16. DECEDENT'S RACE	CAUCASIAN
17. USUAL OCCUPATION	ACTRESS
18. KIND OF BUSINESS OR INDUSTRY	ENTERTAINMENT
19. YEARS IN OCCUPATION	50
20. DECEDENT'S RESIDENCE	4455 LOS FELIZ BLVD. #902
21. CITY	LOS ANGELES
22. COUNTY/PROVINCE	LOS ANGELES
23. ZIP CODE	90027
24. YEARS IN COUNTY	67
25. STATE/FOREIGN COUNTRY	CALIFORNIA
26. INFORMANT'S NAME, RELATIONSHIP	RAYMOND C. WOODSON, SON
27. INFORMANT'S MAILING ADDRESS	1156 WESTERN #C, GLENDALE, CA 91201
31. NAME OF FATHER/PARENT-FIRST	RAYMOND
33. LAST	CONLEY
34. BIRTH STATE	ILLINOIS
35. NAME OF MOTHER/PARENT-FIRST	MELBA
37. LAST (BIRTH NAME)	MANTHEY
38. BIRTH STATE	ILLINOIS
39. DISPOSITION DATE	01/26/2007
40. PLACE OF FINAL DISPOSITION	AT SEA OFF THE COAST OF LOS ANGELES CO.
41. TYPE OF DISPOSITION(S)	CR/SEA
42. SIGNATURE OF EMBALMER	NOT EMBALMED
44. NAME OF FUNERAL ESTABLISHMENT	NEPTUNE SOCIETY
45. LICENSE NUMBER	S.O. FD-1359
47. DATE	01/24/2007
101. PLACE OF DEATH	RESIDENCE
103. IF OTHER THAN HOSPITAL	Decedent's Home
104. COUNTY	LOS ANGELES
105. FACILITY ADDRESS OR LOCATION	4455 LOS FELIZ BOULEVARD #902
106. CITY	LOS ANGELES

107. CAUSE OF DEATH
- (A) IMMEDIATE CAUSE: CARDIOPULMONARY ARREST — MINUTE
- (B) RESPIRATORY FAILURE — MINUTE
- (C) GASTRIC ADENOCARCINOMA — MONTHS
- (D) DEMENTIA - ALZHEIMER'S — MONTHS

108. DEATH REPORTED TO CORONER? NO
109. BIOPSY PERFORMED? NO
110. AUTOPSY PERFORMED? NO
111. USED IN DETERMINING CAUSE? NO

112. OTHER SIGNIFICANT CONDITIONS: NONE
113. WAS OPERATION PERFORMED: NO
113A. IF FEMALE, PREGNANT IN LAST YEAR? NO

116. LICENSE NUMBER: A80255
117. DATE: 01/17/2007
(A) Decedent Attended Since: 01/01/2005
(B) Decedent Last Seen Alive: 01/14/2007
118. TYPE ATTENDING PHYSICIAN'S NAME: KIRKOR KALINDJIAN, MD 1300 N. VERMONT AVE. LOS ANGELES, CA 90027

FAX AUTH.# 195/6214

JAN 2 2 2008

INFORMATIONAL, NOT A VALID DOCUMENT TO ESTABLISH IDENTITY

This copy not valid unless prepared on engraved border displaying the Seal of the Registrar-Recorder/County Clerk.

019042567

CERTIFICATION OF VITAL RECORD

COUNTY OF LOS ANGELES • REGISTRAR-RECORDER/COUNTY CLERK

CERTIFICATE OF DEATH
STATE OF CALIFORNIA

1A. Name of Decedent (First/Given): KEVIN
1B. Middle: JOSEPH
1C. Last (Family): CONNORS
2A. Date of Death: November 10, 1992
2B. Hour: 1354
3. Sex: M
4. Race: Caucasian
5. Hispanic: No
6. Date of Birth: April 10, 1921
7. Age in Years: 71
8. State of Birth: NY
9. Citizen of What Country: USA
10A. Full Name of Father: Alan F. Connors
10B. State of Birth: NFLND
11A. Full Maiden Name of Mother: Marcella Lundegrun
11B. State of Birth: NFLND
12. Military Service: 42 to 45
13. Social Security No.: 067-16-8129
14. Marital Status: Divorced
16A. Usual Occupation: Actor
16B. Usual Kind of Business or Industry: Motion Picture
16C. Usual Employer: Self
16D. Years in Occupation: 40
17. Education: 17

18A. Residence: 27551 Oak Flat Drive, Bear Valley Springs
18B. City: Tehachapi
18C. Zip Code: 93561
18D. County: Kern
18E. Number of Years in This County: 41
18F. State or Foreign Country: California
20. Name, Relationship, Mailing Address of Informant: Jeffrey Connors – Son, 25027 Peachland Avenue #157, Newhall, California 91321

19A. Place of Death: Cedars-Sinai Medical Center
19B. IP
19C. County: Los Angeles
19D. Street Address: 8700 Beverly Blvd.
19E. City: Los Angeles

21. Cause of Death:
- (A) Immediate Cause: Respiratory Arrest — 5 min
- (B) Due to: Oat Cell Carcinoma of the Lung — 8 wks

25. Other Significant Conditions Contributing to Death: Paroxysmal Atrial Fibrillation

27E. Attending Physician's Name and Address: Ashley Lipshutz, M.D., 8737 Beverly Blvd., Los Angeles, Ca. 90048
27A. Decedent Attended Since: 3/17/65
27B. Decedent Last Seen Alive: 11/10/92
27D. Date Signed: 11/11/92

34A. Disposition: Burial
34B. Place of Final Disposition: San Fernando Mission Cemetery, Mission Hills, California
34C. Date: 11-14-1992
35A. Signature of Embalmer: Dale Elstamp
35B. License Number: #4937
36A. Name of Funeral Director: J.T. Oswald Mortuary, N.H., Ca.
36B. License No.: FD-1047
38. Registration Date: NOV 12 1992

NOV 15 1995
19-055597

CERTIFICATION OF VITAL RECORD

COUNTY OF LOS ANGELES • REGISTRAR-RECORDER/COUNTY CLERK

CERTIFICATE OF DEATH
STATE OF CALIFORNIA—DEPARTMENT OF HEALTH
OFFICE OF THE STATE REGISTRAR OF VITAL STATISTICS

State File Number: 0190-017741

DECEDENT PERSONAL DATA

- 1a. Name of Deceased—First Name: Richard
- 1b. Middle Name: Nicholas Peter
- 1c. Last Name: Conte
- 2a. Date of Death: April 15, 1975
- 2b. Hour: 0915
- 3. Sex: male
- 4. Color or Race: cauc
- 5. Birthplace: New Jersey
- 6. Date of Birth: March 24 1910
- 7. Age: 65 years
- 8. Name and Birthplace of Father: Pasquela Conti - Sicily
- 9. Maiden Name and Birthplace of Mother: Julia unknown - Sicily
- 10. Citizen of What Country: U.S.A.
- 11. Social Security Number: 515 30 4879
- 12. Married: married
- 13. Name of Surviving Spouse: Shirlee Colleen Garner
- 14. Last Occupation: Actor
- 15. Number of Years in this Occupation: 36
- 16. Name of Last Employing Company or Firm: Various
- 17. Kind of Industry or Business: Entertainment

PLACE OF DEATH

- 18a. Place of Death: U.C.L.A. Medical Center
- 18b. Street Address: 10833 LeConte St.
- 18d. City or Town: West Los Angeles
- 18e. County: Los Angeles
- 18f. Length of Stay in County of Death: 33 years
- 18g. Length of Stay in California: 33 years

USUAL RESIDENCE

- 19a. Usual Residence—Street Address: 303 N LaPeer Drive
- 19b. Inside City Corporate Limits: yes
- 20. Name and Mailing Address of Informant: Shirlee Colleen Conte - same
- 19c. City or Town: Beverly Hills
- 19d. County: Los Angeles
- 19e. State: Calif

PHYSICIAN'S OR CORONER'S CERTIFICATION

- 21b. Physician: 4-12-75 to 4-15-75, 4-15-75
- 21c. Signature: Charles H. Query MD 4/15/75
- 21e. Address: UCLA Med. Center LA
- 21f. License Number: A-29061

FUNERAL DIRECTOR AND LOCAL REGISTRAR

- 22a. Burial/Entombment: burial
- 22b. Date: 4-19-75
- 23. Cemetery: Westwood Memorial Park
- 24. Embalmer: Leon O Stringer 5239
- 25. Funeral Director: Westwood Village Mortuary
- 26. Reported to Coroner: No
- 28. Date Received: APR 17 1975

CAUSE OF DEATH

- 29. Part I. Death was caused by:
  - (A) Respiratory Arrest — Minutes
  - (B) Pneumonia — 12 DAY
  - (C) Myocardial Infarction & Resuscitation — 12 DAYS
- 31. Operation: No
- 32. Autopsy: No

19-397052

AUG 16 1995

Beatriz Valdez
BEATRIZ VALDEZ
Registrar-Recorder/County Clerk

CERTIFICATION OF VITAL RECORD

COUNTY OF LOS ANGELES • REGISTRAR-RECORDER/COUNTY CLERK

CERTIFICATE OF DEATH — STATE OF CALIFORNIA
State File Number: 39119029758

DECEDENT PERSONAL DATA
- 1A. Name (First): BERNARD
- 1B. Middle: WHALEN
- 1C. Last (Family): CONVY
- 2A. Date of Death: JULY 15, 1991
- 2B. Hour: 0520
- 3. Sex: MALE
- 4. Race: CAUCASIAN
- 5. Hispanic: No (X)
- 6. Date of Birth: JULY 23, 1933
- 7. Age: 57
- 8. State of Birth: MO.
- 9. Citizen of: USA
- 10A. Full Name of Father: BERNARD T. CONVY
- 10B. State of Birth: MO.
- 11A. Full Maiden Name of Mother: MONICA WHALEN
- 11B. State of Birth: MO.
- 12. Military Service: None (X)
- 13. Social Security No.: 565-38-9542
- 14. Marital Status: MARRIED
- 15. Name of Surviving Spouse: CATHERINE HILLS
- 16A. Usual Occupation: ENTERTAINER
- 16B. Usual Kind of Business: ENTERTAINMENT
- 16C. Usual Employer: BERT CONVY PROD.
- 16D. Years in Occupation: 39
- 17. Education—Years Completed: 16

USUAL RESIDENCE
- 18A. Residence: 11737 CRESCENDA STREET
- 18B. City: LOS ANGELES
- 18C. Zip Code: 90049
- 18D. County: LOS ANGELES
- 18E. Number of Years in This County: 50
- 18F. State: CALIFORNIA
- 20. Name, Relationship, Mailing Address of Informant: CATHERINE CONVY — WIFE, 11737 CRESCENDA STREET, LOS ANGELES, CA 90049

PLACE OF DEATH
- 19A. Place of Death: RESIDENCE
- 19C. County: LOS ANGELES
- 19D. Street Address: 11737 CRESCENDA STREET
- 19E. City: LOS ANGELES
- 22. Was Death Reported to Coroner: No (X)

CAUSE OF DEATH
- 21. Death Was Caused By:
  - (A) Immediate Cause: Cardiac Arrest — 5 Min
  - (B) Due To: Glioblastoma Multiforme—Brain — 15 Mos.
- 23. Was Biopsy Performed: No
- 24A. Was Autopsy Performed: No
- 25. Other Significant Conditions: None
- 26. Was Operation Performed: Brain Tumor 7-16-90

PHYSICIAN'S CERTIFICATION
- 27A. Decedent Attended Since: 5/6/1990
- 27B. Decedent Last Seen Alive: 7/1/1991
- 27C. Certifier's License Number: C19015
- 27D. Date Signed: 7-16-91
- 27E. Attending Physician's Name and Address: JOHN DAVID ROMM, M.D., 9735 WILSHIRE BLVD., SUITE 421, BEVERLY HILLS, CA

FUNERAL DIRECTOR AND LOCAL REGISTRAR
- 34A. Disposition: BURIAL
- 34B. Place of Final Disposition: FOREST LAWN MEM PARK—6300 FOREST LAWN DR., HOLLYWOOD HILLS, CA.
- 34C. Date: 7/18/91
- 35A. Signature of Embalmer: James E. Austin
- 35B. License Number: 4350
- 36A. Name of Funeral Director: PIERCE BROTHERS MOELLER-MURPHY
- 36B. License No.: FD-695
- 37. Signature of Local Registrar: Robert C. Gates
- 38. Registration Date: JUL 17 1991

This is to certify that this document is a true copy of the official record filed with the Registrar-Recorder/County Clerk.

Beatriz Valdez
BEATRIZ VALDEZ
Registrar-Recorder/County Clerk

AUG 25 1995
19-399446

This copy not valid unless prepared on engraved border displaying the Seal and Signature of the Registrar-Recorder/County Clerk.

County of San Diego
Certificate of Death

State of California — Department of Public Health

State File Number: 73-054222
Local Registration District and Certificate Number: 8009 03558

1a. Name of Deceased — First Name	Merian
1b. Middle Name	Coldwell
1c. Last Name	Cooper
2a. Date of Death	April 21, 1973
2b. Hour	5 A.M.
3. Sex	male
4. Color or Race	Cauc.
5. Birthplace	Florida
6. Date of Birth	Oct. 24, 1894
7. Age	78 years
8. Name and Birthplace of Father	unkn. unkn.
9. Maiden Name and Birthplace of Mother	Mary Coldwell – Tenn.
10. Citizen of What Country	U.S.A.
11. Social Security Number	547-10-7723 A
12. Married, Never Married, Widowed, Divorced	married
13. Name of Surviving Spouse	Dorothy Jordon
14. Last Occupation	Movie Producer
15. Number of Years in This Occupation	30
16. Name of Last Employing Company or Firm	Cinerama Prod. Corp.
17. Kind of Industry or Business	Movie

Place of Death

18a. Place of Death	Mercy Hospital
18b. Street Address	4077 5th Ave.
18c. Inside City Corporate Limits	yes
18d. City or Town	San Diego
18e. County	San Diego
18f. Length of Stay in County of Death	9 years
18g. Length of Stay in California	30 years

Usual Residence

19a. Usual Residence — Street Address	952 E. Ave.
19b. Inside City Corporate Limits	yes
20. Name and Mailing Address of Informant	Richard M. Cooper, 952 E. Ave. Coronado, Ca.
19c. City or Town	Coronado
19d. County	San Diego
19e. State	Calif.

Physician's or Coroner's Certification

- 21a. (Dates): 10-30-70 / 4-21-73 / 4-20-73
- 21c. Address: 104 Univ. Ave. San Diego Ca.
- 21d. Date Signed: April 23, 1973
- 21r. Physician's California License Number: C 17840

Funeral Director and Local Registrar

- 22a. Specify Burial, Entombment or Cremation: Cremation–Scatter at sea
- 22b. Date: 4/25/73
- 23. Name of Cemetery or Crematory: Cypress View Crematory
- 24. Embalmer: James Carlisle — D127
- 25. Name of Funeral Director: Coronado Mortuary
- 26. Was This Death Reported to Coroner: no
- 28. Date Accepted for Registration by Local Registrar: APR 24 1973

Cause of Death

29. Part I. Death was caused by:
- (A) Immediate Cause: Generalized Carcinomatosis — 4/wks
- (B) Due to: Metastatic Carcinoma — 3 yrs
- (C) Due to: Adeno Carcinoma of Prostate Gland — 4 yrs

30. Part II. Other Significant Conditions: Bilat. Bronchopneumonia

31. Was Operation or Biopsy Performed: ok
32a. Autopsy: yes
32b. Were Findings Considered in Determining Cause of Death: yes

---

December 10, 2008 — Gregory J. Smith, Assessor/Recorder/County Clerk

This copy is not valid unless prepared on an engraved border displaying date, seal and signature of the Recorder/County Clerk

002467437

54

Aneta Corsault

CERTIFICATE OF DEATH
STATE OF CALIFORNIA

1. Name of Decedent—First (Given): ANETA
2. Middle: LOUISE
3. Last (Family): CORSAUT
4. Date of Birth: 11/03/1933
5. Age Yrs.: 62
6. Sex: F
7. Date of Death: 11/06/1995
8. Hour: 2230
9. State of Birth: KANSAS
10. Social Security No.: 511-30-9953
11. Military Service: NONE
12. Marital Status: NEVER MARRIED
13. Education—Years Completed: 14
14. Race: CAUCASIAN
15. Hispanic: No
16. Usual Employer: SELF-EMPLOYED
17. Occupation: ACTRESS
18. Kind of Business: MOTION PICTURES & TV.
19. Years in Occupation: 42
20. Residence: 4312 AGNES AVE.
21. City: STUDIO CITY
22. County: LOS ANGELES
23. Zip Code: 91604
24. Yrs in County: 35
25. State: CALIFORNIA
26. Informant Name, Relationship: ROBERT A. WAGNER - FRIEND
27. Mailing Address: 4312 AGNES AVE. STUDIO CITY, CA 91604
31. Name of Father—First: JESS
32. Middle: HARRISON
33. Last: CORSAUT
34. Birth State: KANSAS
35. Name of Mother—First: OPAL
36. Middle: JANNELE
37. Last (Maiden): SWARENS
38. Birth State: OKLAHOMA
39. Date: 11/10/1995
40. Place of Final Disposition: VALHALLA MEMORIAL PARK 10621 VICTORY BLVD. NORTH HOLLYWOOD, CA
41. Type of Disposition: BURIAL
42. Signature of Embalmer: NOT EMBALMED
44. Name of Funeral Director: PIERCE BROS. VALHALLA MORTUARY
45. License No.: F-916
47. Date: 11/08/1995
101. Place of Death: RESIDENCE (RES.)
104. County: LOS ANGELES
105. Street Address: 4312 AGNES AVE.
106. City: STUDIO CITY

107. Death was caused by:
- (A) CARDIOPULMONARY ARREST — 1 DAY
- (B) METASTATIC BREAST CANCER — 3 YRS

108. Death Reported to Coroner: No
109. Biopsy Performed: No
110. Autopsy Performed: No
112. Other Significant Conditions: NO
113. Operation Performed: NO
114. Decedent Attended Since: 04/16/1992
Decedent Last Seen Alive: 10/19/1995
116. License No.: G036051
117. Date: 11/08/1995
118. Attending Physician: DANIEL LIEBER, M.D. 2601 W. ALAMEDA #210, BURBANK, CA 91505

JOSEPH COTTEN

CERTIFICATE OF DEATH
STATE OF CALIFORNIA

1. NAME OF DECEDENT—FIRST (GIVEN): Joseph
2. MIDDLE: C
3. LAST (FAMILY): Cotten
4. DATE OF BIRTH: 05/15/1905
5. AGE YRS.: 88
6. SEX: M
7. DATE OF DEATH: 02/06/1994
8. HOUR: 0635
9. STATE OF BIRTH: VA
10. SOCIAL SECURITY NO.: 123-01-7286
11. MILITARY SERVICE: NONE
12. MARITAL STATUS: MARRIED
13. EDUCATION—YEARS COMPLETED: 16
14. RACE: WHITE
15. HISPANIC: NO
16. USUAL EMPLOYER: SELF EMPLOYED
17. OCCUPATION: ACTOR
18. KIND OF BUSINESS: MOTION PICTURES
19. YEARS IN OCCUPATION: 70
20. RESIDENCE: 6363 WILSHIRE BLVD. #600
21. CITY: LOS ANGELES
22. COUNTY: LOS ANGELES
23. ZIP CODE: 90048
24. YRS IN COUNTY: 2
25. STATE OR FOREIGN COUNTRY: CALIFORNIA
26. NAME, RELATIONSHIP: PATRICIA M. COTTEN - WIFE
27. MAILING ADDRESS: 6363 WILSHIRE BLVD. #600
28. NAME OF SURVIVING SPOUSE—FIRST: PATRICIA
29. MIDDLE: -
30. LAST (MAIDEN NAME): MEDINA
31. NAME OF FATHER—FIRST: JOSEPH
32. MIDDLE: C
33. LAST: COTTEN
34. BIRTH STATE: NC
35. NAME OF MOTHER—FIRST: SALLY
36. MIDDLE: -
37. LAST (MAIDEN): WILLSON
38. BIRTH STATE: VA
39. DATE: 02/11/1994
40. PLACE OF FINAL DISPOSITION: BLANDFORD CEMETERY - PETERSBURG, VA
41. TYPE OF DISPOSITION(S): CR/TR/BU
42. SIGNATURE OF EMBALMER: NOT EMBALMED
43. LICENSE NO.: NONE
44. NAME OF FUNERAL DIRECTOR: Inglewood Cemetery Mortuary
45. LICENSE NO.: FD 1101
46. SIGNATURE OF LOCAL REGISTRAR: Robert C. Platt
47. DATE: 02/10/1994
101. PLACE OF DEATH: Residence
103. FACILITY OTHER THAN HOSPITAL: RES.
104. COUNTY: Los Angeles
105. STREET ADDRESS: 10590 Wilshire Blvd. #1202
106. CITY: Los Angeles

107. DEATH WAS CAUSED BY:
- IMMEDIATE CAUSE (A): PNEUMONIA — 10 DAYS
- DUE TO (B): COPD — 10 YRS

108. DEATH REPORTED TO CORONER: NO
109. BIOPSY PERFORMED: NO
110. AUTOPSY PERFORMED: NO
111. USED IN DETERMINING CAUSE: NO
112. OTHER SIGNIFICANT CONDITIONS: CARCINOMA OF LARYNX, PROSTATE CANCER
113. WAS OPERATION PERFORMED: LARYNGECTOMY 1990
115. SIGNATURE AND TITLE OF CERTIFIER: Douglas L. Forde MD
116. LICENSE NO.: A10268
117. DATE: 2-9-94
DECEDENT ATTENDED SINCE: 1963
DECEDENT LAST SEEN ALIVE: 02/05/1994
118. TYPE ATTENDING PHYSICIAN'S NAME, MAILING ADDRESS + ZIP: DOUGLAS L. FORDE MD. 2001 SANTA MONICA BLVD. S.M., CA 90404

COUNTY OF LOS ANGELES
DEPARTMENT OF HEALTH SERVICES

CERTIFICATE OF DEATH
STATE OF CALIFORNIA

DECEDENT PERSONAL DATA
- 1. Name of Decedent—First (Given): MARY
- 2. Middle: JANE
- 3. Last (Family): LEWIS
- 4. Date of Birth: 02/15/1916
- 5. Age Yrs.: 83
- 6. Sex: F
- 7. Date of Death: 08/24/1999
- 8. Hour: 1235
- 9. State of Birth: INDIANA
- 10. Social Security No.: 270-01-0857
- 11. Military Service: No
- 12. Marital Status: WIDOW
- 13. Education—Years Completed: 12
- 14. Race: CAUCASIAN
- 15. Hispanic: No
- 16. Usual Employer: SELF EMPLOYED
- 17. Occupation: ACTRESS
- 18. Kind of Business: ENTERTAINMENT
- 19. Years in Occupation: 45

USUAL RESIDENCE
- 20. Residence: 2160 CENTURY PARK EAST #812
- 21. City: LOS ANGELES
- 22. County: LOS ANGELES
- 23. Zip Code: 90067
- 24. Yrs in County: 7
- 25. State: CA

INFORMANT
- 26. Name, Relationship: LARRY J. DRESSLER, EXECUTOR
- 27. Mailing Address: 10390 SANTA MONICA BL. #360, LOS ANGELES, CA 90025

SPOUSE AND PARENT INFORMATION
- 28. Name of Surviving Spouse—First: —
- 29. Middle: —
- 30. Last (Maiden Name): —
- 31. Name of Father—First: JOHN
- 32. Middle: L.
- 33. Last: CROFT
- 34. Birth State: IN
- 35. Name of Mother—First: EVA
- 36. Middle: —
- 37. Last (Maiden): JENSMA
- 38. Birth State: IN

DISPOSITION(S)
- 39. Date: 08/27/1999
- 40. Place of Final Disposition: AT SEA OFF THE COAST OF LOS ANGELES COUNTY
- 41. Type of Disposition: CR/SEA
- 42. Signature of Embalmer: NOT EMBALMED
- 43. License No.: —
- 44. Name of Funeral Director: NEPTUNE SOCIETY OF BURBANK
- 45. License No.: FD-1359
- 47. Date: 08/27/1999

PLACE OF DEATH
- 101. Place of Death: RESIDENCE
- 104. County: LOS ANGELES
- 105. Street Address: 2160 CENTURY PARK EAST #812
- 106. City: LOS ANGELES

CAUSE OF DEATH
- 107. Death was caused by:
  - (A) Immediate Cause: CARDIOPULMONARY ARREST — Minutes
  - (B) Due to: HYPERTENSIVE HEART DISEASE — Years
- 108. Death Reported to Coroner: Yes — Referral Number: 99-57464
- 109. Biopsy Performed: No
- 110. Autopsy Performed: No
- 112. Other Significant Conditions: NONE
- 113. Was Operation Performed: NO

PHYSICIAN'S CERTIFICATION
- 114. Decedent Attended Since: 06/16/1997; Last Seen Alive: 06/30/1999
- 116. License No.: C24698
- 117. Date: 8/27/99
- 118. Physician's Name: RICHARD HAWLEY, MD., 2021 SANTA MONICA BL., SANTA MONICA, CA 90404

Fax Auth. #: 195/1185

Date Issued: SEP 21 1999

COUNTY OF LOS ANGELES
DEPARTMENT OF HEALTH SERVICES

CERTIFICATE OF DEATH

1. Name of Decedent—First (Given)	ROSE
2. Middle	PAULINE
3. Last (Family)	PEACH
4. Date of Birth	12/19/1903
5. Age Yrs.	96
6. Sex	F
7. Date of Death	12/16/2000
8. Hour	0735
9. State of Birth	MA
10. Social Security No.	549-36-2136
11. Military Service	No
12. Marital Status	WIDOWED
13. Education—Years Completed	12
14. Race	CAUCASIAN
15. Hispanic	No
16. Usual Employer	SELF EMPLOYED
17. Occupation	SILENT SCREEN ACTRESS
18. Kind of Business	ENTERTAINMENT
19. Years in Occupation	22
20. Residence	1437 14TH ST
21. City	SANTA MONICA
22. County	LOS ANGELES
23. Zip Code	90404
24. Yrs in County	85
25. State	CA
26. Informant Name, Relationship	KENNETH D PEACH, JR
27. Mailing Address	2501 BEVERLY AVE #5, SANTA MONICA, CA 90405
31. Name of Father—First	JOHN
33. Last	CURLEY
34. Birth State	UNK
35. Name of Mother—First	ROSE
37. Last (Maiden)	FORTIER
38. Birth State	UNK
39. Date of Final Disposition	12/22/2000
40. Place of Final Disposition	FOREST LAWN MEMORIAL PARK, LOS ANGELES, CA 90068
41. Type of Disposition	BURIAL
43. License No.	6449
44. Name of Funeral Director	FOREST LAWN HOLLYWOOD HILLS
45. License No.	FD 904
47. Date	12/20/2000
101. Place of Death	SANTA MONICA UCLA MED CTR
104. County	LOS ANGELES
105. Street Address	1250 16TH ST
106. City	SANTA MONICA

107. Death was caused by:
- (A) CARDIOPULMONARY ARREST — 30 MIN
- (B) PNEUMONIA — DAYS

112. Other significant conditions: ATHEROSCLEROTIC HEART DISEASE, CHRONIC OBSTRUCTIVE PULMONARY DISEASE

113. NO

114. Decedent attended since	09/03/1998
Decedent last seen alive	12/15/2000
116. License No.	A42193
117. Date	12/18/2000
118. Attending Physician	PAUL LEITNER, MD 8540 S SEPULVEDA BLVD #910, LOS ANGELES, CA 90045
Fax Auth. #	273/21746

090392230

CERTIFICATE OF DEATH
STATE OF CALIFORNIA—DEPARTMENT OF PUBLIC HEALTH

Local Registration District and Certificate Number: 7053 14308

Decedent Personal Data
- **Name of Deceased:** Esther Dale Beckhard
- **Date of Death:** July 23, 1961
- **Hour:** 9:00 A.M.
- **Sex:** Female
- **Color or Race:** Cauc.
- **Birthplace:** South Carolina
- **Date of Birth:** November 19, 1885
- **Age:** 75 years
- **Name and Birthplace of Father:** John Dale, Vermont
- **Maiden Name and Birthplace of Mother:** Henrietta Case, Virginia
- **Citizen of What Country:** U.S.A.
- **Social Security Number:** 557-09-9266
- **Last Occupation:** Concert Actress-Artist
- **Number of Years in This Occupation:** 50 yrs
- **Name of Last Employing Company or Firm:** Free Lance
- **Kind of Industry or Business:** Stage and Screen
- **Was Deceased Ever in U.S. Armed Forces:** No
- **Married, Never Married, Widowed, Divorced:** Widowed

Place of Death
- **Name of Hospital:** Queen of Angels Hospital
- **Street Address:** 2301 Bellevue Avenue
- **City or Town:** Los Angeles
- **County:** Los Angeles
- **Length of Stay in County of Death:** 25 years
- **Length of Stay in California:** 25 years

Last Usual Residence
- **Street Address:** 353 South Oakhurst Drive
- **City or Town:** Beverly Hills
- **County:** Los Angeles
- **State:** California
- **Name of Informant:** Miss Alice Dale, sister
- **Address of Informant:** 353 So. Oakhurst Dr., Beverly Hills

Physician's or Coroner's Certification
- Physician attended deceased from 7-3-61 to 7-23-61; last saw deceased alive on 7-23-61
- **Physician Signature:** Henry Lange, M.D.
- **Address:** 6253 Hollywood Blvd, Hollywood
- **Date Signed:** 7-24-61

Funeral Director and Local Registrar
- **Specify Burial, Entombment or Cremation:** Cremation
- **Date:** 7-26-61
- **Name of Cemetery or Crematory:** Grand View Crematory
- **Embalmer Signature / License Number:** Harold V. Schutz 3328
- **Name of Funeral Director:** 6240 Hollywood Boulevard, UTTER-McKINLEY MORTUARIES
- **Date Accepted for Registration:** JUL 26 1961
- **Local Registrar Signature:** George M. Uhl, M.D.

Cause of Death
- **Part I. Death was caused by:**
  - **Immediate Cause (a):** Lower Nephron Nephrosis
  - **Due to (b):** Presumably ischemia associated with hypotension
  - Cardiac arrest (developed suddenly while sitting in bed two days post-operatively) 7-20-61
- **Part II. Other Significant Conditions:** Long standing history of diverticulosis & diverticulitis; Severe diarrhea since 2/3/61 with 22 pound weight loss

Operation and Autopsy
- **Date of Operation:** 7-18-61
- **Autopsy:** No

Certified copy — Conny B. McCormack, Registrar-Recorder/County Clerk, County of Los Angeles. JAN 10 2002, 19-020936.

CERTIFICATE OF DEATH
STATE OF CALIFORNIA

1. Name of Decedent—First (Given): ROYAL
2. Middle: EDWARD
3. Last (Family): DANO, SR.
4. Date of Birth: 11/16/1922
5. Age Yrs: 71
6. Sex: M
7. Date of Death: 05/15/1994
8. Hour: 1015
9. State of Birth: NY
10. Social Security No.: 080-18-4427
11. Military Service: 1943 to 1945
12. Marital Status: MARRIED
13. Education—Years Completed: 12
14. Race: CAUCASIAN
15. Hispanic: NO
16. Usual Employer: VARIOUS
17. Occupation: ACTOR
18. Kind of Business: ENTERTAINMENT
19. Years in Occupation: 50
20. Residence—Street and Number or Location: 517 20TH STREET
21. City: SANTA MONICA
22. County: LOS ANGELES
23. Zip Code: 90402
24. Yrs in County: 39
25. State or Foreign Country: CALIFORNIA
26. Name, Relationship: RICHARD DANO-SON
27. Mailing Address: 909 21ST ST #1 SANTA MONICA, CA 90403
28. Name of Surviving Spouse—First: PEGGY
30. Last (Maiden Name): RANK
31. Name of Father—First: ROYAL
32. Middle: EDWARD
33. Last: DANO
34. Birth State: NY
35. Name of Mother—First: MARY
37. Last (Maiden): O'CONNOR
38. Birth State: IRELAND
39. Date: 05/23/1994
40. Place of Final Disposition: RIVERSIDE NATIONAL CEMETERY 22495 VAN BUREN BLVD RIVERSIDE, CA 95208
41. Type of Disposition(s): CR/BU
42. Signature of Embalmer: NOT EMBALMED
44. Name of Funeral Director: PIERCE BROS. WESTWOOD VILLAGE
45. License No.: F-951
47. Date: 05/19/1994
101. Place of Death: RESIDENCE
103. Facility Other Than Hospital: RES.
104. County: LOS ANGELES
105. Street Address: 517 20TH STREET
106. City: SANTA MONICA

107. Death was caused by:
- (A) IMMEDIATE CAUSE: RESPIRATORY INSUFFICIENCY — 2 YRS
- (B) DUE TO: PULMONARY FIBROSIS — 10 YRS
- (C) DUE TO: EMPHYSEMA — 20 YRS
- (D) DUE TO: CHRONIC BRONCHITIS — 25 YRS

108. Death Reported to Coroner: NO
109. Biopsy Performed: NO
110. Autopsy Performed: NO
111. Used in Determining Cause:
112. Other Significant Conditions: ASHD
113. Was Operation Performed: CORONARY ARTERY BYPASS SURGERY 1985
115. Signature and Title of Certifier: James Blake
116. License No.: G11662
117. Date: 05/18/1994
Decedent Attended Since: 04/09/1975
Decedent Last Seen Alive: 05/15/1994
118. Attending Physician's Name: JAMES BLAKE M.D. 1301 20TH STREET SANTA MONICA, CA 90404

CERTIFICATION OF VITAL RECORD

COUNTY OF LOS ANGELES • REGISTRAR-RECORDER/COUNTY CLERK

CERTIFICATE OF DEATH — STATE OF CALIFORNIA

Local Registration District and Certificate Number: 7037-036381

DECEDENT PERSONAL DATA
- 1A. Name (First): Richard
- 1C. Last: Deacon
- 2A. Date of Death: Aug 8 1984
- 2B. Hour: 1100
- 3. Sex: male
- 4. Race/Ethnicity: cauc
- 5. Spanish/Hispanic: No
- 6. Date of Birth: May 14 1922
- 7. Age: 62 years
- 8. Birthplace of Decedent: Pa.
- 9. Name and Birthplace of Father: J.G. Deacon — Pa
- 10. Birth Name and Birthplace of Mother: Ethel Laughlin — New York
- 11. Citizen of What Country: U.S.A.
- 12. Social Security Number: 113 14 5191
- 13. Marital Status: never married
- 15. Primary Occupation: Actor
- 16. Number of Years in This Occupation: adult life
- 17. Employer (or Self-Employed): Free-lance
- 18. Kind of Industry or Business: Motion Pictures and T.V.

USUAL RESIDENCE
- 19A. Street Address: 9540 Delegrave Drive
- 19B. (number): 198
- 19C. City or Town: Beverly Hills
- 19D. County: Los Angeles
- 19E. State: Calif
- 20. Name and Address of Informant — Relationship: Pre Need by Deceased

PLACE OF DEATH
- 21A. Place of Death: Cedars Sinai Hospital
- 21B. County: Los Angeles
- 21C. Street Address: 8700 Beverly Blvd.
- 21D. City or Town: Los Angeles

CAUSE OF DEATH
- 22. (A) HYPERTENSIVE HEART DISEASE
- 23. Other Significant Conditions: ATHEROSCLEROTIC CORONARY HEART DISEASE
- 24. Was Death Reported to Coroner: 84-9922
- 25. Was Biopsy Performed: No
- 26. Was Autopsy Performed: Yes
- 27. Was Operation Performed: No

CORONER'S USE ONLY
- 35A. Deputy Coroner — Anette Egan — 8-12-84

- 36. Disposition: Cremation
- 37. Date: 8-14-84
- 38. Name and Address of Cemetery or Crematory: Grandview Crematory Glendale Calif
- not embalmed
- 42. Date Accepted by Local Registrar: AUG 13 1984
- 40A. Name of Funeral Director: Westwood Village Mortuary

State Registrar: 9740

OCT 02 1995
19-033395

SANDRA DEE

STATE OF CALIFORNIA
CERTIFICATION OF VITAL RECORD

COUNTY OF VENTURA
VENTURA, CALIFORNIA

CERTIFICATE OF DEATH — 3200556000671

1. Name of Decedent — First	SANDRA
2. Middle	—
3. Last (Family)	DEE
4. Date of Birth	04/23/1942
5. Age	62
6. Sex	F
8. Birth State/Foreign Country	NJ
10. Social Security Number	075-30-5460
11. Ever in U.S. Armed Forces?	NO
12. Marital Status	WIDOWED
7. Date of Death	02/20/2005
8. Hour	0600
13. Education	ASSOCIATE
14/15. Hispanic/Latino	NO
16. Race	WHITE
17. Usual Occupation	ACTRESS
18. Kind of Business/Industry	ENTERTAINMENT
19. Years in Occupation	50
20. Decedent's Residence	201 TRIUNFO CANYON #163
21. City	WESTLAKE VILLAGE
22. County	LOS ANGELES
23. Zip Code	91361
24. Years in County	40
25. State	CA
26. Informant's Name, Relationship	DODD DARIN, SON
27. Informant's Mailing Address	6685 ZUMIREZ DR, MALIBU, CA 90265
31. Name of Father — First	JOHN
33. Last	ZUCK
34. Birth State	NJ
35. Name of Mother — First	MARY
37. Last (Maiden)	CIMBOLIAK
38. Birth State	NJ
39. Disposition Date	03/01/2005
40. Place of Final Disposition	FOREST LAWN MEMORIAL PARK, 6300 FOREST LAWN DR., LOS ANGELES, CA 90068
41. Type of Disposition	BURIAL
43. License Number	8851
44. Name of Funeral Establishment	FOREST LAWN HOLLYWOOD HILLS
45. License Number	FD 904
47. Date	02/28/2005
101. Place of Death	LOS ROBLES HOSP AND MED CTR
102. Hospital	IP
104. County	VENTURA
105. Facility Address	215 W JANSS RD
106. City	THOUSAND OAKS

107. Cause of Death:
- (A) Immediate Cause: CARDIOPULMONARY ARREST — MINS
- (B) HYPOTENSIVE SHOCK — DAYS
- (C) CHRONIC RENAL FAILURE — YRS

112. Other Significant Conditions: VENTRICULAR FIBRILLATION, CARDIAC ARREST S/P, RESPIRATORY FAILURE, LEUKOCYTOSIS

113. Operation Performed: NO

116. Signature and Title of Certifier: Andre Yousefia, MD
118. License Number: A72667
117. Date: 02/22/2005
Decedent Attended Since: 02/08/2005
Decedent Last Seen Alive: 02/19/2005
119. Attending Physician: ANDRE YOUSEFIA, MD 227 W JANSS RD #330, THOUSAND OAKS, CA 91360

CERTIFIED COPY OF VITAL RECORDS
DATE ISSUED: 06/30/2005

STATE OF CALIFORNIA
COUNTY OF VENTURA

HEALTH OFFICER
VENTURA COUNTY, CALIFORNIA

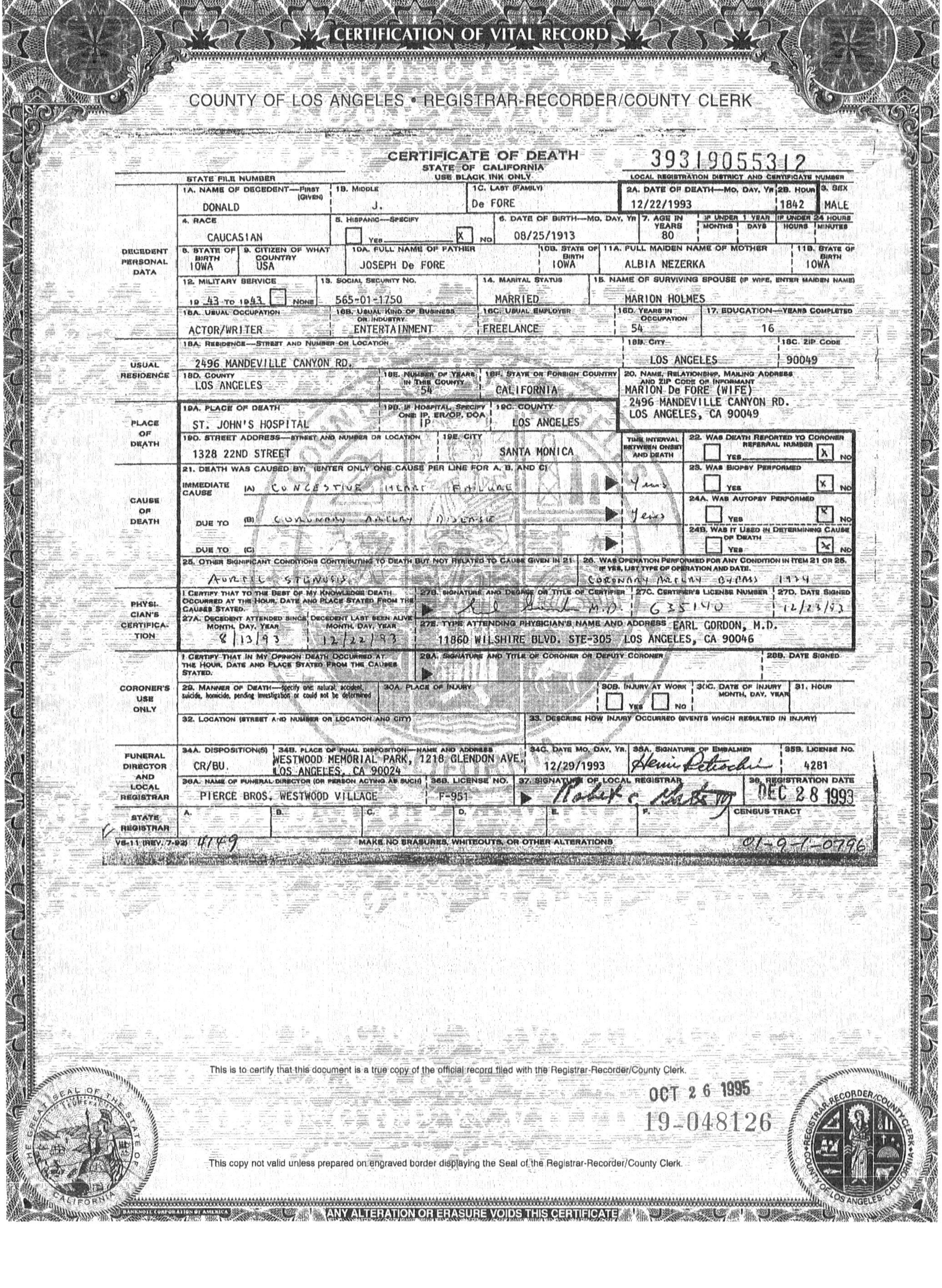

STATE OF CALIFORNIA
CERTIFICATION OF VITAL RECORD

COUNTY OF LOS ANGELES • REGISTRAR-RECORDER/COUNTY CLERK

CERTIFICATE OF DEATH — STATE OF CALIFORNIA

State File Number: 3200919018593

1. Name of Decedent — First	DOM
2. Middle	-
3. Last (Family)	DELUISE
4. Date of Birth	08/01/1933
5. Age	75
6. Sex	M
9. Birth State/Foreign Country	NY
10. Social Security Number	119-24-6157
11. Ever in U.S. Armed Forces?	NO
12. Marital Status	MARRIED
7. Date of Death	05/04/2009
8. Hour (24 Hours)	1844
13. Education	SOME COLLEGE
14/15. Hispanic/Latino	NO
16. Race	CAUCASIAN
17. Usual Occupation	ACTOR
18. Kind of Business/Industry	ENTERTAINMENT
19. Years in Occupation	60
20. Decedent's Residence	1186 CORSICA DR.
21. City	PACIFIC PALISADES
22. County/Province	LOS ANGELES
23. Zip Code	90272
24. Years in County	55
25. State/Foreign Country	CA
26. Informant's Name, Relationship	CAROL A DELUISE, WIFE
27. Informant's Mailing Address	1186 CORSICA DR., PACIFIC PALISADES, CA 90272
28. Name of Surviving Spouse — First	CAROL
29. Middle	A.
30. Last (Maiden Name)	ARATA
31. Name of Father — First	JOHN
32. Middle	-
33. Last	DELUISE
34. Birth State	NY
35. Name of Mother — First	VINCENZA
36. Middle	-
37. Last (Maiden)	DESTEFANO
38. Birth State	ITALY
39. Disposition Date	05/06/2009
40. Place of Final Disposition	RES CAROL A. DELUISE, 1186 CORSICA DR., PACIFIC PALISADES, CA 90272
41. Type of Disposition(s)	CR/RES
42. Signature of Embalmer	NOT EMBALMED
44. Name of Funeral Establishment	NEPTUNE SOCIETY SHERMAN OAKS
45. License Number	FD-1359
46. Signature of Local Registrar	JONATHAN FIELDING, MD
47. Date	05/06/2009
101. Place of Death	ST JOHNS HEALTH CENTER
102. If Hospital, Specify	IP
104. County	LOS ANGELES
105. Facility Address	1328 22ND ST.
106. City	SANTA MONICA

107. Cause of Death
- (A) Immediate Cause: RESPIRATORY FAILURE — DAYS
- (B) CONGESTIVE HEART FAILURE — DAYS
- (C) CORONARY ARTERY DISEASE — YRS

108. Death Reported to Coroner? NO
109. Biopsy Performed? NO
110. Autopsy Performed? NO

112. Other Significant Conditions: NONE
113. Was Operation Performed: NO

114. Decedent Attended Since	04/29/2009
Decedent Last Seen Alive	05/04/2009
115. Signature and Title of Certifier	ELLIOT LAWRENCE GOLDMAN M.D.
116. License Number	G18522
117. Date	05/06/2009
118. Attending Physician's Name, Mailing Address	ELLIOT LAWRENCE GOLDMAN M.D., 1301 20TH STREET #360, SANTA MONICA, CA 90404

INFORMATIONAL, NOT A VALID DOCUMENT TO ESTABLISH IDENTITY

This is to certify that this document is a true copy of the official record filed with the Registrar-Recorder/County Clerk.

SEP 28 2009

DEAN C. LOGAN
Registrar-Recorder/County Clerk

019581420

SANTA BARBARA COUNTY
SANTA BARBARA, CALIFORNIA

CERTIFICATE OF DEATH

- Name of Decedent: JOHN DEREK
- Date of Birth: 08/12/1926
- Age: 71
- Sex: M
- Date of Death: 05/22/1998
- Hour: 1245
- State of Birth: CA
- Social Security No.: 564-30-1984
- Military Service: Yes
- Marital Status: MRD
- Education—Years Completed: 12
- Race: White
- Usual Employer: Self employed
- Occupation: Film Maker
- Kind of Business: Motion Picture Industry
- Years in Occupation: 55
- Residence: 3625 Roblar Avenue
- City: Santa Ynez
- County: Santa Barbara
- ZIP: 93460
- Yrs in County: 18
- State: CA
- Informant: Bo Derek, Wife — 3625 Roblar Ave, Santa Ynez, CA 93460
- Name of Surviving Spouse: Bo — Last (Maiden Name): Collins
- Name of Father: Lawson Harris — Birth State: IN
- Name of Mother: Dolores Johnson — Birth State: CA
- Disposition Date: 05/26/1998 — RES 3625 Roblar Ave. Santa Ynez, CA 93460
- Type of Disposition: CR RES — not embalmed
- Name of Funeral Director: Loper Funeral Chapel — License No.: 1294 — Date: 05/26/1998
- Place of Death: Marian Medical Center — IP
- Street Address: 1400 E Church Street
- County: Santa Barbara — City: Santa Maria

Cause of Death:
- (A) Aortic Dissection Type I — 44 hrs
- (B) Aneurysm — 1 mo
- (C) Arteriosclerotic Heart Disease — 15 yrs

Other significant conditions: Hypertension, Myocardial Infarction 1986

Operation performed: Aortic Dissection Repair 05/20/1998

- Physician: Herbert Tanney, MD, 2030 Viborg Rd, Solvang, CA 93463
- License No.: G4244
- Date: 05/23/1998
- Decedent attended since: 02/09/1979 — Last seen alive: 05/14/1998

State File Number: 3199842001186

S216518

CERTIFIED COPY OF VITAL RECORDS
STATE OF CALIFORNIA
COUNTY OF SANTA BARBARA
DATE ISSUED: JUL 08 1998

KENNETH A. PETTIT
COUNTY CLERK-RECORDER
SANTA BARBARA, CALIFORNIA

This copy not valid unless prepared on engraved border displaying seal and signature of County Clerk-Recorder.

ANY ALTERATION OR ERASURE VOIDS THIS CERTIFICATE

JOE DERITA

STATE OF CALIFORNIA
CERTIFICATION OF VITAL RECORD
COUNTY OF LOS ANGELES • REGISTRAR-RECORDER/COUNTY CLERK

CERTIFICATE OF DEATH
STATE OF CALIFORNIA
USE BLACK INK ONLY

State File Number: 3931 9028876

DECEDENT PERSONAL DATA

- 1A. Name (First): JOE
- 1B. Middle: —
- 1C. Last (Family): DERITA
- 2A. Date of Death: July 3, 1993
- 2B. Hour: 0900
- 3. Sex: M
- 4. Race: Cauc
- 5. Hispanic: No (xx)
- 6. Date of Birth: July 12, 1909
- 7. Age: 83
- 8. State of Birth: PA
- 9. Citizen of: USA
- 10A. Full Name of Father: Franklin Wardell
- 10B. State of Birth: Unk
- 11A. Full Maiden Name of Mother: Florenz DeRita
- 11B. State of Birth: Unk
- 12. Military Service: None (X)
- 13. Social Security No.: 290-01-6624
- 14. Marital Status: Married
- 15. Name of Surviving Spouse: Jean Rase
- 16A. Usual Occupation: Actor
- 16B. Usual Kind of Business or Industry: Entertainment
- 16C. Usual Employer: Self Employed
- 16D. Years in Occupation: 76
- 17. Education—Years Completed: 5

USUAL RESIDENCE

- 18A. Residence—Street and Number or Location: 545 N. Myers St.
- 18B. City: Burbank
- 18C. Zip Code: 91506
- 18D. County: Los Angeles
- 18E. Number of Years in This County: 54
- 18F. State or Foreign Country: California
- 20. Name, Relationship, Mailing Address and Zip Code of Informant: Jean DeRita—wife, 545 N. Myers St., Burbank, Ca. 91506

PLACE OF DEATH

- 19A. Place of Death: Motion Picture/TV Hosp.
- 19B. If Hospital, Specify: IP
- 19C. County: Los Angeles
- 19D. Street Address: 23388 Mulholland Drive
- 19E. City: Woodland Hills
- 22. Was Death Reported to Coroner: No (X)

CAUSE OF DEATH

- 21. Death was caused by:
  - (A) Immediate Cause: Cardiopulmonary Arrest — 6 min.
  - (B) Due to: Bradycardia — 30 min.
  - (C) Due to: Atherosclerotic Cardiovascular Disease — years
- 23. Was Biopsy Performed: No (X)
- 24A. Was Autopsy Performed: No (X)
- 24B. Was It Used in Determining Cause of Death: —
- 25. Other Significant Conditions Contributing to Death But Not Related to Cause Given in 21: Pneumonia, Advanced Dementia
- 26. Was Operation Performed: No

PHYSICIAN'S CERTIFICATION

- 27A. Decedent Attended Since: 10/01/92
- Last Seen Alive: 07/02/93
- 27B. Signature and Degree or Title of Certifier: John Hoh, M.D.
- 27C. Certifier's License Number: G066101
- 27D. Date Signed: 07/06/93
- 27E. Attending Physician's Name and Address: John Hoh, M.D., 23388 Mulholland Drive, Woodland Hills, CA 91364

FUNERAL DIRECTOR AND LOCAL REGISTRAR

- 34A. Disposition: Burial
- 34B. Place of Final Disposition: Valhalla Mem. Park, No. Hollywood, Ca.
- 34C. Date: 7-8-93
- 36A. Name of Funeral Director: Valley Funeral Home
- 36B. License No.: 976
- 38. Registration Date: JUL 07 1993

This is to certify that this document is a true copy of the official record filed with the Registrar-Recorder/County Clerk.

CONNY B. McCORMACK
Registrar-Recorder/County Clerk

OCT 04 2001
19-673792

Certificate of Death

State of California — County of Los Angeles • Registrar-Recorder/County Clerk

District No. 1901   Registrar's No. 7867

1. **Full Name:** Jenny Dolly Vinisski
2. **Place of Death:**
   (A) County: Los Angeles
   (B) City or Town: Los Angeles
   (C) Name of Hospital or Institution: 1735 N Wilcox
   (D) Length of Stay: In this community 5 mo. In California 5 mo.
   (E) If Foreign Born, How Long in the U.S.A.: 36 years
   (E) If Veteran, Name of War: No
   (F) Social Security No.: No
3. **Usual Residence of Deceased:**
   (A) State: California
   (B) County: Los Angeles
   (C) City or Town: Los Angeles
   (D) Street No.: 1735 N Wilcox, Apt. 209
4. **Sex:** Female
5. **Color or Race:** Cauc
6. **Single, Married, Widowed or Divorced:** Married
   (B) Name of Husband or Wife: Bernard W. Vinisski
   (C) Age of Husband or Wife if Alive: 47 years
7. **Birthdate of Deceased:** October 25, 1897
8. **Age:** 43 yrs. 7 mos. 7 days
9. **Birthplace:** Budapest, Hungary
10. **Usual Occupation:** Housewife
11. **Industry or Business:** Home
12. **Father's Name:** Julius Dolly
13. **Father's Birthplace:** Budapest, Hungary
14. **Mother's Maiden Name:** Margaret Weis
15. **Mother's Birthplace:** Budapest, Hungary
16. (A) **Informant:** Irving Netcher
    (B) **Address:** 610 N Beverly Dr, Bev. Hills
17. (A) Cremation — Date: June 4, 1941
    (C) Place: Forest Lawn Crematory
18. Embalmer's Signature: Joseph E Wiley — License No. 2561
    Funeral Director: Pierce Bros. Hollywood
    Address: 5959 Santa Monica Blvd.
    By: C. H. Hess
19. (A) Date Filed: Jun 4 1941 — Registrar: George Parrish M.D.

20. **Date of Death:** Month June, Day 1, Year 1941, Hour 1, Minute PM

21. **Medical Certificate:** [blank]

22. **Coroner's Certificate:** I hereby certify that I held an Exam & Inquiry on the remains of the deceased and find from such action that deceased came to death on the date and hour stated above.
   Immediate Cause of Death: Asphyxia
   Due to: Hanging

23. **If death was due to external causes:**
   (A) Accident, Suicide or Homicide: Suicide
   (B) Date of Injury: 6-1-41
   (C) Where did injury occur: Hollywood, LA, Cal
   (D) Did injury occur in or about home...: Home
   (E) Means of Injury: Hung herself

24. **Coroner's Signature:** Frank A. Nance, Coroner / H. G. Macdonald
    Address: Los Angeles — Date: 6-2-41

SACRAMENTO COUNTY
DEPARTMENT OF HEALTH AND HUMAN SERVICES

STATE OF CALIFORNIA — CERTIFICATION OF VITAL RECORD

State File Number: 3389034006712

Decedent Personal Data
- **1. Name of Decedent—First (Given):** ANNA
- **2. Middle:** LEE
- **3. Last (Family):** DORAN
- **4. Date of Birth:** 07/28/1911
- **5. Age Yrs.:** 89
- **6. Sex:** F
- **7. Date of Death:** 09/19/2000
- **8. Hour:** 0845
- **9. State of Birth:** TX
- **10. Social Security No.:** 564-18-5560
- **11. Military Service:** No
- **12. Marital Status:** Never Married
- **13. Education—Years Completed:** 14
- **14. Race:** Caucasian
- **15. Hispanic:** No
- **16. Usual Employer:** Screen Actors Guild
- **17. Occupation:** Actress
- **18. Kind of Business:** Entertainment
- **19. Years in Occupation:** 77

Usual Residence
- **20. Residence:** 3939 Walnut Ave., Apt. C208
- **21. City:** Carmichael
- **22. County:** Sacramento
- **23. Zip Code:** 95608
- **24. Yrs in County:** 8
- **25. State or Foreign Country:** CA

Informant
- **26. Name, Relationship:** Donna Rae Jennings, 2nd Cousin
- **27. Mailing Address:** 8601 West Camden Dr., Elk Grove, CA 95624

Spouse and Parent Information
- **31. Name of Father—First:** John
- **32. Middle:** Richard
- **33. Last:** Doran
- **34. Birth State:** OK
- **35. Name of Mother—First:** Carrie
- **36. Middle:** Alma
- **37. Last (Maiden):** Barnett
- **38. Birth State:** MO

Disposition(s)
- **39. Date:** 09/21/2000
- **40. Place of Final Disposition:** Res: Donna Rae Jennings, 2nd Cousin, 8601 West Camden Dr., Elk Grove, CA 95624
- **41. Type of Disposition(s):** CR/RES
- **42. Signature of Embalmer:** Not Embalmed
- **44. Name of Funeral Director:** SOUTH EAST LAWN MORTUARY
- **45. License No.:** FD-1455
- **47. Date:** 09/20/2000 TJ

Place of Death
- **101. Place of Death:** Eskaton Village Conv.
- **102. If Hospital, Specify:** CONV. HOSP.
- **104. County:** Sacramento
- **105. Street Address:** 3939 Walnut Avenue
- **106. City:** Carmichael
- **108. Death Reported to Coroner:** No

Cause of Death
- **107. Death was caused by:**
  - (A) Immediate Cause: Cardiac Arrhythmia — secs
  - (B) Due to: Hypertensive Cardiac Disease — 3 yrs
- **109. Biopsy Performed:** No
- **110. Autopsy Performed:** No
- **111. Used in Determining Cause:** —
- **112. Other Significant Conditions:** Acute Cerebrovascular Accident

Physician's Certification
- **114. Decedent Attended Since:** 11/05/1998
- **Last Seen Alive:** 09/15/2000
- **115. Signature and Title of Certifier:** Diana Accinelli, M.D.
- **116. License No.:** G58250
- **117. Date:** 09/20/2000
- **Attending Physician's Name, Mailing Address:** Diana Accinelli, M.D., 5495 Carlson Dr. #B, Sacramento, CA 95819

State Registrar: 338428

Fax Auth. #: 4891

STATE OF CALIFORNIA
COUNTY OF SACRAMENTO SS

This is a true and exact reproduction of the document officially registered and placed on file with SACRAMENTO COUNTY DEPARTMENT OF HEALTH AND HUMAN SERVICES.

DATE ISSUED: December 12, 2000

LOCAL REGISTRAR

This copy not valid unless prepared on engraved border displaying date and signature of Registrar.

ANY ALTERATION OR ERASURE VOIDS THIS CERTIFICATE

Certificate of Death

State of Connecticut — Department of Public Health and Addiction Services

State File Number: 106 96 021833

Deceased Name	Mignon G. Eberhart
Sex	F
Date of Death	10-08-96
Date of Birth	July 6, 1899
Age — Last Birthday	97
Race	White
Hispanic Origin	No
County of Death	Fairfield
Town of Death	Greenwich
Place of Death	Other — Nathaniel Witherell
City & State of Birth	Lincoln, NB
Citizen of	USA
Marital Status	Widowed
Last Spouse	Alanson C. Eberhart
Social Security Number	327-30-5284
Usual Occupation	Author
Kind of Business or Industry	Self Employed
Residence State	Connecticut
County	Fairfield
Town	Greenwich
Number and Street	37 East Lyon Farm
Was Deceased a Veteran	No
Education — Primary/Secondary	12 yrs
College	4 yrs
Father — Name	Thomas W. Good
Mother — Name	Margaret Bruffey
Informant Name	Jane Donovan, Esq.
Mailing Address	666 Summer Street, Stamford, CT 06905
Relationship to Deceased	Executor

Part I. Death was caused by:

Cause	Interval
(a) Immediate Cause: Cardiac Arrest	5 min
(b) Due to: Cardiac arrhythmia	15 min
(c) Due to: Cerebral vascular disease	several years

Part II. Other significant conditions: malnutrition

Autopsy: No

Nurse Pronouncement: Lynn A. Bausch, RN
Date and Time Pronounced: 10/08/96, 8:38 A.M.

Certification — Physician:
- Attended the deceased from: 1-10-85 to 10-8-96
- Last saw him/her alive on: 10-7-96
- Death Occurred: 8:38 A.M., 10-08-1996

Was case referred to Medical Examiner: No

Certifier: Dr. John H. Prunier, M.D.
Mailing: 49 Lake Avenue, Greenwich, Connecticut 06830
Date Signed: 10/9/96

Burial/Cremation	Cemetery or Crematory	Location
Cremation	Stamford Crematory	Stamford, Ct.

Date: 11-4-1996
Funeral Home: Leo P. Gallagher, 2900 Summer St., Stamford, Ct 06905
Name of Embalmer: Not Embalmed
License Number: 2218

This certificate received for record: Nov 4 1996

Attest: Barbara Lowden, Assistant Registrar

THE SEAL OF THE STATE OF CONNECTICUT IS AFFIXED TO CERTIFY THAT THE ABOVE IS A TRUE COPY OF A RECORD FILED WITH THE STATE OF CONNECTICUT DEPARTMENT OF PUBLIC HEALTH PURSUANT TO THE PROVISIONS OF THE GENERAL STATUTES OF CONNECTICUT.

Suzanne Speers, R.H.I.A., M.P.H.
Registrar of Vital Records

Date of Issue: Aug 05 2003

Herb Edelman

CERTIFICATE OF DEATH
STATE OF CALIFORNIA

State File Number: 39619031344

DECEDENT PERSONAL DATA
- **1. Name of Decedent—First (Given):** HERBERT
- **2. Middle:** —
- **3. Last (Family):** EDELMAN
- **4. Date of Birth:** 11/05/1933
- **5. Age Yrs:** 62
- **6. Sex:** M
- **7. Date of Death:** 07/21/1996
- **8. Hour:** 0515
- **9. State of Birth:** NEW YORK
- **10. Social Security No.:** 130-26-2616
- **11. Military Service:** NONE
- **12. Marital Status:** DIVORCED
- **13. Education—Years Completed:** 15
- **14. Race:** CAUCASIAN
- **15. Hispanic:** NO
- **16. Usual Employer:** SELF-EMPLOYED
- **17. Occupation:** ACTOR
- **18. Kind of Business:** ENTERTAINMENT
- **19. Years in Occupation:** 36

USUAL RESIDENCE
- **20. Residence—Street and Number or Location:** 3460 PENINSULA RD.
- **21. City:** OXNARD
- **22. County:** VENTURA
- **23. Zip Code:** 93035
- **24. Yrs in County:** 5
- **25. State or Foreign Country:** CALIFORNIA

INFORMANT
- **26. Name, Relationship:** BETTY T. BENNETT - SISTER
- **27. Mailing Address:** 4269 EMBASSY PARK DR. NW WASHINGTON DC 20016

SPOUSE AND PARENT INFORMATION
- **28-30. Name of Surviving Spouse:** —
- **31. Name of Father—First:** MAYER
- **32. Middle:** —
- **33. Last:** EDELMAN
- **34. Birth State:** RUSSIA
- **35. Name of Mother—First:** JENNIE
- **36. Middle:** DORA
- **37. Last (Maiden):** GREENBERG
- **38. Birth State:** POLAND

DISPOSITION(S)
- **39. Date:** 07/25/1996
- **40. Place of Final Disposition:** AT RESIDENCE OF BETTH T. BENNETT 4269 EMBASSY PARK DR. NW WASHINGTON, DC 20016

FUNERAL DIRECTOR AND LOCAL REGISTRAR
- **41. Type of Disposition(s):** CR/TR/RES
- **42. Signature of Embalmer:** NOT EMBALMED
- **44. Name of Funeral Director:** PIERCE BROS. VALHALLA MORTUARY
- **45. License No.:** F-916
- **47. Date:** 06/25/1996

PLACE OF DEATH
- **101. Place of Death:** MOTION PICTURE & T.V. HOSPITAL
- **103. Facility Other Than Hospital:** CONV. HOSP. (X)
- **104. County:** LOS ANGELES
- **105. Street Address:** 23388 MULHOLLAND DR.
- **106. City:** WOODLAND HILLS

CAUSE OF DEATH
- **107. Death Was Caused By:**
  - (A) IMMEDIATE CAUSE: RESPIRATORY FAILURE — 1 DAY
  - (B) DUE TO: BULLOUS EMPHYSEMA — 1 YR
  - (C) DUE TO: —
  - (D) DUE TO: —
- **108. Death Reported to Coroner:** NO
- **109. Biopsy Performed:** NO
- **110. Autopsy Performed:** NO
- **111. Used in Determining Cause:** NO
- **112. Other Significant Conditions:** ATHEROSCLEROTIC VASCULAR DISEASE
- **113. Was Operation Performed:** NO

PHYSICIAN'S CERTIFICATION
- **115. Signature and Title of Certifier:** Janice Spinner MD
- **116. License No.:** G42727
- **117. Date:** 07/22/1996
- **Decedent Attended Since:** 06/07/1996
- **Decedent Last Seen Alive:** 07/19/1996
- **118. Attending Physician's Name, Mailing Address + Zip:** JANICE SPINNER, M.D. 23388 MULHOLLAND DR. WOODLAND HILLS, CA 91364

FAX AUTH. #: 195/20833

COUNTY OF LOS ANGELES
DEPARTMENT OF HEALTH SERVICES
CERTIFICATE OF DEATH
STATE OF CALIFORNIA

DECEDENT PERSONAL DATA
- 1. Name of Decedent—First (Given): ROSS
- 2. Middle: —
- 3. Last (Family): ELLIOTT
- 4. Date of Birth: 06/18/1917
- 5. Age Yrs.: 82
- 6. Sex: MALE
- 7. Date of Death: 08/12/1999
- 8. Hour: 2356
- 9. State of Birth: NEW YORK
- 10. Social Security No.: 124-12-1214
- 11. Military Service: YES
- 12. Marital Status: MARRIED
- 13. Education—Years Completed: 16
- 14. Race: WHITE
- 15. Hispanic: No
- 16. Usual Employer: SELF EMPLOYED
- 17. Occupation: ACTOR
- 18. Kind of Business: ENTERTAINMENT
- 19. Years in Occupation: 59

(1 OF 2)

USUAL RESIDENCE
- 20. Residence: 5702 GRAVES AVENUE
- 21. City: ENCINO
- 22. County: LOS ANGELES
- 23. Zip Code: 91316
- 24. Yrs in County: 52
- 25. State or Foreign Country: CALIFORNIA

INFORMANT
- 26. Name, Relationship: SUE ELLIOTT - WIFE
- 27. Mailing Address: 5702 GRAVES AVENUE, ENCINO, CALIFORNIA 91316

SPOUSE AND PARENT INFORMATION
- 28. Name of Surviving Spouse—First: SUE
- 29. Middle: —
- 30. Last (Maiden Name): MELLING
- 31. Name of Father—First: HENRY
- 32. Middle: —
- 33. Last: BLUM
- 34. Birth State: POLAND
- 35. Name of Mother—First: CARRIE
- 36. Middle: —
- 37. Last (Maiden): SCHWARTZ
- 38. Birth State: NEW YORK

DISPOSITION(S)
- 39. Date: 08/16/1999
- 40. Place of Final Disposition: RESIDENCE: SUE ELLIOTT - WIFE, 5702 GRAVES AVENUE, ENCINO, CALIFORNIA 91316
- 41. Type of Disposition(s): CREMATION/RESIDENCE
- 42. Signature of Embalmer: NOT EMBALMED
- 43. License No.: —
- 44. Name of Funeral Director: MOUNT SINAI MORTUARY
- 45. License No.: FD-1010
- 47. Date: 08/16/1999

PLACE OF DEATH
- 101. Place of Death: MOTION PICTURE AND TELEVISION HOSP.
- 103. Facility Other Than Hospital: CONV. HOSP. (X)
- 104. County: LOS ANGELES
- 105. Street Address: 23388 MULHOLLAND DRIVE
- 106. City: WOODLAND HILLS

CAUSE OF DEATH
- 107. Death was caused by:
  - Immediate Cause (A): CARDIOPULMONARY ARREST — 15 MINS
  - Due to (B): CEREBRAL METASTASES — 4 MONTHS
  - Due to (C): ADENOCARCINOMA OF THE COLON — 8 YEARS
  - Due to (D): —
- 108. Death Reported to Coroner: No
- 109. Biopsy Performed: No
- 110. Autopsy Performed: No
- 111. Used in Determining Cause: —
- 112. Other Significant Conditions: NONE
- 113. Was Operation Performed: NO

PHYSICIAN'S CERTIFICATION
- 114. Decedent Attended Since: 06/07/1999; Last Seen Alive: 08/12/1999
- 116. License No.: A39209
- 117. Date: 08/13/1999
- 118. Type Attending Physician's Name, Mailing Address, Zip: SAED HUMAYUN, M.D., 23388 MULHOLLAND DRIVE, WOODLAND HILLS, CA 91364

STATE REGISTRAR
- Fax Auth. #: 195/2949
- Census Tract: 090261094

Date Issued: AUG 25 1999

COUNTY OF LOS ANGELES
DEPARTMENT OF HEALTH SERVICES
CERTIFICATE OF DEATH

State File Number: 3 200019 044887

1. Name of Decedent—First (Given)	MURIEL
2. Middle	E.
3. Last (Family)	WORCESTER
4. Date of Birth	07/20/1910
5. Age Yrs.	90
6. Sex	F
7. Date of Death	10/26/2000
8. Hour	0130
9. State of Birth	MN
10. Social Security No.	551-10-2111
11. Military Service	No
12. Marital Status	WIDOWED
13. Education—Years Completed	11
14. Race	CAUCASIAN
15. Hispanic	No
16. Usual Employer	SELF EMPLOYED
17. Occupation	ACTRESS
18. Kind of Business	ENTERTAINMENT
19. Years in Occupation	35
20. Residence	23388 MULHOLLAND DRIVE, #250-2
21. City	WOODLAND HILLS
22. County	LOS ANGELES
23. Zip Code	91364
24. Yrs in County	87
25. State	CA
26. Informant Name, Relationship	KATHLEEN M. COOK, FRIEND
27. Mailing Address	1648 RUTHLOR ROAD, CARDIFF, CA 92007
31. Name of Father—First	JOHN
32. Middle	EDWARD
33. Last	EVANSON
34. Birth State	NORWAY
35. Name of Mother—First	ANNA
37. Last (Maiden)	LEE
38. Birth State	MN
39. Date of Disposition	11/03/2000
40. Place of Final Disposition	SEA SCATTER OFF THE COAST OF ORANGE COUNTY
41. Type of Disposition	CR/SEA
42. Signature of Embalmer	NOT EMBALMED
44. Name of Funeral Director	PRAISWATER MEYER MITCHELL MORT.
45. License No.	FD549
47. Date	10/30/2000
101. Place of Death	MOTION PICTURE HOSPITAL
105. Street Address	23388 MULHOLLAND DRIVE
106. City	WOODLAND HILLS
104. County	LOS ANGELES
107. Cause of Death (A) Immediate	METASTATIC LIVER CANCER
Time Interval	3 MONS.
112. Other Significant Conditions	CEREBROVASCULAR ACCIDENT, MULTI-INFARCT DEMENTIA
113. Operation Performed	NO
114. Decedent Attended Since	07/20/1998
Last Seen	10/24/2000
115. Signature of Certifier	Gerald A. Michaelan M.D.
116. License No.	G061551
117. Date	10/26/2000
118. Attending Physician	GERALD A. MICHAELAN, M.D., 23388 MULHOLLAND DR., WOODLAND HILLS, CA 91364
State Registrar	1552
Fax Auth. #	197/25717
Census Tract	090393440

This is a true certified copy of the record filed in the County of Los Angeles Department of Health Services if it bears the Registrar's signature in purple ink.

DATE ISSUED: JAN 05 2001

Director of Health Services and Registrar

This copy not valid unless prepared on engraved border displaying seal and signature of Registrar.

STATE OF CALIFORNIA — CERTIFICATION OF VITAL RECORD

COUNTY OF LOS ANGELES • REGISTRAR-RECORDER/COUNTY CLERK

CERTIFICATE OF DEATH — 3200919026065

DECEDENT'S PERSONAL DATA
- Name: FARRAH FAWCETT
- Date of Birth: 02/02/1947
- Age: 62
- Sex: F
- Birth State: TX
- Social Security Number: 463-74-6421
- Ever in U.S. Armed Forces: No
- Marital Status: DIVORCED
- Date of Death: 06/25/2009
- Hour: 0928
- Education: SOME COLLEGE
- Hispanic/Latino: No
- Race: CAUCASIAN
- Usual Occupation: ACTRESS
- Kind of Business/Industry: TELEVISION MOTION PICTURES STAGE
- Years in Occupation: 40

USUAL RESIDENCE
- 10580 WILSHIRE BLVD.
- City: LOS ANGELES
- County: LOS ANGELES
- Zip: 90024
- Years in County: 40
- State: CA

INFORMANT
- Name/Relationship: RYAN O'NEAL, FRIEND
- Mailing Address: 21368 PACIFIC COAST HWY, MALIBU, CA 90265

SPOUSE AND PARENT INFORMATION
- Name of Surviving Spouse: —
- Father: JAMES WILLIAM FAWCETT — Birth State: TX
- Mother: PAULINE ALICE EVANS — Birth State: OK

FUNERAL DIRECTOR / LOCAL REGISTRAR
- Disposition Date: 07/01/2009
- Place of Final Disposition: PIERCE BROS. WESTWOOD MEMORIAL PARK, 1218 GLENDON AVE, LOS ANGELES, CA 90024
- Type of Disposition: BURIAL
- Signature of Embalmer: CARLOS SOLORZANO — License No. EMB8704
- Name of Funeral Establishment: PIERCE BROS. WESTWOOD — FD-951
- Signature of Local Registrar: JONATHAN FIELDING, MD — Date: 06/29/2009

PLACE OF DEATH
- ST JOHN'S HEALTH CENTER (IP)
- County: LOS ANGELES
- Facility Address: 1328 22ND STREET
- City: SANTA MONICA

CAUSE OF DEATH
- Immediate Cause (A): METASTATIC ANAL CANCER — Interval: 3 YRS
- Death Reported to Coroner: No
- Biopsy Performed: Yes
- Autopsy Performed: No
- Other Significant Conditions: NONE
- Operation Performed: 11/05/2007 TRANSANAL EXCISION
- If Female, Pregnant in Last Year: No

PHYSICIAN'S CERTIFICATION
- Signature and Title of Certifier: LAWRENCE DOMINIC PIRO M.D. — License No. G52155 — Date: 06/29/2009
- Attending Physician's Mailing Address: 2001 SANTA MONICA BLVD SUITE 560 W, SANTA MONICA, CA 90404
- Decedent Attended Since: 07/06/2007
- Decedent Last Seen Alive: 06/25/2009

This is to certify that this document is a true copy of the official record filed with the Registrar-Recorder/County Clerk.

Dean C. Logan, Registrar-Recorder/County Clerk

JAN 0 4 2010

000179254

INFORMATIONAL, NOT A VALID DOCUMENT TO ESTABLISH IDENTITY

PETER FINCH

CERTIFICATION OF VITAL RECORD

COUNTY OF LOS ANGELES • REGISTRAR-RECORDER/COUNTY CLERK

CERTIFICATE OF DEATH — 0190-004487
STATE OF CALIFORNIA—DEPARTMENT OF HEALTH
OFFICE OF THE STATE REGISTRAR OF VITAL STATISTICS

DECEDENT PERSONAL DATA
- 1a. Name of Deceased—First Name: LARRY
- 1c. Last Name: FINE
- 2a. Date of Death: 1/24/75
- 2b. Hour: 2:00 A.
- 3. Sex: M
- 4. Color or Race: Caucasian
- 5. Birthplace: Pennsylvania
- 6. Date of Birth: 10/05/02
- 7. Age: 72 years
- 8. Name and Birthplace of Father: Joseph Feinberg — Russia
- 9. Maiden Name and Birthplace of Mother: Fannie Lieberman — Russia
- 10. Citizen of What Country: U.S.A.
- 11. Social Security Number: 564-14-1176
- 12. Married, Never Married, Widowed, Divorced: Widower
- 14. Last Occupation: Retired Actor
- 15. Number of Years in this Occupation: 38
- 16. Name of Last Employer: Self-employed — Comedy III Productions
- 17. Kind of Industry or Business: Movies

PLACE OF DEATH
- 18a. Place of Death: Motion Picture & Television Hospital
- 18a. Street Address: 23388 Mulholland Drive
- 18c. Inside City Corporate Limits: Yes
- 18b. City or Town: Woodland Hills, California
- 18c. County: Los Angeles
- 18d. Length of Stay in County: 43 years
- 18e. Length of Stay in California: 43 years

USUAL RESIDENCE
- 19a. Usual Residence—Street Address: 23388 Mulholland Drive
- 19b. Inside City Corporate Limits: Yes
- 19c. City or Town: Woodland Hills
- 19d. County: Los Angeles
- 19e. State: California
- 20. Name and Mailing Address of Informant: Mrs. Phyllis Jo Lamond-Daughter, 12354 Sarah Street, Studio City, CA.

PHYSICIAN'S OR CORONER'S CERTIFICATION
- 21e. Physician or Coroner—Signature: John Messina, M.D.
- 21e. Address: 23388 Mulholland Drive, Woodland Hills, Calif.
- 21d. Date Signed: 1-24-75
- 21f. Physician's California License Number: C 30949
- Investigation dates: 1/15/75 — 1/24/75 — 1/24/75

FUNERAL DIRECTOR AND LOCAL REGISTRAR
- 22a. Specify Burial, Entombment or Cremation: Entombment
- 22b. Date: 1/27/75
- 23. Name of Cemetery or Crematory: Forest Lawn Memorial-Park Assn., Glendale, California
- 25. Name of Funeral Director: Forest Lawn Memorial-Park Assn., Glendale, California
- 26. If Not Certified by Coroner, Was This Death Reported to Coroner: 0
- 28. License Number: 4206
- 28. Date Received for Registration by Local Registrar: JAN 27 1975

CAUSE OF DEATH
- 29. Part I. Death was caused by:
  - (A) Immediate Cause: Cerebral Thrombosis
  - (B) Due to or as a consequence of: Cerebral Arteriosclerosis
- 30. Part II. Other Significant Conditions: —
- 31. Was Operation or Biopsy Performed: NO
- 32a. Autopsy: NO

INJURY INFORMATION
- (blank)

STATE REGISTRAR
- F: 9-1-9

This is to certify that this document is a true copy of the official record filed with the Registrar-Recorder/County Clerk.

BEATRIZ VALDEZ
Registrar-Recorder/County Clerk

AUG 16 1995
19-389400

This copy not valid unless prepared on engraved border displaying the Seal and Signature of the Registrar-Recorder/County Clerk.

ANY ALTERATION OR ERASURE VOIDS THIS CERTIFICATE

STATE OF CALIFORNIA
CERTIFICATION OF VITAL RECORD
COUNTY OF LOS ANGELES • REGISTRAR-RECORDER/COUNTY CLERK

CERTIFICATE OF DEATH

District No. 7901

1. **FULL NAME:** GEORGE FITZMAURICE
2. **PLACE OF DEATH:**
   - (A) County: Los Angeles
   - (B) City or Town: Los Angeles
   - (C) Name of Hospital or Institution: Hospital of the Good Samaritan
   - (D) Length of Stay: In Hospital or Institution: 2 Mos. 3 Days; In this Community: 2 Mos. 3 Days; California: 15 Yrs
   - (E) If Foreign Born, How Long in the U.S.A.: Unknown
3. **USUAL RESIDENCE OF DECEASED:**
   - (A) State: California
   - (B) County: Los Angeles
   - (C) City or Town: Beverly Hills
   - (D) Street No.: 1125 Angelo Drive

3. (A) If Veteran, Name of War: No
3. (B) Social Security No: 569-18-8416
4. **Sex:** Male
5. **Color or Race:** White
6. (A) Single, Married, Widowed or Divorced: Married
6. (B) Name of Husband or Wife: Diana Wilson Fitzmaurice
6. (C) Age of Husband or Wife if Alive: 39 Years
7. **Birthdate of Deceased:** February 13, 1885
8. **Age:** 55 Yrs 4 Mos 0 Days
9. **Birthplace:** Paris, France
10. **Usual Occupation:** Director
11. **Industry or Business:** Motion Picture
12. **Father's Name:** Basil Fitzmaurice
13. **Birthplace:** Unknown
14. **Mother's Maiden Name:** Marguerite Trafford
15. **Birthplace:** Unknown
16. (A) Informant: Diana Wilson Fitzmaurice
    (B) Address: 1125 Angelo Dr., Beverly Hills
17. (A) Burial (B) Date: June 15, 1940
    (C) Place: Forest Lawn Memorial Park
18. (A) Embalmer's Signature: [signature] License No. 2397
    (B) Funeral Director: B. E. DAYTON, INC.
    Address: Beverly Hills, California

20. **Date of Death:** Month: June Day: 13 Year: 1940 Hour: 8 Minute: 45 AM

21. **Medical Certificate:** I hereby certify that I attended the deceased from [April 10] 1940 to June 13, 1940, that I last saw him alive on 13 June 1940, and that death occurred on the date and hour stated above.

Immediate Cause of Death: Acute endocarditis (Str. Viridans)
Due to: Chronic rheumatic endocarditis
Mitral stenosis
Mitral insufficiency

24. Coroner's or Physician's Signature: [signature] R. Mason
    Address: Los Angeles Date: 14 June 40

CONNY B. McCORMACK
Registrar-Recorder/County Clerk

NOV 28 2000
19-118085

CERTIFICATE OF DEATH
STATE OF CALIFORNIA

0190-047186

1A. Name—First	Paul
1B. Middle	Peter
1C. Last	Fix
2A. Date of Death	October 4, 1983
2B. Hour	1330
3. Sex	male
4. Race/Ethnicity	white
5. Spanish/Hispanic	NO XX
6. Date of Birth	March 13, 1901
7. Age	82 years
8. Birthplace of Decedent	New York
9. Name and Birthplace of Father	William Fix – Germany
10. Birth Name and Birthplace of Mother	unknown – Germany
11. Citizen of What Country	U.S.A.
12. Social Security Number	561-12-7198
13. Marital Status	widowed
15. Primary Occupation	actor
16. Number of Years This Occupation	55
17. Employer	Universal Studios
18. Kind of Industry or Business	entertainment
19A. Usual Residence	4513 Vista Del Monte
19C. City or Town	Sherman Oaks
19D. County	Los Angeles
19E. State	California
20. Informant	Marilyn F. Carey – daughter, 4513 Vista DelMonte, Sherman Oaks, California 91403
21A. Place of Death	St. John's Hospital
21B. County	Los Angeles
21C. Street Address	1338 22nd Street
21D. City or Town	Santa Monica

22. Cause of Death:
(A) End-stage renal failure — 23 mo
(B) Chronic glomerulonephritis — 2 yrs

23. Other Conditions: Withdrawal from dialysis with cerebral vascular [illegible]
27. arteriovenous fistula — 11/1/81

Physician: Donald A. Adams, M.D., 11860 Wilshire Blvd., Los Angeles, CA
Attended since 11/20/81; Last saw alive 10/14/83; Date signed 10-17-83; License A16866

36. Disposition: cremation
37. Date: 10/19/83
38. Live Oak Memorial Park, Monrovia, Ca.
39. not embalmed
40A. Gates, Kingsley & Gates, S.M.
40B. F451
42. OCT 17 1983

This is to certify that this document is a true copy of the official record filed with the Registrar-Recorder/County Clerk.

Conny B. McCormack
CONNY B. McCORMACK
Registrar-Recorder/County Clerk

DEC 07 2000
19-149011

Nina Foch

CERTIFICATE OF DEATH
STATE OF CALIFORNIA

State File Number: 3961 9024113

1. NAME OF DECEDENT—FIRST (GIVEN): MICHAEL	2. MIDDLE: —	3. LAST (FAMILY): FOX
4. DATE OF BIRTH: 02/27/1921	5. AGE YRS: 75	6. SEX: M
7. DATE OF DEATH: 06/01/1996	8. HOUR: 0553	
9. STATE OF BIRTH: NY	10. SOCIAL SECURITY NO.: 073-16-1668	11. MILITARY SERVICE: NONE
12. MARITAL STATUS: MARRIED	13. EDUCATION—YEARS COMPLETED: 14	
14. RACE: CAUCASIAN	15. HISPANIC: NO	16. USUAL EMPLOYER: CBS/BELL-PHILLIPS
17. OCCUPATION: ACTOR	18. KIND OF BUSINESS: ENTERTAINMENT	19. YEARS IN OCCUPATION: 50

USUAL RESIDENCE
- 20. RESIDENCE—STREET AND NUMBER OR LOCATION: 6425 NAGLE AVE
- 21. CITY: VAN NUYS
- 22. COUNTY: LOS ANGELES
- 23. ZIP CODE: 91401
- 24. YRS IN COUNTY: 52
- 25. STATE: CA

INFORMANT
- 26. NAME, RELATIONSHIP: HANNAH FOX/WIFE
- 27. MAILING ADDRESS: 6425 NAGLE AVE, VAN NUYS, CA 91401

SPOUSE AND PARENT INFORMATION
- 28. NAME OF SURVIVING SPOUSE—FIRST: HANNAH
- 29. MIDDLE: —
- 30. LAST (MAIDEN NAME): JACOBSON
- 31. NAME OF FATHER—FIRST: JACOB
- 32. MIDDLE: —
- 33. LAST: FOX
- 34. BIRTH STATE: HUNGARY
- 35. NAME OF MOTHER—FIRST: JOSEPHINE
- 36. MIDDLE: —
- 37. LAST (MAIDEN): BERKOWITZ
- 38. BIRTH STATE: PA

DISPOSITION(S)
- 39. DATE: 06/05/1996
- 40. PLACE OF FINAL DISPOSITION: SEA: OFF THE COAST OF MARINA DEL REY, CA

FUNERAL DIRECTOR AND LOCAL REGISTRAR
- 41. TYPE OF DISPOSITION(S): CR/SEA
- 42. SIGNATURE OF EMBALMER: NOT EMBALMED
- 43. LICENSE NO.: —
- 44. NAME OF FUNERAL DIRECTOR: THE ALPHA SOCIETY, INC.
- 45. LICENSE NO.: FD-1274
- 47. DATE: 06/04/1996

PLACE OF DEATH
- 101. PLACE OF DEATH: MOTION PICTURE & T.V. FUND
- 103. FACILITY OTHER THAN HOSPITAL: CONV. HOSP. [X]
- 104. COUNTY: LOS ANGELES
- 105. STREET ADDRESS: 2388 MULHOLLAND DR.
- 106. CITY: WOODLAND HILLS

CAUSE OF DEATH
- 107. DEATH WAS CAUSED BY:
  - IMMEDIATE CAUSE (A): CARDIORESPIRATORY ARREST — 15 MINS
  - DUE TO (B): CONGESTIVE HEART FAILURE — 4 DAYS
  - DUE TO (C): RHEUMATIC HEART DISEASE — 25 YRS
  - DUE TO (D):
- 108. DEATH REPORTED TO CORONER: NO
- 109. BIOPSY PERFORMED: NO
- 110. AUTOPSY PERFORMED: NO
- 111. USED IN DETERMINING CAUSE:
- 112. OTHER SIGNIFICANT CONDITIONS: MYELODYSPLASTIC SYNDROME
- 113. WAS OPERATION PERFORMED: NO

PHYSICIAN'S CERTIFICATION
- 114. DECEDENT ATTENDED SINCE: 11/18/1992; LAST SEEN ALIVE: 05/31/1996
- 115. SIGNATURE AND TITLE OF CERTIFIER: Stanley Rossman, MD
- 116. LICENSE NO.: G25627
- 117. DATE: 06/03/1996
- 118. TYPE ATTENDING PHYSICIAN'S NAME, MAILING ADDRESS + ZIP: S. ROSSMAN, M.D., 6850 SEPULVEDA BLVD., VAN NUYS, CA 91405

COUNTY OF LOS ANGELES
DEPARTMENT OF HEALTH SERVICES

CERTIFICATE OF DEATH — STATE OF CALIFORNIA

State File Number: 3 1998 19 042470

Decedent Personal Data

- **1. Name of Decedent—First (Given):** MARY
- **2. Middle:** —
- **3. Last (Family):** FRANN
- **4. Date of Birth:** 02/27/1943
- **5. Age Yrs.:** 55
- **6. Sex:** F
- **7. Date of Death:** 09/23/1998
- **8. Hour:** 0636
- **9. State of Birth:** MO
- **10. Social Security No.:** 488-44-6141
- **11. Military Service:** No
- **12. Marital Status:** DIVORCED
- **13. Education—Years Completed:** 15
- **14. Race:** CAUCASIAN
- **15. Hispanic:** No
- **16. Usual Employer:** MTM PRODUCTIONS
- **17. Occupation:** ACTRESS
- **18. Kind of Business:** ENTERTAINMENT
- **19. Years in Occupation:** 51

Usual Residence

- **20. Residence:** 2790 HUTTON DR.
- **21. City:** BEVERLY HILLS
- **22. County:** LOS ANGELES
- **23. Zip Code:** 90210
- **24. Yrs in County:** 30
- **25. State or Foreign Country:** CA

Informant

- **26. Name, Relationship:** JACQUELINE ROGERS, SISTER
- **27. Mailing Address:** 19559 CAVA WAY, TOPANGA, CA 90290

Spouse and Parent Information

- **28. Name of Surviving Spouse—First:** —
- **31. Name of Father—First:** HARRY
- **32. Middle:** JOSEPH
- **33. Last:** LUECKE, JR.
- **34. Birth State:** MO
- **35. Name of Mother—First:** ADELE
- **36. Middle:** KATHERINE
- **37. Last (Maiden):** McQUADE
- **38. Birth State:** MO

Funeral Director and Local Registrar

- **39. Date of Disposition:** 09/26/1998
- **40. Place of Final Disposition:** Holy Cross Cemetery 5835 West Slauson Ave. Culver City, California 90230
- **41. Type of Disposition:** Burial
- **42. Signature of Embalmer:** K. A. Krueger
- **43. License No.:** 8130
- **44. Name of Funeral Director:** PIERCE BROS. MOELLER MURPHY
- **47. Date:** 09/25/1998 SH

Place of Death

- **101. Place of Death:** RESIDENCE
- **104. County:** LOS ANGELES
- **105. Street Address:** 2790 HUTTON DRIVE
- **106. City:** BEVERLY HILLS

Cause of Death

- **107. Death was caused by:**
  - (A) Immediate Cause: DEFERRED
  - (B) Due To: —
  - (C) Due To: —
  - (D) Due To: —
- **108. Death Reported to Coroner:** Yes — Referral Number 98-06414
- **109. Biopsy Performed:** —
- **110. Autopsy Performed:** Yes
- **111. Used in Determining Cause:** —

Coroner's Use Only

- **119. Manner of Death:** Pending Investigation
- **126. Signature of Coroner or Deputy Coroner:** Mary T. Macias
- **127. Date:** 09/24/1998
- **128. Typed Name, Title:** MARY T. MACIAS, DEPUTY CORONER
- **Fax Auth. #:** 849-13450
- **Census Tract:** 090198536

Date Issued: NOV 23 1998

COUNTY OF LOS ANGELES
DEPARTMENT OF HEALTH SERVICES
AMENDMENT OF MEDICAL AND HEALTH DATA—DEATH   3 1998 19 042470

PART I — INFORMATION TO LOCATE RECORD

1. NAME—FIRST (GIVEN)	2. MIDDLE	3. LAST (FAMILY)	4. SEX
MARY	–	FRANN	F

5. DATE OF EVENT—MM/DD/CCYY	6. CITY OF OCCURRENCE	7. COUNTY OF OCCURRENCE	
09/23/1998	Beverly Hills	Los Angeles	

PART II — INFORMATION AS IT APPEARS ON RECORD

107. DEATH WAS CAUSED BY:
- IMMEDIATE CAUSE (A): Deferred
- (B):
- (C):
- DUE TO (D):

TIME INTERVAL BETWEEN ONSET AND DEATH:

108. DEATH REPORTED TO CORONER: [X] YES   REFERRAL NUMBER 98-06414
109. BIOPSY PERFORMED: YES / NO
110. AUTOPSY PERFORMED: [X] YES
111. USED IN DETERMINING CAUSE: YES / NO

112. OTHER SIGNIFICANT CONDITIONS CONTRIBUTING TO DEATH BUT NOT RELATED TO CAUSE GIVEN IN 107:

113. WAS OPERATION PERFORMED FOR ANY CONDITION IN ITEM 107 or 112? IF YES, LIST TYPE OF OPERATION AND DATE.

119. MANNER OF DEATH: [X] PENDING INVESTIGATION

PART III — INFORMATION AS IT SHOULD APPEAR

107. DEATH WAS CAUSED BY:
- IMMEDIATE CAUSE (A): SUDDEN CARDIAC DEATH — Rapid
- (B): LIPOMATOSIS WITH FIBROSIS OF ATRIAL SEPTUM — Unk
- (C):
- DUE TO (D):

108. DEATH REPORTED TO CORONER: [X] YES   REFERRAL NUMBER 98-06514
109. BIOPSY PERFORMED: [X] NO
110. AUTOPSY PERFORMED: [X] YES
111. USED IN DETERMINING CAUSE: [X] YES

112. OTHER SIGNIFICANT CONDITIONS CONTRIBUTING TO DEATH BUT NOT RELATED TO CAUSE GIVEN IN 107:
Cardiac Hypertrophy, Clinical History Atrial Fibrillation

113. WAS OPERATION PERFORMED FOR ANY CONDITION IN ITEM 107 or 112? No

119. MANNER OF DEATH: [X] NATURAL

DECLARATION OF CERTIFYING PHYSICIAN OR CORONER

8. SIGNATURE	9. DATE SIGNED	10. TYPED OR PRINTED NAME AND DEGREE/TITLE OF CERTIFIER
Louis A. Pena	10-29-1998	LOUIS A. PENA, M.D. DME

11. ADDRESS	12. CITY	13. STATE	14. ZIP CODE
1104 North Mission Road	Los Angeles	CA	90033

16. DATE ACCEPTED FOR REGISTRATION: 11/05/1998

090198541

This is a true certified copy of the record filed in the County of Los Angeles Department of Health Services if it bears the Registrar's signature in purple ink.

DATE ISSUED NOV 23 1998

Director of Health Service and Registrar

This copy not valid unless prepared on engraved border displaying seal and signature of Registrar.

STATE OF CALIFORNIA — CERTIFICATION OF VITAL RECORD

COUNTY OF LOS ANGELES • REGISTRAR-RECORDER/COUNTY CLERK

CERTIFICATE OF DEATH — 39519022786

Decedent Personal Data
- Name: ISADORE — FRELENG
- Date of Birth: 08/21/1905
- Age: 89
- Sex: M
- Date of Death: 05/26/1995
- Hour: 0610
- State of Birth: MO
- Social Security No: 562-05-6348
- Marital Status: Married
- Education (Years Completed): 12
- Race: White
- Hispanic: No
- Usual Employer: Self Employed
- Occupation: Cartoonist
- Kind of Business: Film Animation
- Years in Occupation: 70

Usual Residence
- 10551 Wilshire Boulevard #701
- City: Los Angeles
- County: Los Angeles
- ZIP: 90024
- Yrs in County: 60
- State: California

Informant
- Lily Freleng, Wife
- 10551 Wilshire Boulevard #701, Los Angeles, CA 90024

Spouse and Parent Information
- Surviving Spouse: Lily — Schonfeld
- Father: Louis Freleng — Birth State: Poland
- Mother: Elka Ribacoff — Birth State: Russia

Disposition(s)
- Date: 05/28/1995
- Place: Hillside Memorial Park, 6001 Centinela Avenue, Los Angeles, CA 90045
- Type: BU
- Not Embalmed
- Funeral Director: Hillside Mortuary — FD 1358
- Date: 05/27/1995

Place of Death
- UCLA MEDICAL CENTER — IP
- 10833 LeConte Avenue
- County: Los Angeles
- City: Los Angeles

Cause of Death
- (A) CARDIAC ARREST — mins
- (B) CARDIAC FAILURE — hours
- (C) RENAL INSUFFICIENCY — days
- (D) ATHEROSCLEROTIC HEART DISEASE — years
- Other significant conditions: Chronic Osteomyelitis
- Operation performed: No
- Biopsy Performed: No
- Autopsy Performed: No

Physician's Certification
- Decedent attended since: 05/05/1995 to 05/26/1995
- Jennifer Reifel, M.D., 10833 LeConte Ave, L.A., CA 90095
- Date: 5/26/1995

CONNY B. McCORMACK
Registrar-Recorder/County Clerk

NOV 28 2000
19-116311

STATE OF CALIFORNIA
CERTIFICATION OF VITAL RECORD

COUNTY OF LOS ANGELES • REGISTRAR-RECORDER/COUNTY CLERK

CERTIFICATE OF DEATH
STATE OF CALIFORNIA—DEPARTMENT OF PUBLIC HEALTH

LOCAL REGISTRATION DISTRICT AND CERTIFICATE NUMBER: 7097-043247

DECEDENT PERSONAL DATA
- 1A. NAME OF DECEASED—FIRST NAME: ROBERT / Bobby
- 1B. MIDDLE NAME: GASTON / Gaston
- 1C. LAST NAME: FULLER AKA
- 2A. DATE OF DEATH: July 18, 1966
- 2B. HOUR: 5:45 PM
- 3. SEX: Male
- 4. COLOR OR RACE: Caucasian
- 5. BIRTHPLACE: Texas
- 6. DATE OF BIRTH: Oct. 22, 1942
- 7. AGE: 23 YEARS
- 8. NAME AND BIRTHPLACE OF FATHER: Lawson S. Fuller, Texas
- 9. MAIDEN NAME AND BIRTHPLACE OF MOTHER: Eva Barrett, Texas
- 10. CITIZEN OF WHAT COUNTRY: USA
- 11. SOCIAL SECURITY NUMBER: 528-52-6591
- 12. LAST OCCUPATION: Entertainer
- 13. NUMBER OF YEARS IN THIS OCCUPATION: Four
- 14. NAME OF LAST EMPLOYING COMPANY OR FIRM: Stereo-Fi Corporation
- 15. KIND OF INDUSTRY OR BUSINESS: Record Production (Musical)
- 16. IF DECEASED WAS EVER IN U.S. ARMED FORCES: None
- 17. SPECIFY MARRIED, NEVER MARRIED, WIDOWED, DIVORCED: Never Married
- 18A. NAME OF PRESENT SPOUSE: --
- 18B. PRESENT OR LAST OCCUPATION OF SPOUSE: --

PLACE OF DEATH
- 19A. PLACE OF DEATH—NAME OF HOSPITAL:
- 19B. STREET ADDRESS: 1776 Sycamore Avenue
- 19C. CITY OR TOWN: Los Angeles
- 19D. COUNTY: Los Angeles
- 19E. LENGTH OF STAY IN COUNTY OF DEATH: two years
- 19F. LENGTH OF STAY IN CALIFORNIA: two years

LAST USUAL RESIDENCE
- 20A. LAST USUAL RESIDENCE—STREET ADDRESS: 1776 Sycamore Ave. #317
- 20B. IF INSIDE CITY CORPORATE LIMITS: CHECK HERE [X]
- 20C. CITY OR TOWN: Los Angeles
- 20D. COUNTY: Los Angeles
- 20E. STATE: California
- 21A. NAME OF INFORMANT: Elsa Keene
- 21B. ADDRESS OF INFORMANT: 6277 Selma Avenue, Hollywood

PHYSICIAN'S OR CORONER'S CERTIFICATION
- 22C. CORONER: Autopsy
- Hall of Justice, Los Angeles
- 22E. DATE SIGNED: 10-17-66

FUNERAL DIRECTOR AND LOCAL REGISTRAR
- 23. SPECIFY BURIAL, ENTOMBMENT, OR CREMATION: Burial
- 24. DATE: 7-22-66
- 25. NAME OF CEMETERY OR CREMATORY: Forest Lawn Mem Pk Cem
- 26. EMBALMER—SIGNATURE: John E. Verdun, LICENSE NUMBER 5317
- 27. NAME OF FUNERAL DIRECTOR: CALLANAN MORTUARY, Hollywood
- 28. DATE ACCEPTED FOR REGISTRATION: OCT 25 1966

CAUSE OF DEATH
- 30. CAUSE OF DEATH
- PART I. DEATH WAS CAUSED BY:
  - IMMEDIATE CAUSE (A): ASPHYXIA
  - DUE TO (B): INHALATION OF GASOLINE

OPERATION AND AUTOPSY
- 31. OPERATION: [X] NO
- 33. AUTOPSY: [XX] YES, DETERMINING ABOVE STATED CAUSES OF DEATH

INJURY INFORMATION
- 34A. SPECIFY ACCIDENT, SUICIDE, OR HOMICIDE: Accident
- 34B. DESCRIBE HOW INJURY OCCURRED: As above.
- 35A. TIME OF INJURY: Prior 5:15 PM July 18, 1966
- 35B. INJURY OCCURRED: [XX] NOT WHILE AT WORK
- 35C. PLACE OF INJURY: Automobile
- 35D. CITY, TOWN, OR LOCATION: Los Angeles
- COUNTY: LA
- STATE: Calif.

This is to certify that this document is a true copy of the official record filed with the Registrar-Recorder/County Clerk.

Conny B. McCormack
CONNY B. McCORMACK
Registrar-Recorder/County Clerk

OCT 0 4 2001
19-673407

STATE OF CALIFORNIA
CERTIFICATION OF VITAL RECORD
COUNTY OF LOS ANGELES • REGISTRAR-RECORDER/COUNTY CLERK

CERTIFICATE OF DEATH
STATE OF CALIFORNIA

State File Number: 0190-015779

DECEDENT PERSONAL DATA
- 1A. Name of Decedent—First: MARVIN
- 1B. Middle: PENZ
- 1C. Last: GAYE, JR.
- 2A. Date of Death: April 1, 1984
- 2B. Hour: 1301
- 3. Sex: Male
- 4. Race/Ethnicity: Black/Negro
- 5. Spanish/Hispanic: No
- 6. Date of Birth: April 2, 1939
- 7. Age: 44 years
- 8. Birthplace of Decedent: Washington D.C.
- 9. Name and Birthplace of Father: Marvin P. Gay — Kentucky
- 10. Birth Name and Birthplace of Mother: Alberta Cooper, No. Carolina
- 11. Citizen of What Country: United States
- 12. Social Security Number: 577-54-8569
- 13. Marital Status: Divorced
- 14. Name of Surviving Spouse: —
- 15. Primary Occupation: Entertainer
- 16. Number of Years This Occupation: 25
- 17. Employer: Columbia Records
- 18. Kind of Industry or Business: Recording

USUAL RESIDENCE
- 19A. Street Address: 2101 South Gramercy Place
- 19C. City or Town: Los Angeles
- 19D. County: Los Angeles
- 19E. State: California
- 20. Name and Address of Informant—Relationship: Edward J. Haddad, friend, 9200 Sunset Boulevard, Suite 1215, Los Angeles, California 90069

PLACE OF DEATH
- 21A. Place of Death: California Medical Center
- 21B. County: Los Angeles
- 21C. Street Address: 1414 South Hope Street
- 21D. City or Town: Los Angeles

CAUSE OF DEATH
- 22. Immediate Cause: (A) Gunshot Wound to Chest Perforating (B) Heart, Lung and Liver
- 24. Was Death Reported to Coroner?: 84-4248
- 25. Was Biopsy Performed?: No
- 26. Was Autopsy Performed?: Yes
- 27. Operation Performed: Left Thoracotomy 4-1-84

INJURY INFORMATION
- 29. Accident, Suicide, Etc.: Homicide
- 30. Place of Injury: Residence
- 31. Injury at Work: No
- 32A. Date of Injury: April 1, 1984
- 32B. Hour: 1220
- 33. Location: 2101 S. Gramercy Place, Los Angeles
- 34. Describe How Injury Occurred: Shot by Known Person

CORONER'S USE ONLY
- 35B. Coroner: Deputy Coroner
- 35C. Date Signed: 4-4-84

- 36. Disposition: Cremation
- 37. Date: April 5, 1984
- 38. Name and Address: Forest Lawn Memorial Park, 1712 S. Glendale Ave., Glendale, CA
- 40A. Name of Funeral Director: Forest Lawn Hollywood Hills Mty
- 40B. License No.: F 904

Registrar: 9654

CONNY B. McCORMACK
Registrar-Recorder/County Clerk

APR 0 7 2000
19-555696

CERTIFICATION OF VITAL RECORD
COUNTY OF LOS ANGELES • REGISTRAR-RECORDER/COUNTY CLERK

CERTIFICATE OF DEATH — STATE OF CALIFORNIA

Local Registration District and Certificate Number: 0190-018173

Decedent Personal Data
- **1A. Name – First:** WILL
- **1B. Middle:** AUGUE
- **1C. Last:** GEER
- **2A. Date of Death:** 4/22/78
- **2B. Hour:** 1835
- **3. Sex:** Male
- **4. Race:** White
- **5. Ethnicity:** American
- **6. Date of Birth:** 3/9/1902
- **7. Age:** 76
- **8. Birthplace of Decedent:** Indiana
- **9. Name and Birthplace of Father:** Roy Geer / Indiana
- **10. Birth Name and Birthplace of Mother:** Unk, Augue / Unk.
- **11. Citizen of What Country:** U.S.A.
- **12. Social Security Number:** 086-03-7015
- **13. Marital Status:** Divorced
- **14. Name of Surviving Spouse:** —
- **15. Primary Occupation:** Actor
- **16. Number of Years This Occupation:** 65yrs.
- **17. Employer:** Folksay, Inc.
- **18. Kind of Industry or Business:** Motion Picture & T.V. Prod.

Usual Residence
- **19A. Street Address:** 1334 No. Stanley Avenue
- **19C. City or Town:** Los Angeles
- **19D. County:** Los Angeles
- **20. Name and Address of Informant – Relationship:** Ms. Ella Ware Geer-Dtr., 21418 Entrada Rd., Topanga, Calif.

Place of Death
- **21A. Place of Death:** Midway Hospital
- **21B. Street Address:** 5925 San Vicente Blvd.
- **21C. City or Town:** Los Angeles
- **21D. County:** Los Angeles

Cause of Death
- **22. Immediate Cause (A):** Cerebro-Vascular Accident — 4 wks
- **(B) Due to:** Cerebral ischemia — 4 wks
- **(C) Due to:** Cardiac Arrhythmia
- **23. Other Conditions:** Hypertensive Heart Dis.
- **24. Reported to Coroner:** No
- **25. Biopsy Performed:** No
- **26. Autopsy Performed:** Yes
- **27. Operation:** Pacemaker Restoration — 4-10-78, 4-11-78

Physician's Certification
- **28A. Attended Decedent Since:** 10-2-64
- **Last Saw Alive:** 4/22/78
- **28B. Physician Signature:** Murray Abowitz, M.D.
- **28C. Date Signed:** 4/24/78
- **28D. License Number:** A08858
- **28E. Address:** 6333 Wilshire Blvd., La 90048

Funeral Director and Local Registrar
- **36. Disposition:** Cremation
- **37. Date:** 4/27/78
- **38. Cemetery/Crematory:** Angeles Abbey Crem. – 1515 E. Compton Blvd., Compton, Calif.
- **39. Embalmer's License Number:** Unembalmed
- **40. Name of Funeral Director:** The Neptune Society
- **41. Local Registrar Signature:** Morrison E. Chamberlin
- **42. Date Accepted by Local Registrar:** APR 25 1978

BEATRIZ VALDEZ
Registrar-Recorder/County Clerk

AUG 10 1995
19-389403

This copy not valid unless prepared on engraved border displaying the Seal and Signature of the Registrar-Recorder/County Clerk.

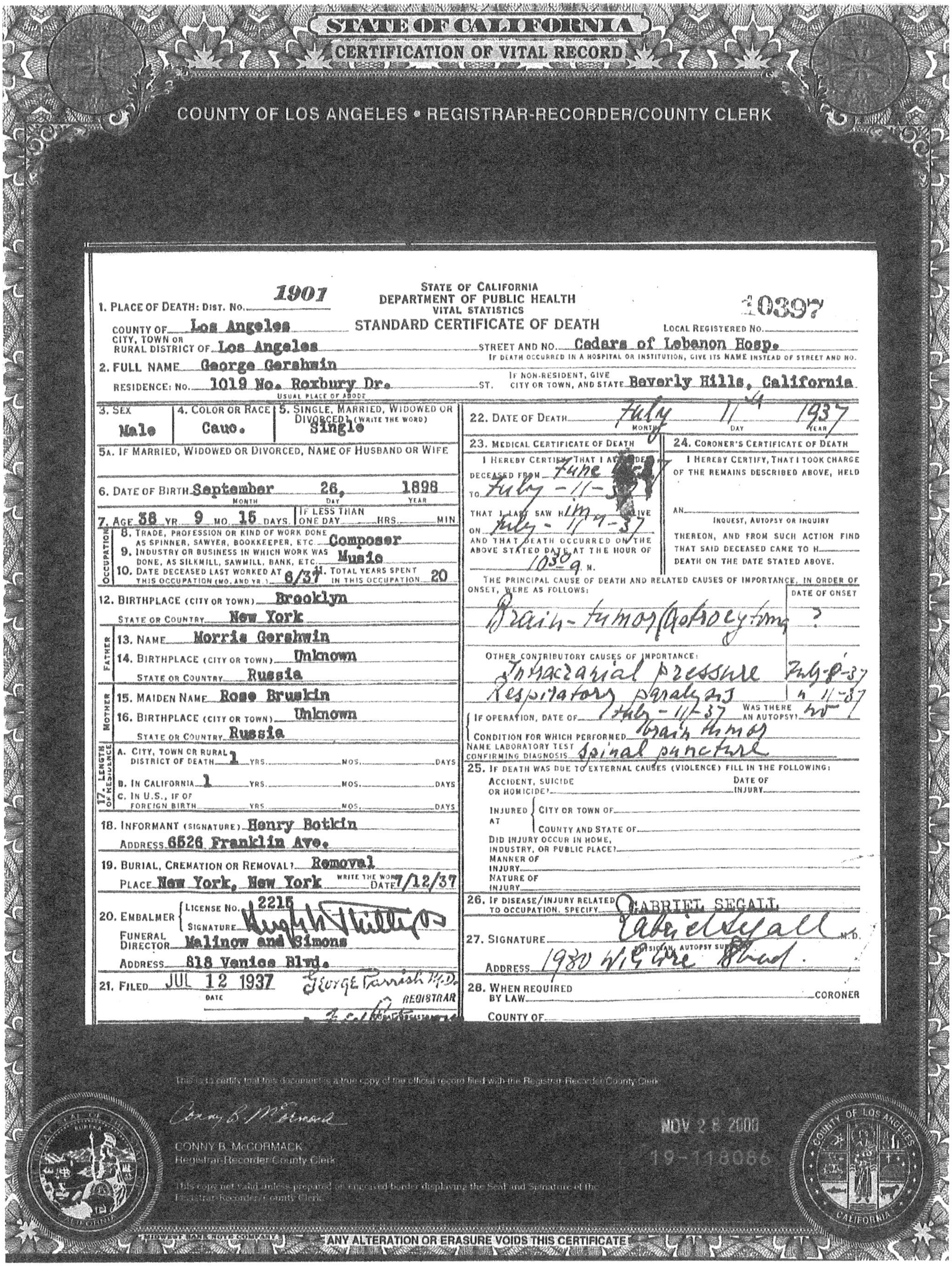

STATE OF CALIFORNIA
CERTIFICATION OF VITAL RECORD
COUNTY OF LOS ANGELES • REGISTRAR-RECORDER/COUNTY CLERK

STATE OF CALIFORNIA
DEPARTMENT OF PUBLIC HEALTH
VITAL STATISTICS
STANDARD CERTIFICATE OF DEATH

10397

1. PLACE OF DEATH: DIST. NO. 1901
COUNTY OF Los Angeles
CITY, TOWN OR RURAL DISTRICT OF Los Angeles
LOCAL REGISTERED NO.
STREET AND NO. Cedars of Lebanon Hosp.
(IF DEATH OCCURRED IN A HOSPITAL OR INSTITUTION, GIVE ITS NAME INSTEAD OF STREET AND NO.)
2. FULL NAME George Gershwin
RESIDENCE: NO. 1019 No. Roxbury Dr. ST. (USUAL PLACE OF ABODE) IF NON-RESIDENT, GIVE CITY OR TOWN, AND STATE Beverly Hills, California
3. SEX Male
4. COLOR OR RACE Cauc.
5. SINGLE, MARRIED, WIDOWED OR DIVORCED (WRITE THE WORD) Single
5A. IF MARRIED, WIDOWED OR DIVORCED, NAME OF HUSBAND OR WIFE
6. DATE OF BIRTH September 26, 1898 (MONTH, DAY, YEAR)
7. AGE 38 YR. 9 MO. 15 DAYS. IF LESS THAN ONE DAY HRS. MIN.
OCCUPATION
8. TRADE, PROFESSION OR KIND OF WORK DONE AS SPINNER, SAWYER, BOOKKEEPER, ETC. Composer
9. INDUSTRY OR BUSINESS IN WHICH WORK WAS DONE, AS SILKMILL, SAWMILL, BANK, ETC. Music
10. DATE DECEASED LAST WORKED AT THIS OCCUPATION (MO. AND YR.) 6/37
11. TOTAL YEARS SPENT IN THIS OCCUPATION 20
12. BIRTHPLACE (CITY OR TOWN) Brooklyn
STATE OR COUNTRY New York
FATHER
13. NAME Morris Gershwin
14. BIRTHPLACE (CITY OR TOWN) Unknown
STATE OR COUNTRY Russia
MOTHER
15. MAIDEN NAME Rose Bruskin
16. BIRTHPLACE (CITY OR TOWN) Unknown
STATE OR COUNTRY Russia
17. LENGTH OF RESIDENCE
A. CITY, TOWN OR RURAL DISTRICT OF DEATH 1 YRS. MOS. DAYS
B. IN CALIFORNIA 1 YRS. MOS. DAYS
C. IN U.S., IF OF FOREIGN BIRTH YRS. MOS. DAYS
18. INFORMANT (SIGNATURE) Henry Botkin
ADDRESS 6526 Franklin Ave.
19. BURIAL, CREMATION OR REMOVAL? Removal
PLACE New York, New York WRITE THE WORD DATE 7/12/37
20. EMBALMER LICENSE NO. 2215
SIGNATURE Hugh W. Phillips
FUNERAL DIRECTOR Malinow and Simons
ADDRESS 818 Venice Blvd.
21. FILED JUL 12 1937 (DATE) George Parrish M.D. REGISTRAR

22. DATE OF DEATH July 11 1937 (MONTH, DAY, YEAR)
23. MEDICAL CERTIFICATE OF DEATH
I HEREBY CERTIFY THAT I ATTENDED DECEASED FROM June 1937 TO July-11-37 THAT I LAST SAW HIM ALIVE ON July-11?-37 AND THAT DEATH OCCURRED ON THE ABOVE STATED DATE AT THE HOUR OF 10:35 A. M.
THE PRINCIPAL CAUSE OF DEATH AND RELATED CAUSES OF IMPORTANCE, IN ORDER OF ONSET, WERE AS FOLLOWS: DATE OF ONSET
Brain tumor (Astrocytoma) ?
OTHER CONTRIBUTORY CAUSES OF IMPORTANCE:
Intracranial pressure July-8-37
Respiratory paralysis " 11-37
IF OPERATION, DATE OF July-11-37 WAS THERE AN AUTOPSY? no
CONDITION FOR WHICH PERFORMED brain tumor
NAME LABORATORY TEST CONFIRMING DIAGNOSIS spinal puncture
24. CORONER'S CERTIFICATE OF DEATH
I HEREBY CERTIFY, THAT I TOOK CHARGE OF THE REMAINS DESCRIBED ABOVE, HELD AN INQUEST, AUTOPSY OR INQUIRY THEREON, AND FROM SUCH ACTION FIND THAT SAID DECEASED CAME TO H DEATH ON THE DATE STATED ABOVE.
25. IF DEATH WAS DUE TO EXTERNAL CAUSES (VIOLENCE) FILL IN THE FOLLOWING:
ACCIDENT, SUICIDE OR HOMICIDE? DATE OF INJURY
INJURED AT CITY OR TOWN OF COUNTY AND STATE OF
DID INJURY OCCUR IN HOME, INDUSTRY, OR PUBLIC PLACE?
MANNER OF INJURY
NATURE OF INJURY
26. IF DISEASE/INJURY RELATED TO OCCUPATION, SPECIFY GABRIEL SEGALL
27. SIGNATURE Gabriel Segall M.D. PHYSICIAN, AUTOPSY SURGEON
ADDRESS 1930 Wilshire Blvd.
28. WHEN REQUIRED BY LAW CORONER
COUNTY OF

This is to certify that this document is a true copy of the official record filed with the Registrar-Recorder/County Clerk.

Conny B. McCormack
CONNY B. McCORMACK
Registrar-Recorder/County Clerk

NOV 2 8 2000
19-118086

This copy not valid unless prepared on engraved border displaying the Seal and Signature of the Registrar-Recorder/County Clerk.

ANY ALTERATION OR ERASURE VOIDS THIS CERTIFICATE

STATE OF CALIFORNIA — CERTIFICATION OF VITAL RECORD

COUNTY OF LOS ANGELES • REGISTRAR-RECORDER/COUNTY CLERK

CERTIFICATE OF DEATH — State File Number: 3200819030849

DECEDENT'S PERSONAL DATA
- Name of Decedent: ESTELLE — GETTLEMAN
- AKA: ESTELLE GETTY
- Date of Birth: 07/25/1923
- Age: 84
- Sex: F
- Birth State: NY
- Social Security Number: 052-18-3356
- Ever in U.S. Armed Forces: No
- Marital Status: WIDOWED
- Date of Death: 07/22/2008
- Hour: 0535
- Education: HS GRADUATE
- Hispanic/Latino: No
- Race: CAUCASIAN
- Usual Occupation: ACTRESS
- Kind of Business/Industry: MOTION PICTURE AND TELEVISION
- Years in Occupation: 60

USUAL RESIDENCE
- 7560 HOLLYWOOD BLVD.
- City: LOS ANGELES
- County: LOS ANGELES
- ZIP: 90046
- Years in County: 25
- State: CA

INFORMANT
- Name/Relationship: BARRY LEWIS GETTLEMAN, SON
- Mailing Address: 3923 NE 166TH ST. #N110, MIAMI BEACH, FL 33160

SPOUSE AND PARENT INFORMATION
- Name of Surviving Spouse: —
- Father: CHARLES SCHER — POLAND
- Mother: SARAH LACHER — POLAND

FUNERAL DIRECTOR / LOCAL REGISTRAR
- Disposition Date: 07/24/2008
- Place of Final Disposition: HOLLYWOOD FOREVER CEMETERY, 6000 SANTA MONICA BLVD., LOS ANGELES, CA 90038
- Type of Disposition: BU
- Signature of Embalmer: NOT EMBALMED
- Funeral Establishment: HOLLYWOOD FUNERAL HOME — FD1651
- Local Registrar: JONATHAN FIELDING, MD — 07/23/2008

PLACE OF DEATH
- Place of Death: RESIDENCE — Decedent's Home
- County: LOS ANGELES
- Facility Address: 7560 HOLLYWOOD BLVD.
- City: LOS ANGELES

CAUSE OF DEATH
- Immediate Cause (A): END STAGE LEWY BODY DEMENTIA — MOS
- Death Reported to Coroner: No
- Biopsy Performed: No
- Autopsy Performed: No
- Used in Determining Cause: No
- Other Significant Conditions: NONE
- Was Operation Performed: NONE
- If Female Pregnant in Last Year: No

PHYSICIAN'S CERTIFICATION
- Certifier: LLORENS JOSEPH PEMBROOK M.D.
- License Number: A37585
- Date: 07/23/2008
- Decedent Attended Since: 05/20/2008
- Decedent Last Seen Alive: 07/22/2008
- Physician's Address: 4849 VAN NUYS BLVD STE 102, SHERMAN OAKS, CA 91403
- Manner of Death: Natural

INFORMATIONAL, NOT A VALID DOCUMENT TO ESTABLISH IDENTITY

This is to certify that this document is a true copy of the official record filed with the Registrar-Recorder/County Clerk.

DEAN C. LOGAN, Registrar-Recorder/County Clerk — JAN 0 4 2010

000179252

STATE OF CALIFORNIA
CERTIFICATION OF VITAL RECORD

COUNTY OF LOS ANGELES • REGISTRAR-RECORDER/COUNTY CLERK

CERTIFICATE OF DEATH
STATE OF CALIFORNIA—DEPARTMENT OF PUBLIC HEALTH

LOCAL REGISTRATION DISTRICT AND CERTIFICATE NUMBER: 7013 369

DECEDENT PERSONAL DATA
- 1a. Name of Deceased—First Name: Harold Jerry
- 1b. Middle Name: Lee
- 1c. Last Name: Giesler, aka Giesler
- 2a. Date of Death: Jan. 1, 1962
- 2b. Hour: 5:45 A.M.
- 3. Sex: Male
- 4. Color or Race: Cauc.
- 5. Birthplace: Iowa
- 6. Date of Birth: Nov. 2, 1886
- 7. Age: 75 years
- 8. Name and Birthplace of Father: James L. Giesler – Iowa
- 9. Maiden Name and Birthplace of Mother: Mildred Hilbert – Iowa
- 10. Citizen of What Country: USA
- 11. Social Security Number: (Unknown)
- 12. Last Occupation: Attorney
- 13. Number of Years in This Occupation: 50
- 14. Name of Last Employing Company or Firm: Self Employed
- 15. Kind of Industry or Business: Law
- 16. If Deceased Was Ever in U.S. Armed Forces: No
- 17. Married
- 18a. Name of Present Spouse: Ruth M. Giesler
- 18b. Present or Last Occupation of Spouse: Housewife

PLACE OF DEATH
- 19a. Place of Death: (None)
- 19b. Street Address: 901 Benedict Canyon Drive
- 19c. City or Town: Beverly Hills
- 19d. County: Los Angeles
- 19e. Length of Stay in County of Death: 55 years
- 19f. Length of Stay in California: 55 years

LAST USUAL RESIDENCE
- 20a. Last Usual Residence—Street Address: 901 Benedict Canyon Dr.
- 20c. City or Town: Beverly Hills
- 20d. County: Los Angeles
- 20e. State: Calif.
- 21a. Name of Informant: Mr. Michael J. Giesler
- 21b. Address of Informant: 3351 Mentone Ave, Los Angeles, Calif.

PHYSICIAN'S OR CORONER'S CERTIFICATION
- 22a. Physician: ... deceased from 3-1-57 to 1-1-62 ... last saw deceased alive on 1-1-62
- 22c. Physician or Coroner Signature: Jacob A. Shejupf, M.D.
- 22d. Address: Beverly Hills
- 22e. Date Signed: 1-2-62

- 23. Specify Burial: Entombment
- 24. Date: Jan. 4, 1962
- 25. Name of Cemetery or Crematory: Forest Lawn Memorial Park
- 26. Embalmer Signature / License Number: Virginia K. [illegible] 4498
- 27. Name of Funeral Director: Pierce Bros, Beverly Hills
- 28. Date Accepted for Registration: JAN 3 1962
- 29. Local Registrar Signature: R. H. Sutherland

CAUSE OF DEATH
- Part I. Death was caused by:
  - Immediate Cause (a): Congestive Heart Failure — wk
  - Due to (b): Myocardial Infarction, Recent — 5 wks
  - Due to (c): Coronary Heart Disease — 3 yrs

OPERATION AND AUTOPSY
- 31. No Operation Performed
- 33. No Autopsy Performed

Filed FEB 2, 1962 RAY E. LEE, COUNTY RECORDER

This is to certify that this document is a true copy of the official record filed with the Registrar-Recorder/County Clerk.

CONNY B. McCORMACK
Registrar-Recorder/County Clerk

OCT 04 2001
19-676575

COUNTY OF LOS ANGELES • REGISTRAR-RECORDER/COUNTY CLERK

CERTIFICATE OF DEATH
State File Number: 0190-004047

DECEDENT PERSONAL DATA
- 1A. Name of Deceased — First Name: SAMUEL
- 1C. Last Name: GOLDWYN
- 2A. Date of Death: January 31, 1974
- 2B. Hour: 1:30 A.M.
- 3. Sex: Male
- 4. Color or Race: Caucasian
- 5. Birthplace: Poland
- 6. Date of Birth: August 27, 1882
- 7. Age: 91 Years
- 8. Name and Birthplace of Father: Arron Goldfish — Poland
- 9. Maiden Name and Birthplace of Mother: Anna Reben — Poland
- 10. Citizen of What Country: U.S.A.
- 11. Social Security Number: 563-18-3282
- 12. Married
- 13. Name of Surviving Spouse: Frances McLaughlin
- 14. Last Occupation: Producer
- 15. Number of Years in This Occupation: 69
- 16. Name of Last Employing Company or Firm: Self-employed
- 17. Kind of Industry or Business: Motion Pictures

PLACE OF DEATH
- 18B. Street Address: 1200 Laurel Lane
- 18C. Inside City Corporate Limits: Yes
- 18D. City or Town: Beverly Hills
- 18E. County: Los Angeles
- 18F. Length of Stay in County of Death: 54 Years
- 18G. Length of Stay in California: 54 Years

USUAL RESIDENCE
- 19A. Usual Residence — Street Address: 1200 Laurel Lane
- 19B. Inside City Corporate Limits: Yes
- 20. Name and Mailing Address of Informant: Samuel J. Goldwyn, Jr. — Son, 966 Oakmont Drive, Los Angeles, California
- 19C. City or Town: Beverly Hills
- 19D. County: Los Angeles
- 19E. State: California

PHYSICIAN'S OR CORONER'S CERTIFICATION
- 21B. Physician From: Jan '70 To: 31 Jan 74 Last Seen: 26 Jan 74
- 21C. Physician Signature: R.K. Barton, M.D.
- 21D. Date Signed: 31 Jan 74
- 21E. Address: 9730 Wilshire Boulevard
- 21F. License Number: C8974

FUNERAL DIRECTOR AND LOCAL REGISTRAR
- 22A. Specify Burial: Burial
- 22B. Date: 2/1/74
- 23. Name of Cemetery: Forest Lawn Memorial-Park Assn., Glendale, California
- 25. Name of Funeral Director: Forest Lawn Memorial-Park Assn., Glendale, California
- 28. Date Accepted for Registration: FEB 1 1974

CAUSE OF DEATH
- 29. Part I. Death was caused by:
  - (A) Immediate Cause: Cerebral vascular accident — Interval: 2 weeks
  - (B) Due to: Arteriosclerotic heart disease — Interval: 20 yrs
- 31. Was Operation Performed: No
- 32A. Autopsy: No

Registrar-Recorder/County Clerk: Conny B. McCormack
APR 0 7 2000
19-552324

STATE OF CALIFORNIA
CERTIFICATION OF VITAL RECORD

COUNTY OF LOS ANGELES • REGISTRAR-RECORDER/COUNTY CLERK

CERTIFICATE OF DEATH
State File Number: 7097-026152

DECEDENT PERSONAL DATA
- 1A. Name of Deceased — First Name: Thomas
- 1B. Middle Name:
- 1C. Last Name: Gomez
- 2A. Date of Death: June 18 1971
- 2B. Hour: 9:20 P.M.
- 3. Sex: male
- 4. Color or Race: cauc
- 5. Birthplace: New York
- 6. Date of Birth: July 10 1905
- 7. Age: 65
- 8. Name and Birthplace of Father: Sabino Thomas - La.
- 9. Maiden Name and Birthplace of Mother: Ida Thoman - N.Y
- 10. Citizen of What Country: U.S.A.
- 11. Social Security Number: 088-05-7593
- 12. Married, Never Married, Widowed, Divorced: never married
- 13. Name of Surviving Spouse:
- 14. Last Occupation: Actor
- 15. Number of Years in This Occupation: 47
- 16. Name of Last Employing Company or Firm: Free lance
- 17. Kind of Industry or Business: Motion Pictures

PLACE OF DEATH
- 18A. Place of Death: St Johns Hospital
- 18B. Street Address: 1328 22nd St.
- 18C. Inside City Corporate Limits: yes
- 18D. City or Town: Santa Monica
- 18E. County: Los Angeles
- 18F. Length of Stay in County of Death: 29 YEARS
- 18G. Length of Stay in California: 29 YEARS

USUAL RESIDENCE
- 19A. Usual Residence — Street Address: 8560 Ridpath Dr.
- 19B. Inside City Corporate Limits: yes
- 20. Name and Mailing Address of Informant: Leocadia Smock, 172-90 Highland, Jamaica New York
- 19C. City or Town: Hollywood
- 19D. County: Los Angeles
- 19E. State: Calif

PHYSICIAN'S OR CORONER'S CERTIFICATION
- 21A. Coroner:
- From: 1/13/49
- To: 6/18/71
- And: 6/18/71
- 21C. Address: 2021 Santa Monica Blvd. Santa Monica, Calif. 90404
- 21D. Date Signed: 6-21-71
- 21E. Physician's California License Number: A 05-525

FUNERAL DIRECTOR AND LOCAL REGISTRAR
- 22A. Specify Burial, Entombment or Cremation: cremation
- 22B. Date: 6-22-71
- 23. Name of Cemetery or Crematory: Westwood Memorial Park
- 24. Embalmer: not embalmed
- 25. Name of Funeral Director: Westwood Village Mortuary
- 26. If Not Certified by Coroner: no
- 28. Date Accepted for Registration: JUN 21 1971

CAUSE OF DEATH
- 29. Part I. Death was Caused by:
  - (A) Multiple Cerebral Embolization — 1 mo
  - (B) Carotid artery disease — years
  - (C) Diabetes Mellitus — years
- 31. Was Operation or Biopsy Performed: no
- 32A. Autopsy: yes
- 32B. If Yes, Were Findings Considered in Determining Cause of Death: no

STATE REGISTRAR
- F. 1942

This is to certify that this document is a true copy of the official record filed with the Registrar-Recorder/County Clerk.

Conny B. McCormack
Registrar-Recorder/County Clerk

APR 0 7 2000
19-552334

COUNTY OF LOS ANGELES
DEPARTMENT OF HEALTH SERVICES

CERTIFICATE OF DEATH — STATE OF CALIFORNIA

State File Number: 3 2001 9 035331

Decedent Personal Data
- Name: GERALD GORDON
- Date of Birth: 07/12/1934
- Age: 67
- Sex: M
- Date of Death: 08/17/2001
- Hour: 0455
- State of Birth: ILL
- Social Security No.: 331-26-3508
- Military Service: No
- Marital Status: MARRIED
- Education: 14
- Race: CAUCASIAN
- Hispanic: No
- Usual Employer: SELF EMPLOYED
- Occupation: ACTOR
- Kind of Business: ENTERTAINMENT
- Years in Occupation: 42

Usual Residence
- 2514 VASANTA WAY
- City: LOS ANGELES
- County: LOS ANGELES
- Zip: 90068
- Yrs in County: 27
- State: CA

Informant
- Name, Relationship: NANCY McCORMICK-GORDON, WIFE
- Mailing Address: 2514 VASANTA WAY, LOS ANGELES, CA 90068

Spouse and Parent Information
- Surviving Spouse: NANCY ANN McCORMICK
- Father: ALBERT GOLDMAN — Birth State: ILL
- Mother: RAE ZLOTNICK — Birth State: ILL

Disposition(s)
- Date: 08/30/2001
- Place of Final Disposition: CATHOLIC CEMETERY, FORT WAYNE, INDIANA
- Type of Disposition: CR/TR/BU
- Signature of Embalmer: NOT EMBALMED
- Funeral Director: PIERCE BROTHERS CUNNINGHAM & O'CONNOR
- License No.: FD-8
- Date: 08/30/2001

Place of Death
- CEDARS-SINAI MEDICAL CENTER
- IP
- Street Address: 8700 BEVERLY BLVD.
- City: LOS ANGELES
- County: LOS ANGELES

Cause of Death
- Immediate Cause (A): PNEUMONIA — 2 WKS
- Due to (B): UROSEPSIS — 2 WKS
- Death Reported to Coroner: No
- Biopsy Performed: No
- Autopsy Performed: No
- Used in Determining Cause: No

- Other Significant Conditions: EMPHYSEMA
- Operation Performed: LUNG TRANSPLANTATION — 06/07/1999

N39.0

Physician's Certification
- Decedent Attended Since: 07/01/1999
- Decedent Last Seen Alive: 08/17/2001
- Certifier: Manmohan Biring, MD
- License No.: A054442
- Date: 08/28/2001
- Attending Physician: MANMOHAN BIRING, MD, 8700 BEVERLY BL., ST. 6732, LOS ANGELES, CA 90048

599.0

Census Tract: 90471170

This is a true certified copy of the record filed in the County of Los Angeles Department of Health Services if it bears the Registrar's signature in purple ink.

Date Issued: OCT 15 2001

Director of Health Services and Registrar: Jonathan E. Fielding

This copy not valid unless prepared on engraved border displaying seal and signature of Registrar.

COUNTY OF LOS ANGELES
DEPARTMENT OF HEALTH SERVICES

CERTIFICATE OF DEATH
STATE OF CALIFORNIA

DECEDENT PERSONAL DATA
- 1. Name of Decedent—First (Given): LEO
- 2. Middle: VINCENT
- 3. Last (Family): GORDON, JR.
- 4. Date of Birth: 12/02/1922
- 5. Age: 78
- 6. Sex: MALE
- 7. Date of Death: 12/26/2000
- 8. Hour: 1345
- 9. State of Birth: NEW YORK
- 10. Social Security No.: 549-32-7758
- 11. Military Service: X YES
- 12. Marital Status: MARRIED
- 13. Education—Years Completed: UNKNOWN
- 14. Race: CAUCASIAN
- 15. Hispanic: No
- 16. Usual Employer: SELF EMPLOYED
- 17. Occupation: ACTOR/SCREEN WRITER
- 18. Kind of Business: ENTERTAINMENT
- 19. Years in Occupation: 50

USUAL RESIDENCE
- 20. Residence: 9977 WORNOM AVE.
- 21. City: SUNLAND
- 22. County: LOS ANGELES
- 23. Zip Code: 91040
- 24. Yrs in County: 48
- 25. State: CALIFORNIA

INFORMANT
- 26. Name, Relationship: TARA GORDON/DAUGHTER
- 27. Mailing Address: 9977 WORNOM AVE., SUNLAND, CA. 91040

SPOUSE AND PARENT INFORMATION
- 28. Name of Surviving Spouse—First: DORA LYN
- 29. Middle: EMMA
- 30. Last (Maiden Name): CARTWRIGHT
- 31. Name of Father—First: LEO
- 32. Middle: VINCENT
- 33. Last: GORDON, SR.
- 34. Birth State: UNK
- 35. Name of Mother—First: ANN
- 36. Middle: —
- 37. Last (Maiden): QUALY
- 38. Birth State: UNK

DISPOSITION(S)
- 39. Date: 12/29/2000
- 40. Place of Final Disposition: HOLLYWOOD FOREVER CEMETERY 6000 SANTA MONICA BLVD., LA., CA. 90038

FUNERAL DIRECTOR AND LOCAL REGISTRAR
- 41. Type of Disposition: CR/BU
- 42. Signature of Embalmer: NOT EMBALMED
- 44. Name of Funeral Director: HOLLYWOOD FUNERAL HOME
- 45. License No.: FD-1651
- 47. Date: 12/28/2000

PLACE OF DEATH
- 101. Place of Death: RESIDENCE
- 104. County: LOS ANGELES
- 105. Street Address: 9977 WORNOM AVE.
- 106. City: SUNLAND

CAUSE OF DEATH
- 107. Death was caused by:
  - (A) RESPIRATORY FAILURE — HOURS
  - (B) CHRONIC OBSTRUCTIVE PULMONARY DISEASE — YEARS
- 108. Death Reported to Coroner: No
- 109. Biopsy Performed: No
- 110. Autopsy Performed: No
- 111. Used in Determining Cause: No
- 112. Other Significant Conditions: SEVERE AUTONOMIC INSUFFICIENCY, SPINAL STENOSIS, CORONARY ARTERY DISEASE
- 113. Was Operation Performed: NONE

PHYSICIAN'S CERTIFICATION
- 114. Decedent attended since: 06/09/1999; Decedent last seen alive: 12/26/2000
- 115. Signature and Title of Certifier: Keith G. Kauhanen, M.D.
- 116. License No.: G35385
- 117. Date: 12/27/2000
- 118. K. KAUHANEN, MD 4323 RIVERSIDE DRIVE, BURBANK, CA. 91505

FAX AUTH. #: 344-27113

090399525

COUNTY OF LOS ANGELES
DEPARTMENT OF HEALTH SERVICES
CERTIFICATE OF DEATH

STATE FILE NUMBER: 3 1999 19 030532

1. Name of Decedent—First (Given)	SANDRA
2. Middle	GOULD
3. Last (Family)	MORSE
4. Date of Birth	07/23/1921
5. Age Yrs.	77
6. Sex	FE
7. Date of Death	07/20/1999
8. Hour	0742
9. State of Birth	NY
10. Social Security No.	114-05-7220
11. Military Service	No
12. Marital Status	WIDOWED
13. Education—Years Completed	12
14. Race	WHITE
15. Hispanic	No
16. Usual Employer	SELF EMPLOYED
17. Occupation	ACTRESS
18. Kind of Business	SHOW BUSINESS
19. Years in Occupation	70
20. Residence	3219 OAKDELL LANE
21. City	STUDIO CITY
22. County	LOS ANGELES
23. Zip Code	91604
24. Yrs in County	57
25. State	CA
26. Informant Name, Relationship	MICHAEL BERNS – SON
27. Mailing Address	4929 CARTWRIGHT AVE., NORTH HOLLYWOOD, CA 91601
31. Name of Father	UNK.
32. Middle	UNK.
33. Last	UNK.
34. Birth State	UNK.
35. Name of Mother	ANNE
36. Middle	UNK.
37. Last (Maiden)	UNK.
38. Birth State	UNK.
39. Date of Disposition	07/28/1999
40. Place of Final Disposition	RES. MICHAEL BERNS, 4929 CARTWRIGHT AVE., NORTH HOLLYWOOD, CA 91601
41. Type of Disposition	CR/RES
42. Signature of Embalmer	NOT EMBALMED
44. Name of Funeral Director	AARON CREMATION & BURIAL SERV.
45. License No.	FD-1531
47. Date	07/28/1999
101. Place of Death	ST. JOSEPH MEDICAL CTR.
104. County	LOS ANGELES
105. Street Address	501 S. BUENA VISTA ST.
106. City	BURBANK

107. Death was caused by:

	Cause	Time Interval
Immediate Cause (A)	CARDIOPULMONARY ARREST	1 HR
Due to (B)	MASSIVE CEREBROVASCULAR INFARCTION	4 DAYS
Due to (C)	CARDIAC THROMBOEMBOLISM	4 DAYS
Due to (D)	AORTIC VALVE THROMBOSIS	4 DAYS

112. Other Significant Conditions: AORTIC STENOSIS, MITRAL REGURGITATION, CORONARY ARTERY DISEASE

113. Operation Performed: AORTIC VALVE REPLACEMENT & CORONARY BYPASS / 07/15/1999

Decedent Attended Since	06/25/1999
Decedent Last Seen Alive	07/20/1999
116. License No.	G049875
117. Date	07/26/1999
118. Attending Physician	MARC L. LADENHEIM, MD 2625 W. ALAMEDA AVE., BURBANK, CA 91505

CENSUS TRACT: 090266702
FAX AUTH. #: 197/3061

DATE ISSUED: SEP 14 1999

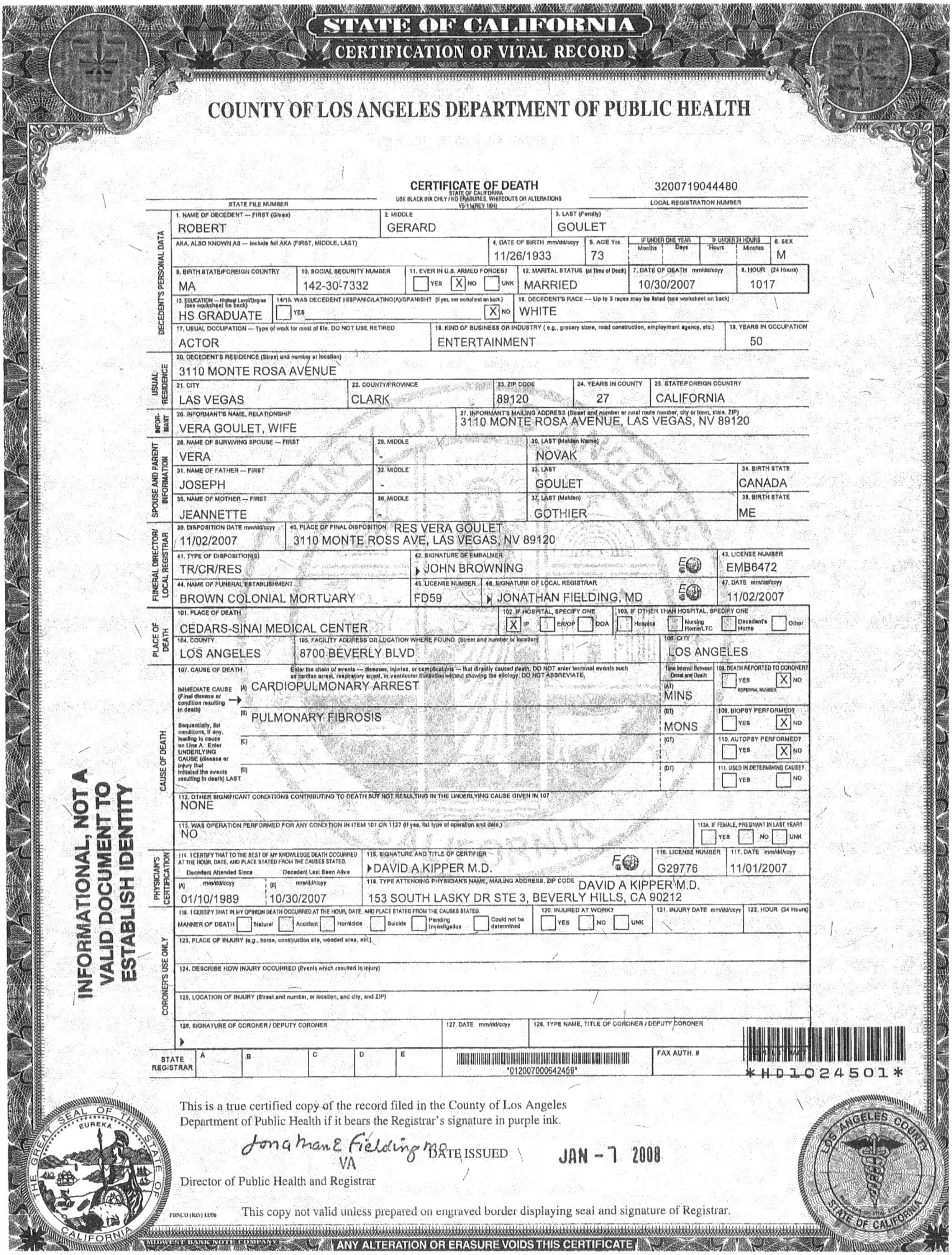

STATE OF CALIFORNIA
CERTIFICATION OF VITAL RECORD
COUNTY OF LOS ANGELES • REGISTRAR-RECORDER/COUNTY CLERK

CERTIFICATE OF DEATH

Registration District No. 1901
Registrar's Number: 1007

DECEDENT PERSONAL DATA
- 1A. Name (First): Sidney
- 1B. Middle Name: P.
- 1C. Last Name: Grauman
- 2A. Date of Death: March 5, 1950
- 2B. Hour: 3:30 P.M.
- 3. Sex: Male
- 4. Color or Race: Cauc.
- 5. Married/Never Married/Widowed/Divorced: Never Married
- 6. Date of Birth: Mar. 17, 1879
- 7. Age (last birthday): 70 years
- 8A. Usual Occupation: Owner
- 8B. Kind of Business or Industry: Theatre
- 9. Birthplace: Indiana
- 10. Citizen of What Country: U.S.A.
- 11. Name of Father: David Grauman
- 12. Maiden Name of Mother: Rosa Goldsmith
- 13. Name of Spouse:
- 14. Was Deceased Ever in U.S. Armed Forces: No
- 15. Social Security Number: 550-01-6606
- 16. Informant: Mrs. Gertrude Skall, Los Angeles, California

PLACE OF DEATH
- 17A. Place of Death: Los Angeles
- 17B. Length of Stay: 34 yrs
- 17C. County: Los Angeles
- 17D. Full Name and Address of Hospital or Institution: Cedars of Lebanon Hospital, 4833 Fountain Ave.

USUAL RESIDENCE
- 18A. Street Address: 3045 W. 8th Street
- 18B. City or Town: Los Angeles
- 18C. County: Los Angeles
- 18D. State: California

CAUSE OF DEATH
- 19.I(a) Disease or Condition Directly Leading to Death: Coronary Occlusion — Approximate Interval: Burst

OPERATIONS / AUTOPSY
- 21. Autopsy: Yes

PHYSICIAN'S OR CORONER'S CERTIFICATION
- 23. Physician: I hereby certify that I attended the deceased from 3/5/50, that I last saw the deceased alive on March 5, 1950
- 23B. Signature: Myron Prinzmetal M.D.
- 23C. Degree or Title: Judo Civers Dr
- 23E. Date Signed: March 6, '50

FUNERAL DIRECTOR AND REGISTRAR
- 24. Burial
- 24B. Date: 3/9/50
- Cemetery or Crematory: Forest Lawn Mausoleum
- 25. Signature of Embalmer: Arthur L. Woodmansee, License Number 3065
- 26. Signature of Funeral Director: Pierce Bros., Los Angeles
- 27. Date Received by Local Registrar: MAR 7 1950

Conny B. McCormack
Registrar-Recorder/County Clerk
DEC 07 2000
19-147106

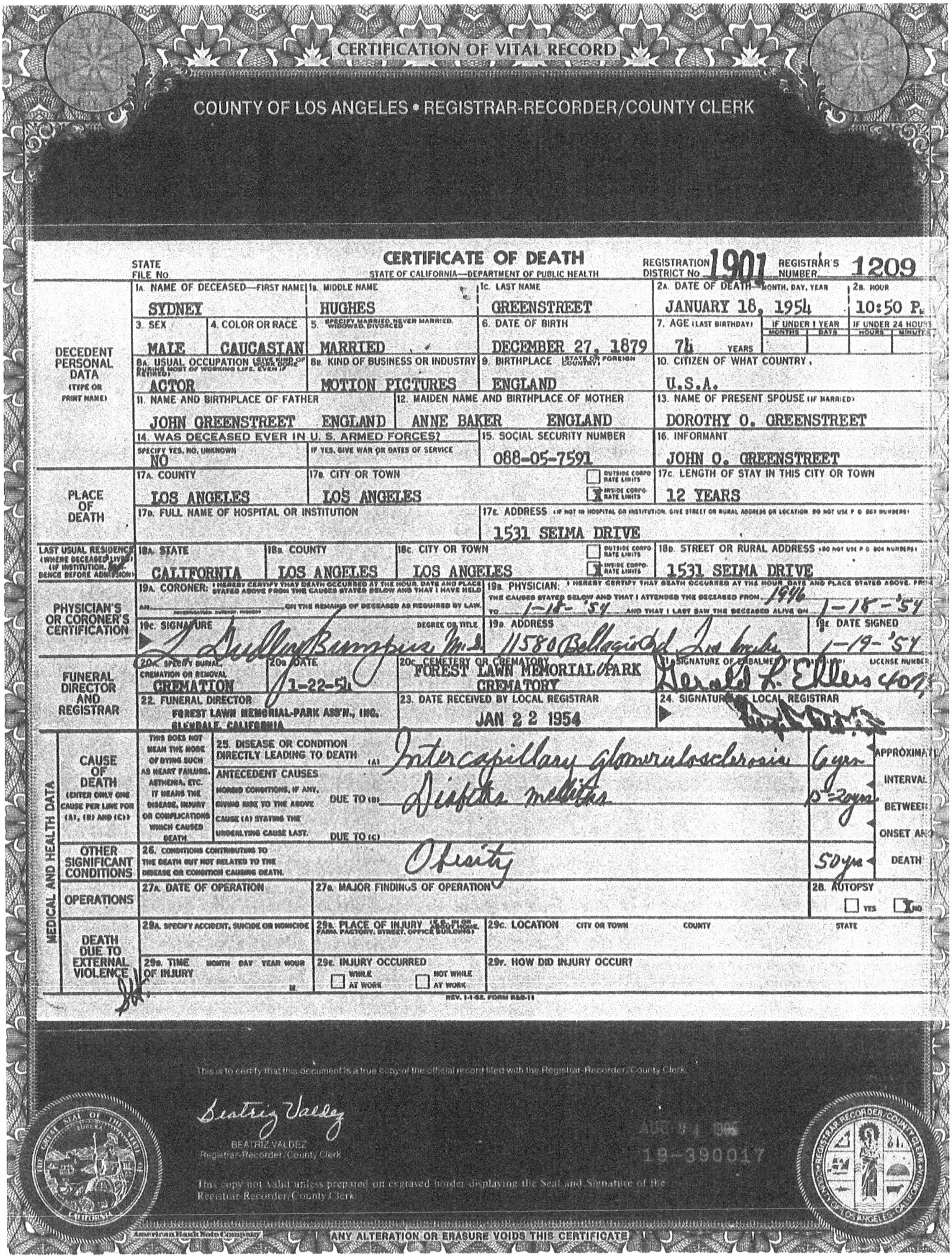

JANE GREER

101

STATE OF CALIFORNIA
CERTIFICATION OF VITAL RECORD

COUNTY OF LOS ANGELES • REGISTRAR-RECORDER/COUNTY CLERK

CERTIFICATE OF DEATH — STATE OF CALIFORNIA

State File Number: 3200819006273

DECEDENT'S PERSONAL DATA
- 1. Name of Decedent — First (Given): DAVID
- 2. Middle: L.
- 3. Last (Family): GROH
- 4. Date of Birth: 05/21/1939
- 5. Age Yrs: 68
- 6. Sex: M
- 9. Birth State/Foreign Country: NEW YORK
- 10. Social Security Number: 101-30-8307
- 11. Ever in U.S. Armed Forces: YES (X)
- 12. Marital Status at Time of Death: MARRIED
- 7. Date of Death: 02/12/2008
- 8. Hour (24 Hours): 1845
- 13. Education: BACHELOR
- 14/15. Was Decedent Hispanic/Latino(a)/Spanish: NO (X)
- 16. Decedent's Race: WHITE
- 17. Usual Occupation: ACTOR
- 18. Kind of Business or Industry: ENTERTAINMENT
- 19. Years in Occupation: 45

USUAL RESIDENCE
- 20. Decedent's Residence: 1411 N. HARPER AVE. #5
- 21. City: WEST HOLLYWOOD
- 22. County/Province: LOS ANGELES
- 23. ZIP Code: 90046
- 24. Years in County: 33
- 25. State/Foreign Country: CA

INFORMANT
- 26. Informant's Name/Relationship: KRISTEN ANDERSEN-GROH, WIFE
- 27. Informant's Mailing Address: 1411 N. HARPER AVE. #5, WEST HOLLYWOOD, CA 90046

SPOUSE AND PARENT INFORMATION
- 28. Name of Surviving Spouse — First: KRISTEN
- 30. Last (Maiden Name): ANDERSEN
- 31. Name of Father — First: BENJAMIN
- 33. Last: GROH
- 34. Birth State: IOWA
- 35. Name of Mother — First: MILDRED
- 37. Last (Maiden): WEINBERG
- 38. Birth State: NEW YORK

FUNERAL DIRECTOR / LOCAL REGISTRAR
- 39. Disposition Date: 02/15/2008
- 40. Place of Final Disposition: MOUNT SINAI MEMORIAL PARK, 5950 FOREST LAWN DR., LOS ANGELES, CA 90068
- 41. Type of Disposition: CR/BU
- 42. Signature of Embalmer: NOT EMBALMED
- 44. Name of Funeral Establishment: MOUNT SINAI MORTUARY
- 45. License Number: FD1010
- 46. Signature of Local Registrar: JONATHAN FIELDING, MD
- 47. Date: 02/13/2008

PLACE OF DEATH
- 101. Place of Death: CEDARS-SINAI MEDICAL CENTER
- 102. If Hospital, Specify One: IP (X)
- 104. County: LOS ANGELES
- 105. Facility Address: 8700 BEVERLY BLVD
- City: LOS ANGELES

CAUSE OF DEATH
- 107. Immediate Cause (A): METASTATIC RENAL CARCINOMA — 20 MOS
- 108. Death Reported to Coroner: NO (X)
- 109. Biopsy Performed: NO (X)
- 110. Autopsy Performed: NO (X)
- 112. Other Significant Conditions: NONE
- 113. Was Operation Performed: NO

PHYSICIAN'S CERTIFICATION
- 114. Decedent Attended Since: 12/13/2006; Decedent Last Seen Alive: 02/12/2008
- 115. Signature and Title of Certifier: BARRY EUGENE ROSENBLOOM M.D.
- 116. License Number: G22745
- 117. Date: 02/13/2008
- 118. Type Attending Physician's Name, Mailing Address: BARRY EUGENE ROSENBLOOM M.D., 9090 WILSHIRE BLVD STE 200, BEVERLY HILLS, CA 90211

This is to certify that this document is a true copy of the official record filed with the Registrar-Recorder/County Clerk.

SEP 16 2009

DEAN C. LOGAN
Registrar-Recorder/County Clerk

This copy not valid unless prepared on engraved border displaying the Seal and Signature of the Registrar-Recorder/County Clerk.

000004564

INFORMATIONAL, NOT A VALID DOCUMENT TO ESTABLISH IDENTITY

STATE OF CALIFORNIA
CERTIFICATION OF VITAL RECORD

COUNTY OF LOS ANGELES • REGISTRAR-RECORDER/COUNTY CLERK

CERTIFICATE OF DEATH — STATE OF CALIFORNIA—DEPARTMENT OF PUBLIC HEALTH

State File Number: 7097-052854

DECEDENT PERSONAL DATA
- 1A. Name of Deceased—First Name: Charles
- 1B. Middle Name: William
- 1C. Last Name: Haines
- 2A. Date of Death: Dec. 26, 1973
- 2B. Hour: 6:45 P.M.
- 3. Sex: Male
- 4. Color or Race: Cauc.
- 5. Birthplace: Virginia
- 6. Date of Birth: Jan. 1, 1900
- 7. Age (Last Birthday): 73 Years
- 8. Name and Birthplace of Father: George Haines — Virginia
- 9. Maiden Name and Birthplace of Mother: Laura Matthews — Virginia
- 10. Citizen of What Country: U.S.A.
- 11. Social Security Number: 563-01-6455
- 12. Married, Never Married, Widowed, Divorced: Never Married
- 13. Name of Surviving Spouse: —
- 14. Last Occupation: Designer
- 15. Number of Years in This Occupation: 40
- 16. Name of Last Employing Company or Firm: Self Employed
- 17. Kind of Industry or Business: Interior Designs

PLACE OF DEATH
- 18A. Place of Death—Name of Hospital: Saint Johns Hospital
- 18B. Street Address: 1328 22nd Street
- 18C. Inside City Corporate Limits: Yes
- 18D. City or Town: Santa Monica
- 18E. County: Los Angeles
- 18F. Length of Stay in County: 52 Years
- 18G. Length of Stay in California: 52 Years

USUAL RESIDENCE
- 19A. Usual Residence—Street Address: 601 Lorna Lane
- 19B. Inside City Corporate Limits: Yes
- 19C. City or Town: Los Angeles
- 19D. County: Los Angeles
- 19E. State: California
- 20. Name and Mailing Address of Informant: George Haines, 220 12th Street, Santa Monica, Ca

PHYSICIAN'S OR CORONER'S CERTIFICATION
- 21B. Physician — 12/26/73
- 21E. Address: 2001 Santa Monica Blvd
- Date Signed: 12-26-73
- License Number: A-05525

FUNERAL DIRECTOR AND LOCAL REGISTRAR
- 22A. Specify Burial, Entombment or Cremation: Cremation
- 22B. Date: Dec. 28, 1973
- 23. Name of Cemetery or Crematory: Live Oak Crematory and Woodlawn Mausoleum
- 24. Embalmer: Not Embalmed
- 25. Name of Funeral Director: Gates, Kingsley & Gates
- 26. Reported to Coroner: No
- 28. Date Accepted for Registration: DEC 27 1973

CAUSE OF DEATH
- 29. Part I. Death Was Caused By:
  - (A) Immediate Cause: Cardiac arrest
  - (B) Due to: [illegible] Ca. Ockell
  - Interval: 6 mos
- 31. Operation: No
- 32A. Autopsy: No

This is to certify that this document is a true copy of the official record filed with the Registrar-Recorder/County Clerk.

Conny B. McCormack
CONNY B. McCORMACK
Registrar-Recorder/County Clerk

NOV 28 2000
19-113446

CERTIFICATE OF DEATH — STATE OF CALIFORNIA

State File Number: 3 2003 19 000649

DECEDENT'S PERSONAL DATA
- 1. Name of Decedent — First (Given): CONRAD
- 2. Middle: LAFCADIO
- 3. Last (Family): HALL
- 4. Date of Birth: 06/21/1926
- 5. Age: 76
- 6. Sex: M
- 7. Date of Death: 01/04/2003
- 8. Hour: 1909
- 9. Birth State/Foreign Country: TAHITI
- 10. Social Security Number: 572-28-1939
- 11. Ever in U.S. Armed Forces?: NO
- 12. Marital Status: MARRIED
- 13. Education: MASTER'S
- 14/15. Hispanic/Latino?: NO
- 16. Race: CAUCASIAN
- 17. Usual Occupation: DIRECTOR OF PHOTOGRAPHY
- 18. Kind of Business/Industry: FILM MAKING
- 19. Years in Occupation: 50

USUAL RESIDENCE
- 20. Residence: 1310 N. SWEETZER AVE APT. 603
- 21. City: LOS ANGELES
- 22. County: LOS ANGELES
- 23. Zip Code: 90069
- 24. Years in County: 55
- 25. State/Foreign Country: CA

INFORMANT
- 26. Informant's Name, Relationship: SUSAN C HALL, WIFE
- 27. Mailing Address: 1310 N SWEETZER AVE APT. 603 LOS ANGELES CA 90069

SPOUSE AND PARENT INFORMATION
- 28. Name of Surviving Spouse — First: SUSAN
- 29. Middle: C
- 30. Last (Maiden): KOWARSH
- 31. Name of Father — First: JAMES
- 32. Middle: NORMAN
- 33. Last: HALL
- 34. Birth State: IOWA
- 35. Name of Mother — First: SARAH
- 36. Middle: —
- 37. Last (Maiden): WINCHESTER
- 38. Birth State: TAHITI

FUNERAL DIRECTOR / LOCAL REGISTRAR
- 39. Disposition Date: 01/10/2003
- 40. Place of Final Disposition: AT SEA OFF THE COAST OF TAHITI
- 41. Type of Disposition: CR/TR/SEA
- 42. Signature of Embalmer: NOT EMBALMED
- 44. Name of Funeral Establishment: FOREST LAWN HOLLYWOOD HILLS
- 45. License Number: FD 904
- 46. Signature of Local Registrar: Thomas Garthwaite
- 47. Date: 01/09/2003

PLACE OF DEATH
- 101. Place of Death: ST. JOHN'S HOSPITAL
- 102. If Hospital, Specify: IP
- 104. County: LOS ANGELES
- 105. Facility Address: 1328 22ND ST
- 106. City: SANTA MONICA

CAUSE OF DEATH
- 107. Immediate Cause (A): METASTATIC BLADDER CANCER — 6 MOS
- 108. Death Reported to Coroner: NO
- 109. Biopsy Performed: YES
- 110. Autopsy Performed: NO
- 111. Used in Determining Cause: NO
- 112. Other Significant Conditions: PNEUMONIA
- 113. Operation Performed: TRANSURETHRAL RESECTION OF BLADDER TUMOR 11/01/2002

PHYSICIAN'S CERTIFICATION
- 114. Decedent Attended Since: 11/04/2002; Last Seen Alive: 01/04/2003
- 115. Signature and Title of Certifier: D. Piro MD
- 116. License Number: G52155
- 117. Date: 01/08/2003
- 118. Attending Physician's Name/Address: LAWRENCE D PIRO MD 2001 SANTA MONICA BL STE. 560W SANTA MONICA CA 90404

State Registrar Fax Auth #: 273/1991

INFORMATIONAL, NOT A VALID DOCUMENT TO ESTABLISH IDENTITY

JAN 2 2 2008

019042559

STATE OF CALIFORNIA
CERTIFICATION OF VITAL RECORD

COUNTY OF LOS ANGELES
DEPARTMENT OF HEALTH SERVICES

CERTIFICATE OF DEATH
STATE OF CALIFORNIA

DECEDENT PERSONAL DATA
- 1. Name (Given): CARRIE
- 2. Middle: LOUISE
- 3. Last (Family): HAMILTON
- 4. Date of Birth: 12/05/1963
- 5. Age: 38
- 6. Sex: F
- 7. Date of Death: 01/20/2002
- 8. Hour: 0730
- 9. State of Birth: NY
- 10. Social Security No.: 572-04-6678
- 11. Military Service: No
- 12. Marital Status: DIVORCED
- 13. Education—Years Completed: 14
- 14. Race: CAUC
- 15. Hispanic: No
- 16. Usual Employer: SELF EMPLOYED
- 17. Occupation: ACTRESS/WRITER/DIRECTOR
- 18. Kind of Business: ENTERTAINMENT
- 19. Years in Occupation: 20

USUAL RESIDENCE
- 20. Residence: 15497 BLUE MESA ROAD
- 21. City: GUNNISON
- 22. County: GUNNISON
- 23. Zip Code: 81230
- 24. Yrs in County: 7
- 25. State: CO

INFORMANT
- 26. Name/Relationship: CAROL C. BURNETT — MOTHER
- 27. Mailing Address: 5750 WILSHIRE BLVD. SUITE 590, LOS ANGELES, CA. 90036

SPOUSE AND PARENT INFORMATION
- 31. Father First: JOSEPH
- 32. Middle: HENRY
- 33. Last: HAMILTON
- 34. Birth State: CA
- 35. Mother First: CAROL
- 36. Middle: C.
- 37. Last (Maiden): BURNETT
- 38. Birth State: TX

DISPOSITION(S)
- 39. Date: 01/25/2002
- 40. Place of Final Disposition: RES: BRIAN MILLER 15497 BLUE MESA ROAD GUNNISON, CO. 81230
- 41. Type of Disposition: CR/TR/RES
- 42. Signature of Embalmer: NOT EMBALMED
- 44. Name of Funeral Director: PIERCE BROS. WESTWOOD
- 45. License No.: FD-951
- 47. Date: 01/24/2002

PLACE OF DEATH
- 101. Place of Death: CEDARS SINAI MEDICAL CENTER
- 102. Hospital: IP
- 104. County: LOS ANGELES
- 105. Street Address: 8700 BEVERLY BLVD.
- 106. City: LOS ANGELES

CAUSE OF DEATH
- 107. Immediate Cause (A): CANCER OF LUNG — 5 MOS.
- 108. Death Reported to Coroner: No
- 109. Biopsy Performed: Yes
- 110. Autopsy Performed: No
- 112. Other Significant Conditions: NONE
- 113. Was Operation Performed: NO

PHYSICIAN'S CERTIFICATION
- 114. Decedent Attended Since: 07/30/2001; Last Seen Alive: 01/20/2002
- 115. Signature: Richard N. Gold M.D.
- 116. License No.: G25597
- 117. Date: 01/22/2002
- 118. Type Attending Physician's Name: RICHARD N. GOLD, M.D. 8631 W. 3rd ST. LOS ANGELES, CA. 90048

090502881

COUNTY OF SAN DIEGO

GREGORY J. SMITH
ASSESSOR/RECORDER/COUNTY CLERK

CERTIFICATE OF DEATH — STATE OF CALIFORNIA
Local Registration District and Certificate Number: 8000 011084

Decedent Personal Data

- **Name of Decedent:** James Neil Hamilton
- **Date of Death:** September 24, 1984
- **Hour:** 2215
- **Sex:** Male
- **Race/Ethnicity:** Caucasian
- **Spanish/Hispanic:** No
- **Date of Birth:** September 9, 1899
- **Age:** 85 years
- **Birthplace of Decedent:** MA
- **Name and Birthplace of Father:** Alexander Hamilton — NY
- **Birth Name and Birthplace of Mother:** Unk. O'Neill — MA
- **Citizen of What Country:** USA
- **Social Security Number:** 573-09-5935
- **Marital Status:** Married
- **Name of Surviving Spouse:** Elsa Whitner
- **Primary Occupation:** Actor
- **Number of Years This Occupation:** 50
- **Employer:** 20th Century Fox
- **Kind of Industry or Business:** Motion Picture

Usual Residence

- **Street Address:** 920 E Washington #203
- **City or Town:** Escondido
- **County:** San Diego
- **State:** Ca
- **Informant:** Elsa Hamilton — wife, 920 E Washington #203, Escondido, Ca 92025

Place of Death

- **Place of Death:** 920 E Washington #203
- **County:** San Diego
- **City or Town:** Escondido

Cause of Death

- **Immediate Cause (A):** Cardiogenic Shock — 2 min
- **(B):** Arrhythmia — 3 min
- **(C):** Arteriosclerotic heart disease — 30 yrs
- **Other Significant Conditions:** Senile Dementia, Emphysema
- **Was Death Reported to Coroner?** No
- **Was Biopsy Performed?** No
- **Was Autopsy Performed?** No
- **Was Operation Performed?** No

Physician's Certification

- Attended decedent since Jan 27 1972
- Last saw decedent alive Sept 24 1984
- Physician: Arthur M Nicolaysen, MD, 815 E Pennsylvania, Escondido, Ca
- Date Signed: 9-26-84
- License Number: A19306

Disposition

- **Disposition:** Cremation
- **Date:** 9-26-84
- **Cemetery/Crematory:** Leneda Inc, El Cajon, Ca
- **Embalmer:** not embalmed
- **Funeral Director:** NEPTUNE OF SAN DIEGO
- **License No.:** F-1352
- **Date Accepted by Local Registrar:** SEP 26 1984

663062

This is a true and exact reproduction of the document officially registered and placed on file in the office of the San Diego County Recorder/Clerk

October 19, 2001

Gregory J. Smith
Assessor/Recorder/County Clerk

This copy is not valid unless prepared on an engraved border displaying date, seal and signature of the Recorder/County Clerk

CERTIFICATE OF DEATH

STATE OF CALIFORNIA—DEPARTMENT OF PUBLIC HEALTH

STATE FILE No. — REGISTRATION DISTRICT No. 7053 — REGISTRAR'S NUMBER 14579

DECEDENT PERSONAL DATA

- 1A. Name of Deceased—First Name: Oliver
- 1B. Middle Name: Norvell
- 1C. Last Name: Hardy
- 2A. Date of Death: Aug. 7, 1957
- 2B. Hour: 7.25 A
- 3. Sex: Male
- 4. Color or Race: Cauc.
- 5. Married
- 6. Date of Birth: January 18, 1892
- 7. Age (Last Birthday): 65 Years
- 8A. Usual Occupation: Actor
- 8B. Kind of Business or Industry: Motion Pictures
- 9. Birthplace: Harlem, Georgia
- 10. Citizen of What Country: U.S.A.
- 11. Name and Birthplace of Father: Oliver Hardy, Sr. — Georgia
- 12. Maiden Name and Birthplace of Mother: Emily Norvell — Georgia
- 13. Name of Present Spouse (if married): Lucille Hardy
- 14. Was Deceased Ever in U.S. Armed Forces?: No
- 15. Social Security Number: 547-10-9581
- 16. Informant: Lucille Hardy

PLACE OF DEATH

- 17A. County: Los Angeles
- 17B. City or Town: North Hollywood — Inside Corpo. Date Limits
- 17C. Length of Stay in This City or Town: 38 yrs.
- 17D. Full Name of Hospital or Institution: —
- 17E. Address: 5421 Auckland Avenue

LAST USUAL RESIDENCE

- 18A. State: California
- 18B. County: Los Angeles
- 18C. City or Town: North Hollywood
- 18D. Street or Rural Address: 5421 Auckland Avenue

PHYSICIAN'S OR CORONER'S CERTIFICATION

- 19B. Physician: Attended deceased from April 1955 to Aug 7 '57, last saw alive July 15-57
- 19C. Signature: Wm. Gobbell, M.D.
- 19D. Address: 16100 Ventura Blvd, Encino, California
- 19E. Date Signed: Aug 7, 1957

FUNERAL DIRECTOR AND REGISTRAR

- 20A. Burial/Cremation: Cremation
- 20B. Date: 8-9-1957
- 20C. Cemetery or Crematory: Chapel of the Pines
- 21. Signature of Embalmer: C. Morrison, License 235
- 22. Funeral Director: Pierce Brothers Beverly Hills
- 23. Date Received by Local Registrar: AUG 8 1957
- 24. Signature of Local Registrar: George M. Uhl, M.D.

MEDICAL AND HEALTH DATA — CAUSE OF DEATH

- 25. Disease or Condition Directly Leading to Death:
  - (a) Acute Cerebral Vascular Accident (Thrombosis) superimposed — Interval: 24 hrs
  - Due to (b): Chronic Right-sided Hemiplegia c̄ aphasia — 11 months
  - Due to (c): Atherosclerosis generalized — 5-10 y
- 26. Other Significant Conditions Contributing: Arteriosclerotic Heart disease with auricular fibrillation and cardiac decompensation — 3 years
- 28. Autopsy: No

This is to certify that this document is a true copy of the official record filed with the Registrar-Recorder/County Clerk.

Beatriz Valdez, Registrar-Recorder/County Clerk

AUG 0 4 199?
19-390021

CERTIFICATE OF DEATH
STATE OF CALIFORNIA — DEPARTMENT OF PUBLIC HEALTH

State File Number: 7097-021331

DECEDENT PERSONAL DATA
- 1a. Name (First): Vinton
- 1b. Middle: Jackson
- 1c. Last: Hayworth
- 2a. Date of Death: May 21, 1970
- 2b. Hour: 9:15 PM
- 3. Sex: Male
- 4. Color or Race: Cauc.
- 5. Birthplace: Washington D.C.
- 6. Date of Birth: June 4, 1906
- 7. Age: 63 years
- 8. Name and Birthplace of Father: Allyn Daru Hayworth – Ind.
- 9. Maiden Name and Birthplace of Mother: Margaret O'Rare – Washington D.C.
- 10. Citizen of What Country: USA
- 11. Social Security Number: 562-14-8904
- 12. Married
- 13. Name of Surviving Spouse: Jean Owens
- 14. Last Occupation: Actor
- 15. Number of Years in This Occupation: 50
- 16. Name of Last Employing Company or Firm: Screen Jems
- 17. Kind of Industry or Business: Motion Pictures

PLACE OF DEATH
- 18a. Place of Death: (hospital/facility)
- 18b. Street Address: 4645 Ethel Ave.
- 18c. Inside City Corporate Limits: Yes
- 18d. City or Town: Studio City
- 18e. County: Los Angeles
- 18f. Length of Stay in County: 13 years
- 18g. Length of Stay in California: 13 years

USUAL RESIDENCE
- 19a. Street Address: 4645 Ethel Ave.
- 19a. Inside City Corporate Limits: Yes
- 20. Name and Mailing Address of Informant: Jean O. Hayworth
- 19c. City or Town: No. Hollywood
- 19d. County: Los Angeles
- 19e. State: Calif.
- Informant: Same

PHYSICIAN'S OR CORONER'S CERTIFICATION
- Date Occurred At: 1958
- From: 5-20-70
- To: 5-14-70
- Physician: Frances J. Baker MD
- Date Signed: 5-21-70
- Address: 3701 W. Alameda
- License Number: 10878

FUNERAL DIRECTOR AND LOCAL REGISTRAR
- 22a. Cremation
- 22b. Date: 5-25-70
- 23. Name of Cemetery or Crematory: Chapel of the Pines
- 24. Embalmer: Thomas M. Dewhirst — 5676
- 25. Funeral Director: PIERCE BROTHERS-VALHALLA
- 26. Reported to Coroner: No
- 27. Local Registrar Signature: Schedbecker MD
- 28. Date Accepted for Registration: MAY 24 1970

CAUSE OF DEATH
- 29. Part I. Immediate Cause (a): Myocardial infarction — 1 day
- Due to (b): Arteriosclerotic heart disease — 6 yrs

State Registrar: 1434

JAN 0 4 2001
19-180311

Conny B. McCormack
Registrar-Recorder/County Clerk

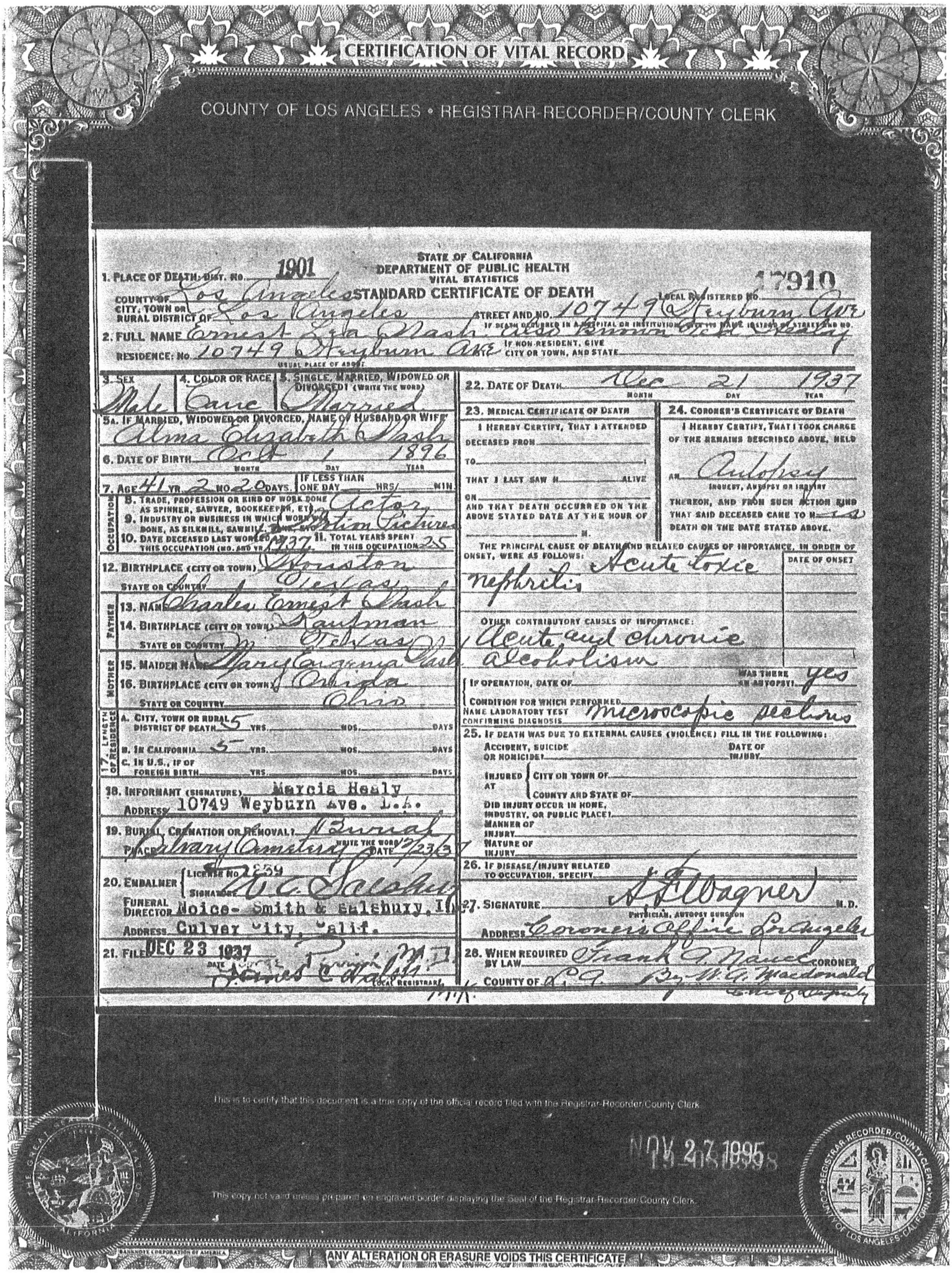

Certificate of Death — Leona Helmsley

State of Connecticut, Department of Public Health
VS-4 REV. 1/04
State File Number: 413

1. Decedent's Legal Name	Leona Helmsley
2. Sex	Female
3. Actual or Presumed Date of Death	August 20, 2007
4. Actual or Presumed Time of Death	12:40 AM
5. Age Last Birthday	87
7. Date of Birth	July 4, 1920
8. Birthplace	Marbletown, New York
9. Residence (State)	New York
10. Residence (County)	New York
11. Residence (City or Town)	New York
12. Residence (Street and No.)	36 Central Park South
14. Zip Code	10019
15. Ever in US Armed Forces?	No
16. Marital Status at Time of Death	Widowed
17. Surviving Spouse's Name	not applicable
18. Father's Name	Morris Rosenthol
19. Mother's Name Prior to First Marriage	Ida Popkin
20. Informant's Name	Mr. John Codey
21. Informant's Relationship to Decedent	Executor
22. Mailing Address	315 Port Washington Blvd. Port Washington, N.Y. 11050
23. If Death Occurred in a Hospital	ER/Outpatient
25. Facility Name	Round Hill Rd. Greenwich, CT
26. City or Town of Death	Greenwich
Zip Code	06831
27. County of Death	Fairfield
28. Method of Disposition	Entombment
29. Disposition	Sleepy Hollow Cemetery
30. Location	Tarrytown, New York
31. Date	8/22/07
32. Was Body Embalmed?	Yes — Melissa Fahey
33. Funeral Facility	Frank E. Campbell The Funeral Chapel, 1076 Madison Avenue, NY NY
35. License Number	2637
36. Date Pronounced Dead	8/20/07
37. Time Pronounced	00:40
41. Was Medical Examiner Contacted?	No
42. Was an Autopsy Performed?	No
43. Were the Autopsy Findings Available	No

44. Cause of Death

Part I	Cause	Approximate Interval Onset to Death
(a) Immediate Cause	Cardiopulmonary Arrest	Minutes
(b) Due to	Myocardial Infarction	Days

Part II: Peripheral Vascular Disease, Weak Valvular Disease

46. If Female	Not pregnant within past year
47. Did Tobacco Use Contribute to Death?	No
48. Certifier	Pronouncing & Certifying Practitioner
Date Certified	8/20/07
This Certificate was Received for Record on	AUG 20 2007
Registrar	Barbara Lowden, CT
50. Decedent's Education	High School Graduate/GED
51. Decedent of Hispanic Origin?	No, Not Spanish/Hispanic/Latino
52. Decedent's Race	White

I HEREBY CERTIFY THAT THE FOREGOING IS A TRUE COPY OF THE RECORD ON FILE IN THE GREENWICH TOWN CLERK'S OFFICE, EXCEPT SUCH INFORMATION THAT IS NONDISCLOSABLE BY LAW, ATTESTED BY THE RAISED SEAL OF THE TOWN OF GREENWICH.

Barbara Lowden, Assistant Registrar — December 2, 2008

LEGAL FEE: $10.00
THIS CERTIFICATE NOT VALID WITHOUT SEAL

CERTIFICATION OF VITAL RECORD

COUNTY OF LOS ANGELES • REGISTRAR-RECORDER/COUNTY CLERK

CERTIFICATE OF DEATH — STATE OF CALIFORNIA

State File Number: 39619034428

Decedent Personal Data

- 1. Name of Decedent—First (Given): MARGOT
- 2. Middle: LOUISE
- 3. Last (Family): HEMINGWAY
- 4. Date of Birth: 02/16/1954
- 5. Age Yrs.: 42
- 6. Sex: FEM
- 7. Date of Death: 07/01/1996 FND
- 8. Hour: 1355
- 9. State of Birth: OR
- 10. Social Security No.: 518-68-6195
- 11. Military Service: NONE
- 12. Marital Status: DIVORCED
- 13. Education—Years Completed: 12
- 14. Race: CAUC.
- 15. Hispanic: No
- 16. Usual Employer: SELF EMPLOYED
- 17. Occupation: ACTRESS
- 18. Kind of Business: ENTERTAINMENT
- 19. Years in Occupation: 20

Usual Residence

- 20. Residence—Street and Number or Location: 102 W. CHANNEL LANE
- 21. City: SUN VALLEY
- 22. County: BLAINE
- 23. Zip Code: 83353
- 24. Yrs in County: 41
- 25. State or Foreign Country: IDAHO

Informant

- 26. Name, Relationship: JOHN HEMINGWAY - FATHER
- 27. Mailing Address: 411 ONYX ST., KETCHUM, ID 83340

Spouse and Parent Information

- 31. Name of Father—First: JOHN
- 32. Middle: H.
- 33. Last: HEMINGWAY
- 34. Birth State: CN
- 35. Name of Mother—First: BYRA
- 36. Middle: L.
- 37. Last (Maiden): WHITTLESEY
- 38. Birth State: ID

Disposition(s)

- 39. Date: 07/05/1996
- 40. Place of Final Disposition: KETCHUM CEMETERY, KETCHUM, ID 83340
- 41. Type of Disposition(s): CR/TR/BU
- 43. License No.: 5249
- 44. Name of Funeral Director: FOREST LAWN MTY GLENDALE
- 45. License No.: FD-656
- 47. Date: 07/03/1996

Place of Death

- 101. Place of Death: RESIDENCE, Second home
- 104. County: LOS ANGELES
- 105. Street Address: 139 FRASER ST.
- 106. City: SANTA MONICA

Cause of Death

- 107. Death was Caused by:
  - Immediate Cause (A): DEFERRED
- 108. Death Reported to Coroner: YES
  - Referral Number: 96-04985
- 110. Autopsy Performed: YES

Coroner's Use Only

- 119. Manner of Death: PENDING INVESTIGATION
- 126. Signature of Coroner or Deputy Coroner: Mary T. Macias
- 127. Date: 07/03/1996
- 128. Typed Name, Title of Coroner or Deputy Coroner: MARY T. MACIAS/DEPUTY CORONER
- Fax Auth. #: 273/33223

State Registrar: 9501

CONNY B. McCORMACK
Registrar-Recorder/County Clerk

OCT 11 1996
19-393903

CERTIFICATION OF VITAL RECORD

COUNTY OF LOS ANGELES • REGISTRAR-RECORDER/COUNTY CLERK

AMENDMENT OF MEDICAL AND HEALTH DATA—DEATH 39619034428

PART I — INFORMATION TO LOCATE RECORD

1. NAME—FIRST (GIVEN): MARGOT
2. MIDDLE: LOUISE
3. LAST (FAMILY): HEMINGWAY
4. SEX: FEM
5. DATE OF EVENT—MM/DD/CCYY: 07/01/1996 FND
6. CITY OF OCCURRENCE: Santa Monica
7. COUNTY OF OCCURRENCE: Los Angeles

PART II — INFORMATION AS IT APPEARS ON RECORD

107. DEATH WAS CAUSED BY:
- IMMEDIATE CAUSE (A): Deferred
- (B):
- (C):
- DUE TO (D):

108. DEATH REPORTED TO CORONER: YES — REFERRAL NUMBER 96-04985
109. BIOPSY PERFORMED: YES
110. AUTOPSY PERFORMED: YES
111. USED IN DETERMINING CAUSE: YES

112. OTHER SIGNIFICANT CONDITIONS CONTRIBUTING TO DEATH BUT NOT RELATED TO CAUSE GIVEN IN 107:

113. WAS OPERATION PERFORMED FOR ANY CONDITION IN ITEM 107 or 112?:

119. MANNER OF DEATH: PENDING INVESTIGATION
120. INJURY AT WORK:
121. INJURY DATE—MM/DD/CCYY:
122. HOUR:
123. PLACE OF INJURY:
124. DESCRIBE HOW INJURY OCCURRED:
125. LOCATION:

PART III — INFORMATION AS IT SHOULD APPEAR

107. DEATH WAS CAUSED BY:
- IMMEDIATE CAUSE (A): ACUTE PHENOBARBITAL INTOXICATION
- (B):
- (C):
- DUE TO (D):

TIME INTERVAL BETWEEN ONSET AND DEATH: Unk

108. DEATH REPORTED TO CORONER: YES — REFERRAL NUMBER 96-04985
109. BIOPSY PERFORMED: NO
110. AUTOPSY PERFORMED: YES
111. USED IN DETERMINING CAUSE: YES

112. OTHER SIGNIFICANT CONDITIONS CONTRIBUTING TO DEATH BUT NOT RELATED TO CAUSE GIVEN IN 107: None

113. WAS OPERATION PERFORMED FOR ANY CONDITION IN ITEM 107 or 112?: No

119. MANNER OF DEATH: SUICIDE
120. INJURY AT WORK: NO
121. INJURY DATE: Unknown
122. HOUR: Unk
123. PLACE OF INJURY: Residence, Second home
124. DESCRIBE HOW INJURY OCCURRED: Ingestion
125. LOCATION: 139 Fraser St., Santa Monica CA 90405

DECLARATION OF CERTIFYING PHYSICIAN OR CORONER

8. SIGNATURE OF CERTIFYING PHYSICIAN OR CORONER: Christopher Rogers
9. DATE SIGNED: 8-20-96
10. TYPED OR PRINTED NAME AND DEGREE/TITLE OF CERTIFIER: CHRISTOPHER B. ROGERS, M.D. DME
11. ADDRESS—STREET AND NUMBER: 1104 North Mission Road
12. CITY: Los Angeles
13. STATE: CA
14. ZIP CODE: 90033

STATE/LOCAL REGISTRAR USE ONLY

15. OFFICE OF STATE REGISTRAR OR SIGNATURE OF LOCAL REGISTRAR
16. DATE ACCEPTED FOR REGISTRATION: 08/27/1996

STATE OF CALIFORNIA, DEPARTMENT OF HEALTH SERVICES, OFFICE OF STATE REGISTRAR

This is to certify that this document is a true copy of the official record filed with the Registrar-Recorder/County Clerk.

OCT 11 1996
19-393904

CONNY B. McCORMACK
Registrar-Recorder/County Clerk

This copy not valid unless prepared on engraved border displaying the Seal and Signature of the Registrar-Recorder/County Clerk.

Certificate of Death

State of California — County of Los Angeles • Registrar-Recorder/County Clerk

State File Number: 3 199919 053911

Decedent Personal Data
- 1. Name (First): Shirley
- 2. Middle: Ann
- 3. Last (Family): Hemphill
- 4. Date of Birth: 07/01/1947
- 5. Age: 52
- 6. Sex: F
- 7. Date of Death: 12/10/1999
- 8. Hour: 0947
- 9. State of Birth: NC
- 10. Social Security No.: 239-80-7090
- 11. Military Service: No
- 12. Marital Status: Never Married
- 13. Education—Years Completed: 13
- 14. Race: Black
- 15. Hispanic: No
- 16. Usual Employer: Self Employed
- 17. Occupation: Comedian / Actress
- 18. Kind of Business: Entertainment
- 19. Years in Occupation: 25

Usual Residence
- 20. Residence: 397 Trona Ave.
- 21. City: West Covina
- 22. County: Los Angeles
- 23. Zip Code: 91793
- 24. Yrs in County: 25
- 25. State: California

Informant
- 26. Name, Relationship: William A. Hemphill, Brother
- 27. Mailing Address: 1206 Whatcoat St., Baltimore, Maryland 21207

Spouse and Parent Information
- 31. Father—First: Richard
- 33. Last: Hemphill
- 34. Birth State: NC
- 35. Mother—First: Mozella
- 37. Last (Maiden): Greenly
- 38. Birth State: NC

Disposition
- 39. Date: 12/17/1999
- 40. Place of Final Disposition: Res: William A. Hemphill, 1206 Whatcoat St., Baltimore, MD 21207
- 41. Type of Disposition: CR/RES
- 42. Signature of Embalmer: Wendi Smith
- 43. License No.: 8273
- 44. Funeral Director: Forest Lawn Mortuary-Covina
- 45. License No.: FD1150
- 47. Date: 12/15/1999

Place of Death
- 101. Place of Death: Residence
- 103. Facility: Other
- 104. County: Los Angeles
- 105. Street Address: 397 Trona Ave.
- 106. City: West Covina

Cause of Death
- 107. Immediate Cause (A): Deferred
- 108. Death Reported to Coroner: Yes — Referral Number 99-08456
- 109. Biopsy Performed: (blank)
- 110. Autopsy Performed: Yes
- 111. Used in Determining Cause: (blank)

Coroner's Use Only
- 119. Manner of Death: Pending Investigation
- 126. Signature of Coroner: Juana Garcia
- 127. Date: 12/13/1999
- 128. Typed Name: Juana Garcia/Deputy Coroner
- Fax Auth. #: 545-6822

Conny B. McCormack
Registrar-Recorder/County Clerk

OCT 0 4 200[?]
19-673783

State of California
Certification of Vital Record

COUNTY OF LOS ANGELES • REGISTRAR-RECORDER/COUNTY CLERK

Amendment of Medical and Health Data—Death

No. 0002556

PART I — Information to Locate Record
- Name: SHIRLEY ANN HEMPHILL
- Sex: F
- Date of Event: 12/10/1999
- City of Occurrence: WEST COVINA
- County of Occurrence: LOS ANGELES

PART II — Information as it Appears on Record
- Immediate Cause (A): DEFERRED (2 OF 2)
- Death Reported to Coroner: YES (Referral No. 99-08456)
- Autopsy Performed: YES
- Manner of Death: Pending Investigation

PART III — Information as it Should Appear
- Immediate Cause:
  - (A) ACUTE CARDIAC DYSFUNCTION — UNK
  - (B) HYPERTROPHIC CARDIOMYOPATHY — YEARS
- Other Significant Conditions: ACUTE PYELONEPHRITIS, FATTY LIVER, OBESITY
- Operation Performed: NO
- Death Reported to Coroner: YES (Referral No. 99-08456)
- Biopsy Performed: NO
- Autopsy Performed: YES
- Used in Determining Cause: YES
- Manner of Death: Natural

Declaration of Certifying Physician or Coroner
- Date Signed: 02/08/2000
- Certifier: PEDRO M. ORTIZ-COLON, M.D., DMB
- Address: 1104 NORTH MISSION ROAD, LOS ANGELES, CA 90033

Office of the State Registrar — Date Accepted: 03/17/2000

This is to certify that this document is a true copy of the official record filed with the Registrar-Recorder/County Clerk.

CONNY B. McCORMACK
Registrar-Recorder/County Clerk

OCT 04 2001
19-673781

This copy not valid unless prepared on engraved border displaying the Seal and Signature of the Registrar-Recorder/County Clerk.

STATE OF CALIFORNIA — CERTIFICATION OF VITAL RECORD

COUNTY OF LOS ANGELES • REGISTRAR-RECORDER/COUNTY CLERK

CERTIFICATE OF DEATH — State File Number: 3200819015410

1. Name of Decedent — First	CHARLTON
2. Middle	—
3. Last	HESTON
4. Date of Birth	10/04/1923
5. Age	84
6. Sex	M
9. Birth State/Foreign Country	ILLINOIS
10. Social Security Number	320-12-0313
11. Ever in U.S. Armed Forces?	YES
12. Marital Status	MARRIED
7. Date of Death	04/05/2008
8. Hour	1720
13. Education	SOME COLLEGE
14/15. Hispanic/Latino	NO
16. Race	CAUCASIAN
17. Usual Occupation	ACTOR
18. Kind of Business or Industry	ENTERTAINMENT
19. Years in Occupation	65
20. Decedent's Residence	2859 COLDWATER CANYON DR
21. City	BEVERLY HILLS
22. County	LOS ANGELES
23. Zip Code	90210
24. Years in County	55
25. State	CA
26. Informant's Name / Relationship	FRASER HESTON, SON
27. Informant's Mailing Address	7990 BRIAR SUMMIT DR, LOS ANGELES, CA 90046
28. Surviving Spouse — First	LYDIA
29. Middle	MARIE
30. Last (Maiden)	CLARKE
31. Father — First	RUSSEL
32. Middle	WHITFORD
33. Last	CARTER
34. Birth State	CA
35. Mother — First	LILLA
36. Middle	UNK
37. Last (Maiden)	BAINES
38. Birth State	IL
39. Disposition Date	04/09/2008
40. Place of Final Disposition	ST. MATTHEW'S EPISCOPAL CHURCH, 1031 BIENVENEDA AVE, PACIFIC PALISADES, CA 90272
41. Type of Disposition	CR/BU
42. Signature of Embalmer	NOT EMBALMED
44. Name of Funeral Establishment	PIERCE BROTHERS WESTWOOD
45. License Number	FD-951
46. Signature of Local Registrar	JONATHAN FIELDING, MD
47. Date	04/07/2008
101. Place of Death	RESIDENCE
104. County	LOS ANGELES
105. Facility Address	2859 COLDWATER CANYON DR
106. City	BEVERLY HILLS
107. Cause of Death — Immediate Cause (A)	PNEUMONIA
Interval	DAYS
108. Death Reported to Coroner?	NO
110. Autopsy Performed?	NO
112. Other Significant Conditions	NONE
113. Operation Performed?	NO
115. Signature and Title of Certifier	JAMES WILLIAM DAVIS M.D.
116. License Number	G32480
117. Date	04/07/2008
118. Attending Physician	JAMES WILLIAM DAVIS M.D., 200 MEDICAL PLAZA STE 420, LOS ANGELES, CA 90095
Decedent Attended Since	04/23/1996
Decedent Last Seen Alive	04/05/2008

INFORMATIONAL, NOT A VALID DOCUMENT TO ESTABLISH IDENTITY

This is to certify that this document is a true copy of the official record filed with the Registrar-Recorder/County Clerk.

SEP 16 2009

DEAN C. LOGAN
Registrar-Recorder/County Clerk

000004576

Certificate of Death

State of California

State File Number: 39619030574

Decedent Personal Data
- Name: DANA LYNNE GOETZ
- Date of Birth: 05/06/1964
- Age: 32
- Sex: F
- Date of Death: 07/15/1996
- Hour: 0230
- State of Birth: CA
- Social Security No: 556-78-3063
- Military Service: None
- Marital Status: NEVER MARRIED
- Education: 12
- Race: CAUCASIAN
- Usual Employer: SELF EMPLOYED
- Occupation: ACTRESS
- Kind of Business: ENTERTAINMENT
- Years in Occupation: 18

Usual Residence
- 11763 CANTON PL
- STUDIO CITY, LOS ANGELES, 91604
- Yrs in County: 32
- State: CA

Informant
- AMY L. GOETZ, SISTER
- 12205 SUMMER TIME LANE, CULVER CITY, CA 90230

Spouse and Parent Information
- Father: THEODORE A. GOETZ — Birth State: NY
- Mother: SANDRA K. HILL — Birth State: WA

Disposition(s)
- Date: 07/23/1996
- Place of Final Disposition: RES: AMY L. GOETZ, SISTER 12205 SUMMER TIME LANE, CULVER CITY, CA 90230
- Type of Disposition: CR/RES
- Signature of Embalmer: NOT EMBALMED
- Funeral Director: FOREST LAWN HOLLYWOOD HILLS — License No. F 904
- Date: 07/19/1996

Place of Death
- ST JOSEPH MED CTR (IP)
- 501 S. BUENA VISTA
- County: LOS ANGELES
- City: BURBANK

Cause of Death
- (A) Cardiopulmonary Arrest — 10 mins
- (B) Recurrent Pneumonia — 1 wk
- (C) Pontine Myelinolysis — Yrs

Other Significant Conditions: Diabetes Mellitus, Renal Failure

Operation Performed: No

Physician's Certification
- Death Occurred: 06/14/1996 to 07/14/1996
- License No: G49561
- Date: 07/16/1996
- Physician: G. Fischmann, MD 5525 Etiwanda #320, Tarzana, CA 91356

Fax Auth #: 273/38434

This is to certify that this document is a true copy of the official record filed with the Registrar-Recorder/County Clerk.

CONNY B. McCORMACK
Registrar-Recorder/County Clerk

OCT 04 2001
19-673791

Certificate of Death

State of California — Certification of Vital Record
County of Los Angeles • Registrar-Recorder/County Clerk

INFORMATIONAL, NOT A VALID DOCUMENT TO ESTABLISH IDENTITY

State File Number: 3 1998 19 007878

Decedent Personal Data
- 1. Name (First): Jonathan
- 2. Middle: F.
- 3. Last: Hole
- 4. Date of Birth: 08/13/1904
- 5. Age: 93
- 6. Sex: M
- 7. Date of Death: 02/12/1998
- 8. Hour: 0630
- 9. State of Birth: Iowa
- 10. Social Security No.: 083-03-2790
- 11. Military Service: No
- 12. Marital Status: Widowed
- 13. Education: 14
- 14. Race: Caucasian
- 15. Hispanic: No
- 16. Usual Employer: Various
- 17. Occupation: Actor
- 18. Kind of Business: Radio, Television And Film
- 19. Years in Occupation: 65

Usual Residence
- 20. Residence: 5024 Balboa Blvd.
- 21. City: Encino
- 22. County: Los Angeles
- 23. Zip Code: 91316
- 24. Yrs in County: 47
- 25. State: California

Informant
- 26. Name, Relationship: Jennifer Leonard – Daughter
- 27. Mailing Address: 686 Blue Oak Ave. Thousand Oaks, CA 91320

Spouse and Parent Information
- 28–30. Name of Surviving Spouse: –
- 31. Name of Father: Jonathan
- 32. Middle: F.
- 33. Last: Hole
- 34. Birth State: Iowa
- 35. Name of Mother: Fern
- 37. Last (Maiden): Foreman
- 38. Birth State: USA-UNK

Disposition
- 39. Date: 03/10/1998
- 40. Place of Final Disposition: Westwood Memorial Park 1218 Glendon Ave. Los Angeles, CA 90024
- 41. Type of Disposition: CR/BU
- 42. Signature of Embalmer: Not Embalmed
- 44. Name of Funeral Director: Pierce Bros. Westwood Village
- 45. License No.: FD 951
- 47. Date: 03/04/1998 SN

Place of Death
- 101. Place of Death: N. Hollywood MED CTR
- 102. ER/OP
- 104. County: Los Angeles
- 105. Street Address: 12629 Riverside Dr.
- 106. City: N. Hollywood

Cause of Death
- 107. (A) Immediate Cause: Blunt Head Trauma — Interval: 1 Day
- 108. Death Reported to Coroner: Yes — Referral No. 98-01249
- 109. Biopsy Performed: No
- 110. Autopsy Performed: No
- 111. Used in Determining Cause: No
- 112. Other Significant Conditions: None
- 113. Operation Performed: No

Coroner's Use Only
- 119. Manner of Death: Accident
- 120. Injury at Work: No
- 121. Injury Date: 02/11/1998
- 122. Hour: UNK
- 123. Place of Injury: Residence
- 124. How Injury Occurred: Fell To The Floor.
- 125. Location: 5024 Balboa Blvd. Encino, CA 91316
- 126. Signature of Coroner: Selena Barros
- 127. Date: 03/02/1998
- 128. Typed Name: SELENA BARROS, DEPUTY CORONER
- Fax Auth. #: 849-5632

State Registrar: 885

This is to certify that this document is a true copy of the official record filed with the Registrar-Recorder/County Clerk.

CONNY B. McCORMACK
Registrar-Recorder/County Clerk

JUL 22 2005

019408513

This copy not valid unless prepared on engraved border displaying the Seal and Signature of the Registrar-Recorder/County Clerk.

ANY ALTERATION OR ERASURE VOIDS THIS CERTIFICATE

Certificate of Death
State of California

State File Number: 39519049549

1. Name of Decedent—First (Given): FRED	3. Last (Family): HOLLIDAY
4. Date of Birth: 01/01/1936	5. Age Yrs.: 59
6. Sex: MALE	7. Date of Death: 11/21/1995	8. Hour: 1529
9. State of Birth: PA	10. Social Security No.: 178-26-5438
11. Military Service: None	12. Marital Status: MARRIED	13. Education—Years Completed: 13
14. Race: WHITE	15. Hispanic: No	16. Usual Employer: SELF EMPLOYED
17. Occupation: ACTOR	18. Kind of Business: ENTERTAINMENT	19. Years in Occupation: 40
20. Residence: 4610 FORMAN AVENUE	
21. City: TOLUCA LAKE	22. County: LOS ANGELES	23. Zip Code: 91602	24. Yrs in County: 35	25. State: CALIFORNIA
26. Name, Relationship: JUDY HOLLIDAY - WIFE	27. Mailing Address: 4610 FORMAN AVENUE, TOLUCA LAKE, CA 91602
28. Name of Surviving Spouse—First: JUDY	30. Last (Maiden Name): KAPLER
31. Name of Father—First: SAMUEL	33. Last: GROSSINGER	34. Birth State: AUSTRIA
35. Name of Mother—First: ESTHER	37. Last (Maiden): MARTIN	38. Birth State: PA
39. Date: 11/24/1995	40. Place of Final Disposition: MOUNT SINAI MEMORIAL PARK 5950 FOREST LAWN DRIVE, L.A., CA 90068
41. Type of Disposition: BURIAL	42. Signature of Embalmer: NOT EMBALMED
44. Name of Funeral Director: MOUNT SINAI MORTUARY	45. License No.: FD-1010	47. Date: 11/24/1995
101. Place of Death: NORTHRIDGE HOSPITAL MED. CENTER	102. ER/OP	104. County: LOS ANGELES
105. Street Address: 18300 ROSCOE BLVD.	106. City: NORTHRIDGE

107. Death was caused by:
- (A) Immediate Cause: ARTERIOSCLEROTIC CARDIOVASCULAR DISEASE — Time Interval: UNK

108. Death Reported to Coroner: Yes — Referral Number: 95-09127
109. Biopsy Performed: No
110. Autopsy Performed: No

112. Other Significant Conditions: NONE
113. Was Operation Performed: No

119. Manner of Death: NATURAL

126. Signature of Coroner: Leilana Aranda
127. Date: 11/23/1995
128. Typed Name: LEILANA ARANDA, DEP. CORONER

STATE OF CALIFORNIA
CERTIFICATION OF VITAL RECORD
COUNTY OF LOS ANGELES • REGISTRAR-RECORDER/COUNTY CLERK

CERTIFICATE OF DEATH — 7097-039671

DECEDENT PERSONAL DATA
- 1A. Name (First): EDWARD
- 1B. Middle: EVERETT
- 1C. Last: HORTON
- 2A. Date of Death: September 29, 1970
- 2B. Hour: 3:00 A.M.
- 3. Sex: Male
- 4. Color or Race: Caucasian
- 5. Birthplace: New York
- 6. Date of Birth: March 18, 1886
- 7. Age (last birthday): 84 years
- 8. Name and Birthplace of Father: Edward Everett Horton — Maryland
- 9. Maiden Name and Birthplace of Mother: Isabella D. Matanzas — Cuba
- 10. Citizen of What Country: USA
- 11. Social Security Number: 564-16-7787
- 12. Married, Never Married, Widowed, Divorced: Never Married
- 13. Name of Surviving Spouse: ---
- 14. Last Occupation: Actor
- 15. Number of Years in This Occupation: 63
- 16. Name of Last Employing Company or Firm: Self Employed
- 17. Kind of Industry or Business: Entertainment

PLACE OF DEATH
- 18A. Place of Death: None
- 18B. Street Address: 5521 Edward Everett Horton Lane
- 18C. Inside City Corporate Limits: Yes
- 18D. City or Town: Encino
- 18E. County: Los Angeles
- 18F. Length of Stay in County of Death: 64 years
- 18G. Length of Stay in California: 64 years

USUAL RESIDENCE
- 19A. Street Address: 5521 Edward Everett Horton Lane
- 19B. Inside City Corporate Limits: Yes
- 19C. City or Town: Encino
- 19D. County: Los Angeles
- 19E. State: California
- 20. Name and Mailing Address of Informant: Isabella H. Grant — Niece, P.O. Box 6, Encino, California

PHYSICIAN'S OR CORONER'S CERTIFICATION
- 21A. Coroner — From: 2/14/66 To: 9/29/70
- 21B. Physician — 9/28/70
- 21D. Date Signed: 9/29/70
- 21E. Address: 16550 Ventura, Encino, Ca.
- 21F. Physician's California License Number: G4269

FUNERAL DIRECTOR AND LOCAL REGISTRAR
- 22A. Specify Burial, Entombment or Cremation: Burial
- 22B. Date: 10-1-70
- 23. Name of Cemetery or Crematory: Forest Lawn Memorial Park
- 24. Embalmer — Signature: Fredric McPhillips, License 4801
- 25. Name of Funeral Director: Forest Lawn Memorial Park, Glendale, California
- 28. Date Accepted for Registration: OCT 1 1970

CAUSE OF DEATH
- 29. Part I. Death was caused by:
  - (A) Immediate Cause: Cancer of prostate — 1 yr.
- 30. Part II. Other Significant Conditions: none
- 32A. Autopsy: no

STATE REGISTRAR
F. 1591

This is to certify that this document is a true copy of the official record filed with the Registrar-Recorder/County Clerk.

CONNY B. McCORMACK
Registrar-Recorder/County Clerk

NOV 2 8 2000
19-113368

This copy not valid unless prepared on engraved border displaying the Seal and Signature of the Registrar-Recorder/County Clerk.

ANY ALTERATION OR ERASURE VOIDS THIS CERTIFICATE

COUNTY OF RIVERSIDE
RIVERSIDE, CALIFORNIA

CERTIFICATE OF DEATH — STATE OF CALIFORNIA

State File Number: 3200733002627

1. Name of Decedent — First (Given)	BETTY
2. Middle	-
3. Last (Family)	HUTTON
AKA	-
4. Date of Birth	02/26/1921
5. Age	86 Yrs.
6. Sex	F
9. Birth State/Foreign Country	MI
10. Social Security Number	377-12-9280
11. Ever in U.S. Armed Forces?	NO
12. Marital Status	DIVORCED
7. Date of Death	03/12/2007
8. Hour (24 Hours)	0015
13. Education	DOCTORATE
14/15. Hispanic/Latino?	NO
16. Decedent's Race	WHITE
17. Usual Occupation	ACTRESS AND SINGER
18. Kind of Business or Industry	ENTERTAINMENT
19. Years in Occupation	33
20. Decedent's Residence	2080 S. CAMINO REAL #6
21. City	PALM SPRINGS
22. County/Province	RIVERSIDE
23. Zip Code	92264
24. Years in County	7
25. State/Foreign Country	CA
26. Informant's Name, Relationship	CARL BRUNO, DPOA
27. Informant's Mailing Address	915 ALTA CRESTA, PALM SPRINGS, CA 92262
28. Name of Surviving Spouse — First	-
31. Name of Father — First	PERCY
33. Last	THORNBURG
34. Birth State	NE
35. Name of Mother — First	MABEL
37. Last (Maiden)	LUX
38. Birth State	NE
39. Disposition Date	03/13/2007
40. Place of Final Disposition	DESERT MEMORIAL PARK, 31705 DA VALL DRIVE, CATHEDRAL CITY, CA 92234
41. Type of Disposition	BURIAL
42. Signature of Embalmer	NOT EMBALMED
44. Name of Funeral Establishment	FOREST LAWN CATHEDRAL CITY
45. License Number	FD 1847
46. Signature of Local Registrar	ERIC K. FRYKMAN, M.D.
47. Date	03/13/2007
101. Place of Death	RESIDENCE
103. If Other Than Hospital	Decedent's Home
104. County	RIVERSIDE
105. Facility Address	2080 S. CAMINO REAL #6
106. City	PALM SPRINGS
107. Cause of Death (A) Immediate Cause	RESPIRATORY ARREST — MINS.
(B)	PLEURAL EFFUSIONS — WKS.
(C)	METASTATIC BREAST CANCER — MOS.
108. Death Reported to Coroner?	YES — 2007-01893
109. Biopsy Performed?	NO
110. Autopsy Performed?	NO
112. Other Significant Conditions	ANEMIA, BONE PAIN, WEIGHT LOSS
113. Was Operation Performed	NO
113. If Female, Pregnant in Last Year?	NO
114. Decedent Attended Since	06/18/2004
Decedent Last Seen Alive	03/02/2007
116. Signature and Title of Certifier	DAVID NEUMANN, M.D.
118. License Number	G27957
117. Date	03/12/2007
118. Type Attending Physician's Name, Mailing Address	DAVID NEUMANN, M.D., 1180 N. INDIAN CANYON DRIVE #E314, PALM SPRINGS, CA 92262

Barcode: *01200700044 1969*

CERTIFIED COPY OF VITAL RECORDS
STATE OF CALIFORNIA, COUNTY OF RIVERSIDE

0 3 3 8 5 7 4 5 0

This is a true and exact reproduction of the document officially registered and placed on file in the office of the County of Riverside, County Clerk-Recorder.

DATE ISSUED: MAY 29 2008

LARRY W. WARD
ASSESSOR-COUNTY CLERK-RECORDER
RIVERSIDE COUNTY, CALIFORNIA

This copy is not valid unless prepared on engraved border displaying date, seal and signature of the County Clerk-Recorder.

INFORMATIONAL, NOT A VALID DOCUMENT TO ESTABLISH IDENTITY

STATE OF CALIFORNIA — CERTIFICATION OF VITAL RECORD

COUNTY OF LOS ANGELES • REGISTRAR-RECORDER/COUNTY CLERK

CERTIFICATE OF DEATH — State File Number: 3200919027107

DECEDENT'S PERSONAL DATA
- Name: MICHAEL JOSEPH JACKSON
- Date of Birth: 08/29/1958
- Age: 50
- Sex: M
- Birth State: IN
- Social Security Number: 303-62-5728
- Ever in U.S. Armed Forces: No
- Marital Status: DIVORCED
- Date of Death: 06/25/2009
- Hour: 1426
- Education: HS GRADUATE
- Hispanic/Latino: No
- Race: BLACK
- Usual Occupation: MUSICIAN
- Kind of Business/Industry: ENTERTAINMENT
- Years in Occupation: 45

USUAL RESIDENCE
- Street: 4641 HAYVENHURST AVENUE
- City: ENCINO
- County: LOS ANGELES
- Zip Code: 91436
- Years in County: 35
- State: CA

INFORMANT
- Name/Relationship: LATOYA JACKSON, SISTER
- Mailing Address: 8306 WILSHIRE BLVD, SUITE 528, BEVERLY HILLS, CA 90211

SPOUSE AND PARENT INFORMATION
- Name of Father: JOSEPH WALTER JACKSON — Birth State: AR
- Name of Mother: KATHERINE ESTHER SCRUSE — Birth State: AL

FUNERAL DIRECTOR / LOCAL REGISTRAR
- Disposition Date: 07/07/2009
- Place of Final Disposition: FOREST LAWN MEMORIAL PARK, 6300 FOREST LAWN DRIVE, LOS ANGELES, CA 90068
- Type of Disposition: TEMP
- Signature of Embalmer: JESUS MIGUEL RUIZ
- License Number: 8473
- Name of Funeral Establishment: FOREST LAWN MEMR PRKS & MTYS
- License Number: FD 904
- Signature of Local Registrar: JONATHAN FIELDING, MD
- Date: 07/07/2009

PLACE OF DEATH
- Place of Death: RONALD REAGAN/UCLA MEDICAL CENTER
- ER/OP
- County: LOS ANGELES
- Facility Address: 757 WESTWOOD PLAZA DRIVE
- City: LOS ANGELES

CAUSE OF DEATH
- Immediate Cause (A): DEFERRED
- Death Reported to Coroner: Yes — Referral Number: 2009-04415
- Biopsy Performed: No
- Autopsy Performed: Yes
- Used in Determining Cause: Yes

CORONER'S USE ONLY
- Signature of Coroner/Deputy Coroner: CHERYL MACWILLIE
- Date: 07/07/2009
- Type Name/Title: CHERYL MACWILLIE, DEPUTY CORONER

This is to certify that this document is a true copy of the official record filed with the Registrar-Recorder/County Clerk.

JAN 0 4 2010

Dean C. Logan
DEAN C. LOGAN
Registrar-Recorder/County Clerk

000179258

STATE OF CALIFORNIA — CERTIFICATION OF VITAL RECORD

COUNTY OF LOS ANGELES • REGISTRAR-RECORDER/COUNTY CLERK

PHYSICIAN/CORONER'S AMENDMENT
NO ERASURES, WHITEOUTS, PHOTOCOPIES, OR ALTERATIONS

STATE FILE NUMBER: 3052009085414
LOCAL REGISTRATION NUMBER: 3200919027107
1.1

☐ BIRTH ☒ DEATH ☐ FETAL DEATH

TYPE OR PRINT CLEARLY IN BLACK INK ONLY – THIS AMENDMENT BECOMES AN ACTUAL PART OF THE OFFICIAL RECORD

PART I — INFORMATION TO LOCATE RECORD

INFORMATION AS IT APPEARS ON ORIGINAL RECORD

1A NAME—FIRST	1B MIDDLE	1C LAST	2 SEX
MICHAEL	JOSEPH	JACKSON	M

3 DATE OF EVENT—MM/DD/CCYY	4 CITY OF EVENT	5 COUNTY OF EVENT
06/25/2009	LOS ANGELES	LOS ANGELES

PART II — STATEMENT OF CORRECTIONS

LIST ONE ITEM PER LINE

6 CERTIFICATE ITEM NUMBER	7 INFORMATION AS IT APPEARS ON ORIGINAL RECORD	8 INFORMATION AS IT SHOULD APPEAR
107A	DEFERRED	ACUTE PROPOFOL INTOXICATION
107AT	-	UNKNOWN
112	-	BENZODIAZEPINE EFFECT
119	--	HOMICIDE
120		NO
121		06/25/2009
122		UNK
123		RESIDENCE
124		INTRAVENOUS INJECTION BY ANOTHER
125		100 NORTH CAROLWOOD DRIVE, LOS ANGELES, CA 90077

2 of 2

DECLARATION OF CERTIFYING PHYSICIAN OR CORONER

I HEREBY DECLARE UNDER PENALTY OF PERJURY THAT THE ABOVE INFORMATION IS TRUE AND CORRECT TO THE BEST OF MY KNOWLEDGE.

9 SIGNATURE OF CERTIFYING PHYSICIAN OR CORONER	10 DATE SIGNED—MM/DD/CCYY	11 TYPED OR PRINTED NAME AND TITLE/DEGREE OF CERTIFIER
► CHRISTOPHER ROGERS MD	08/31/2009	DME

12 ADDRESS—STREET and NUMBER	13 CITY	14 STATE	15 ZIP CODE
1104 NORTH MISSION ROAD	LOS ANGELES	CA	90033

STATE/LOCAL REGISTRAR USE ONLY

16 OFFICE OF VITAL RECORDS OR LOCAL REGISTRAR	17 DATE ACCEPTED FOR REGISTRATION—MM/DD/CCYY
► STATE REGISTRAR - OFFICE OF VITAL RECORDS	08/31/2009

STATE OF CALIFORNIA, DEPARTMENT OF PUBLIC HEALTH, OFFICE OF VITAL RECORDS
020101001301749
FORM VS 24Ae (REV. 1/08)
1.1

INFORMATIONAL, NOT A VALID DOCUMENT TO ESTABLISH IDENTITY

This is to certify that this document is a true copy of the official record filed with the Registrar-Recorder/County Clerk.

JAN 0 4 2018

DEAN C. LOGAN
Registrar-Recorder/County Clerk

This copy not valid unless prepared on engraved border displaying the Seal and Signature of the Registrar-Recorder/County Clerk.

000179259

ANY ALTERATION OR ERASURE VOIDS THIS CERTIFICATE

COUNTY OF LOS ANGELES
DEPARTMENT OF HEALTH SERVICES
CERTIFICATE OF DEATH
STATE OF CALIFORNIA

1. Name of Decedent—First (Given)	Brion
2. Middle	Howard
3. Last (Family)	James
4. Date of Birth	02/20/1945
5. Age Yrs.	54
6. Sex	M
7. Date of Death	08/07/1999
8. Hour	0638
9. State of Birth	CA
10. Social Security No.	557-48-4826
11. Military Service	X Yes
12. Marital Status	Divorced
13. Education—Years Completed	16
14. Race	White
15. Hispanic—Specify	X No
16. Usual Employer	Self-employed
17. Occupation	Actor
18. Kind of Business	Film Industry
19. Years in Occupation	27
20. Residence	6135 Bonsall Road
21. City	Malibu
22. County	Los Angeles
23. Zip Code	90265
24. Yrs in County	12
25. State or Foreign Country	CA
26. Name, Relationship	Chester L. James, Jr. (Brother)
27. Mailing Address	123 W. 12th St., Beaumont, CA 92223
31. Name of Father—First	Chester
32. Middle	Leroy
33. Last	James
34. Birth State	PA
35. Name of Mother—First	Ida
36. Middle	Mae
37. Last (Maiden)	Buckelew
38. Birth State	OK
39. Date	08/10/1999
40. Place of Final Disposition	Mt. View Cemetery 1315 Edgar Ave Beaumont CA
41. Type of Disposition(s)	CR/BU
42. Signature of Embalmer	Not embalmed
44. Name of Funeral Director	Weaver Mortuary - Beaumont
45. License No.	FD-644
47. Date	08/10/1999
101. Place of Death	U.C.L.A. Medical Center
102. If Hospital, Specify One	X IP
104. County	Los Angeles
105. Street Address	10833 LeConte Ave.
106. City	Los Angeles

107. Death Was Caused By:

	Cause	Time Interval
Immediate Cause (A)	Acute Myocardial Infarction	1 hr
Due to (B)	Hypertensive Heart Disease	5 yrs
Due to (C)	Essential Hypertension	10 yrs

108. Death Reported to Coroner: X No
109. Biopsy Performed: X No
110. Autopsy Performed: X No

112. Other Significant Conditions: None
113. Was Operation Performed: No

114. Decedent Attended Since: 01/01/1995 — Last Seen Alive: 08/05/1999
116. License No. G7277
117. Date: 08/07/1999
118. Type Attending Physician's Name: Robert Karns, MD 8920 Wilshire Blvd Beverly Hills CA 90211

Census Tract 090261093

This is a true certified copy of the record filed in the County of Los Angeles Department of Health Services if it bears the Registrar's signature in purple ink.

263 DATE ISSUED AUG 25 1999

Director of Health Service and Registrar

This copy not valid unless prepared on engraved border displaying seal and signature of Registrar.

STATE OF CALIFORNIA — CERTIFICATION OF VITAL RECORD
COUNTY OF RIVERSIDE
RIVERSIDE, CALIFORNIA

CERTIFICATE OF DEATH
State File Number: 3 1997 33 004715

DECEDENT PERSONAL DATA
- 1. Name (First): DENNIS
- 2. Middle: —
- 3. Last (Family): JAMES
- 4. Date of Birth: 08/24/1917
- 5. Age: 79
- 6. Sex: M
- 7. Date of Death: 06/03/1997
- 8. Hour: 2230
- 9. State of Birth: NJ
- 10. Social Security No.: 152-05-9249
- 11. Military Service: YES
- 12. Marital Status: MAR
- 13. Education—Years Completed: 17
- 14. Race: WHITE
- 15. Hispanic: No
- 16. Usual Employer: SELF EMPLOYED
- 17. Occupation: ENTERTAINER
- 18. Kind of Business: TELEVISION
- 19. Years in Occupation: 59

USUAL RESIDENCE
- 20. Street: 3581 CARIBETH DRIVE
- 21. City: ENCINO
- 22. County: LOS ANGELES
- 23. Zip Code: 91436
- 24. Yrs in County: 35
- 25. State: CA

INFORMANT
- 26. Name, Relationship: MARJORIE JAMES, WIFE
- 27. Mailing Address: 3581 CARIBETH DRIVE, ENCINO, CA 91436

SPOUSE AND PARENT INFORMATION
- 28. Name of Surviving Spouse—First: MARJORIE
- 30. Last (Maiden Name): CRAWFORD
- 31. Name of Father—First: DEMETRIO
- 33. Last: SPOSA
- 34. Birth State: IT
- 35. Name of Mother—First: THERESA
- 37. Last (Maiden): AMOROSI
- 38. Birth State: NY

DISPOSITION(S)
- 39. Date: 06/04/1997
- 40. Place of Final Disposition: FOREST LAWN HOLLYWOOD HILLS, 6300 FOREST LAWN DRIVE, LOS ANGELES, CA
- 41. Type of Disposition(s): CR/BU
- 42. Signature of Embalmer: NOT EMBALMED
- 44. Name of Funeral Director: PALM SPRINGS MORTUARY, CATHEDRAL CITY
- 45. License No.: FD1513
- 47. Date: 06/04/1997

PLACE OF DEATH
- 101. Place of Death: RESIDENCE
- 104. County: RIVERSIDE
- 105. Street Address: 742 INVERNESS DRIVE
- 106. City: RANCHO MIRAGE

CAUSE OF DEATH
- 107(A) Immediate Cause: CARDIOPULMONARY ARREST — MINS
- 107(B) Due to: RESPIRATORY FAILURE — DAYS
- 107(C) Due to: ADENOCARCINOMA OF LUNG — MONS
- 107(D) Due to: CARCINOMA OF LUNG — MONS
- 108. Death Reported to Coroner: YES — Referral Number 9712949
- 109. Biopsy Performed: YES
- 110. Autopsy Performed: NO
- 112. Other Significant Conditions: NONE
- 113. Was Operation Performed: NO

PHYSICIAN'S CERTIFICATION
- 114. Decedent Attended Since: 01/31/1997; Last Seen Alive: 06/03/1997
- 116. License No.: G4006
- 117. Date: 06/03/1997
- 118. Attending Physician: JOEL HIRSCHBERG M.D., 39000 BOB HOPE DRIVE, RANCHO MIRAGE, CA 92270

Fax Auth. #: 163549

STATE OF CALIFORNIA, COUNTY OF RIVERSIDE
This is a true and exact reproduction of the document officially registered and placed on file in the office of County of Riverside, Department of Health.

Date Issued: 09/10/1997

Gary Feldman M.D.
Local Registrar
RIVERSIDE COUNTY, CALIFORNIA

STATE OF CALIFORNIA
CERTIFICATION OF VITAL RECORD

COUNTY OF LOS ANGELES • REGISTRAR-RECORDER/COUNTY CLERK

CERTIFICATE OF DEATH — STATE OF CALIFORNIA

State File Number: 3 2003 19 018737

1. NAME OF DECEDENT — FIRST: MICHAEL
2. MIDDLE: —
3. LAST: JETER
4. DATE OF BIRTH: 08/26/1952
5. AGE: 50
6. SEX: M
7. DATE OF DEATH: 03/30/2003
8. HOUR: 1640
9. BIRTH STATE: TN
10. SOCIAL SECURITY NUMBER: 412-94-7652
11. EVER IN U.S. ARMED FORCES?: UNK
12. MARITAL STATUS: NEVER MARRIED
13. EDUCATION: BACHELOR'S
14/15. HISPANIC: NO
16. RACE: WHITE
17. USUAL OCCUPATION: ACTOR
18. KIND OF BUSINESS OR INDUSTRY: ENTERTAINMENT
19. YEARS IN OCCUPATION: 30
20. DECEDENT'S RESIDENCE: 2300 CASTILIAN DR
21. CITY: LOS ANGELES
22. COUNTY: LOS ANGELES
23. ZIP CODE: 90068
24. YEARS IN COUNTY: 12
25. STATE: CA
26. INFORMANT'S NAME, RELATIONSHIP: BRIAN BLUE, FRIEND
27. INFORMANT'S MAILING ADDRESS: 3410 W VIEWMONT WAY W SEATTLE WA 98199
31. NAME OF FATHER — FIRST: WILLIAM
33. LAST: JETER
34. BIRTH STATE: TN
35. NAME OF MOTHER — FIRST: VIRGINIA
37. LAST (Maiden): RAINES
38. BIRTH STATE: TN
39. DISPOSITION DATE: 04/08/2003
40. PLACE OF FINAL DISPOSITION: RESIDENCE, SEAN BLUE. 2300 CASTILIAN DR LOS ANGELES CA 90068
41. TYPE OF DISPOSITION: CR/RES
42. SIGNATURE OF EMBALMER: NOT EMBALMED
44. NAME OF FUNERAL ESTABLISHMENT: FOREST LAWN HOLLYWOOD HILLS
45. LICENSE NUMBER: FD 904
47. DATE: 04/07/2003

101. PLACE OF DEATH: RESIDENCE
103. IF OTHER THAN HOSPITAL: Decedent's Home
104. COUNTY: LOS ANGELES
105. FACILITY ADDRESS OR LOCATION WHERE FOUND: 2300 CASTILIAN DRIVE
106. CITY: LOS ANGELES

107. CAUSE OF DEATH:
IMMEDIATE CAUSE (A): DEFERRED

108. DEATH REPORTED TO CORONER: YES
REFERRAL NUMBER: 2003-02506
109. BIOPSY PERFORMED?: —
110. AUTOPSY PERFORMED?: NO

120. MANNER OF DEATH: Pending Investigation

127. DATE: 04/02/2003
128. TYPE NAME, TITLE OF CORONER / DEPUTY CORONER: BRYAN HILL DEPUTY CORONER

FAX AUTH #: 273/7059

This is to certify that this document is a true copy of the official record filed with the Registrar-Recorder/County Clerk.

CONNY B. McCORMACK
Registrar-Recorder/County Clerk

OCT 27 2003

190249592

STATE OF CALIFORNIA
CERTIFICATION OF VITAL RECORD

COUNTY OF LOS ANGELES • REGISTRAR-RECORDER/COUNTY CLERK

AMENDMENT OF MEDICAL AND HEALTH DATA—DEATH

STATE FILE NUMBER: 3 052003 102054
LOCAL REGISTRATION DISTRICT AND CERTIFICATE NUMBER: 3200319018737 / 03-010434

PART I — INFORMATION TO LOCATE RECORD

1. NAME—FIRST (GIVEN): MICHAEL
2. MIDDLE:
3. LAST (FAMILY): JETER
4. SEX: M
5. DATE OF EVENT: 03/30/2003
6. CITY OF OCCURRENCE: LOS ANGELES
7. COUNTY OF OCCURRENCE: LOS ANGELES

PART II — INFORMATION AS IT APPEARS ON RECORD

107. DEATH WAS CAUSED BY:
- IMMEDIATE CAUSE (A): DEFERRED
- (B):
- (C):
- DUE TO (D):

2 of 2

108. DEATH REPORTED TO CORONER: YES — REFERRAL NUMBER 2003-02506
109. BIOPSY PERFORMED:
110. AUTOPSY PERFORMED:
111. USED IN DETERMINING CAUSE:

112. OTHER SIGNIFICANT CONDITIONS CONTRIBUTING TO DEATH BUT NOT RELATED TO CAUSE GIVEN IN 107:
113. WAS OPERATION PERFORMED FOR ANY CONDITION IN ITEM 107 or 112?
119. MANNER OF DEATH: [X] PENDING INVESTIGATION
120. INJURY AT WORK:
121. INJURY DATE:
122. HOUR:
123. PLACE OF INJURY:
124. DESCRIBE HOW INJURY OCCURRED:
125. LOCATION:

PART III — INFORMATION AS IT SHOULD APPEAR

107. DEATH WAS CAUSED BY:
- IMMEDIATE CAUSE (A): MULTIPLE DRUG INTOXICATION
- (B):
- (C):
- DUE TO (D):

TIME INTERVAL BETWEEN ONSET AND DEATH: UNK
108. DEATH REPORTED TO CORONER: [X] YES — REFERRAL NUMBER 2003-02506
109. BIOPSY PERFORMED: [X] NO
110. AUTOPSY PERFORMED: [X] NO
111. USED IN DETERMINING CAUSE: [X] NO

112. OTHER SIGNIFICANT CONDITIONS CONTRIBUTING TO DEATH BUT NOT RELATED TO CAUSE GIVEN IN 107: IDIOPATHIC EPILEPSY
113. WAS OPERATION PERFORMED FOR ANY CONDITION IN ITEM 107 or 112? NO
119. MANNER OF DEATH: [X] ACCIDENT
120. INJURY AT WORK: [X] NO
121. INJURY DATE: UNKNOWN
122. HOUR: UNK
123. PLACE OF INJURY: UNKNOWN
124. DESCRIBE HOW INJURY OCCURRED: INTAKE OF DRUGS
125. LOCATION: UNKNOWN

DECLARATION OF CERTIFYING PHYSICIAN OR CORONER

8. SIGNATURE OF CERTIFYING PHYSICIAN OR CORONER: Louis A. Pena
9. DATE SIGNED: 06/27/2003
10. TYPED OR PRINTED NAME AND DEGREE/TITLE OF CERTIFIER: LOUIS A. PENA, M.D. DME
11. ADDRESS: 1104 N. MISSION ROAD
12. CITY: LOS ANGELES
13. STATE: CA
14. ZIP CODE: 90033

15. OFFICE OF STATE REGISTRAR OR SIGNATURE OF LOCAL REGISTRAR: OFFICE OF STATE REGISTRAR OF VITAL STATISTICS
16. DATE ACCEPTED FOR REGISTRATION: 10/09/2003

This is to certify that this document is a true copy of the official record filed with the Registrar-Recorder/County Clerk.

CONNY B. McCORMACK
Registrar-Recorder/County Clerk

OCT 27 2003

190249389

COUNTY OF LOS ANGELES
DEPARTMENT OF HEALTH SERVICES
CERTIFICATE OF DEATH
STATE OF CALIFORNIA

1. Name of Decedent—First (Given)	HENRY
2. Middle	BURK
3. Last (Family)	JONES
4. Date of Birth	08/01/1912
5. Age Yrs.	86
6. Sex	M
7. Date of Death	05/17/1999
8. Hour	1620
9. State of Birth	PA
10. Social Security No.	204-07-0821
11. Military Service	X Yes
12. Marital Status	DIVORCED
13. Education—Years Completed	16
14. Race	CAUCASIAN
15. Hispanic—Specify	X No
16. Usual Employer	SELF-EMPLOYED
17. Occupation	ACTOR
18. Kind of Business	ENTERTAINMENT
19. Years in Occupation	65
20. Residence	502 9TH ST.
21. City	SANTA MONICA
22. County	LOS ANGELES
23. Zip Code	90402
24. Yrs in County	36
25. State or Foreign Country	CA
26. Name, Relationship	JOCELYN JONES WATKINS/DAUGHTER
27. Mailing Address	502 9TH ST. SANTA MONICA, CA 90402
28. Name of Surviving Spouse—First	—
29. Middle	—
30. Last (Maiden Name)	—
31. Name of Father—First	JOHN
32. Middle	FRANCES XAVIER
33. Last	JONES
34. Birth State	PA
35. Name of Mother—First	HELEN
36. Middle	REGINA
37. Last (Maiden)	BURK
38. Birth State	PA
39. Date	05/21/1999
40. Place of Final Disposition	RES:JOCELYN JONES WATKINS-502 9TH ST. SANTA MONICA, CA 90402
41. Type of Disposition(s)	CR/RES
42. Signature of Embalmer	NOT EMBALMED
43. License No.	—
44. Name of Funeral Director	THE ALPHA SOCIETY, INC.
45. License No.	FD-1274
47. Date	05/21/1999
101. Place of Death	UCLA MEDICAL CENTER
102. If Hospital, Specify One	X IP
104. County	Los Angeles
105. Street Address	10833 LeConte Avenue
106. City	Los Angeles

107. Death Was Caused By:
- (A) Immediate Cause: PNEUMONIA — days
- (B) Due to: EMPHYSEMA — years
- (C) Due to: INTERSTITIAL PULMONARY FIBROSIS — years

108. Death Reported to Coroner: X Yes — Referral Number 99-03524
109. Biopsy Performed: X No
110. Autopsy Performed: X Yes
111. Used in Determining Cause: X Yes

112. Other Significant Conditions: Fall with Minor Head Trauma
113. Was Operation Performed: No

120. Injury at Work: X No
121. Injury Date: 05/14/1999
122. Hour: 0320
123. Place of Injury: Residence
124. Describe How Injury Occurred: Fall at residence
125. Location: 502 9th St. Santa Monica, CA 90402
126. Signature of Coroner: Michael C Fishbein, MD
127. Date: 05/20/1999
128. Typed Name: Michael C. Fishbein, Deputy Coroner

Manner of Death: X Accident

Fax Auth. #: 135/9810
Census Tract: 090240463

This is a true certified copy of the record filed in the County of Los Angeles Department of Health Services if it bears the Registrar's signature in purple ink.

Director of Health Service and Registrar

This copy not valid unless prepared on engraved border displaying seal and signature of Registrar.

CERTIFICATION OF VITAL RECORD

COUNTY OF LOS ANGELES • REGISTRAR-RECORDER/COUNTY CLERK

CERTIFICATE OF DEATH
STATE OF CALIFORNIA—DEPARTMENT OF PUBLIC HEALTH

Local Registration District: 7013
Certificate Number: 18333

DECEDENT PERSONAL DATA
- 1a. Name of Deceased—First Name: LINDLEY (Aka: Spike)
- 1b. Middle Name: ARMSTRONG
- 1c. Last Name: JONES
- 2a. Date of Death: MAY 1, 1965
- 2b. Hour: 3:15 A.M.
- 3. Sex: Male
- 4. Color or Race: Cauc.
- 5. Birthplace: California
- 6. Date of Birth: December 14, 1911
- 7. Age: 53 years
- 8. Name and Birthplace of Father: Lindley M. Jones, Iowa
- 9. Maiden Name and Birthplace of Mother: Ada Armstrong, Iowa
- 10. Citizen of What Country: USA
- 11. Social Security Number: 561-09-1728
- 12. Last Occupation: Orchestra Leader
- 13. Number of Years in this Occupation: 30
- 14. Name of Last Employing Company or Firm: Self-employed
- 15. Kind of Industry or Business: Music-entertainment
- 16. If Deceased Was Ever in U.S. Armed Forces: No
- 17. Never Married, Widowed, Divorced: Married
- 18a. Name of Present Spouse: Helen Grayco
- 18b. Present or Last Occupation of Spouse: Vocalist

PLACE OF DEATH
- 19b. Street Address: 409 North Martin Lane
- 19c. City or Town: Beverly Hills
- 19d. County: Los Angeles
- 19e. Length of Stay in County of Death: Life
- 19f. Length of Stay in California: Life

LAST USUAL RESIDENCE
- 20a. Last Usual Residence—Street Address: 409 North Martin Lane
- 20b. Inside City Corporate Limits: (checked)
- 20c. City or Town: Beverly Hills 8713
- 20d. County: Los Angeles
- 20e. State: California

PHYSICIAN'S OR CORONER'S CERTIFICATION
- 22a. Physician: attended deceased from 1957 to May 1, 1965, last saw alive May 1, 1965
- 22c. Physician—Signature: Joseph A Schwartz M.D.
- 22d. Address: 9600 Wilshire Blvd Los Angeles
- 22e. Date Signed: May 3, 1965

FUNERAL DIRECTOR AND LOCAL REGISTRAR
- 23. Specify Burial, Entombment or Cremation: Entombment
- 24. Date: 5-4-65
- 25. Name of Cemetery or Crematory: Holy Cross Mausoleum
- 26. Embalmer—Signature: Roy L. Logan
- License Number: 4927
- 27. Name of Funeral Director: CALLANAN MORTUARY
- 28. Date Accepted for Registration: MAY 4 1965

CAUSE OF DEATH
- 30. Death was caused by:
  - Immediate Cause (a): Hypercarbondioxide emia with respiratory insufficiency — 1 month
  - Due to (b): Pulmonary emphysema and Cor pulmonale — 5 yrs
  - Due to (c): Bronchial asthma — 33 yrs

OPERATION AND AUTOPSY
- 31. Operation: No operation performed (checked)
- 33. Autopsy: No autopsy performed (checked)

Filed MAY 28 1965 RAY E. LEE, COUNTY RECORDER

This is to certify that this document is a true copy of the official record filed with the Registrar-Recorder/County Clerk.

Beatriz Valdez
BEATRIZ VALDEZ
Registrar-Recorder/County Clerk

AUG 10 1995
19-389279

This copy not valid unless prepared on engraved border displaying the Seal and Signature of the Registrar-Recorder/County Clerk.

STATE OF CALIFORNIA
CERTIFICATION OF VITAL RECORD
COUNTY OF LOS ANGELES • REGISTRAR-RECORDER/COUNTY CLERK

CERTIFICATE OF DEATH — 7097-043582

DECEDENT PERSONAL DATA
- 1A. Name (First): Janis
- 1B. Middle: Lyn
- 1C. Last: Joplin
- 2A. Date of Death: October 4, 1970
- 2B. Hour: 2110 hrs.
- 3. Sex: Female
- 4. Color or Race: Caucasian
- 5. Birthplace: Texas
- 6. Date of Birth: Jan 19, 1943
- 7. Age: 27 years
- 8. Name and Birthplace of Father: Seth Ward – Texas
- 9. Maiden Name and Birthplace of Mother: Dorothy Bonita East – Oklahoma
- 10. Citizen of What Country: USA
- 11. Social Security Number: Unknown
- 12. Married, Never Married, Widowed, Divorced: Never Married
- 14. Last Occupation: Singer
- 15. Number of Years in This Occupation: 15
- 16. Name of Last Employing Company or Firm: Self-Employed
- 17. Kind of Industry or Business: Entertainment

AMENDED 1 OF

PLACE OF DEATH
- 18B. Street Address: 7047 Franklin Avenue, Apt. 105
- 18C. Inside City Corporate Limits: Yes
- 18D. City or Town: Los Angeles
- 18E. County: Los Angeles
- 18F. Length of Stay in County of Death: 1 year
- 18G. Length of Stay in California: 10 years

USUAL RESIDENCE
- 19A. Street Address: 380 Baltimore
- 19B. Inside City Corporate Limits: yes
- 19C. City or Town: Larkspur
- 19D. County: Marin
- 19E. State: California
- 20. Name and Mailing Address of Informant: Robert E. Gordon, 9418 Wilshire Boulevard, Beverly Hills, California

PHYSICIAN'S OR CORONER'S CERTIFICATION
- 21A. Coroner: Investigation
- 21D. Date Signed: 10-6-70
- Justice, Los Angeles

FUNERAL DIRECTOR AND LOCAL REGISTRAR
- 22A. Cremation
- 22B. Date: 10-8-70
- 23. Name of Cemetery or Crematory: Scatter Over The Ocean — Westwood Memorial Park Crem.
- 24. Embalmer: Claude C. Yates 5697
- 25. Name of Funeral Director: Westwood Village Mortuary
- 28. Date Accepted for Registration: OCT 7 1970

CAUSE OF DEATH
- 29. Part I. Immediate Cause (A): Deferred

INJURY INFORMATION
- 32A. Autopsy: Yes
- 38. Were Laboratory Tests Done for Drugs: Yes
- 39. Were Laboratory Tests (Alcohol): Yes

This is to certify that this document is a true copy of the official record filed with the Registrar-Recorder/County Clerk.

Conny B. McCormack
Registrar-Recorder/County Clerk

NOV 28 2000
19-113367

STATE OF CALIFORNIA
CERTIFICATION OF VITAL RECORD
COUNTY OF LOS ANGELES • REGISTRAR-RECORDER/COUNTY CLERK

AMENDMENT OF MEDICAL AND HEALTH SECTION DATA—DEATH

State Certificate Number: 10284
Local Registration District and Certificate Number: 7097 043582

IDENTIFICATION OF THE RECORD

- 1a. FIRST NAME: Janis
- 1b. MIDDLE NAME: Lyn
- 1c. LAST NAME: Joplin
- 2. PLACE OF OCCURRENCE—CITY OR COUNTY: Los Angeles
- 3. DATE OF EVENT: Oct. 4, 1970
- 4. DATE ORIGINAL FILED: 10-7-70

ORIGINALLY REPORTED INFORMATION

29. PART I. DEATH WAS CAUSED BY:
- (A) IMMEDIATE CAUSE: Deferred
- (B) DUE TO, OR AS A CONSEQUENCE OF:
- (C) DUE TO, OR AS A CONSEQUENCE OF:

32a. AUTOPSY: Yes

INFORMATION AS IT SHOULD BE STATED ON THE ORIGINALLY REGISTERED CERTIFICATE

29. PART I. DEATH WAS CAUSED BY:
- (A) IMMEDIATE CAUSE: Acute heroin-morphine intoxication
- (B) DUE TO, OR AS A CONSEQUENCE OF: Injection of overdose
- (C) DUE TO, OR AS A CONSEQUENCE OF:

31. WAS OPERATION OR BIOPSY PERFORMED: No
32a. AUTOPSY: Yes

- 33. SPECIFY ACCIDENT, SUICIDE OR HOMICIDE: ACCIDENT
- 34. PLACE OF INJURY: Apartment House
- 35. INJURY AT WORK: No
- 36a. DATE OF INJURY: October 4, 1970
- 36b. HOUR: Prior to 2110 hrs
- 37a. PLACE OF INJURY (STREET AND NUMBER OR LOCATION AND CITY OR TOWN): 7047 Franklin Ave., Apt. 105, Los Angeles
- 37b. DISTANCE FROM PLACE OF INJURY TO USUAL RESIDENCE: 340 MILES
- 38. WERE LABORATORY TESTS DONE FOR DRUGS OR TOXIC CHEMICALS: Yes
- 39. WERE LABORATORY TESTS DONE FOR ALCOHOL: Yes
- 40. DESCRIBE HOW INJURY OCCURRED: As above

DECLARATION OF CERTIFYING PHYSICIAN OR CORONER

5. I, THE CERTIFYING PHYSICIAN OR CORONER HAVING PERSONAL KNOWLEDGE OF SUPPLEMENTAL INFORMATION WHICH MODIFIES THE INFORMATION ORIGINALLY REPORTED, DECLARE UNDER PENALTY OF PERJURY THAT THE ABOVE INFORMATION IS TRUE AND CORRECT TO THE BEST OF MY KNOWLEDGE.

- 6a. SIGNATURE OF PHYSICIAN OR CORONER: [signed] Thomas T. Noguchi M.D.
- 6b. DATE SIGNED: 10/29/70
- 7a. NAME OF PHYSICIAN OR CORONER: THOMAS T. NOGUCHI, M.D.
- 7b. DEGREE OR TITLE: CORONER
- 7c. ADDRESS: HALL OF JUSTICE LOS ANGELES, CALIFORNIA

REGISTRAR'S OFFICE

- 8a. OFFICE OF STATE OR LOCAL REGISTRAR: [signed]
- 8b. DATE ACCEPTED: OCT 29 1970

This is to certify that this document is a true copy of the official record filed with the Registrar-Recorder/County Clerk.

CONNY B. McCORMACK
Registrar-Recorder/County Clerk

NOV 28 2000
19-113366

STATE OF CALIFORNIA
CERTIFICATION OF VITAL RECORD

COUNTY OF LOS ANGELES • REGISTRAR-RECORDER/COUNTY CLERK

CERTIFICATE OF DEATH — STATE OF CALIFORNIA

State File Number: — Local Registration Number: 3200819016001

DECEDENT'S PERSONAL DATA
- 1. Name of Decedent — First (Given): STANLEY
- 2. Middle: M.
- 3. Last (Family): KAMEL
- 4. Date of Birth: 01/01/1943
- 5. Age: 65
- 6. Sex: M
- 7. Date of Death: 04/08/2008 FND
- 8. Hour: 0900 EST
- 9. Birth State/Foreign Country: NJ
- 10. Social Security Number: 146-34-3220
- 11. Ever in U.S. Armed Forces?: NO
- 12. Marital Status: NEVER MARRIED
- 13. Education: BACHELOR
- 14/15. Hispanic/Latino: NO
- 16. Race: CAUCASIAN
- 17. Usual Occupation: ACTOR
- 18. Kind of Business/Industry: ENTERTAINMENT INDUSTRY
- 19. Years in Occupation: 40

USUAL RESIDENCE
- 20. Decedent's Residence: 6341 BRYN-MAWR DR.
- 21. City: LOS ANGELES
- 22. County: LOS ANGELES
- 23. Zip Code: 90068
- 24. Years in County: 40
- 25. State: CA

INFORMANT
- 26. Informant's Name / Relationship: STEPHEN KAMEL, BROTHER
- 27. Mailing Address: 22 KEVIN RD, EAST BRUNSWICK, NJ 08816

SPOUSE AND PARENT INFORMATION
- 31. Name of Father — First: SYDNEY
- 33. Last: KAMEL
- 34. Birth State: NY
- 35. Name of Mother — First: LILLIAN
- 37. Last (Maiden): PERLMUTTER
- 38. Birth State: NY

FUNERAL DIRECTOR / LOCAL REGISTRAR
- 39. Disposition Date: 04/11/2008
- 40. Place of Final Disposition: ANSHE EMETH CEMETERY, CRANBURY RD., EAST BRUNSWICK, NJ 08816
- 41. Type of Disposition: TR/BU
- 42. Signature of Embalmer: NOT EMBALMED
- 44. Name of Funeral Establishment: HOLLYWOOD FUNERAL HOME
- 45. License Number: FD1651
- 46. Signature of Local Registrar: JONATHAN FIELDING, MD
- 47. Date: 04/10/2008

PLACE OF DEATH
- 101. Place of Death: RESIDENCE
- 103. Other Than Hospital: Decedent's Home (X)
- 104. County: LOS ANGELES
- 105. Facility Address or Location Where Found: 6341 BRYN-MAWR DR
- 106. City: LOS ANGELES

CAUSE OF DEATH
- 107. Immediate Cause (A): HYPEROSMOLAR STATE
- (B): HUMAN IMMUNODEFICIENCY VIRUS — 20 YRS
- 108. Death Reported to Coroner: NO
- 109. Biopsy Performed: NO
- 110. Autopsy Performed: NO
- 112. Other Significant Conditions: CARDIOVASCULAR HEART DISEASE, DIABETES MELLITUS TYPE 2.
- 113. Was Operation Performed: NONE

PHYSICIAN'S CERTIFICATION
- 114. Physician Attended Since: 11/--/2006; Decedent Last Seen Alive: 04/04/2008
- 115. Signature and Title of Certifier: JAMES ERNEST GAEDE M.D.
- 116. License Number: G86232
- 117. Date: 04/10/2008
- 118. Attending Physician Name, Mailing Address: JAMES ERNEST GAEDE M.D., 150 N ROBERTSON BLVD 300, BEVERLY HILLS, CA 90211

State Registrar document number: *012008000787574*

INFORMATIONAL, NOT A VALID DOCUMENT TO ESTABLISH IDENTITY

This is to certify that this document is a true copy of the official record filed with the Registrar-Recorder/County Clerk.

SEP 16 2009

DEAN C. LOGAN
Registrar-Recorder/County Clerk

000004566

CERTIFICATE OF DEATH — STATE OF CALIFORNIA

State File Number: 0190-022472

1A. Name (First)	Andrew
1B. Middle	G.
1C. Last	Kaufman
2A. Date of Death	May 16, 1984
2B. Hour	1827
3. Sex	Male
4. Race/Ethnicity	White/Jewish
5. Spanish/Hispanic	No
6. Date of Birth	January 17, 1949
7. Age	35 Years
8. Birthplace of Decedent	New York
9. Name and Birthplace of Father	Stanley Kaufman, New York
10. Birth Name and Birthplace of Mother	Janice Bernstein, New York
11. Citizen of What Country	USA
12. Social Security Number	112-36-5432
13. Marital Status	Never Married
15. Primary Occupation	Entertainer
16. Number of Years This Occupation	12
17. Employer	Self Employed
18. Kind of Industry or Business	Entertainment
19A. Usual Residence—Street Address	300 Lombard Ave.
19C. City or Town	Pacific Palisades
19D. County	Los Angeles
19E. State	California
20. Name and Address of Informant	Stanley Kaufman, father, 21 Grassfield Rd., Great Neck, New York 11024
21A. Place of Death	Cedars Sinai Medical Center
21B. County	Los Angeles
21C. Street Address	8700 Beverly Blvd.
21D. City or Town	Los Angeles

Cause of Death:
- (A) Immediate Cause: renal failure — 48 hrs
- (B) Due to: metastatic carcinoma — 4 mos
- (C) Due to: primary bronchogenic carcinoma — 5 mo

24. Was Death Reported to Coroner? no
25. Was Biopsy Performed? yes
26. Was Autopsy Performed? no
27. Was Operation Performed? no

Physician's Certification:
- Attended Decedent Since: 1-11-79
- Last Saw Decedent Alive: 5-16-84
- Physician: Steven B Rubin MD
- Date Signed: 5-17-84
- License Number: G13497
- Address: 435 No. Roxbury Dr. #300, Beverly Hills, CA 90210

Disposition: Burial
Date: 5/17/84
Cemetery: Beth David Cemetery, Elmont, New York
Funeral Director: Hillside Mem. Pk. Mort., License 1358
Date Accepted by Local Registrar: MAY 17 1984

INFORMATIONAL, NOT A VALID DOCUMENT TO ESTABLISH IDENTITY

FEB 02 2005

Conny B. McCormack
Registrar-Recorder/County Clerk

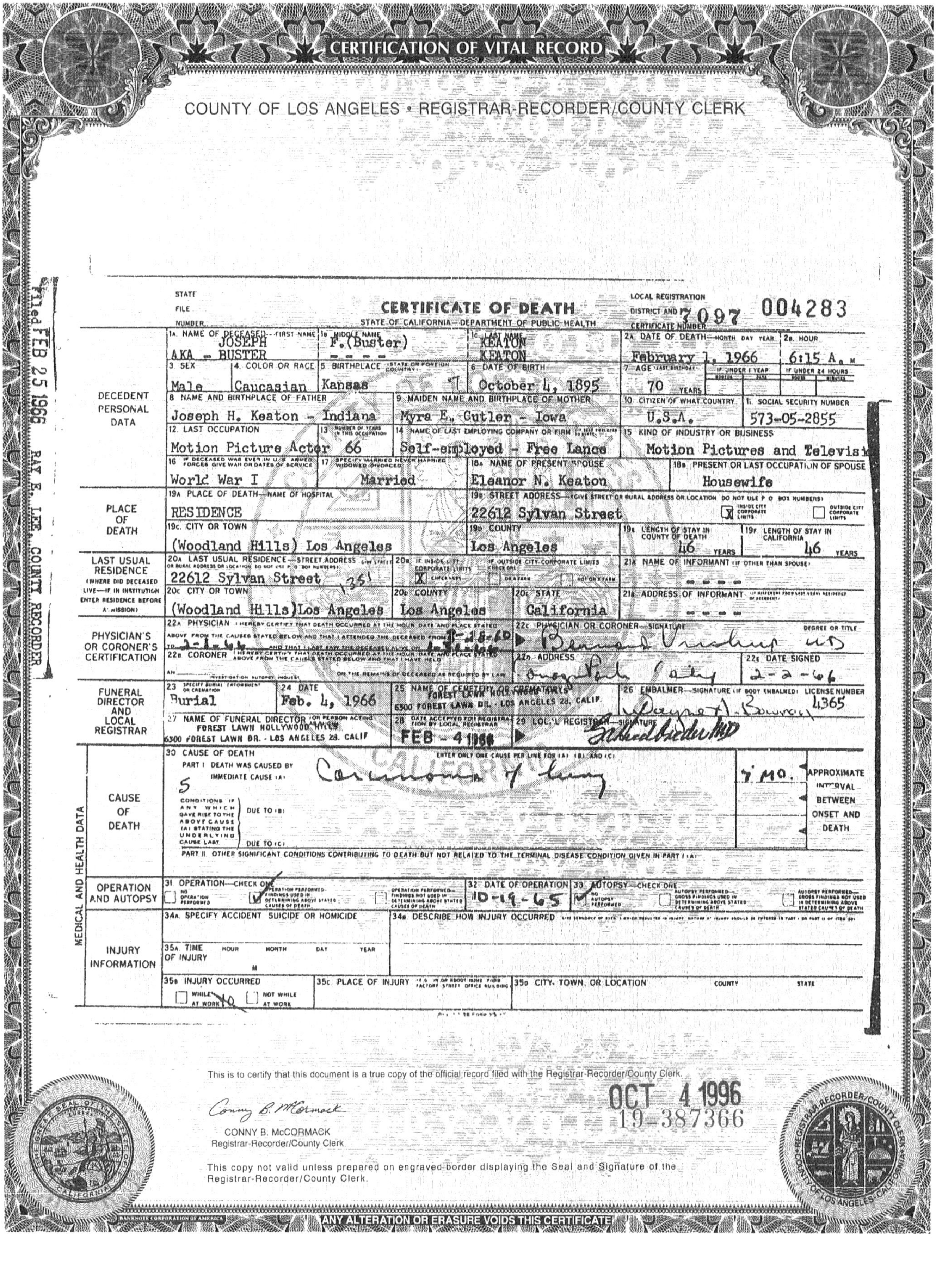

CERTIFICATION OF VITAL RECORD

COUNTY OF LOS ANGELES • REGISTRAR-RECORDER/COUNTY CLERK

Filed FEB 25 1966 RAY E. LEE, COUNTY RECORDER

STATE FILE NUMBER

CERTIFICATE OF DEATH

STATE OF CALIFORNIA—DEPARTMENT OF PUBLIC HEALTH

LOCAL REGISTRATION DISTRICT AND CERTIFICATE NUMBER 7097 004283

DECEDENT PERSONAL DATA

1A. NAME OF DECEASED—FIRST NAME: JOSEPH / AKA – BUSTER
1B. MIDDLE NAME: F. (Buster)
1C. LAST NAME: KEATON / KEATON
2A. DATE OF DEATH—MONTH DAY YEAR: February 1, 1966
2B. HOUR: 6:15 A.M.
3. SEX: Male
4. COLOR OR RACE: Caucasian
5. BIRTHPLACE (STATE OR FOREIGN COUNTRY): Kansas
6. DATE OF BIRTH: October 4, 1895
7. AGE (LAST BIRTHDAY): 70 YEARS
IF UNDER 1 YEAR: MONTHS DAYS
IF UNDER 24 HOURS: HOURS MINUTES
8. NAME AND BIRTHPLACE OF FATHER: Joseph H. Keaton – Indiana
9. MAIDEN NAME AND BIRTHPLACE OF MOTHER: Myra E. Cutler – Iowa
10. CITIZEN OF WHAT COUNTRY: U.S.A.
11. SOCIAL SECURITY NUMBER: 573-05-2855
12. LAST OCCUPATION: Motion Picture Actor
13. NUMBER OF YEARS IN THIS OCCUPATION: 66
14. NAME OF LAST EMPLOYING COMPANY OR FIRM: Self-employed – Free Lance
15. KIND OF INDUSTRY OR BUSINESS: Motion Pictures and Televis[ion]
16. IF DECEASED WAS EVER IN U.S. ARMED FORCES GIVE WAR OR DATES OF SERVICE: World War I
17. SPECIFY MARRIED, NEVER MARRIED, WIDOWED, DIVORCED: Married
18A. NAME OF PRESENT SPOUSE: Eleanor N. Keaton
18B. PRESENT OR LAST OCCUPATION OF SPOUSE: Housewife

PLACE OF DEATH

19A. PLACE OF DEATH—NAME OF HOSPITAL: RESIDENCE
19B. STREET ADDRESS (GIVE STREET OR RURAL ADDRESS OR LOCATION. DO NOT USE P.O. BOX NUMBERS): 22612 Sylvan Street [X] INSIDE CITY CORPORATE LIMITS [ ] OUTSIDE CITY CORPORATE LIMITS
19C. CITY OR TOWN: (Woodland Hills) Los Angeles
19D. COUNTY: Los Angeles
19E. LENGTH OF STAY IN COUNTY OF DEATH: 46 YEARS
19F. LENGTH OF STAY IN CALIFORNIA: 46 YEARS

LAST USUAL RESIDENCE (WHERE DID DECEASED LIVE—IF IN INSTITUTION ENTER RESIDENCE BEFORE ADMISSION)

20A. LAST USUAL RESIDENCE—STREET ADDRESS: 22612 Sylvan Street
20B. IF INSIDE CITY CORPORATE LIMITS CHECK BOX: [X]
20C. CITY OR TOWN: (Woodland Hills) Los Angeles
20D. COUNTY: Los Angeles
20E. STATE: California
21A. NAME OF INFORMANT (IF OTHER THAN SPOUSE): – – – –
21B. ADDRESS OF INFORMANT: – – – –

PHYSICIAN'S OR CORONER'S CERTIFICATION

22A. PHYSICIAN: I HEREBY CERTIFY THAT DEATH OCCURRED AT THE HOUR, DATE AND PLACE STATED ABOVE FROM THE CAUSES STATED BELOW AND THAT I ATTENDED THE DECEASED FROM ... TO ... AND THAT I LAST SAW THE DECEASED ALIVE ON ...
22B. CORONER: I HEREBY CERTIFY THAT DEATH OCCURRED AT THE HOUR, DATE AND PLACE STATED ABOVE FROM THE CAUSES STATED BELOW AND THAT I HAVE HELD AN INVESTIGATION, AUTOPSY, INQUEST ON THE REMAINS OF DECEASED AS REQUIRED BY LAW
22C. PHYSICIAN OR CORONER—SIGNATURE, DEGREE OR TITLE: MD
22D. ADDRESS
22E. DATE SIGNED: 2-2-66

FUNERAL DIRECTOR AND LOCAL REGISTRAR

23. SPECIFY BURIAL, ENTOMBMENT OR CREMATION: Burial
24. DATE: Feb. 4, 1966
25. NAME OF CEMETERY OR CREMATORY: FOREST LAWN HOLLYWOOD HILLS, 6300 FOREST LAWN DR. - LOS ANGELES 28, CALIF.
26. EMBALMER—SIGNATURE (IF BODY EMBALMED), LICENSE NUMBER: 4365
27. NAME OF FUNERAL DIRECTOR (OR PERSON ACTING AS SUCH): FOREST LAWN HOLLYWOOD HILLS, 6300 FOREST LAWN DR. - LOS ANGELES 28, CALIF
28. DATE ACCEPTED FOR REGISTRATION BY LOCAL REGISTRAR: FEB - 4 1966
29. LOCAL REGISTRAR—SIGNATURE: MD

MEDICAL AND HEALTH DATA

CAUSE OF DEATH

30. CAUSE OF DEATH — ENTER ONLY ONE CAUSE PER LINE FOR (A), (B) AND (C)
PART I. DEATH WAS CAUSED BY: IMMEDIATE CAUSE (A)
CONDITIONS, IF ANY, WHICH GAVE RISE TO THE ABOVE CAUSE (A), STATING THE UNDERLYING CAUSE LAST: DUE TO (B), DUE TO (C)
APPROXIMATE INTERVAL BETWEEN ONSET AND DEATH: 5 MO.
PART II. OTHER SIGNIFICANT CONDITIONS CONTRIBUTING TO DEATH BUT NOT RELATED TO THE TERMINAL DISEASE CONDITION GIVEN IN PART I (A)

OPERATION AND AUTOPSY

31. OPERATION—CHECK ONE: [ ] NO OPERATION PERFORMED [✓] OPERATION PERFORMED—FINDINGS USED IN DETERMINING ABOVE STATED CAUSES OF DEATH [ ] OPERATION PERFORMED—FINDINGS NOT USED IN DETERMINING ABOVE STATED CAUSES OF DEATH
32. DATE OF OPERATION: 10-19-65
33. AUTOPSY—CHECK ONE: [✓] NO AUTOPSY PERFORMED [ ] AUTOPSY PERFORMED—GROSS FINDINGS USED IN DETERMINING ABOVE STATED CAUSES OF DEATH [ ] AUTOPSY PERFORMED—GROSS FINDINGS NOT USED IN DETERMINING ABOVE STATED CAUSES OF DEATH

INJURY INFORMATION

34A. SPECIFY ACCIDENT, SUICIDE OR HOMICIDE
34B. DESCRIBE HOW INJURY OCCURRED
35A. TIME OF INJURY: HOUR MONTH DAY YEAR
35B. INJURY OCCURRED: [ ] WHILE AT WORK [ ] NOT WHILE AT WORK
35C. PLACE OF INJURY
35D. CITY, TOWN, OR LOCATION: COUNTY STATE

This is to certify that this document is a true copy of the official record filed with the Registrar-Recorder/County Clerk.

OCT 4 1996

19-387366

CONNY B. McCORMACK
Registrar-Recorder/County Clerk

This copy not valid unless prepared on engraved border displaying the Seal and Signature of the Registrar-Recorder/County Clerk.

ANY ALTERATION OR ERASURE VOIDS THIS CERTIFICATE

COUNTY OF LOS ANGELES
DEPARTMENT OF HEALTH SERVICES
CERTIFICATE OF DEATH
STATE OF CALIFORNIA

1. Name of Decedent—First (Given)	JACKSON
2. Middle	DeFOREST
3. Last (Family)	KELLEY
4. Date of Birth	01/20/1920
5. Age Yrs.	79
6. Sex	MALE
7. Date of Death	06/11/1999
8. Hour	1215
9. State of Birth	GA
10. Social Security No.	252-01-3786
11. Military Service	X YES
12. Marital Status	MARRIED
13. Education—Years Completed	12
14. Race	CAUCASIAN
15. Hispanic	No
16. Usual Employer	VARIOUS MOTION PICTURE STUDIOS
17. Occupation	ACTOR
18. Kind of Business	MOTION PICTURE/ENTERTAINMENT
19. Years in Occupation	54
20. Residence	15463 GREENLEAF ST.
21. City	SHERMAN OAKS
22. County	LOS ANGELES
23. Zip Code	91403
24. Yrs in County	60
25. State	CA
26. Name, Relationship	CAROLYN M. KELLEY, WIFE
27. Mailing Address	23388 MULHOLLAND DR. WOODLAND HILLS, CA 91364
28. Name of Surviving Spouse—First	CAROLYN
30. Last (Maiden Name)	MEAGHER
31. Name of Father—First	ERNEST
32. Middle	DAVID
33. Last	KELLEY
34. Birth State	GA
35. Name of Mother—First	CLORA
37. Last (Maiden)	CASEY
38. Birth State	GA
39. Date	06/15/1999
40. Place of Final Disposition	AT SEA OFF THE COAST OF LOS ANGELES COUNTY
41. Type of Disposition	CR/SEA
42. Signature of Embalmer	NOT EMBALMED
44. Name of Funeral Director	BURBANK NEPTUNE SOCIETY
45. License No.	FD-1359
47. Date	06/14/1999
101. Place of Death	MOTION PICTURE & T.V. HOSP.
102.	IP
104. County	LOS ANGELES
105. Street Address	23388 MULHOLLAND DR.
106. City	WOODLAND HILLS

107. Death Was Caused By:
- (A) Immediate Cause: RESPIRATORY FAILURE — 2 YRS.
- (B) Due to: CARCINOID TUMOR WITH METASTASIS – ILEUM — 3 YRS.

108. Death Reported to Coroner	No
109. Biopsy Performed	No
110. Autopsy Performed	No
111. Used in Determining Cause	No
112. Other Significant Conditions	NONE
113. Was Operation Performed	RESECTION OF ILEOCECAL CARCINOID NEOPLASM 05/12/1996
116. License No.	A39209
117. Date	06/11/1999
118. Attending Physician	SAEED HUMAYUN, MD 23388 MULHOLLAND DR. WOODLAND HILLS CA 91364
Decedent Attended Since	03/19/1999
Decedent Last Seen Alive	06/11/1999
Fax Auth. #	195/4924
Census Tract	090242216

DATE ISSUED: JUN 24 1999

STATE OF CALIFORNIA — CERTIFICATION OF VITAL RECORD

COUNTY OF LOS ANGELES • REGISTRAR-RECORDER/COUNTY CLERK

District No. 1903 — Registrar's No. 18305

1. FULL NAME: Edgar L. Kennedy
2. PLACE OF DEATH:
   (A) County: Los Angeles
   (B) City or Town: Los Angeles
   (C) Name of Hospital or Institution: 23430 Ventura Blvd, Motion Picture Country House
   (D) Length of Stay: In Hospital or Institution: 1 month 24 days; In this Community: same; In California: Life
   (E) If Foreign Born, How Long in the U.S.A.: —
3. (E) If Veteran, Name of War: World War I
   (F) Social Security No.: 568-12-0520
4. Sex: Male
5. Color or Race: White
6. (A) Single, Married, Widowed or Divorced: Married
   (B) Name of Husband or Wife: Patricia Allyn Kennedy
   (C) Age of Husband or Wife if Alive: 50
7. Birthdate of Deceased: April 26, 1890
8. Age: 58 Yrs. 6 Mos. 14 Days
9. Birthplace: Monterey, California
10. Usual Occupation: Actor
11. Industry or Business: Motion Picture
12. Father Name: Neil Kennedy
13. Birthplace: Canada
14. Mother Maiden Name: Annie Quinn
15. Birthplace: California
16. (A) Informant: Mrs. Patricia Allyn Kennedy
    (B) Address: 362 C So. Doheny Dr. Beverly Hills
17. (A) Burial (B) Date: Nov. 12, 1948
    (C) Place: Holy Cross Cemetery
18. Embalmer's Signature: [signature] License No. 3661
    (B) Funeral Director: Cunningham & O'Connor
    Address: Los Angeles, California
    By: Edward P. Cunningham
19. Date Filed: NOV 10 1948

3. USUAL RESIDENCE OF DECEASED:
   (A) State: California
   (B) County: Los Angeles
   (C) City or Town: Beverly Hills
   (D) Street No.: 362 C So. Doheny Drive

20. Date of Death: Month November, Day 9, Year 1948, Hour 2, Minute 40 AM

21. MEDICAL CERTIFICATE: I hereby certify that I attended the deceased from 9/16/48 to 11/9/48. That I last saw h— alive on 11/8/48, and that death occurred on the date and hour stated above.
    Immediate Cause of Death: Bronchogenic Carcinoma — Duration: 6 mo.

22. CORONER'S CERTIFICATE: —
    Autopsy: None performed

24. Physician's Signature: Arthur L. Kolal, M.D.
    Address: 17003 Ventura Blvd., Encino, Calif.
    Date: 11/9/48

CERTIFICATE OF DEATH
DEPARTMENT OF PUBLIC HEALTH — FEDERAL SECURITY AGENCY, U.S. PUBLIC HEALTH SERVICE

Conny B. McCormack, Registrar-Recorder/County Clerk
NOV 28 2000
19-118060

STATE OF CONNECTICUT
DEPARTMENT OF PUBLIC HEALTH
VS-4 REV. 1/04

CERTIFICATE OF DEATH

STATE FILE NUMBER (For State Use only. Do not write in this box)

1. DECEDENT'S LEGAL NAME (Include AKAs if any) (First, Middle, Last): **Eartha Kitt**
2. SEX: ☒ Female
3. ACTUAL OR PRESUMED DATE OF DEATH: **December 25, 2008**
4. ACTUAL OR PRESUMED TIME OF DEATH: **2:15** ☒ PM
5. AGE LAST BIRTHDAY: **81**
7. DATE OF BIRTH: **January 17, 1927**
8. BIRTHPLACE: **Columbia, South Carolina**
9. RESIDENCE (State): **Connecticut**
10. RESIDENCE (County): **Fairfield**
11. RESIDENCE (City or Town): **Weston**
12. RESIDENCE (Street and No.): **2 Nordholm Dr.**
14. ZIP CODE: **06883**
15. EVER IN US ARMED FORCES?: ☒ No
16. MARITAL STATUS AT TIME OF DEATH: ☒ Divorced
17. SURVIVING SPOUSE'S NAME: **NA**
18. FATHER'S NAME: **Unobtainable**
19. MOTHER'S NAME PRIOR TO FIRST MARRIAGE: **Unobtainable**
20. INFORMANT'S NAME: **Kitt Shapiro**
21. INFORMANT'S RELATIONSHIP TO DECEDENT: **Daughter**
22. MAILING ADDRESS: **1 Hockanum Rd., Westport, CT 06880**
24. IF DEATH OCCURRED SOMEWHERE OTHER THAN A HOSPITAL: ☒ Decedent's Home
25. FACILITY NAME: **2 Nordholm Dr.**
26. CITY OR TOWN OF DEATH / ZIP CODE: **Weston, Connecticut 06883**
27. COUNTY OF DEATH: **Fairfield**
28. METHOD OF DISPOSITION: ☒ Cremation
29. DISPOSITION: **Mt. Grove Crematory**
30. LOCATION: **Bridgeport, Connecticut**
31. DATE: **12/29/08**
32. WAS BODY EMBALMED?: ☒ No
33. FUNERAL FACILITY: **Harding Funeral Home, 210 Post Rd. Westport, CT 06880**
34. SIGNATURE OF FUNERAL DIRECTOR OR EMBALMER: *Neil F. Harding*
35. LICENSE NUMBER: **1942**
36. DATE PRONOUNCED DEAD: **12-25-08**
37. TIME PRONOUNCED: **1415**
38. NURSE PRONOUNCEMENT NAME: **Claire F. LoMaglio RN**
39. SIGNATURE: *Claire F. LoMaglio RN*
40. DATE SIGNED: **122508**
41. WAS MEDICAL EXAMINER CONTACTED?: ☒ No
42. WAS AN AUTOPSY PERFORMED?: ☒ No

44. IMMEDIATE CAUSE: (a) **Colon cancer** — years

48. CERTIFIER: Myra L. Skluth, MD — 12/26/08
49. MAILING - CERTIFIER: **87 East Ave, Norwalk, CT 06851**

THIS CERTIFICATE WAS RECEIVED FOR RECORD ON: **December 29, 2008**

50. DECEDENT'S EDUCATION: ☒ High School Graduate/GED
51. DECEDENT OF HISPANIC ORIGIN?: ☒ No, Not Spanish/Hispanic/Latino
52. DECEDENT'S RACE: ☒ Black or African American
53. DECEDENT'S USUAL OCCUPATION: **Entertainer**
54. KIND OF BUSINESS/INDUSTRY: **Entertainment**

I CERTIFY THAT THIS IS A TRUE COPY OF THE CERTIFICATE RECEIVED FOR RECORD.

Attest *[signature]*
Registrar, Town of Weston
January 2, 2009

Ted Knight

STATE OF CALIFORNIA — CERTIFICATION OF VITAL RECORD

COUNTY OF LOS ANGELES • REGISTRAR-RECORDER/ COUNTY CLERK

CERTIFICATE OF DEATH — STATE OF CALIFORNIA — 3861093031

DECEDENT PERSONAL DATA
- 1A. Name (First): THEODORE — AKA: THEODORE
- 1B. Middle: CHARLES — CHARLES
- 1C. Last: KONOPKA — KNIGHT
- 2A. Date of Death: AUGUST 26, 1986
- 2B. Hour: 1317
- 3. Sex: MALE
- 4. Race/Ethnicity: WHITE/POLISH
- 5. Spanish/Hispanic: NO
- 6. Date of Birth: DECEMBER 7, 1923
- 7. Age: 62 YEARS
- 8. Birthplace of Decedent: CONNECTICUT
- 9. Name and Birthplace of Father: CHARLES KONOPKA – POLAND
- 10. Birth Name and Birthplace of Mother: SOPHIA KOWALESKA – POLAND
- 11A. Citizen of What Country: USA
- 11B. Military Service Dates: 1943 TO 1945
- 12. Social Security Number: 046-14-5481
- 13. Marital Status: MARRIED
- 14. Name of Surviving Spouse: DOROTHY C. KNIGHT
- 15. Primary Occupation: ACTOR
- 16. Number of Years in Occupation: 37
- 17. Employer: SELF-EMPLOYED
- 18. Kind of Industry or Business: TELEVISION

USUAL RESIDENCE
- 19A. Street Address: 17416 CAMINO DE YATASTO
- 19C. City or Town: PACIFIC PALISADES
- 19D. County: LOS ANGELES
- 19E. State: CALIFORNIA
- 20. Informant: TED C. KNIGHT, JR. – SON, 1351 AVENIDA DE CORTEZ, PACIFIC PALISADES, CALIF. 90272

PLACE OF DEATH
- 21A. Place of Death: RESIDENCE
- 21B. County: LOS ANGELES
- 21C. Street Address: 17416 CAMINO DE YATASTO
- 21D. City or Town: PACIFIC PALISADES

CAUSE OF DEATH
- 22. (A) CARDIOPULMONARY FAILURE — Approximate interval: 1 HOUR
- (B) METASTATIC TRANSITIONAL CELL CANCER OF THE BLADDER — 10 YEARS
- 23. Other Significant Conditions: NONE
- 24. Was death reported to Coroner? NO
- 25. Was biopsy performed? YES
- 26. Was autopsy performed? NO
- 27. Operation: PARTIAL CYSTECTOMY — Date: JULY 8, 1976

PHYSICIAN'S CERTIFICATION
- 28A. Attended decedent since MAY 5, 1981; Last saw alive AUGUST 11, 1986
- 28B. Physician's signature: Stanley Brosman MD
- 28C. Date Signed: 8-28-86
- 28D. License Number: C 22619
- 28E. Physician's Name and Address: S. Brosman, M.D. 2001 Santa Monica Blvd. Santa Monica, Ca.

DISPOSITION
- 36. Disposition: Burial
- 37. Date: 8/29/86
- 38. Cemetery: FOREST LAWN MEMORIAL PARK, 1712 S. GLENDALE AVE., GLENDALE, CA 91209
- 39. Embalmer's License Number and Signature: 5249 Robert P. Hoggerty
- 40A. Funeral Establishment: FOREST LAWN MEMORIAL PARK, 1712 S. GLENDALE AVE., GLENDALE, CA 91209
- 40B. License No.: 656
- 42. Date Accepted by Local Registrar: AUG 28 1986

This is to certify that this document is a true copy of the official record filed with the Registrar-Recorder/County Clerk.

Conny B. McCormack
CONNY B. McCORMACK
Registrar-Recorder/County Clerk

NOV 06 1998
19-602412

This copy not valid unless prepared on engraved border displaying the Seal and Signature of the Registrar-Recorder/County Clerk.

ANY ALTERATION OR ERASURE VOIDS THIS CERTIFICATE

State of California — Certification of Vital Record

County of Los Angeles • Registrar-Recorder/County Clerk

Certificate of Death

State File Number: 3200819023569

Name of Decedent	HARVEY HERSCHEL KORMAN
Date of Birth	02/15/1927
Age	81
Sex	M
Birth State	IL
Social Security Number	326-18-1131
Ever in U.S. Armed Forces	YES
Marital Status	MARRIED
Date of Death	05/29/2008
Hour	1147
Education	ASSOCIATE
Hispanic/Latino	NO
Race	WHITE
Usual Occupation	ACTOR
Kind of Business/Industry	ENTERTAINMENT
Years in Occupation	60
Decedent's Residence	10960 WILSHIRE BLVD., #1100
City	LOS ANGELES
County	LOS ANGELES
Zip Code	90024
Years in County	50
State	CA
Informant's Name, Relationship	DEBORAH KORMAN, WIFE
Informant's Mailing Address	10960 WILSHIRE BLVD., #1100, LOS ANGELES, CA 90024
Name of Surviving Spouse	DEBORAH KATHERINE FRITZ
Name of Father	CYRIL RAYMOND KORMAN — Birth State: UKRAINE
Name of Mother	ELLEN — (Maiden) BLECHER — Birth State: FRANCE
Disposition Date	06/03/2008
Place of Final Disposition	WOODLAWN CEMETERY, 1847 14TH STREET, SANTA MONICA, CA 90404
Type of Disposition	BURIAL
Signature of Embalmer	DAVID SWEETIN
License Number	EMB9021
Name of Funeral Establishment	MIDGLEY-GARDENSIDE MORTUARY
License Number	FD1557
Signature of Local Registrar	JONATHAN FIELDING, MD
Date	06/02/2008
Place of Death	UCLA MEDICAL CENTER
Facility Address	10833 LECONTE AVENUE
County	LOS ANGELES
City	LOS ANGELES

Cause of Death

- (A) Immediate Cause: SEPTIC SHOCK — MINS
- (B) BACTEREMIA — DAYS
- (C) MULTIPLE INTRAABDOMINAL ABSCESSES — MONS
- (D) ABDOMINAL AORTIC ANEURYSM — MONS

Other Significant Conditions: HYPERTENSION, BENIGN LEFT FRONTAL MENINGIOMA

Operation Performed: ABDOMINAL AORTIC ANEURYSM REPAIR 02/07/2008, CRANIOTOMY 01/26/2008

Death Reported to Coroner: NO
Biopsy Performed: NO
Autopsy Performed: NO

Physician's Certification

Decedent Attended Since: 02/07/2008
Decedent Last Seen Alive: 05/29/2008
Certifier: ALI ZARRINPAR M.D.
License Number: A97784
Date: 06/02/2008
Attending Physician's Mailing Address: 10833 LECONTE AVENUE, LOS ANGELES, CA 90095

INFORMATIONAL, NOT A VALID DOCUMENT TO ESTABLISH IDENTITY

This is to certify that this document is a true copy of the official record filed with the Registrar-Recorder/County Clerk.

SEP 16 2009

DEAN C. LOGAN
Registrar-Recorder/County Clerk

000004565

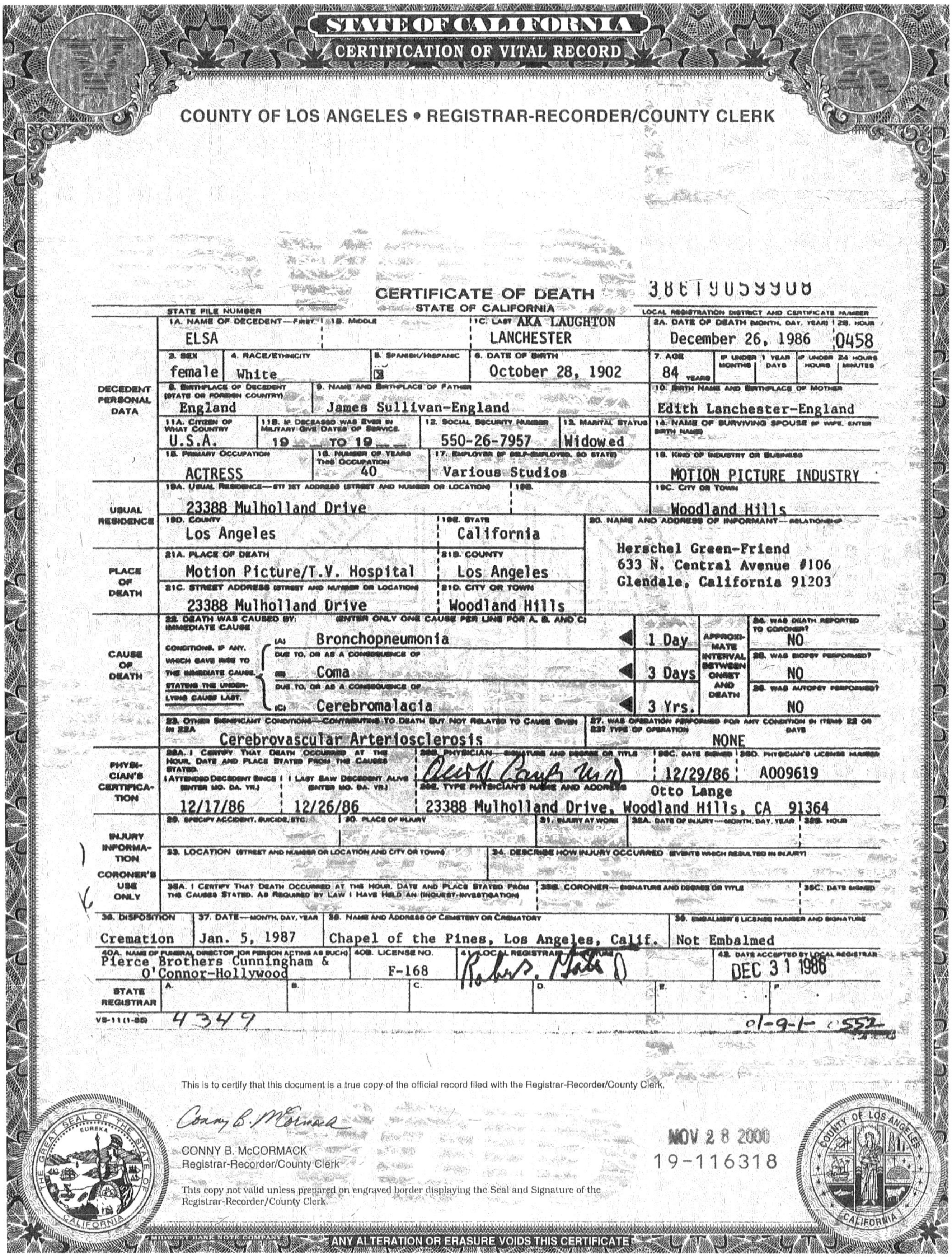

STATE OF CALIFORNIA
CERTIFICATION OF VITAL RECORD
COUNTY OF LOS ANGELES • REGISTRAR-RECORDER/COUNTY CLERK

CERTIFICATE OF DEATH

DISTRICT NO. 1901

1. FULL NAME: Carole Landis Schmidlapp
2. PLACE OF DEATH:
   (A) COUNTY: Los Angeles
   (B) CITY OR TOWN: Los Angeles (Pacific Palisades)
   (C) NAME OF HOSPITAL OR INSTITUTION: 1465 N. Capri Drive
   IN THIS COMMUNITY: 13 years — IN CALIFORNIA: 27 years
3. USUAL RESIDENCE OF DECEASED:
   (A) STATE: California
   (B) COUNTY: Los Angeles
   (C) CITY OR TOWN: Los Angeles (Pac. Palisades)
   (D) STREET NO.: 1465 N. Capri Drive
3. (E) IF VETERAN, NAME OF WAR: none
3. (F) SOCIAL SECURITY NO.: 565-14-5742
4. SEX: Female
5. COLOR OR RACE: white
6. (A) SINGLE, MARRIED, WIDOWED OR DIVORCED: Married
6. (B) NAME OF HUSBAND OR WIFE: Horace Schmidlapp
6. (C) AGE OF HUSBAND OR WIFE IF ALIVE: 33 YEARS
7. BIRTHDATE OF DECEASED: January 1, 1919
8. AGE: 29 YRS 6 MOS 4 DAYS
9. BIRTHPLACE: Fairchild, Wisconsin
10. USUAL OCCUPATION: Actress
11. INDUSTRY OR BUSINESS: Cinema
12. FATHER'S NAME: Alfred L. Ridste
13. BIRTHPLACE: Dawson, Minn.
14. MOTHER'S MAIDEN NAME: Clara Sentek
15. BIRTHPLACE: Fairchild, Wisconsin
16. (A) INFORMANT: Mrs. Clara Ridste
    (B) ADDRESS: 1506 E. 64th St., Long Beach
17. (A) Burial (B) DATE: 7-10-48
    (C) PLACE: Forest Lawn Memorial Park
18. (A) EMBALMER SIGNATURE: Robert Maslmeyer LICENSE 1878
    (B) FUNERAL DIRECTOR: Boggs & Nashmeyer's Wilshire Funeral Home
    ADDRESS: Santa Monica, Calif.
    BY: John C. Boggs
19. (A) DATE FILED: JUL 13 1948

20. DATE OF DEATH: (found) July 5, 1948

21. MEDICAL CERTIFICATE
22. CORONER'S CERTIFICATE — Autopsy
    IMMEDIATE CAUSE OF DEATH: Barbiturate Poisoning
    DUE TO: Ingestion of Overdose of Seconal
    OF AUTOPSY: As above

23. IF DEATH WAS DUE TO EXTERNAL CAUSES:
    (A) ACCIDENT, SUICIDE OR HOMICIDE: Suicide
    (B) DATE OF INJURY: 7-4-48
    (C) WHERE DID INJURY OCCUR: Los Angeles, L.A., Calif.
    (D) DID INJURY OCCUR IN OR ABOUT HOME: home — WHILE AT WORK: no
    (E) MEANS OF INJURY: Took sleeping tablets

24. CORONER'S OR PHYSICIAN'S SIGNATURE: BEN H. BROWN, CORONER / Schrenkrans DEPUTY
    ADDRESS: LOS ANGELES
    DATE: 7-9-48

STATE OF CALIFORNIA — DEPARTMENT OF PUBLIC HEALTH
FEDERAL SECURITY AGENCY — U.S. PUBLIC HEALTH SERVICE

CONNY B. McCORMACK
Registrar-Recorder/County Clerk

STATE OF CALIFORNIA
CERTIFICATION OF VITAL RECORD

COUNTY OF LOS ANGELES • REGISTRAR-RECORDER/COUNTY CLERK

CERTIFICATE OF DEATH
STATE OF CALIFORNIA
USE BLACK INK ONLY / NO ERASURES, WHITEOUTS OR ALTERATIONS
VS-11 (REV 3/06)

STATE FILE NUMBER — LOCAL REGISTRATION NUMBER 3200719029096

DECEDENT'S PERSONAL DATA

1 NAME OF DECEDENT—FIRST (Given): CHARLES
2 MIDDLE: G
3 LAST (Family): LANE
AKA, ALSO KNOWN AS – Include full AKA (FIRST, MIDDLE, LAST): -
4 DATE OF BIRTH mm/dd/ccyy: 01/26/1905
5 AGE Yrs: 102
IF UNDER ONE YEAR Months / Days; IF UNDER 24 HOURS Hours / Minutes
6 SEX: M
9 BIRTH STATE/FOREIGN COUNTRY: CALIFORNIA
10 SOCIAL SECURITY NUMBER: 563-14-1368
11 EVER IN U.S. ARMED FORCES? [X] YES [ ] NO [ ] UNK
12 MARITAL STATUS/SRDP (at Time of Death): WIDOWED
7 DATE OF DEATH mm/dd/ccyy: 07/09/2007
8 HOUR (24 Hours): 2110
13 EDUCATION – Highest Level/Degree (see worksheet on back): SOME COLLEGE
14/15 WAS DECEDENT HISPANIC/LATINO(A)/SPANISH? (If yes, see worksheet on back) [ ] YES [X] NO
16 DECEDENT'S RACE – Up to 3 races may be listed (see worksheet on back): CAUCASIAN
17 USUAL OCCUPATION – Type of work for most of life. DO NOT USE RETIRED: ACTOR
18 KIND OF BUSINESS OR INDUSTRY (e.g. grocery store, road construction, employment agency, etc.): MOTION PICTURES
19 YEARS IN OCCUPATION: 50

USUAL RESIDENCE

20 DECEDENT'S RESIDENCE (Street and number, or location): 321 GRETNA GREEN WAY
21 CITY: LOS ANGELES
22 COUNTY/PROVINCE: LOS ANGELES
23 ZIP CODE: 90049
24 YEARS IN COUNTY: 77
25 STATE/FOREIGN COUNTRY: CALIFORNIA

INFORMANT

26 INFORMANT'S NAME, RELATIONSHIP: THOMAS LANE - D.P.O.A.
27 INFORMANT'S MAILING ADDRESS (Street and number, or rural route number, city or town, state and zip): 725 7TH STREET #12, SANTA MONICA, CA 90402

SPOUSE/SRDP AND PARENT INFORMATION

28 NAME OF SURVIVING SPOUSE/SRDP—FIRST: -
29 MIDDLE: -
30 LAST (BIRTH NAME): -
31 NAME OF FATHER/PARENT—FIRST: JACOB
32 MIDDLE: B
33 LAST: LEVISION
34 BIRTH STATE: NEVADA
35 NAME OF MOTHER/PARENT—FIRST: ALICE
36 MIDDLE: -
37 LAST (BIRTH NAME): GERSTLE
38 BIRTH STATE: CALIFORNIA

FUNERAL DIRECTOR/LOCAL REGISTRAR

39 DISPOSITION DATE mm/dd/ccyy: 07/19/2007
40 PLACE OF FINAL DISPOSITION: HOME OF PEACE CEMETERY, 1229 EL CAMINO REAL, COLMA, CA 94014
41 TYPE OF DISPOSITION(S): CR/BU
42 SIGNATURE OF EMBALMER: NOT EMBALMED
43 LICENSE NUMBER: -
44 NAME OF FUNERAL ESTABLISHMENT: PIERCE BROTHERS VALHALLA MORTUARY
45 LICENSE NUMBER: FD-916
46 SIGNATURE OF LOCAL REGISTRAR: Jonathan E Fielding
47 DATE mm/dd/ccyy: 07/13/2007

PLACE OF DEATH

101 PLACE OF DEATH: RESIDENCE
102 IF HOSPITAL, SPECIFY ONE: [ ] IP [ ] ER/OP [ ] DOA
103 IF OTHER THAN HOSPITAL, SPECIFY ONE: [ ] Hospice [ ] Nursing Home/LTC [X] Decedent's Home [ ] Other
104 COUNTY: LOS ANGELES
105 FACILITY ADDRESS OR LOCATION WHERE FOUND (Street and number, or location): 321 GRETNA GREEN WAY
106 CITY: LOS ANGELES

CAUSE OF DEATH

107 CAUSE OF DEATH — Enter the chain of events – diseases, injuries, or complications – that directly caused death. DO NOT enter terminal events such as cardiac arrest, respiratory arrest, or ventricular fibrillation without showing the etiology. DO NOT ABBREVIATE.
IMMEDIATE CAUSE (Final disease or condition resulting in death) (A): CONGESTIVE HEART FAILURE — Time Interval Between Onset and Death (AT): YRS
Sequentially, list conditions, if any, leading to cause on Line A. Enter UNDERLYING CAUSE (disease or injury that initiated the events resulting in death) LAST: (B) (C) (D)
108 DEATH REPORTED TO CORONER? [ ] YES [X] NO
109 BIOPSY PERFORMED? [ ] YES [X] NO
110 AUTOPSY PERFORMED? [ ] YES [X] NO
111 USED IN DETERMINING CAUSE? [ ] YES [X] NO
112 OTHER SIGNIFICANT CONDITIONS CONTRIBUTING TO DEATH BUT NOT RESULTING IN THE UNDERLYING CAUSE GIVEN IN 107: NONE
113 WAS OPERATION PERFORMED FOR ANY CONDITION IN ITEM 107 OR 112? (If yes, list type of operation and date.): NO
113A IF FEMALE, PREGNANT IN LAST YEAR? [ ] YES [ ] NO [ ] UNK

PHYSICIAN'S CERTIFICATION

114 I CERTIFY THAT TO THE BEST OF MY KNOWLEDGE DEATH OCCURRED AT THE HOUR, DATE, AND PLACE STATED FROM THE CAUSES STATED.
Decedent Attended Since (A) mm/dd/ccyy: 08/22/2002
Decedent Last Seen Alive (B) mm/dd/ccyy: 06/20/2007
115 SIGNATURE AND TITLE OF CERTIFIER: W. Harrell
116 LICENSE NUMBER: G64492
117 DATE mm/dd/ccyy: 07/12/2007
118 TYPE ATTENDING PHYSICIAN'S NAME, MAILING ADDRESS, ZIP CODE: WILLIAM C. HARRELL, MD 2021 SANTA MONICA BLVD. #337, SANTA MONICA, CA 90404

CORONER'S USE ONLY

119 I CERTIFY THAT IN MY OPINION DEATH OCCURRED AT THE HOUR, DATE, AND PLACE STATED FROM THE CAUSES STATED. MANNER OF DEATH [ ] Natural [ ] Accident [ ] Homicide [ ] Suicide [ ] Pending Investigation [ ] Could not be determined
120 INJURED AT WORK? [ ] YES [ ] NO [ ] UNK
121 INJURY DATE mm/dd/ccyy
122 HOUR (24 Hours)
123 PLACE OF INJURY (e.g. home, construction site, wooded area, etc.)
124 DESCRIBE HOW INJURY OCCURRED (Events which resulted in injury)
125 LOCATION OF INJURY (Street and number, or location, and city, and zip)
126 SIGNATURE OF CORONER / DEPUTY CORONER
127 DATE mm/dd/ccyy
128 TYPE NAME, TITLE OF CORONER / DEPUTY CORONER

STATE REGISTRAR: A B C D E — FAX AUTH #: 195/3556 — CENSUS TRACT

This is to certify that this document is a true copy of the official record filed with the Registrar-Recorder/County Clerk. JAN 22 2008

INFORMATIONAL, NOT A VALID DOCUMENT TO ESTABLISH IDENTITY

019042568

This copy not valid unless prepared on engraved border displaying the Seal of the Registrar-Recorder/County Clerk.

PBNCO (Rev) 11/06

MIDWEST BANK NOTE COMPANY

ANY ALTERATION OR ERASURE VOIDS THIS CERTIFICATE

STATE OF CALIFORNIA
CERTIFICATION OF VITAL RECORD
COUNTY OF LOS ANGELES • REGISTRAR-RECORDER/COUNTY CLERK

DISTRICT No. 7901 **REGISTRAR'S No.** 19851

1. **FULL NAME:** Harry Philmore Langdon
2. **PLACE OF DEATH:**
   - (A) COUNTY: Los Angeles
   - (B) CITY OR TOWN: Los Angeles
   - (C) NAME OF HOSPITAL OR INSTITUTION: St Vincents Hosp.
   - (D) LENGTH OF STAY: IN HOSPITAL OR INSTITUTION: 1 day; IN THIS COMMUNITY: 22 yrs; IN CALIFORNIA: 22 yrs
3. **USUAL RESIDENCE OF DECEASED:**
   - (A) STATE: California
   - (B) COUNTY: Los Angeles
   - (C) CITY OR TOWN: Los Angeles
   - (D) STREET No.: 3365 Oak Glen Drive
3. (E) IF VETERAN, NAME OF WAR: No
3. (F) SOCIAL SECURITY NO: 571-10-5901
4. **SEX:** Male
5. **COLOR OR RACE:** Cauc
6. (A) **SINGLE, MARRIED, WIDOWED OR DIVORCED:** Married
6. (B) **NAME OF HUSBAND OR WIFE:** Mabel Langdon
6. (C) **AGE OF HUSBAND OR WIFE IF ALIVE:** 38 YEARS
7. **BIRTHDATE OF DECEASED:** June 15, 1884
8. **AGE:** 60 yrs 6 mos 7 days
9. **BIRTHPLACE:** Unknown
10. **USUAL OCCUPATION:** Actor
11. **INDUSTRY OR BUSINESS:** Motion Pictures
12. **FATHER NAME:** William W. Langdon
13. **BIRTHPLACE:** Unknown
14. **MOTHER MAIDEN NAME:** Lavina Lockinbill
15. **BIRTHPLACE:** Unknown
16. (A) **INFORMANT:** Mabel Langdon
    (B) **ADDRESS:** 3365 Oak Glen Drive
17. (A) BURIAL, CREMATION OR REMOVAL: Cremation
    (B) DATE: 12/26/44
    (C) PLACE: Pierce Brothers Crematory
18. (A) **EMBALMER'S SIGNATURE:** Joseph E. Wiley LICENSE No. 2561
    (B) **FUNERAL DIRECTOR:** Pierce Bros. Hollywood
    ADDRESS: 5959 Santa Monica Blvd.
19. (A) **DATE FILED:** Dec 25 1944

20. **DATE OF DEATH:** MONTH: Dec. DAY: 22 YEAR: 1944 HOUR: 8 MINUTE: 25 A.M.

21. **MEDICAL CERTIFICATE:** I HEREBY CERTIFY, THAT I ATTENDED THE DECEASED FROM Dec 11 1944 TO Dec 21 1944; THAT I LAST SAW H- ALIVE ON Dec 21 1944; AND THAT DEATH OCCURRED ON THE DATE AND HOUR STATED ABOVE.

IMMEDIATE CAUSE OF DEATH: Cerebral Thrombosis — DURATION: 11 days
DUE TO: Cerebral Arteriosclerosis — Unknown

22. **CORONER'S CERTIFICATE**

24. **CORONER'S OR PHYSICIAN'S SIGNATURE:** J.M. Wheelis
    ADDRESS: Beverly Hills DATE: 12-23-44

CERTIFICATE OF DEATH

STATE OF CALIFORNIA — DEPARTMENT OF PUBLIC HEALTH
U.S. DEPT. OF COMMERCE — BUREAU OF THE CENSUS

CONNY B. McCORMACK, Registrar-Recorder/County Clerk
NOV 28 2000

CERTIFICATE OF DEATH
STATE OF CALIFORNIA—DEPARTMENT OF PUBLIC HEALTH

Local Registration District: 7053
Certificate Number: 21729

Decedent Personal Data
- 1a. Name of Deceased—First Name: CHARLES
- 1c. Last Name: LAUGHTON
- 2a. Date of Death: 12/15/62
- 2b. Hour: 10:30 P.
- 3. Sex: MALE
- 4. Color or Race: CAUCASIAN
- 5. Birthplace: ENGLAND
- 6. Date of Birth: JULY 1, 1899
- 7. Age: 63
- 8. Name and Birthplace of Father: ROBERT LAUGHTON, ENGLAND
- 9. Maiden Name and Birthplace of Mother: ELIZA CONLON, IRELAND
- 10. Citizen of What Country: U.S.A.
- 11. Social Security Number: 549-20-1262
- 12. Last Occupation: ACTOR
- 13. Number of Years in this Occupation: 37
- 14. Name of Last Employing Company or Firm: SELF EMPLOYED
- 15. Kind of Industry or Business: STAGE & MOTION PICTURES
- 16. Armed Forces: WORLD WAR I (ENGLAND)
- 17. Specify Married, Never Married, Widowed, Divorced: MARRIED
- 18a. Name of Present Spouse: ELSA LANCHESTER LAUGHTON
- 18b. Present or Last Occupation of Spouse: ACTRESS

Place of Death
- 19a. Place of Death: RESIDENCE
- 19b. Street Address: 1825 NORTH CURSON AVENUE
- 19c. City or Town: LOS ANGELES (HOLLYWOOD)
- 19d. County: LOS ANGELES
- 19e. Length of Stay in County of Death: 25 YEARS
- 19f. Length of Stay in California: 25 YEARS

Last Usual Residence
- 20a. Street Address: 1825 NORTH CURSON AVENUE
- 20c. City or Town: HOLLYWOOD
- 20d. County: LOS ANGELES
- 20e. State: CALIFORNIA
- 21a. Name of Informant: FRANCIS LAUGHTON, BROTHER

Physician's or Coroner's Certification
- 22a. Physician: Death occurred 12/15/62, attended deceased from 5/18/62 to 12/15/62
- 22c. Physician or Coroner—Signature: Harold Bernstein M.D.
- 22d. Address: 436 N. ROXBURY DR., BEVERLY HILLS CALIF.
- 22e. Date Signed: 12/17/62

Funeral Director and Local Registrar
- 23. Burial, Cremation: BURIAL
- 24. Date: DEC. 19, 1962
- 25. Name of Cemetery or Crematory: FOREST LAWN HOLLYWOOD HILLS
- 26. Embalmer License Number: 2375
- 27. Name of Funeral Director: FOREST LAWN HOLLYWOOD HILLS
- 28. Date Accepted by Local Registrar: DEC 19 1962

Cause of Death
- 30. Cause of Death Part I(a): Metastatic renal carcinoma — 11 mos.

- 31. Operation: (checked)
- 32. Date of Operation: 7/30/62
- 33. Autopsy: NO

Beatriz Valdez
Registrar-Recorder/County Clerk

AUG 04 1995
19-390012

Certificate of Death

State of California — Department of Public Health

Local Registration District and Certificate Number: 7080 8928

Decedent Personal Data

- **1a. Name of Deceased — First Name:** Stan
- **1c. Last Name:** Laurel
- **2a. Date of Death:** February 23, 1965
- **2b. Hour:** 7:45
- **3. Sex:** Male
- **4. Color or Race:** Caucasian
- **5. Birthplace:** England
- **6. Date of Birth:** June 16, 1890
- **7. Age (Last Birthday):** 74 Years
- **8. Name and Birthplace of Father:** Arthur Jefferson — England
- **9. Maiden Name and Birthplace of Mother:** Madge Metcalf — England
- **10. Citizen of What Country:** England
- **11. Social Security Number:** 547-10-8329
- **12. Last Occupation:** Movie Actor
- **13. Number of Years in This Occupation:** 50
- **14. Name of Last Employing Company or Firm:** Laurel & Hardy Productions
- **15. Kind of Industry or Business:** Movies
- **16. If Deceased Was Ever in U.S. Armed Forces:** None
- **17. Specify Married, Never Married, Widowed, Divorced:** Married
- **18a. Name of Present Spouse:** Ida K. Laurel
- **18b. Present or Last Occupation of Spouse:** Homemaker

Place of Death

- **19a. Place of Death — Name of Hospital:** (Not in a Hospital)
- **19b. Street Address:** 849 Ocean Avenue
- **19c. City or Town:** Santa Monica
- **19d. County:** Los Angeles
- **19e. Length of Stay in County of Death:** 50 Years
- **19f. Length of Stay in California:** 50 Years

Last Usual Residence

- **20a. Last Usual Residence — Street Address:** 849 Ocean Blvd.
- **20b. Inside City Corporate Limits:** Check here
- **20c. City or Town:** Santa Monica
- **20d. County:** Los Angeles
- **20e. State:** California
- **21a. Name of Informant:** Ida K. Laurel

Physician's or Coroner's Certification

- **22b. Physician or Coroner — Signature:** [signature] M.D.
- **22c. Address:** 225 Santa Monica, Santa Monica, Cal.
- **22e. Date Signed:** 2/24/65

Funeral Director and Local Registrar

- **23. Specify Burial, Entombment or Cremation:** Cremation
- **24. Date:** February 26, 1965
- **25. Name of Cemetery or Crematory:** Forest Lawn Crematory — Los Angeles
- **26. Embalmer — Signature / License Number:** Harris O. Small — 2856
- **27. Name of Funeral Director:** Forest Lawn Hollywood Hills, 6300 Forest Lawn Dr., Los Angeles 28, Calif.
- **28. Date Accepted for Registration:** FEB 26 1965
- **29. Local Registrar Signature:** R. H. Sutherland, M.D.

Cause of Death

Part I. Death was caused by:

- **Immediate Cause (a):** Myocardial Infarction, Massive (Posterior) — 28 hours
- **Due to (b):** Arteriosclerosis — Long Bundle Branch Block — 20 years
- **Due to (c):** Atherosclerosis — Advanced — 12 years

Part II. Other significant conditions contributing to death but not related to the terminal disease condition given in Part I(a):
Diabetes Mellitus — Brittle

Operation and Autopsy

- **31. Operation:** No Operation Performed
- **33. Autopsy:** No Autopsy Performed

Local Registration Number: 19-389280

Date stamped: AUG 10 1995

Beatriz Valdez, Registrar-Recorder/County Clerk

STATE OF CALIFORNIA
CERTIFICATION OF VITAL RECORD

COUNTY OF LOS ANGELES
DEPARTMENT OF HEALTH SERVICES

CERTIFICATE OF DEATH
STATE OF CALIFORNIA

1. Name of Decedent—First (Given)	Anthony
2. Middle	Dwain
3. Last (Family)	Lee
4. Date of Birth	07/17/1961
5. Age	39
6. Sex	Male
7. Date of Death	10/28/2000
8. Hour	0104
9. State of Birth	CA
10. Social Security No.	561-35-6974
11. Military Service	No
12. Marital Status	Divorced
13. Education—Years Completed	12
14. Race	African-American
15. Hispanic	No
16. Usual Employer	S.A.G – Aftra
17. Occupation	Actor
18. Kind of Business	Entertainment
19. Years in Occupation	20
20. Residence	7201 Lennox Ave., #315
21. City	Van Nuys
22. County	Los Angeles
23. Zip Code	91405
24. Yrs in County	6
25. State	California
26. Informant Name, Relationship	Tina F. Lee-Vogt, Sister
27. Mailing Address	8977 Vista Campo Way Elk Grove, Ca., 95758
31. Name of Father—First	Willard
32. Middle	Bernard
33. Last	Lee
34. Birth State	LA
35. Name of Mother—First	Frances
36. Middle	Faye
37. Last (Maiden)	Hayes
38. Birth State	TX
39. Date	11/10/2000
40. Place of Final Disposition	At residence, Tina F. Lee-Vogt 8977 Vista Campo Way, Elk Grove, CA 95758
41. Type of Disposition	CR/RES
42. Signature of Embalmer	Not Embalmed
44. Name of Funeral Director	Angelus Funeral Home
45. License No.	FD 243
47. Date	11/09/2000
101. Place of Death	Residence
104. County	Los Angeles
105. Street Address	9701 Yoakum Drive
106. City	Los Angeles
107. Immediate Cause (A)	Deferred
108. Death Reported to Coroner	Yes – Referral Number 2000-07602
110. Autopsy Performed	Yes
119. Manner of Death	Pending Investigation
126. Signature of Coroner	[signed]
127. Date	11/02/2000
128. Typed Name	Rachel Zaragoza Deputy Coroner
Census Tract	090382235

This is a true certified copy of the record filed in the County of Los Angeles Department of Health Services if it bears the Registrar's signature in purple ink.

DATE ISSUED DEC 06 2000

Director of Health Services and Registrar

This copy not valid unless prepared on engraved border displaying seal and signature of Registrar.

ANY ALTERATION OR ERASURE VOIDS THIS CERTIFICATE

COUNTY OF LOS ANGELES
DEPARTMENT OF HEALTH SERVICES
AMENDMENT OF MEDICAL AND HEALTH DATA—DEATH

PART I — INFORMATION TO LOCATE RECORD
- 1. NAME—FIRST (GIVEN): Anthony
- 2. MIDDLE: Dwain
- 3. LAST (FAMILY): Lee
- 4. SEX: Male
- 5. DATE OF EVENT—MM/DD/CCYY: 10/28/2000
- 6. CITY OF OCCURRENCE: Los Angeles
- 7. COUNTY OF OCCURRENCE: Los Angeles
- 2 OF 2

PART II — INFORMATION AS IT APPEARS ON RECORD
- 107. DEATH WAS CAUSED BY:
  - (A) IMMEDIATE CAUSE: Deferred
- 108. DEATH REPORTED TO CORONER: YES — REFERRAL NUMBER 2000-07602
- 109. BIOPSY PERFORMED: (blank)
- 110. AUTOPSY PERFORMED: YES
- 111. USED IN DETERMINING CAUSE: (blank)
- 112. OTHER SIGNIFICANT CONDITIONS: (blank)
- 113. WAS OPERATION PERFORMED: (blank)
- 119. MANNER OF DEATH: PENDING INVESTIGATION
- 120. INJURY AT WORK: (blank)
- 121. INJURY DATE: (blank)
- 122. HOUR: (blank)
- 123. PLACE OF INJURY: (blank)
- 124. DESCRIBE HOW INJURY OCCURRED: (blank)
- 125. LOCATION: (blank)

PART III — INFORMATION AS IT SHOULD APPEAR
- 107. DEATH WAS CAUSED BY:
  - (A) IMMEDIATE CAUSE: Multiple Gunshot Wounds
- TIME INTERVAL BETWEEN ONSET AND DEATH: Rapid
- 108. DEATH REPORTED TO CORONER: YES — REFERRAL NUMBER 2000-07602
- 109. BIOPSY PERFORMED: NO
- 110. AUTOPSY PERFORMED: YES
- 111. USED IN DETERMINING CAUSE: YES
- 112. OTHER SIGNIFICANT CONDITIONS: None
- 113. WAS OPERATION PERFORMED: No
- 119. MANNER OF DEATH: HOMICIDE
- 120. INJURY AT WORK: NO
- 121. INJURY DATE: 10/28/2000
- 122. HOUR: 0045
- 123. PLACE OF INJURY: Residence
- 124. DESCRIBE HOW INJURY OCCURRED: Shot By Officer
- 125. LOCATION: 9701 Yoakum Drive, Los Angeles 90210

DECLARATION OF CERTIFYING PHYSICIAN OR CORONER
- 8. SIGNATURE OF CERTIFYING PHYSICIAN OR CORONER: Jeffrey Gutstadt MD
- 9. DATE SIGNED: 11/30/2000
- 10. TYPED OR PRINTED NAME AND DEGREE/TITLE OF CERTIFIER: Jeffrey P. Gutstadt, M.D. DME
- 11. ADDRESS: 1104 North Mission Road
- 12. CITY: Los Angeles
- 13. STATE: Calif.
- 14. ZIP CODE: 90033

STATE/LOCAL REGISTRAR USE ONLY
- 15. OFFICE OF STATE REGISTRAR OR SIGNATURE OF LOCAL REGISTRAR: Mark Finnman rh
- 16. DATE ACCEPTED FOR REGISTRATION: 12/01/2000

090382322

COUNTY OF LOS ANGELES
DEPARTMENT OF HEALTH SERVICES

CERTIFICATE OF DEATH
STATE OF CALIFORNIA

DECEDENT PERSONAL DATA
- 1. Name of Decedent—First (Given): PHILIP
- 3. Last (Family): LEEDS
- 4. Date of Birth: 04/06/1906
- 5. Age: 92
- 6. Sex: MALE
- 7. Date of Death: 08/16/1998
- 8. Hour: 1413
- 9. State of Birth: NY
- 10. Social Security No.: 061-07-9153
- 11. Military Service: No
- 12. Marital Status: WIDOWER
- 13. Education—Years Completed: 17
- 14. Race: CAUCASIAN
- 15. Hispanic: No
- 16. Usual Employer: SELF EMPLOYED
- 17. Occupation: ACTOR
- 18. Kind of Business: MOTION PICTURE & TELEVISION
- 19. Years in Occupation: 60

USUAL RESIDENCE
- 20. Residence: 7135 HOLLYWOOD BL. #102
- 21. City: LOS ANGELES
- 22. County: LOS ANGELES
- 23. Zip Code: 90046
- 24. Yrs in County: 22
- 25. State: CALIFORNIA

INFORMANT
- 26. Name, Relationship: HONEY SHAPIRO – EXECUTRIX
- 27. Mailing Address: 7135 HOLLYWOOD BL. PENTHOUSE 2, L.A., CA. 90046

SPOUSE AND PARENT INFORMATION
- 31. Name of Father—First: UNKNOWN
- 32. Middle: UNKNOWN
- 33. Last: UNKNOWN
- 34. Birth State: NY
- 35. Name of Mother—First: UNKNOWN
- 36. Middle: UNKNOWN
- 37. Last (Maiden): UNKNOWN
- 38. Birth State: NY

DISPOSITION(S)
- 39. Date: 08/28/1998
- 40. Place of Final Disposition: HONEY SHAPIRO RES: 7135 HOLLYWOOD BL. PENTHOUSE 2, L.A., CA.
- 41. Type of Disposition(s): CR/RES
- 42. Signature of Embalmer: NOT EMBALMED
- 44. Name of Funeral Director: NEPTUNE SOCIETY
- 45. License No.: FD 1359
- 47. Date: 08/27/1998

PLACE OF DEATH
- 101. Place of Death: CEDARS SINAI MED CTR
- 102. IP
- 104. County: LOS ANGELES
- 105. Street Address: 8700 BEVERLY BL.
- 106. City: LOS ANGELES

CAUSE OF DEATH
- 107. Death was caused by:
  - (A) Immediate Cause: RESPIRATORY FAILURE — IMMED.
  - (B) Due to: PNEUMONIA — 1 WEEK
  - (C) Due to: ASPIRATION PNEUMONIA — 1 WEEK
  - (D) Due to: HIATAL HERNIA — 10 YRS
- 108. Death Reported to Coroner: YES — Referral Number 98-55910
- 109. Biopsy Performed: No
- 110. Autopsy Performed: No
- 111. Used in Determining Cause: No
- 112. Other Significant Conditions: EMPHYSEMA, CORONARY ARTERY DISEASE
- 113. Was Operation Performed: NO

PHYSICIAN'S CERTIFICATION
- Decedent Attended Since: 08/07/1998
- Decedent Last Seen Alive: 08/16/1998
- 116. License No.: A20389
- 117. Date: 08/25/1998
- Attending Physician: C. J. BURSTIN, MD, 9091 WILSHIRE BL #203, L.A., CA. 90211

CORONER'S USE ONLY
- 119. Manner of Death: NATURAL

Date Issued: SEP 01 1998

Census: 090167888
Fax Auth. #: 195/7672

COUNTY OF LOS ANGELES
DEPARTMENT OF HEALTH SERVICES

CERTIFICATE OF DEATH
STATE FILE NUMBER: 3 2002 19 003000

DECEDENT PERSONAL DATA
1. Name of Decedent—First (Given): QUEENIE
2. Middle: —
3. Last (Family): LEONARD
4. Date of Birth: 02/18/1905
5. Age Yrs.: 96
6. Sex: F
7. Date of Death: 01/19/2002
8. Hour: 1030
9. State of Birth: ENGLAND
10. Social Security No.: 560-26-1166
11. Military Service: No
12. Marital Status: DIVORCED
13. Education—Years Completed: UNK
14. Race: CAUCASIAN
15. Hispanic: No
16. Usual Employer: SELF-EMPLOYED
17. Occupation: ACTRESS
18. Kind of Business: SHOW BUSINESS
19. Years in Occupation: 50

USUAL RESIDENCE
20. Residence: 1330 FEDERAL AVE., APT. #12
21. City: LOS ANGELES
22. County: LOS ANGELES
23. Zip Code: 90025
24. Yrs in County: 60
25. State or Foreign Country: CA

INFORMANT
26. Name, Relationship: PATIENCE CLEVELAND, POA
27. Mailing Address: 21321 PROVIDENCIA ST., WOODLAND HILLS, CA 91364

SPOUSE AND PARENT INFORMATION
28-30. Name of Surviving Spouse: —
31. Name of Father—First: JOHN
32. Middle: L.
33. Last: WALKER
34. Birth State: ENGLAND
35. Name of Mother—First: LOUISE
36. Middle: —
37. Last (Maiden): CLEGG
38. Birth State: ENGLAND

DISPOSITION(S)
39. Date: 01/28/2002
40. Place of Final Disposition: WESTWOOD VILLAGE MEMORIAL PARK 1218 GLENDON AVE., LOS ANGELES, CA
41. Type of Disposition(s): CR/BU
42. Signature of Embalmer: NOT EMBALMED

FUNERAL DIRECTOR AND LOCAL REGISTRAR
44. Name of Funeral Director: PIERCE BROTHERS CUNNINGHAM & O'CONNOR
45. License No.: FD-8
46. Signature of Local Registrar: Frez Leaf
47. Date: 01/25/2002

PLACE OF DEATH
101. Place of Death: RES
105. Street Address: 1330 FEDERAL AVE., APT. #12
106. City: LOS ANGELES
104. County: LOS ANGELES

CAUSE OF DEATH
107. Death was caused by:
(A) Immediate Cause: CARDIOPULMONARY COLLAPSE — 1 MIN
(B) Due to: HYPERTENSION — 1 YR
(C) Due to: CONGESTIVE HEART FAILURE — 5 YRS
108. Death Reported to Coroner: Yes — Referral Number 2002-50760
109. Biopsy Performed: No
110. Autopsy Performed: No
112. Other Significant Conditions: HYPOTHYROIDISM; ATRIAL FIBRILLATION
113. Was Operation Performed: NO

I119

PHYSICIAN'S CERTIFICATION
114. Decedent Attended Since: 01/05/1990; Last Seen Alive: 07/27/2001
115. Signature and Title of Certifier: [signature]
116. License No.: A21573
117. Date: 01/25/2002
118. Attending Physician: ROLAND E. WALLEN, MD 2001 SANTA MONICA BLVD., STE. #1060W, SANTA MONICA, CA 90404

CORONER'S USE ONLY
119. Manner of Death: 5

FAX AUTH. #: 092-B415

This is a true certified copy of the record filed in the County of Los Angeles Department of Health Services if it bears the Registrar's signature in purple ink.

DATE ISSUED: MAY 01 2002

Director of Health Services and Registrar

This copy not valid unless prepared on engraved border displaying seal and signature of Registrar.

State of California Certification of Vital Record

County of Los Angeles • Registrar-Recorder/County Clerk

Certificate of Death — State of California

State File Number: 0190-026534

1A. Name of Decedent—First	ALLEN
1B. Middle	
1C. Last	LUDDEN
2A. Date of Death	JUNE 9, 1981
2B. Hour	0124
3. Sex	Male
4. Race	White
6. Date of Birth	October 5, 1917
7. Age	63 years
8. Birthplace of Decedent	Wisconsin
9. Name and Birthplace of Father	Elmer Ellsworth – Wisconsin
10. Birth Name and Birthplace of Mother	Leila Allen – Wisconsin
11. Citizen of What Country	United States
12. Social Security Number	461-02-2186
13. Marital Status	Married
14. Name of Surviving Spouse	Betty White
15. Primary Occupation	Actor
16. Number of Years This Occupation	30
17. Employed	Self-employed
18. Kind of Industry or Business	Entertainment

Usual Residence:
- 19A. 506 North Carmelina Avenue
- 19C. Los Angeles
- 19D. County: Los Angeles
- 19E. State: California

20. Informant: Mr. Richard D. Keesling, friend — 11940 San Vicente Boulevard, Los Angeles, California 90049

Place of Death:
- 21A. Hospital of the Good Samaritan
- 21B. Los Angeles
- 21C. 616 South Witmer
- 21D. Los Angeles

22. Cause of Death:
- (A) FIBROSARCOMA — 2½ yrs
- 24. Was Death Reported to Coroner? NO
- 25. Was Biopsy Performed? YES
- 26. Was Autopsy Performed? NO

23. Other Conditions: HYPERCALCEMIA

27. Operation: LAPARATOMY — 4/7/80

Physician's Certification:
- 28A. Attended 2/19/80; Last saw alive 5/29/81
- 28B. Edward E. Harnagel
- 28C. Date signed: 6/10/81
- 28D. License: C-9775
- 28E. Edward E. Harnagel, M.D., 2010 Wilshire, L.A., CA 90057

36. Disposition: Burial
37. Date: Shipped June 11, 1981
38. Cemetery: Graceland Cemetery, Mineral Point, Wisconsin 7154
40. Funeral Director: Forest Lawn-Hollywood Hills
42. Date Accepted by Local Registrar: JUN 11 1981

CONNY B. McCORMACK
Registrar-Recorder/County Clerk

APR 06 2000

19-557852

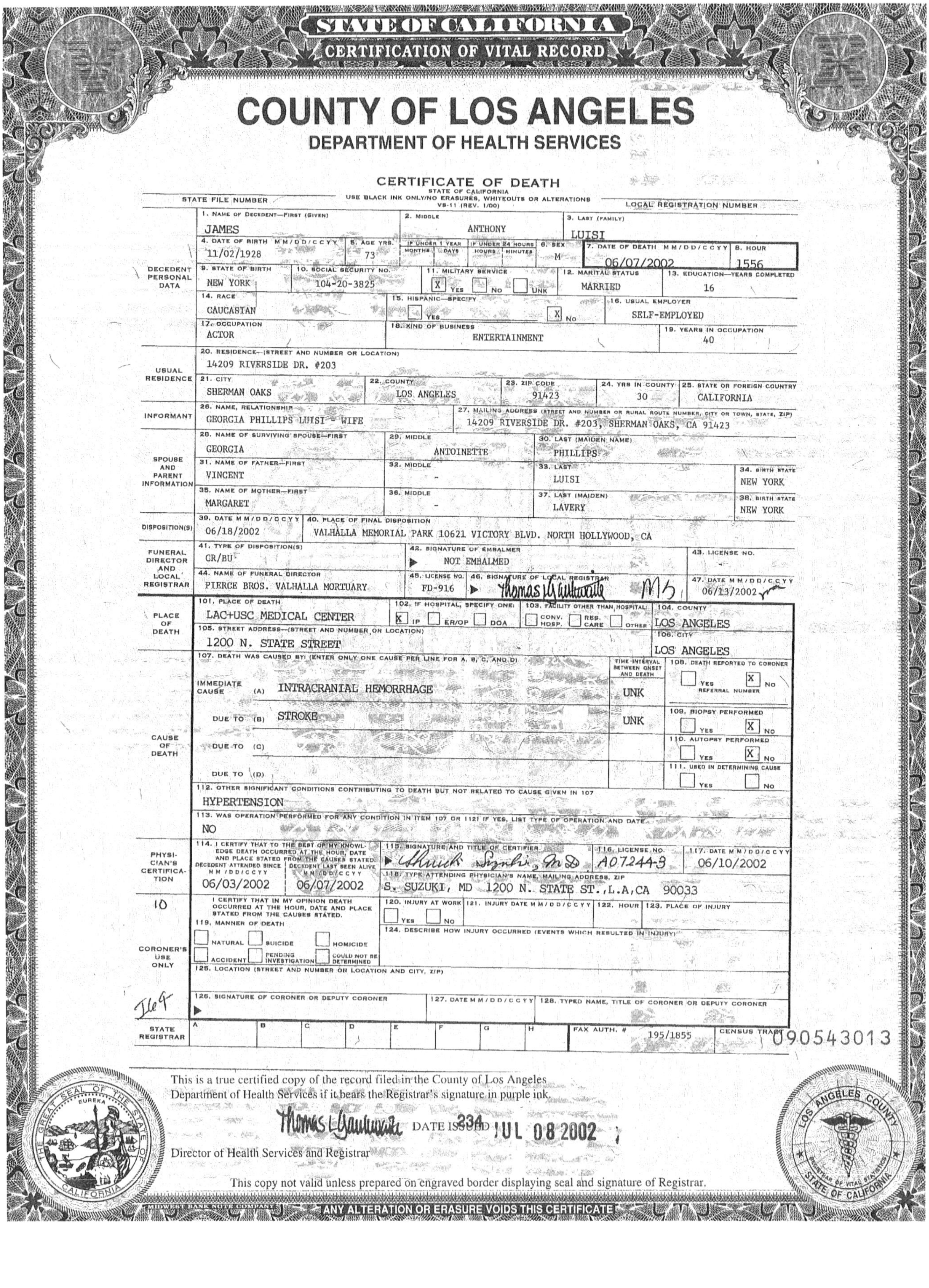

STATE OF CALIFORNIA
CERTIFICATION OF VITAL RECORD

COUNTY OF LOS ANGELES

DEPARTMENT OF HEALTH SERVICES

CERTIFICATE OF DEATH
STATE OF CALIFORNIA
USE BLACK INK ONLY/NO ERASURES, WHITEOUTS OR ALTERATIONS
VS-11 (REV. 1/00)

STATE FILE NUMBER — LOCAL REGISTRATION NUMBER

DECEDENT PERSONAL DATA

1. NAME OF DECEDENT—FIRST (GIVEN): JAMES
2. MIDDLE: ANTHONY
3. LAST (FAMILY): LUISI
4. DATE OF BIRTH MM/DD/CCYY: 11/02/1928
5. AGE YRS.: 73
6. SEX: M
7. DATE OF DEATH MM/DD/CCYY: 06/07/2002
8. HOUR: 1556
9. STATE OF BIRTH: NEW YORK
10. SOCIAL SECURITY NO.: 104-20-3825
11. MILITARY SERVICE: [X] YES [ ] NO [ ] UNK
12. MARITAL STATUS: MARRIED
13. EDUCATION—YEARS COMPLETED: 16
14. RACE: CAUCASIAN
15. HISPANIC—SPECIFY: [ ] YES [X] NO
16. USUAL EMPLOYER: SELF-EMPLOYED
17. OCCUPATION: ACTOR
18. KIND OF BUSINESS: ENTERTAINMENT
19. YEARS IN OCCUPATION: 40

USUAL RESIDENCE

20. RESIDENCE—(STREET AND NUMBER OR LOCATION): 14209 RIVERSIDE DR. #203
21. CITY: SHERMAN OAKS
22. COUNTY: LOS ANGELES
23. ZIP CODE: 91423
24. YRS IN COUNTY: 30
25. STATE OR FOREIGN COUNTRY: CALIFORNIA

INFORMANT

26. NAME, RELATIONSHIP: GEORGIA PHILLIPS LUISI - WIFE
27. MAILING ADDRESS (STREET AND NUMBER OR RURAL ROUTE NUMBER, CITY OR TOWN, STATE, ZIP): 14209 RIVERSIDE DR. #203, SHERMAN OAKS, CA 91423

SPOUSE AND PARENT INFORMATION

28. NAME OF SURVIVING SPOUSE—FIRST: GEORGIA
29. MIDDLE: ANTOINETTE
30. LAST (MAIDEN NAME): PHILLIPS
31. NAME OF FATHER—FIRST: VINCENT
32. MIDDLE: -
33. LAST: LUISI
34. BIRTH STATE: NEW YORK
35. NAME OF MOTHER—FIRST: MARGARET
36. MIDDLE: -
37. LAST (MAIDEN): LAVERY
38. BIRTH STATE: NEW YORK

DISPOSITION(S)

39. DATE MM/DD/CCYY: 06/18/2002
40. PLACE OF FINAL DISPOSITION: VALHALLA MEMORIAL PARK 10621 VICTORY BLVD. NORTH HOLLYWOOD, CA

FUNERAL DIRECTOR AND LOCAL REGISTRAR

41. TYPE OF DISPOSITION(S): CR/BU
42. SIGNATURE OF EMBALMER: NOT EMBALMED
43. LICENSE NO.:
44. NAME OF FUNERAL DIRECTOR: PIERCE BROS. VALHALLA MORTUARY
45. LICENSE NO.: FD-916
46. SIGNATURE OF LOCAL REGISTRAR: Thomas L Garthwaite MD
47. DATE MM/DD/CCYY: 06/13/2002

PLACE OF DEATH

101. PLACE OF DEATH: LAC+USC MEDICAL CENTER
102. IF HOSPITAL, SPECIFY ONE: [X] IP [ ] ER/OP [ ] DOA
103. IF FACILITY OTHER THAN HOSPITAL: [ ] CONV. HOSP. [ ] RES. CARE [ ] OTHER
104. COUNTY: LOS ANGELES
105. STREET ADDRESS—(STREET AND NUMBER OR LOCATION): 1200 N. STATE STREET
106. CITY: LOS ANGELES

CAUSE OF DEATH

107. DEATH WAS CAUSED BY: (ENTER ONLY ONE CAUSE PER LINE FOR A, B, C, AND D)

	Cause	Time interval between onset and death
IMMEDIATE CAUSE (A)	INTRACRANIAL HEMORRHAGE	UNK
DUE TO (B)	STROKE	UNK
DUE TO (C)		
DUE TO (D)		

108. DEATH REPORTED TO CORONER: [ ] YES [X] NO — REFERRAL NUMBER
109. BIOPSY PERFORMED: [ ] YES [X] NO
110. AUTOPSY PERFORMED: [ ] YES [X] NO
111. USED IN DETERMINING CAUSE: [ ] YES [ ] NO
112. OTHER SIGNIFICANT CONDITIONS CONTRIBUTING TO DEATH BUT NOT RELATED TO CAUSE GIVEN IN 107: HYPERTENSION
113. WAS OPERATION PERFORMED FOR ANY CONDITION IN ITEM 107 OR 112? IF YES, LIST TYPE OF OPERATION AND DATE: NO

PHYSICIAN'S CERTIFICATION

114. I CERTIFY THAT TO THE BEST OF MY KNOWLEDGE DEATH OCCURRED AT THE HOUR, DATE AND PLACE STATED FROM THE CAUSES STATED.
DECEDENT ATTENDED SINCE MM/DD/CCYY: 06/03/2002
DECEDENT LAST SEEN ALIVE MM/DD/CCYY: 06/07/2002
115. SIGNATURE AND TITLE OF CERTIFIER: Shinichi Suzuki, MD
116. LICENSE NO.: A072443
117. DATE MM/DD/CCYY: 06/10/2002
118. TYPE ATTENDING PHYSICIAN'S NAME, MAILING ADDRESS, ZIP: S. SUZUKI, MD 1200 N. STATE ST., L.A, CA 90033

10

CORONER'S USE ONLY

I CERTIFY THAT IN MY OPINION DEATH OCCURRED AT THE HOUR, DATE AND PLACE STATED FROM THE CAUSES STATED.
119. MANNER OF DEATH: [ ] NATURAL [ ] SUICIDE [ ] HOMICIDE [ ] ACCIDENT [ ] PENDING INVESTIGATION [ ] COULD NOT BE DETERMINED
120. INJURY AT WORK: [ ] YES [ ] NO
121. INJURY DATE MM/DD/CCYY
122. HOUR
123. PLACE OF INJURY
124. DESCRIBE HOW INJURY OCCURRED (EVENTS WHICH RESULTED IN INJURY)
125. LOCATION (STREET AND NUMBER OR LOCATION AND CITY, ZIP)
126. SIGNATURE OF CORONER OR DEPUTY CORONER
127. DATE MM/DD/CCYY
128. TYPED NAME, TITLE OF CORONER OR DEPUTY CORONER

Jk4

STATE REGISTRAR: A B C D E F G H — FAX AUTH. # — 195/1855 — CENSUS TRACT

090543013

This is a true certified copy of the record filed in the County of Los Angeles Department of Health Services if it bears the Registrar's signature in purple ink.

Thomas L Garthwaite — DATE ISSUED 334 JUL 08 2002

Director of Health Services and Registrar

This copy not valid unless prepared on engraved border displaying seal and signature of Registrar.

ANY ALTERATION OR ERASURE VOIDS THIS CERTIFICATE

COUNTY OF SONOMA
SANTA ROSA, CALIFORNIA

CERTIFICATE OF DEATH

State File Number: 3-1999-49-002289

DECEDENT PERSONAL DATA
- 1. Name of Decedent—First (Given): Charles
- 2. Middle: —
- 3. Last (Family): Macauley
- 4. Date of Birth: 09/26/1927
- 5. Age Yrs.: 71
- 6. Sex: M
- 7. Date of Death: 08/13/1999
- 8. Hour: 0512
- 9. State of Birth: KY
- 10. Social Security No.: 407-28-3723
- 11. Military Service: Yes
- 12. Marital Status: Never Married
- 13. Education—Years Completed: 12
- 14. Race: White
- 15. Hispanic: No
- 16. Usual Employer: Viacom
- 17. Occupation: Actor
- 18. Kind of Business: Entertainment
- 19. Years in Occupation: 40

USUAL RESIDENCE
- 20. Residence: 8339 West Dry Creek Road
- 21. City: Healdsburg
- 22. County: Sonoma
- 23. Zip Code: 95448
- 24. Yrs in County: 6
- 25. State: CA

INFORMANT
- 26. Name, Relationship: Robert Benevides – Executor
- 27. Mailing Address: 8339 West Dry Creek Rd, Healdsburg, CA 95448

SPOUSE AND PARENT INFORMATION
- 31. Name of Father—First: Charles
- 32. Middle: H.
- 33. Last: McCawley
- 34. Birth State: KY
- 35. Name of Mother—First: Charlotte
- 36. Middle: E.
- 37. Last (Maiden): Richards
- 38. Birth State: KY

- 39. Date: 08/20/1999
- 40. Place of Final Disposition: RES, Robert Benevides, 8339 W. Dry Creek Rd, Healdsburg, CA 95448
- 41. Type of Disposition: CR/RES
- 42. Signature of Embalmer: Not Embalmed
- 44. Name of Funeral Director: Adobe Creek Funeral Home
- 45. License No.: FD-1646
- 47. Date: 08/17/1999

PLACE OF DEATH
- 101. Place of Death: Healdsburg General Hospital
- 102. IP
- 104. County: Sonoma
- 105. Street Address: 1375 University Avenue
- 106. City: Healdsburg

CAUSE OF DEATH
- 107. Immediate Cause (A): Metastatic Adenocarcinoma Abdomen — 3 Mos.
- 108. Death Reported to Coroner: No
- 109. Biopsy Performed: Yes
- 110. Autopsy Performed: No

PHYSICIAN'S CERTIFICATION
- 114. Decedent Attended Since: 09/27/1994
- Decedent Last Seen Alive: 08/12/1999
- 116. License No.: G30658
- 117. Date: 08/16/1999
- 118. Attending Physician: Richard Ganz MD, 455 March Ave., Healdsburg, CA 95448

275650

Fax Auth. #: 4780

CERTIFIED COPY OF VITAL RECORDS
Date Issued: 09/02/1999

KARL MALDEN

STATE OF CALIFORNIA — CERTIFICATION OF VITAL RECORD

COUNTY OF LOS ANGELES • REGISTRAR-RECORDER/COUNTY CLERK

CERTIFICATE OF DEATH — State File Number 3200919026561

1. Name of Decedent — First	KARL
2. Middle	-
3. Last	MALDEN
4. Date of Birth	03/22/1912
5. Age	97
6. Sex	M
9. Birth State/Foreign Country	IL
10. Social Security Number	311-03-8904
11. Ever in U.S. Armed Forces	YES
12. Marital Status	MARRIED
13. Date of Death	07/01/2009
14. Hour (24 Hours)	0335
Education	BACHELOR
Hispanic/Latino/Spanish	NO
Race	CAUCASIAN
17. Usual Occupation	ACTOR
18. Kind of Business/Industry	ENTERTAINMENT
19. Years in Occupation	75
20. Decedent's Residence	1845 MANDEVILLE CANYON RD
21. City	LOS ANGELES
22. County	LOS ANGELES
23. Zip Code	90049
24. Years in County	50
25. State	CA
26. Informant's Name, Relationship	MONA MALDEN, WIFE
27. Informant's Mailing Address	1845 MANDEVILLE CANYON RD, LOS ANGELES, CA 90049
28. Name of Surviving Spouse — First	MONA
30. Last (Maiden Name)	GREENBERG
31. Name of Father — First	PETAR
33. Last	SEKULOVICH
34. Birth State	YUGOSLVIA
35. Name of Mother — First	MINNIE
37. Last (Maiden)	SEBERA
38. Birth State	CZECH REP
39. Disposition Date	07/04/2009
40. Place of Final Disposition	PIERCE BROS. WESTWOOD MEMORIAL PARK, 1218 GLENDON AVE, LOS ANGELES, CA 90024
41. Type of Disposition	CREMATION/BURIAL
42. Signature of Embalmer	NOT EMBALMED
44. Name of Funeral Establishment	PIERCE BROS WESTWOOD
45. License Number	951
46. Signature of Local Registrar	JONATHAN FIELDING, MD
47. Date	07/01/2009
101. Place of Death	RESIDENCE — Decedent's Home
104. County	LOS ANGELES
105. Facility Address	1845 MANDEVILLE CANYON RD
106. City	LOS ANGELES
107. Cause of Death (Immediate)	METASTATIC PROSTATE CANCER
Time Interval	20 YRS
108. Death Reported to Coroner	YES
Referral Number	2009-54442
109. Biopsy Performed	NO
110. Autopsy Performed	NO
112. Other Significant Conditions	CORONARY ARTERY DISEASE
113. Operation Performed	NO
115. Signature and Title of Certifier	MARK HOWARD BISCOW M.D.
116. License Number	G49268
117. Date	07/01/2009
Decedent Attended Since	03/09/2000
Decedent Last Seen Alive	03/25/2009
118. Attending Physician's Name/Address	MARK HOWARD BISCOW M.D., 2121 WILSHIRE BLVD STE 305, SANTA MONICA, CA 90403

This is to certify that this document is a true copy of the official record filed with the Registrar-Recorder/County Clerk.

DEAN C. LOGAN, Registrar-Recorder/County Clerk

Date: JAN 0 4 2010

000179257

INFORMATIONAL, NOT A VALID DOCUMENT TO ESTABLISH IDENTITY

CERTIFICATE OF DEATH
STATE OF CALIFORNIA

State File Number: 39519049899

1. Name of Decedent—First (Given)	Louis
2. Middle	Marie
3. Last (Family)	Malle
4. Date of Birth	10/30/1932
5. Age Yrs.	63
6. Sex	M
7. Date of Death	11/23/1995
8. Hour	2115
9. State of Birth	FRANCE
10. Social Security No.	554-41-4383
11. Military Service	NONE
12. Marital Status	MARRIED
13. Education—Years Completed	15
14. Race	WHITE
15. Hispanic	No
16. Usual Employer	SELF EMPLOYED
17. Occupation	FILM DIRECTOR
18. Kind of Business	MOVIE
19. Years in Occupation	40
20. Residence—Street and Number or Location	955 SOUTH CARRILLO DR.
21. City	LOS ANGELES
22. County	LOS ANGELES
23. Zip Code	90048
24. Yrs in County	7
25. State or Foreign Country	CALIFORNIA
26. Name, Relationship	CANDICE BERGEN, WIFE
27. Mailing Address	955 SOUTH CARRILLO DR., LOS ANGELES, CA. 90048
28. Name of Surviving Spouse—First	CANDICE
29. Middle	-
30. Last (Maiden Name)	BERGEN
31. Name of Father—First	PIERRE
32. Middle	-
33. Last	MALLE
34. Birth State	FRANCE
35. Name of Mother—First	FRANCOISE
36. Middle	-
37. Last (Maiden)	BEGHIN
38. Birth State	FRANCE
39. Date	11/27/1995
40. Place of Final Disposition	RES: CANDICE BERGEN, 15 RUE DU LOUVRE, 75001 PARIS, FRANCE
41. Type of Disposition(s)	TR/CR/RES
42. Signature of Embalmer	Elizabeth Derrick
43. License No.	7435
44. Name of Funeral Director	FOREST LAWN HOLLYWOOD HILLS
45. License No.	F 904
47. Date	11/27/1995
101. Place of Death	RESIDENCE
103. Facility Other Than Hospital	RES
104. County	LOS ANGELES
105. Street Address	9091 ALTO CEDRO DR.
106. City	BEVERLY HILLS

107. Death was caused by:

	Cause	Time Interval Between Onset and Death
Immediate Cause (A)	Progressive Multifocal Leukoencephalopathy	8 mons
Due to (B)	T-cell Non-Hodgkin's Lymphoma	8 mons
Due to (C)		
Due to (D)		

- 108. Death Reported to Coroner: No
- 109. Biopsy Performed: No
- 110. Autopsy Performed: No
- 111. Used in Determining Cause: No
- 112. Other Significant Conditions: None
- 113. Was Operation Performed: No
- 116. License No.: G22745
- 117. Date: 11/24/1995
- Decedent Attended Since: 03/01/1995
- Decedent Last Seen Alive: 11/21/1995
- 118. Attending Physician's Name: BARRY E. ROSENBLOOM, MD, 8635 W. THIRD ST. STE. 665W, LOS ANGELES, CA. 90048

CERTIFICATION OF VITAL RECORD

COUNTY OF LOS ANGELES • REGISTRAR-RECORDER/COUNTY CLERK

CERTIFICATE OF DEATH — STATE OF CALIFORNIA—DEPARTMENT OF PUBLIC HEALTH

State File Number: 7097 002772

DECEDENT PERSONAL / DATA
- 1a. Name of Deceased—First Name: Hal
- 1b. Middle Name: (blank)
- 1c. Last Name: March
- 2a. Date of Death: January 19, 1970
- 2b. Hour: 0415
- 3. Sex: Male
- 4. Color or Race: Cauc.
- 5. Birthplace: California
- 6. Date of Birth: April 22, 1920
- 7. Age: 49 Years
- 8. Name and Birthplace of Father: Leon Mendelson, Rumania
- 9. Maiden Name and Birthplace of Mother: Ethel Schinfield, Rumania
- 10. Citizen of What Country: USA
- 11. Social Security Number: 566-09-2341
- 12. Married, Never Married, Widowed, Divorced: Married
- 13. Name of Surviving Spouse: Florence Ann Tockstein
- 14. Last Occupation: Entertainer
- 15. Number of Years in This Occupation: 35
- 16. Name of Last Employing Company or Firm: Self Employed
- 17. Kind of Industry or Business: Entertainment

PLACE OF DEATH
- 18a. Place of Death: U.C.L.A. Medical Center
- 18b. Street Address: 10860 LeConte Ave.
- 18c. Inside City Corporate Limits: yes
- 18d. City or Town: West Los Angeles
- 18e. County: Los Angeles
- 18f. Length of Stay in County of Death: 10 Years
- 18g. Length of Stay in California: 10 Years

USUAL RESIDENCE
- 19a. Usual Residence—Street Address: 909 N. Roxbury Dr.
- 19b. Inside City Corporate Limits: yes
- 19c. City or Town: Beverly Hills
- 19d. County: Los Angeles
- 19e. State: California
- 20. Name and Mailing Address of Informant: Andrew Morgan Maree, 1322 Benedict Canyon BH

PHYSICIAN'S OR CORONER'S CERTIFICATION
- 21a. From: 12/22/69 To: 1/19/70 And: 1/18/70
- 21c. Physician or Coroner Signature: James R Blake
- 21d. Date Signed: 1/19/70
- 21e. Address: 9735 Wilshire Blvd
- 21f. Physician's California License Number: G11662

FUNERAL DIRECTOR AND LOCAL REGISTRAR
- 22a. Burial
- 22b. Date: 1/21/70
- 23. Name of Cemetery or Crematory: Hillside Memorial Park
- 24. Embalmer: H W Lowry, License 2350
- 25. Name of Funeral Director: Groman Mortuary bb
- 26. If not certified by coroner, was this death reported to coroner: No
- 28. Date Accepted for Registration by Local Registrar: JAN 21 1970

CAUSE OF DEATH
- 29. Part I. Immediate Cause (a): Bronchogenic carcinoma — Interval: 8mo
- Due to (b): Pneumonia — Interval: 8 Days
- 30. Part II. Other Significant Conditions: no
- 31. Was Operation or Biopsy Performed: no
- 32a. Autopsy: yes
- 32b. Were Findings Considered in Determining Cause of Death: no

---

This is to certify that this document is a true copy of the official record filed with the Registrar-Recorder/County Clerk.

Beatriz Valdez
BEATRIZ VALDEZ
Registrar-Recorder/County Clerk

AUG 10 1995

19-388004

This copy not valid unless prepared on engraved border displaying the Seal and Signature of the Registrar-Recorder/County Clerk.

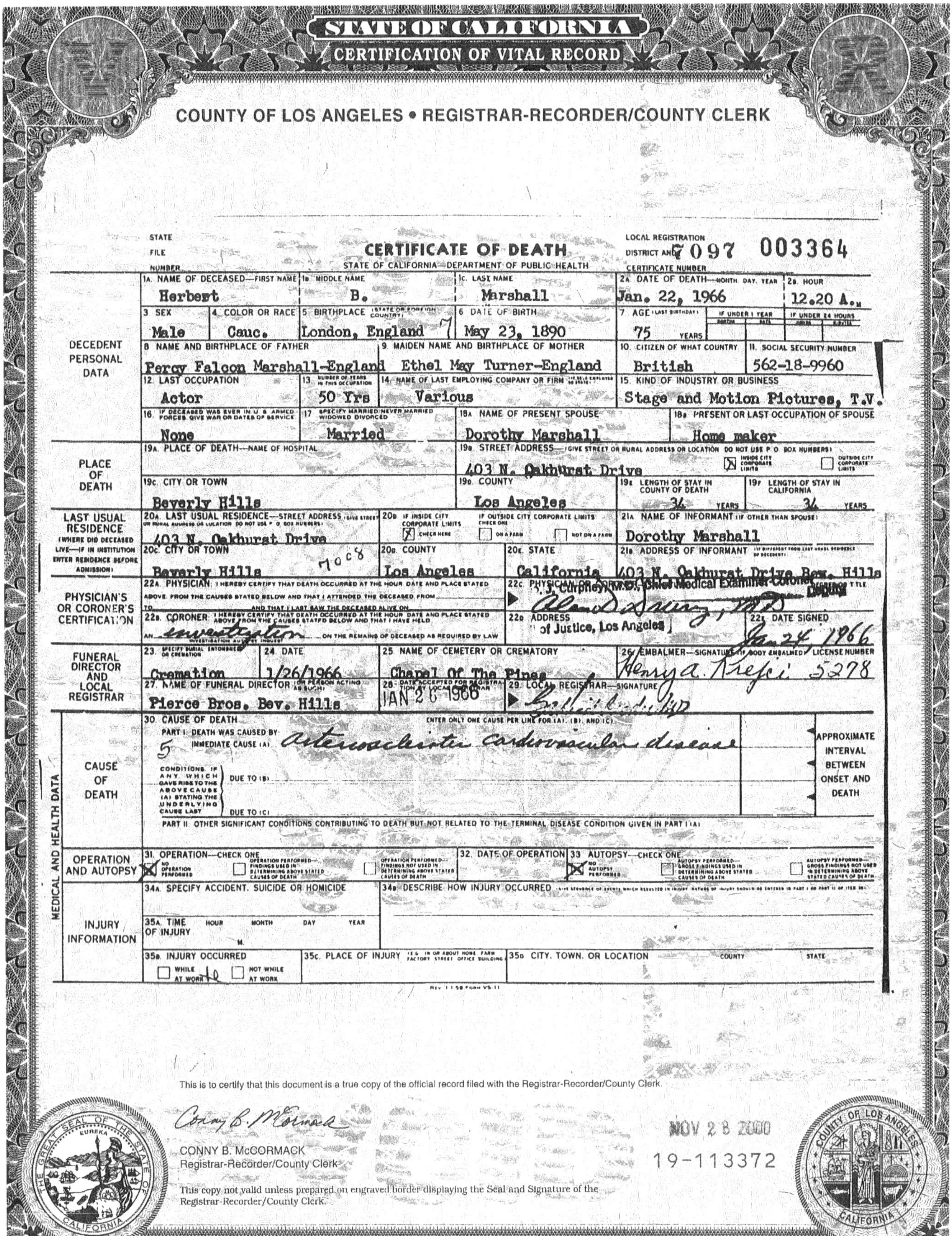

STATE OF CALIFORNIA
CERTIFICATION OF VITAL RECORD

COUNTY OF LOS ANGELES • REGISTRAR-RECORDER/COUNTY CLERK

CERTIFICATE OF DEATH
STATE OF CALIFORNIA
USE BLACK INK ONLY / NO ERASURES, WHITEOUTS OR ALTERATIONS
VS 11 (REV 1/06)

STATE FILE NUMBER — LOCAL REGISTRATION NUMBER: 3200819023285

DECEDENT'S PERSONAL DATA

1. NAME OF DECEDENT — FIRST (Given): DICK
2. MIDDLE: -
3. LAST (Family): MARTIN

AKA. ALSO KNOWN AS — Include full AKA (FIRST, MIDDLE, LAST): THOMAS RICHARD MARTIN
4. DATE OF BIRTH mm/dd/ccyy: 01/30/1922
5. AGE Yrs: 86
IF UNDER ONE YEAR: Months / Days — IF UNDER 24 HOURS: Hours / Minutes
6. SEX: M

9. BIRTH STATE/FOREIGN COUNTRY: MICHIGAN
10. SOCIAL SECURITY NUMBER: 375-12-4357
11. EVER IN U.S. ARMED FORCES?: ☐ YES ☒ NO ☐ UNK
12. MARITAL STATUS (at Time of Death): MARRIED
7. DATE OF DEATH mm/dd/ccyy: 05/24/2008
8. HOUR (24 Hours): 1811

13. EDUCATION — Highest Level/Degree (see worksheet on back): SOME COLLEGE
14/15. WAS DECEDENT HISPANIC/LATINO(A)/SPANISH? (If yes, see worksheet on back): ☐ YES ☒ NO
16. DECEDENT'S RACE — Up to 3 races may be listed (see worksheet on back): CAUCASIAN

17. USUAL OCCUPATION — Type of work for most of life. DO NOT USE RETIRED: COMEDIAN AND DIRECTOR
18. KIND OF BUSINESS OR INDUSTRY (e.g., grocery store, road construction, employment agency, etc.): ENTERTAINMENT
19. YEARS IN OCCUPATION: 70

USUAL RESIDENCE

20. DECEDENT'S RESIDENCE (Street and number or location): 31026 BROAD BEACH ROAD
21. CITY: MALIBU
22. COUNTY/PROVINCE: LOS ANGELES
23. ZIP CODE: 90265
24. YEARS IN COUNTY: 56
25. STATE/FOREIGN COUNTRY: CA

INFORMANT

26. INFORMANT'S NAME, RELATIONSHIP: DOLLY MARTIN, WIFE
27. INFORMANT'S MAILING ADDRESS (Street and number or rural route number, city or town, state, ZIP): 31026 BROAD BEACH ROAD, MALIBU, CA 90265

SPOUSE AND PARENT INFORMATION

28. NAME OF SURVIVING SPOUSE — FIRST: DOLLY
29. MIDDLE: -
30. LAST (Maiden Name): READ

31. NAME OF FATHER — FIRST: WILLIAM
32. MIDDLE: J.
33. LAST: MARTIN
34. BIRTH STATE: MICHIGAN

35. NAME OF MOTHER — FIRST: ETHEL
36. MIDDLE: -
37. LAST (Maiden): CARSON
38. BIRTH STATE: MICHIGAN

FUNERAL DIRECTOR/ LOCAL REGISTRAR

39. DISPOSITION DATE mm/dd/ccyy: 05/30/2008
40. PLACE OF FINAL DISPOSITION: RESIDENCE DOLLY MARTIN, 31026 BROAD BEACH ROAD, MALIBU, CA 90265
41. TYPE OF DISPOSITION(S): CREMATION/RESIDENCE
42. SIGNATURE OF EMBALMER: NOT EMBALMED
43. LICENSE NUMBER: -
44. NAME OF FUNERAL ESTABLISHMENT: NEPTUNE SOCIETY
45. LICENSE NUMBER: FD1359
46. SIGNATURE OF LOCAL REGISTRAR: JONATHAN FIELDING, MD
47. DATE mm/dd/ccyy: 05/30/2008

PLACE OF DEATH

101. PLACE OF DEATH: SANTA MONICA UCLA MEDICAL CENTER
102. IF HOSPITAL, SPECIFY ONE: ☒ IP ☐ ER/OP ☐ DOA
103. IF OTHER THAN HOSPITAL, SPECIFY ONE: ☐ Hospice ☐ Nursing Home/LTC ☐ Decedent's Home ☐ Other
104. COUNTY: LOS ANGELES
105. FACILITY ADDRESS OR LOCATION WHERE FOUND (Street and number or location): 1225 16TH STREET
106. CITY: SANTA MONICA

CAUSE OF DEATH

107. CAUSE OF DEATH — Enter the chain of events — diseases, injuries, or complications — that directly caused death. DO NOT enter terminal events such as cardiac arrest, respiratory arrest, or ventricular fibrillation without showing the etiology. DO NOT ABBREVIATE

	Cause	Time Interval Between Onset and Death
IMMEDIATE CAUSE (Final disease or condition resulting in death) → (A)	RESPIRATORY ARREST	(AT) MINS
Sequentially, list conditions, if any, leading to cause on Line A. Enter UNDERLYING CAUSE (disease or injury that initiated the events resulting in death) LAST (B)	RESPIRATORY FAILURE	(BT) DYS
(C)	PNEUMONIA	(CT) DYS
(D)		(DT)

108. DEATH REPORTED TO CORONER? ☐ YES ☒ NO — REFERRAL NUMBER
109. BIOPSY PERFORMED? ☐ YES ☒ NO
110. AUTOPSY PERFORMED? ☐ YES ☒ NO
111. USED IN DETERMINING CAUSE? ☐ YES ☐ NO

112. OTHER SIGNIFICANT CONDITIONS CONTRIBUTING TO DEATH BUT NOT RESULTING IN THE UNDERLYING CAUSE GIVEN IN 107: ANOXIC BRAIN INJURY SECONDARY TO CARDIOPULMONARY ARREST, TUBURCULOSIS ASSOCIATED WITH PULMONARY FIBROSIS
113. WAS OPERATION PERFORMED FOR ANY CONDITION IN ITEM 107 OR 112? (If yes, list type of operation and date.): NO
113A. IF FEMALE, PREGNANT IN LAST YEAR? ☐ YES ☐ NO ☐ UNK

PHYSICIAN'S CERTIFICATION

114. I CERTIFY THAT TO THE BEST OF MY KNOWLEDGE DEATH OCCURRED AT THE HOUR, DATE AND PLACE STATED FROM THE CAUSES STATED. Decedent Attended Since (A) mm/dd/ccyy: 05/17/2008 — Decedent Last Seen Alive (B) mm/dd/ccyy: 05/24/2008
115. SIGNATURE AND TITLE OF CERTIFIER: YU CHING WEN, MD
116. LICENSE NUMBER: G080088
117. DATE mm/dd/ccyy: 05/30/2008
118. TYPE ATTENDING PHYSICIAN'S NAME, MAILING ADDRESS, ZIP CODE: YU CHING WEN, MD, 1245 16TH STREET, SANTA MONICA, CA 90404

CORONER'S USE ONLY

119. I CERTIFY THAT IN MY OPINION DEATH OCCURRED AT THE HOUR, DATE, AND PLACE STATED FROM THE CAUSES STATED. MANNER OF DEATH ☐ Natural ☐ Accident ☐ Homicide ☐ Suicide ☐ Pending Investigation ☐ Could not be determined
120. INJURED AT WORK? ☐ YES ☐ NO ☐ UNK
121. INJURY DATE mm/dd/ccyy
122. HOUR (24 Hours)
123. PLACE OF INJURY (e.g., home, construction site, wooded area, etc.)
124. DESCRIBE HOW INJURY OCCURRED (Events which resulted in injury)
125. LOCATION OF INJURY (Street and number, or location, and city, and ZIP)
126. SIGNATURE OF CORONER / DEPUTY CORONER
127. DATE mm/dd/ccyy
128. TYPE NAME, TITLE OF CORONER / DEPUTY CORONER

STATE REGISTRAR: A B C D E — *012008000826816* — FAX AUTH # — CENSUS TRACT

INFORMATIONAL, NOT A VALID DOCUMENT TO ESTABLISH IDENTITY

This is to certify that this document is a true copy of the official record filed with the Registrar-Recorder/County Clerk.

SEP 16 2009

DEAN C. LOGAN
Registrar-Recorder/County Clerk

000004577

This copy not valid unless prepared on engraved border displaying the Seal and Signature of the Registrar-Recorder/County Clerk.

PBNCO (Rev) 07/09

ANY ALTERATION OR ERASURE VOIDS THIS CERTIFICATE

COUNTY OF LOS ANGELES
DEPARTMENT OF HEALTH SERVICES
CERTIFICATE OF DEATH

1. Name of Decedent: RODERICK ANDREW McDOWALL
4. Date of Birth: 09/17/1928
5. Age: 70
6. Sex: M
7. Date of Death: 10/03/1998
8. Hour: 0730
9. State of Birth: ENGLAND
10. Social Security No.: 558-22-0529
11. Military Service: No
12. Marital Status: NM
13. Education—Years Completed: 12
14. Race: CAUCASIAN
15. Hispanic: No
16. Usual Employer: SELF EMPLOYED
17. Occupation: ACTOR
18. Kind of Business: MOTION PICTURE
19. Years in Occupation: 63
20. Residence: 3110 BROOKDALE RD.
21. City: STUDIO CITY
22. County: LOS ANGELES
23. Zip Code: 91604
24. Yrs in County: 42
25. State or Foreign Country: CA
26. Informant—Name, Relationship: VIRGINIA McDOWALL - SISTER
27. Mailing Address: 23388 MULHOLLAND DR. WOODLAND HILLS CA 91364
31. Name of Father: THOMAS McDOWALL
34. Birth State: ENGLAND
35. Name of Mother: WINSFRIEDE
37. Last (Maiden): CORCORAN
38. Birth State: IRELAND
39. Date of Disposition: 10/07/1998
40. Place of Final Disposition: AT SEA OFF COAST OF LOS ANGELES COUNTY
41. Type of Disposition: CR/SEA
42. Signature of Embalmer: NOT EMBALMED
44. Name of Funeral Director: NEPTUNE SOCIETY
45. License No.: FD1359
47. Date: 10/06/1998

101. Place of Death: RESIDENCE
104. County: LOS ANGELES
105. Street Address: 3110 BROOKDALE ROAD
106. City: STUDIO CITY
107. Death Was Caused By:
(A) CANCER OF THE LUNG — 6 MOS
108. Death Reported to Coroner: No
109. Biopsy Performed: Yes
110. Autopsy Performed: No
111. Used in Determining Cause: No
112. Other Significant Conditions: BONE & BRAIN METASTASES
113. Was Operation Performed: YES — LEFT LUNG AND SKIN BIOPSY — 04/30/1998
114. Decedent Attended Since: 09/16/1998 **Decedent Last Seen Alive:** 09/29/1998
116. License No.: G15859
117. Date: 10/05/1998
118. Attending Physician: AVRUM Z. BLUMING M.D., 16133 VENTURA BL. #470, ENCINO, CA 91436

Fax Auth. #: 195/7433
Census Tract: 090181041

DATE ISSUED OCT 16 1998

CERTIFICATE OF DEATH
STATE OF CALIFORNIA

State File Number: 39419030149

DECEDENT PERSONAL DATA

- **1. Name of Decedent—First (Given):** CAMERON
- **2. Middle:** McDOWELL
- **3. Last (Family):** MITCHELL
- **4. Date of Birth:** 11/04/1918
- **5. Age Yrs.:** 75
- **6. Sex:** M
- **7. Date of Death:** 07/06/1994
- **8. Hour:** 2150
- **9. State of Birth:** PA
- **10. Social Security No.:** 125-07-2753
- **11. Military Service:** 1942 to 1945
- **12. Marital Status:** DIVORCED
- **13. Education—Years Completed:** 12
- **14. Race:** WHITE
- **15. Hispanic:** No
- **16. Usual Employer:** SELF EMPLOYED
- **17. Occupation:** ACTOR
- **18. Kind of Business:** ENTERTAINMENT
- **19. Years in Occupation:** 60

USUAL RESIDENCE

- **20. Residence:** 14948 ALTATA DRIVE
- **21. City:** PACIFIC PALISADES
- **22. County:** LOS ANGELES
- **23. Zip Code:** 90272
- **24. Yrs in County:** 56
- **25. State:** CA

INFORMANT

- **26. Name, Relationship:** CAMILLE MITCHELL, DAUGHTER
- **27. Mailing Address:** BOX 850, SASKATOON, SASKATCHEWAN, CAN. SZK3V4

SPOUSE AND PARENT INFORMATION

- **28-30. Name of Surviving Spouse:** —
- **31. Name of Father—First:** CHARLES
- **33. Last:** MITZELL
- **34. Birth State:** PA
- **35. Name of Mother—First:** KATHARINE
- **37. Last (Maiden):** EHRHARDT
- **38. Birth State:** PA

DISPOSITION(S)

- **39. Date:** 07/11/1994
- **40. Place of Final Disposition:** DESERT MEMORIAL PARK, 69 920 E. RAMON RD., CATHEDRAL CITY, CA 92234

FUNERAL DIRECTOR AND LOCAL REGISTRAR

- **41. Type of Disposition(s):** BU
- **42. Signature of Embalmer:** David McKnight
- **43. License No.:** E7371
- **44. Name of Funeral Director:** PALM SPRINGS MORTUARY
- **45. License No.:** FD 1513
- **46. Signature of Local Registrar:** Robert C. Bates
- **47. Date:** 07/08/1994

PLACE OF DEATH

- **101. Place of Death:** COUNTRY VILLA WESTWOOD
- **103. Facility:** CONV. HOSP. [X]
- **104. County:** LOS ANGELES
- **105. Street Address:** 12121 SANTA MONICA BLVD.
- **106. City:** LOS ANGELES

CAUSE OF DEATH

- **107. Death was caused by:**
  - (A) Immediate Cause: CARCINOMA of the LUNG — Time Interval: 1 year
- **108. Death Reported to Coroner:** No
- **109. Biopsy Performed:** No
- **110. Autopsy Performed:** No
- **111. Used in Determining Cause:** —
- **112. Other Significant Conditions:** None
- **113. Was Operation Performed:** No

PHYSICIAN'S CERTIFICATION

- **114. Decedent Attended Since:** 06/01/1994
- **Decedent Last Seen Alive:** 07/06/1994
- **115. Signature and Title of Certifier:** Raynard Kington MD
- **116. License No.:** G70864
- **117. Date:** 07/08/1994
- **118. Attending Physician's Name:** Raynard Kington, M.D., 10833 LeConte Ave L.A. CA 90024

STATE OF CALIFORNIA — CERTIFICATION OF VITAL RECORD

COUNTY OF LOS ANGELES DEPARTMENT OF PUBLIC HEALTH

CERTIFICATE OF DEATH

State File Number: 3200919041310

1. Name of Decedent — First (Given): **VICTOR**
2. Middle: —
3. Last (Family): **MIZZY**
4. Date of Birth: 01/09/1916
5. Age Yrs: 93
6. Sex: M
8. Birth State/Foreign Country: NEW YORK
10. Social Security Number: 085-09-8177
11. Ever in U.S. Armed Forces? YES [X]
12. Marital Status: DIVORCED
7. Date of Death: 10/17/2009
8. Hour (24 Hours): 1330
13. Education: BACHELOR
14/15. Hispanic: NO
16. Decedent's Race: WHITE
17. Usual Occupation: COMPOSER
18. Kind of Business or Industry: ENTERTAINMENT
19. Years in Occupation: 80
20. Decedent's Residence: 2170 STRADELLA RD.
21. City: LOS ANGELES
22. County/Province: LOS ANGELES
23. Zip Code: 90077
24. Years in County: 46
25. State/Foreign Country: CALIFORNIA
26. Informant's Name, Relationship: LYNN MIZZY JONAS, DAUGHTER
27. Informant's Mailing Address: 42 ST. AUSTINS PL., STATEN ISLAND, NY 10310

31. Name of Father — First: ABRAM
33. Last: MIZANSKY
34. Birth State: LITHUANIA
35. Name of Mother — First: GUSSIE
37. Last (Maiden): MUNITZ
38. Birth State: LITHUANIA

39. Disposition Date: 10/20/2009
40. Place of Final Disposition: EDEN MEMORIAL PARK, 11500 SEPULVEDA BLVD, MISSION HILLS, CA 91345
41. Type of Disposition: BU
42. Signature of Embalmer: NOT EMBALMED
44. Name of Funeral Establishment: MALINOW & SILVERMAN MORTUARY
45. License Number: FD-467
46. Signature of Local Registrar: JONATHAN FIELDING, MD
47. Date: 10/19/2009

101. Place of Death: RESIDENCE
103. County: LOS ANGELES
105. Facility Address: 2170 STRADELLA RD
City: LOS ANGELES

107. Cause of Death:
- Immediate Cause (A): CARDIAC ARREST — MINS
- (B): ISCHEMIC CARDIOMYOPATHY — YRS
- (C): CONGESTIVE HEART FAILURE — YRS

108. Death Reported to Coroner: NO
109. Biopsy Performed: NO
110. Autopsy Performed: NO

112. Other Significant Conditions: ATRIAL FIBRILLATION
113. Was Operation Performed: NO

114. I certify that to the best of my knowledge death occurred at the hour, date and place stated from the causes stated.
Decedent Attended Since: 03/15/2009
Decedent Last Seen Alive: 10/14/2009
115. Signature and Title of Certifier: RICHARD HARDING LANDER M.D.
116. License Number: G70491
117. Date: 10/18/2009
118. Type Attending Physician's Name, Mailing Address, Zip Code: RICHARD HARDING LANDER M.D., 23388 MULHOLLAND DR, WOODLAND HILLS, CA 91364

010001001335148

This is a true certified copy of the record filed in the County of Los Angeles Department of Public Health if it bears the Registrar's signature in purple ink.

Jonathan E. Fielding, MD
Director of Public Health and Registrar

Date Issued: OCT 21 2009

HD1977687

This copy not valid unless prepared on engraved border displaying seal and signature of Registrar.

INFORMATIONAL, NOT A VALID DOCUMENT TO ESTABLISH IDENTITY

STATE OF CALIFORNIA
CERTIFICATION OF VITAL RECORD

COUNTY OF LOS ANGELES • REGISTRAR-RECORDER/COUNTY CLERK

CERTIFICATE OF DEATH — State File Number: 3200919001549

1. Name of Decedent — First	RICARDO
3. Last (Family)	MONTALBAN
4. Date of Birth	11/25/1920
5. Age	88
6. Sex	M
7. Date of Death	01/14/2009
8. Hour (24 Hours)	0630
9. Birth State/Foreign Country	MEXICO
10. Social Security Number	067-18-0231
11. Ever in U.S. Armed Forces?	NO
12. Marital Status	WIDOWED
13. Education	HS GRADUATE
14/15. Hispanic/Latino	YES — MEXICAN
16. Race	CAUCASIAN
17. Usual Occupation	ACTOR
18. Kind of Business or Industry	ENTERTAINMENT
19. Years in Occupation	60
20. Decedent's Residence	1423 ORIOLE DR
21. City	LOS ANGELES
22. County	LOS ANGELES
23. Zip Code	90069
24. Years in County	65
25. State	CA
26. Informant's Name / Relationship	ANITA SMITH, DAUGHTER
27. Informant's Mailing Address	2079 PROSSER AVE, LOS ANGELES, CA 90025
31. Name of Father — First	JENARO
33. Last	MONTALBAN
34. Birth State	SPAIN
35. Name of Mother — First	RICARDA
37. Last (Maiden)	MERINO
38. Birth State	SPAIN
39. Disposition Date	01/22/2009
40. Place of Final Disposition	HOLY CROSS CEMETERY, 5835 W. SLAUSON AVE, CULVER CITY, CA 90230
41. Type of Disposition	BU
42. Signature of Embalmer	NOT EMBALMED
44. Name of Funeral Establishment	PIERCE BROTHERS WESTWOOD
45. License Number	FD-951
46. Signature of Local Registrar	JONATHAN FIELDING, MD
47. Date	01/15/2009
101. Place of Death	RESIDENCE
103. If Other Than Hospital	Decedent's Home
104. County	LOS ANGELES
105. Facility Address	1423 ORIOLE DR
106. City	LOS ANGELES
107. Cause of Death — Immediate	(A) CONGESTIVE HEART FAILURE — 4 MOS
	(B) CORONARY ARTERY DISEASE — 8 MOS
112. Other Significant Conditions	NONE
113. Was Operation Performed	NO
108. Death Reported to Coroner	YES
Referral Number	2009-50455
109. Biopsy Performed	NO
110. Autopsy Performed	NO
114. Certifier	ERNEST LOUIS PRUDENTE M.D.
116. License Number	A70695
117. Date	01/15/2009
118. Attending Physician's Address	2121 WILSHIRE BL STE 304, SANTA MONICA, CA 90403
(A) Decedent Attended Since	10/15/2001
(B) Decedent Last Seen Alive	09/26/2008

INFORMATIONAL, NOT A VALID DOCUMENT TO ESTABLISH IDENTITY

This is to certify that this document is a true copy of the official record filed with the Registrar-Recorder/County Clerk.

SEP 28 2009

Dean C. Logan
Registrar-Recorder/County Clerk

019581421

CERTIFICATION OF VITAL RECORD

COUNTY OF LOS ANGELES • REGISTRAR-RECORDER/COUNTY CLERK

CERTIFICATE OF DEATH
STATE OF CALIFORNIA

State File Number: 39519021721

DECEDENT PERSONAL DATA
- 1. Name of Decedent (First): ELIZABETH
- 2. Middle: A.
- 3. Last (Family): MONTGOMERY
- 4. Date of Birth: 04/15/1938
- 5. Age: 57
- 6. Sex: F
- 7. Date of Death: 05/18/1995
- 8. Hour: 0827
- 9. State of Birth: CA
- 10. Social Security No.: 079-28-5301
- 11. Military Service: None
- 12. Marital Status: MARRIED
- 13. Education – Years Completed: 12
- 14. Race: CAUCASIAN
- 15. Hispanic: No
- 16. Usual Employer: SELF EMPLOYED
- 17. Occupation: ACTOR
- 18. Kind of Business: MOTION PICTURES & TELEVISION
- 19. Years in Occupation: 40

USUAL RESIDENCE
- 20. Residence – Street and Number or Location: 1230 BENEDICT CANYON
- 21. City: BEVERLY HILLS
- 22. County: LOS ANGELES
- 23. Zip Code: 90210
- 24. Yrs in County: 57
- 25. State or Foreign Country: CA

INFORMANT
- 26. Name, Relationship: ROBERT H. FOXWORTH (HUSBAND)
- 27. Mailing Address: 1230 BENEDICT CANYON, BEVERLY HILLS, CA 90210

SPOUSE AND PARENT INFORMATION
- 28. Name of Surviving Spouse – First: ROBERT
- 29. Middle: H.
- 30. Last (Maiden Name): FOXWORTH
- 31. Name of Father – First: ROBERT
- 33. Last: MONTGOMERY
- 34. Birth State: NY
- 35. Name of Mother – First: ELIZABETH
- 37. Last (Maiden): ALLEN
- 38. Birth State: KY

DISPOSITION(S)
- 39. Date: 05/22/1995
- 40. Place of Final Disposition: ROBERT H. FOXWORTH FOR RES: 1230 BENEDICT CANYON, BEVERLY HILLS, CA 90210
- 41. Type of Disposition: CR/RES
- 42. Signature of Embalmer: NOT EMBALMED
- 44. Name of Funeral Director: PIERCE BROS. WESTWOOD VILLAGE
- 45. License No.: F-951
- 47. Date: 05/19/1995

PLACE OF DEATH
- 101. Place of Death: RESIDENCE
- 103. Facility Other Than Hospital: RES
- 104. County: LOS ANGELES
- 105. Street Address: 1230 BENEDICT CANYON
- 106. City: BEVERLY HILLS

CAUSE OF DEATH
- 107. Death Was Caused By:
  - (A) Immediate Cause: RESPIRATORY ARREST — Seconds
  - (B) Due To: MALNUTRITION — Months
  - (C) Due To: METASTATIC COLON CANCER — Years
- 108. Death Reported to Coroner: No
- 109. Biopsy Performed: No
- 110. Autopsy Performed: No
- 111. Used in Determining Cause: No
- 112. Other Significant Conditions Contributing to Death: ANASARCA
- 113. Was Operation Performed: NO

PHYSICIAN'S CERTIFICATION
- 115. Signature of Certifier: Gary Hoffman, MD
- 116. License No.: G 040007
- 117. Date: 05/18/1995
- Decedent Attended Since: 07/01/1995
- Decedent Last Seen Alive: 05/18/1995
- 118. Type/Attending Physician's Name, Mailing Address: GARY HOFFMAN, M.D., 9400 BRIGHTON WAY, #307, BEVERLY HILLS, CA

This is to certify that this document is a true copy of the official record filed with the Registrar-Recorder/County Clerk.

Beatriz Valdez
BEATRIZ VALDEZ
Registrar-Recorder/County Clerk

AUG 24 1995
19-004338

This copy not valid unless prepared on engraved border displaying the Seal and Signature of the Registrar-Recorder/County Clerk.

ANY ALTERATION OR ERASURE VOIDS THIS CERTIFICATE

STATE OF CALIFORNIA
CERTIFICATION OF VITAL RECORD

COUNTY OF LOS ANGELES
DEPARTMENT OF HEALTH SERVICES

CERTIFICATE OF DEATH — STATE OF CALIFORNIA
State File Number: 3 1999 19 054770

Decedent Personal Data
- 1. Name (First/Given): Harry
- 2. Middle: Hymie
- 3. Last (Family): Lichenstein
- 4. Date of Birth: 03/14/1902
- 5. Age: 97
- 6. Sex: Male
- 7. Date of Death: 12/28/1999
- 8. Hour: 0445
- 9. State of Birth: Texas
- 10. Social Security No.: 545-24-4310
- 11. Military Service: No
- 12. Marital Status: Never Married
- 13. Education – Years Completed: 12
- 14. Race: Cauc
- 15. Hispanic: No
- 16. Usual Employer: Screen Actors Guild
- 17. Occupation: Actor
- 18. Kind of Business: Movie Industry
- 19. Years in Occupation: 60
- 20. Residence: 1600 N. Bronson Ave. #17
- 21. City: Hollywood
- 22. County: Los Angeles
- 23. Zip Code: 90028
- 24. Yrs in County: 65
- 25. State or Foreign Country: Calif.

Informant
- 26. Name, Relationship: Joy Parker – Niece
- 27. Mailing Address: 12416-A Coronet St. Austin, Texas 78727

Spouse and Parent Information
- 28. Name of Surviving Spouse: –
- 31. Name of Father – First: Frank
- 33. Last: Lichenstein
- 34. Birth State: Poland
- 35. Name of Mother – First: Lydia
- 37. Last (Maiden): Unk.
- 38. Birth State: Poland

Disposition
- 39. Date: 12/30/1999
- 40. Place of Final Disposition: Shearith Israel Cem. – Dallas, Texas
- 41. Type of Disposition: Tr/Bu
- 42. Signature of Embalmer: Not Embalmed
- 44. Name of Funeral Director: Chevra Kadisha Mortuary
- 45. License No.: FD-1326
- 47. Date: 12/29/1999

Place of Death
- 101. Place of Death: Beverly Hills Rehb. Ctr.
- 103. Facility Other Than Hospital: Conv. Hosp.
- 104. County: Los Angeles
- 105. Street Address: 580 San Vicente Blvd.
- 106. City: Los Angeles

Cause of Death
- 107. Immediate Cause (A): Senile Dementia — Time Interval: 6 Months
- 108. Death Reported to Coroner: No
- 109. Biopsy Performed: No
- 110. Autopsy Performed: No
- 112. Other Significant Conditions: Hypertension
- 113. Was Operation Performed: No

Physician's Certification
- 114. Decedent Attended Since: 10/03/1991
- Decedent Last Seen Alive: 12/16/1999
- 115. Signature: P. Levine, M.D.
- 116. License No.: G 035171
- 117. Date: 12/28/1999
- 118. Attending Physician: Phillip Levine, M.D. 8631 W. 3rd St. #815E L.A., CA 90048

State Registrar
Census Tract: 090317091

COUNTY OF RIVERSIDE
RIVERSIDE, CALIFORNIA

CERTIFICATE OF DEATH — STATE OF CALIFORNIA — VS-11 (REV. 7/97)

State File Number: 3 1999 33003032

Decedent Personal Data
- **1. Name of Decedent—First (Given):** Gary
- **2. Middle:** —
- **3. Last (Family):** Morton
- **4. Date of Birth:** 12/19/1924
- **5. Age Yrs.:** 74
- **6. Sex:** M
- **7. Date of Death:** 03/30/1999
- **8. Hour:** 1415
- **9. State of Birth:** NY
- **10. Social Security No.:** 091-18-5014
- **11. Military Service:** Yes
- **12. Marital Status:** Married
- **13. Education—Years Completed:** 12
- **14. Race:** White
- **15. Hispanic:** No
- **16. Usual Employer:** Self-Employed
- **17. Occupation:** Producer
- **18. Kind of Business:** Motion Pictures & Television
- **19. Years in Occupation:** 20
- **20. Residence:** 40241 Club View Drive
- **21. City:** Rancho Mirage
- **22. County:** Riverside
- **23. Zip Code:** 92270
- **24. Yrs in County:** 10
- **25. State or Foreign Country:** CA

Informant
- **26. Name, Relationship:** Susie Morton – Wife
- **27. Mailing Address:** 40241 Club View Drive, Rancho Mirage, CA 92270

Spouse and Parent Information
- **28. Name of Surviving Spouse—First:** Susie
- **29. Middle:** —
- **30. Last (Maiden Name):** McAllister
- **31. Name of Father—First:** Morris
- **32. Middle:** —
- **33. Last:** Goldaper
- **34. Birth State:** NY
- **35. Name of Mother—First:** Rose
- **36. Middle:** —
- **37. Last (Maiden):** Greenfader
- **38. Birth State:** NY

Disposition(s)
- **39. Date:** 04/02/1999
- **40. Place of Final Disposition:** Res., Susie Morton, 40241 Club View Dr., Rancho Mirage, CA 92270
- **41. Type of Disposition(s):** Cr/Res
- **42. Signature of Embalmer:** Not embalmed
- **43. License No.:** —
- **44. Name of Funeral Director:** Wiefels & Son, Palm Springs
- **45. License No.:** FD 836
- **46. Signature of Local Registrar:** Gary Feldman MD
- **47. Date:** 04/02/1999

Place of Death
- **101. Place of Death:** Eisenhower Memorial Hosp.
- **102. If Hospital, Specify One:** IP
- **104. County:** Riverside
- **105. Street Address:** 39000 Bob Hope Drive
- **106. City:** Rancho Mirage

Cause of Death
- **107. Death was caused by:**
  - (A) Immediate Cause: Respiratory Failure — 7 Days
  - (B) Due to: Advanced Lung Cancer — 2 Yrs
- **108. Death Reported to Coroner:** No
- **109. Biopsy Performed:** No
- **110. Autopsy Performed:** No
- **112. Other Significant Conditions:** Chronic Obstructive Lung Disease
- **113. Was Operation Performed:** No

Physician's Certification
- **114. Decedent Attended Since:** 03/24/1999
- **Decedent Last Seen Alive:** 03/30/1999
- **115. Signature and Title of Certifier:** Khaldoun Alnabelsi
- **116. License No.:** A061138
- **117. Date:** 04/01/1999
- **118. Type Attending Physician's Name, Mailing Address, Zip:** Khaldoun Alnabelsi, M.D., 39000 Bob Hope Drive, K-305, Rancho Mirage, CA 92270

State Registrar: 889973

STATE OF CALIFORNIA, COUNTY OF RIVERSIDE

This is a true and exact reproduction of the document officially registered and placed on file in the office of County of Riverside, Department of Health.

DATE ISSUED: 04/28/1999

Gary Feldman M.D.
Local Registrar
RIVERSIDE COUNTY, CALIFORNIA

STATE OF CALIFORNIA
CERTIFICATION OF VITAL RECORD

COUNTY OF LOS ANGELES
DEPARTMENT OF HEALTH SERVICES

CERTIFICATE OF DEATH — STATE OF CALIFORNIA
State File Number: 3 2000 19 040554

DECEDENT PERSONAL DATA
- 1. Name (First): RICHARD
- 2. Middle: DANA MICHAEL
- 3. Last: MULLIGAN
- 4. Date of Birth: 11/13/1932
- 5. Age: 67
- 6. Sex: M
- 7. Date of Death: 09/26/2000
- 8. Hour: 1430
- 9. State of Birth: NY
- 10. Social Security No.: 075-26-0145
- 11. Military Service: Yes
- 12. Marital Status: DIVORCED
- 13. Education—Years Completed: 14
- 14. Race: CAUCASIAN
- 15. Hispanic: No
- 16. Usual Employer: WARNER BROTHERS
- 17. Occupation: ACTOR
- 18. Kind of Business: ENTERTAINMENT
- 19. Years in Occupation: 40

USUAL RESIDENCE
- 20. Residence: 145 S BEACHWOOD DR
- 21. City: LOS ANGELES
- 22. County: LOS ANGELES
- 23. Zip Code: 90004
- 24. Yrs in County: 26
- 25. State: CA

INFORMANT
- 26. Name, Relationship: PAUL PRICE, FRIEND
- 27. Mailing Address: 463 S COCHRAN AVE, LOS ANGELES, CA 90036

SPOUSE AND PARENT INFORMATION
- 31. Father—First: ROBERT
- 32. Middle: EDWARD
- 33. Last: MULLIGAN
- 34. Birth State: NY
- 35. Mother—First: ANN
- 36. Middle: ELIZABETH
- 37. Last (Maiden): GINGELL
- 38. Birth State: NY

DISPOSITION(S)
- 39. Date: 10/04/2000
- 40. Place of Final Disposition: RESIDENCE: JAMES MULLIGAN, 14 WINTER ST WEST, WEST LEBANON, NH 03784
- 41. Type of Disposition: CR/TR/RES
- 42. Signature of Embalmer: NOT EMBALMED
- 44. Name of Funeral Director: FOREST LAWN HOLLYWOOD HILLS
- 45. License No.: FD 904
- 47. Date: 10/03/2000

PLACE OF DEATH
- 101. Place of Death: RESIDENCE
- 104. County: LOS ANGELES
- 105. Street Address: 145 S BEACHWOOD DR
- 106. City: LOS ANGELES

CAUSE OF DEATH
- 107. Immediate Cause (A): METASTATIC COLON CARCINOMA — YRS
- 108. Death Reported to Coroner: No
- 109. Biopsy Performed: Yes
- 110. Autopsy Performed: No
- 111. Used in Determining Cause: No
- 112. Other Significant Conditions: TYPE I DIABETES
- 113. Operation Performed: RIGHT HEMICOLECTOMY --/--/1994

PHYSICIAN'S CERTIFICATION
- 114. Decedent Attended Since: 08/05/1988; Decedent Last Seen Alive: 09/24/2000
- 115. Signature: Michael O Bush MD
- 116. License No.: G38124
- 117. Date: 09/27/2000
- 118. Attending Physician: MICHAEL A BUSH, MD 8920 WILSHIRE BLVD, BEVERLY HILLS, CA

CORONER'S USE ONLY
- 119. Manner of Death: (blank)

STATE REGISTRAR
- Fax Auth. #: 273/6917

Date Issued: NOV 1 2000

This is a true certified copy of the record filed in the County of Los Angeles Department of Health Services if it bears the Registrar's signature in purple ink.

Director of Health Services and Registrar

This copy not valid unless prepared on engraved border displaying seal and signature of Registrar.

090380018

CERTIFICATE OF DEATH
STATE OF CALIFORNIA

1. Name of Decedent—First (Given)	Gene
2. Middle	–
3. Last (Family)	Nelson
4. Date of Birth	03/24/1920
5. Age Yrs.	76
6. Sex	M
7. Date of Death	09/16/1996
8. Hour	1600
9. State of Birth	Washington
10. Social Security No.	550-12-3568
11. Military Service	None
12. Marital Status	Divorced
13. Education—Years Completed	12
14. Race	Caucasian
15. Hispanic	No
16. Usual Employer	Self Employed
17. Occupation	Director
18. Kind of Business	Entertainment
19. Years in Occupation	61
20. Residence	14155 Magnolia Blvd. #I
21. City	Sherman Oaks
22. County	Los Angeles
23. Zip Code	91423
24. Yrs in County	73
25. State or Foreign Country	California
26. Name, Relationship	Christopher Nelson-Son
27. Mailing Address	750 S. Griffith Park Dr., Burbank, CA. 91506
28-30. Surviving Spouse	–
31. Name of Father—First	Leander
32. Middle	–
33. Last	Berg
34. Birth State	Sweden
35. Name of Mother—First	Lenore
36. Middle	–
37. Last (Maiden)	Nelson
38. Birth State	Oregon
39. Date	09/22/1996
40. Place of Final Disposition	RES: Christopher Nelson-750 S. Griffith Park Dr., Burbank, CA. 91506
41. Type of Disposition(s)	CR/RES
42. Signature of Embalmer	Not Embalmed
43. License No.	–
44. Name of Funeral Director	Neptune Society-Burbank
45. License No.	F-1289
47. Date	09/19/1996
101. Place of Death	Motion Picture & Telev. Hosp
102. IP	X
104. County	Los Angeles
105. Street Address	23388 Mulholland Drive
106. City	Woodland Hills

107. Death Was Caused By:

	Cause	Interval
Immediate Cause (A)	Cardiopulmonary Arrest	5 Mins.
Due to (B)	Leiomyosarcoma, Abdomen	13 Mos.
Due to (C)		
Due to (D)		

- 108. Death Reported to Coroner: No
- 109. Biopsy Performed: Yes
- 110. Autopsy Performed: No
- 111. Used in Determining Cause: No
- 112. Other Significant Conditions: None
- 113. Operation Performed: Laparotomy & Excision Abdominal Tumor 08/13/1995
- 115. Signature: David L. Smith, M.D.
- 116. License No.: G11277
- 117. Date: 09/19/1996
- Decedent Attended Since: 06/16/1995
- Decedent Last Seen Alive: 09/16/1996
- 118. Attending Physician: D.L. Smith, MD 23388 Mulholland Dr, Woodland Hills, CA 91364

STATE OF CALIFORNIA

CERTIFICATION OF VITAL RECORD

COUNTY OF LOS ANGELES • REGISTRAR-RECORDER/COUNTY CLERK

STATE FILE NUMBER

CERTIFICATE OF DEATH

STATE OF CALIFORNIA—DEPARTMENT OF PUBLIC HEALTH

LOCAL REGISTRATION DISTRICT AND CERTIFICATE NUMBER 7097-002506

DECEDENT PERSONAL DATA

1A. NAME OF DECEASED—FIRST NAME: EVELYN
1B. MIDDLE NAME: FLORENCE
1C. LAST NAME: NESBIT
2A. DATE OF DEATH—MONTH, DAY, YEAR: January 17, 1967
2B. HOUR: 4:00 P M.
3. SEX: Female
4. COLOR OR RACE: Cauc.
5. BIRTHPLACE (STATE OR FOREIGN COUNTRY): Pennsylvania
6. DATE OF BIRTH: December 25, 1885
7. AGE (LAST BIRTHDAY): 81 YEARS
8. NAME AND BIRTHPLACE OF FATHER: Unk - Nesbit / Penn.
9. MAIDEN NAME AND BIRTHPLACE OF MOTHER: Eva MacKenzie / Penn.
10. CITIZEN OF WHAT COUNTRY: U.S.A.
11. SOCIAL SECURITY NUMBER: 279-18-8920A
12. LAST OCCUPATION: Actress
13. NUMBER OF YEARS IN THIS OCCUPATION: 25
14. NAME OF LAST EMPLOYING COMPANY OR FIRM: Unknown
15. KIND OF INDUSTRY OR BUSINESS: Theater Productions
16. IF DECEASED WAS EVER IN U.S. ARMED FORCES, GIVE WAR OR DATES OF SERVICE: No
17. SPECIFY MARRIED, NEVER MARRIED, WIDOWED, DIVORCED: Widowed
18A. NAME OF PRESENT SPOUSE:
18B. PRESENT OR LAST OCCUPATION OF SPOUSE:

PLACE OF DEATH

19A. PLACE OF DEATH—NAME OF HOSPITAL: Casa Contenta Rest Home
19B. STREET ADDRESS—(GIVE STREET OR RURAL ADDRESS OR LOCATION. DO NOT USE P. O. BOX NUMBERS): 1338 20th Street — INSIDE CITY CORPORATE LIMITS [X]; OUTSIDE CITY CORPORATE LIMITS [ ]
19C. CITY OR TOWN: Santa Monica
19D. COUNTY: Los Angeles
19E. LENGTH OF STAY IN COUNTY OF DEATH: 15 YEARS
19F. LENGTH OF STAY IN CALIFORNIA: 15 YEARS

LAST USUAL RESIDENCE (WHERE DID DECEASED LIVE—IF IN INSTITUTION ENTER RESIDENCE BEFORE ADMISSION)

20A. LAST USUAL RESIDENCE—STREET ADDRESS (GIVE STREET OR RURAL ADDRESS OR LOCATION. DO NOT USE P. O. BOX NUMBERS): 654 Walther Way
20B. IF INSIDE CITY CORPORATE LIMITS CHECK HERE [X]; IF OUTSIDE CITY CORPORATE LIMITS CHECK ONE: [ ] ON A FARM [ ] NOT ON A FARM
20C. CITY OR TOWN: Los Angeles
20D. COUNTY: Los Angeles
20E. STATE: California
21A. NAME OF INFORMANT (IF OTHER THAN SPOUSE): Russell W. Thaw
21B. ADDRESS OF INFORMANT (IF DIFFERENT FROM LAST USUAL RESIDENCE OF DECEASED): 654 Walther Way

PHYSICIAN'S OR CORONER'S CERTIFICATION

22A. PHYSICIAN: I HEREBY CERTIFY THAT DEATH OCCURRED AT THE HOUR, DATE AND PLACE STATED ABOVE FROM THE CAUSES STATED BELOW AND THAT I ATTENDED THE DECEASED FROM 2-17-66 TO 1-17-67 AND THAT I LAST SAW THE DECEASED ALIVE ON 1-16-67
22B. CORONER: I HEREBY CERTIFY THAT DEATH OCCURRED AT THE HOUR, DATE AND PLACE STATED ABOVE FROM THE CAUSES STATED BELOW AND THAT I HAVE HELD AN INVESTIGATION AUTOPSY INQUEST ON THE REMAINS OF DECEASED AS REQUIRED BY LAW
22C. PHYSICIAN OR CORONER—SIGNATURE: Robert A. Moore — DEGREE OR TITLE: MD
22D. ADDRESS: 2210 Santa Monica Blvd Santa Monica - Calif
22E. DATE SIGNED: 1-18-67

FUNERAL DIRECTOR AND LOCAL REGISTRAR

23. SPECIFY BURIAL, ENTOMBMENT OR CREMATION: Burial
24. DATE: Jan. 19, 1967
25. NAME OF CEMETERY OR CREMATORY: Holy Cross Cemetery
26. EMBALMER—SIGNATURE (IF BODY EMBALMED) LICENSE NUMBER: Audrey M. Smith 4233
27. NAME OF FUNERAL DIRECTOR (OR PERSON ACTING AS SUCH): Gates, Kingsley, & Gates SM
28. DATE ACCEPTED FOR REGISTRATION BY LOCAL REGISTRAR: JAN 19 1967
29. LOCAL REGISTRAR—SIGNATURE: Alfred Buchner MD L.R.

MEDICAL AND HEALTH DATA

CAUSE OF DEATH

30. CAUSE OF DEATH — ENTER ONLY ONE CAUSE PER LINE FOR (A), (B), AND (C)

PART I. DEATH WAS CAUSED BY:
IMMEDIATE CAUSE (A): bronchopneumonia - recurrent — 1 mo
CONDITIONS, IF ANY, WHICH GAVE RISE TO THE ABOVE CAUSE (A) STATING THE UNDERLYING CAUSE LAST — DUE TO (B): Cerebral Thrombosis - Mesencephalic — 1+ mo
DUE TO (C): Arteriosclerosis — years

APPROXIMATE INTERVAL BETWEEN ONSET AND DEATH

PART II. OTHER SIGNIFICANT CONDITIONS CONTRIBUTING TO DEATH BUT NOT RELATED TO THE TERMINAL DISEASE CONDITION GIVEN IN PART I (A): Onset of hemiplegia due to old major stroke

OPERATION AND AUTOPSY

31. OPERATION—CHECK ONE: [X] OPERATION PERFORMED; [ ] OPERATION PERFORMED—FINDINGS USED IN DETERMINING ABOVE STATED CAUSES OF DEATH; [ ] OPERATION PERFORMED—FINDINGS NOT USED IN DETERMINING ABOVE STATED CAUSES OF DEATH
32. DATE OF OPERATION:
33. AUTOPSY—CHECK ONE: [X] AUTOPSY PERFORMED; [ ] AUTOPSY PERFORMED—GROSS FINDINGS USED IN DETERMINING ABOVE STATED CAUSES OF DEATH; [ ] AUTOPSY PERFORMED—GROSS FINDINGS NOT USED IN DETERMINING ABOVE STATED CAUSES OF DEATH

INJURY INFORMATION

34A. SPECIFY ACCIDENT, SUICIDE OR HOMICIDE
34B. DESCRIBE HOW INJURY OCCURRED (ENTER SEQUENCE OF EVENTS WHICH RESULTED IN INJURY. NATURE OF INJURY SHOULD BE ENTERED IN PART I OR PART II OF ITEM 30)
35A. TIME OF INJURY — HOUR MONTH DAY YEAR M.
35B. INJURY OCCURRED [ ] WHILE AT WORK [ ] NOT WHILE AT WORK
35C. PLACE OF INJURY (E.G. IN OR ABOUT HOME, FARM, FACTORY, STREET, OFFICE BUILDING)
35D. CITY, TOWN, OR LOCATION — COUNTY — STATE

This is to certify that this document is a true copy of the official record filed with the Registrar-Recorder/County Clerk.

Conny B. McCormack

CONNY B. McCORMACK
Registrar-Recorder/County Clerk

NOV 28 2000

19-113371

This copy not valid unless prepared on engraved border displaying the Seal and Signature of the Registrar-Recorder/County Clerk.

MIDWEST BANK NOTE COMPANY

ANY ALTERATION OR ERASURE VOIDS THIS CERTIFICATE

Certificate of Death

State of Connecticut — Department of Public Health
VS-4 REV. 1/04

1. **Decedent's Legal Name:** Paul L. Newman
2. **Sex:** Male
3. **Actual or Presumed Date of Death:** September 26, 2008
4. **Actual or Presumed Time of Death:** 6:45 PM
5. **Age Last Birthday:** 83
7. **Date of Birth:** 01/26/1925
8. **Birthplace:** Cleveland Heights, Ohio
9. **Residence (State):** Connecticut
10. **Residence (County):** Fairfield
11. **Residence (City or Town):** Westport
12. **Residence (Street and No.):** 274 North Ave
14. **Zip Code:** 06880
15. **Ever in US Armed Forces:** Yes
16. **Marital Status at Time of Death:** Married
17. **Surviving Spouse's Name:** Joanne Woodward
18. **Father's Name:** Arthur S. Newman
19. **Mother's Name Prior to First Marriage:** Theresa Fetzer
20. **Informant's Name:** Ms. Joanne Woodward Newman
21. **Informant's Relationship to Decedent:** Wife
22. **Mailing Address:** 274 North Avenue, Westport, CT 06880
23. **If Death Occurred in a Hospital:** N/A
24. **If Death Occurred Somewhere Other Than a Hospital:** Decedent's Home
25. **Facility Name:** 274 North Avenue
26. **City or Town of Death:** Westport — **Zip Code:** 06880
27. **County of Death:** Fairfield
28. **Method of Disposition:** Cremation
29. **Disposition:** Ferncliff Crematory
30. **Location:** Hartsdale, New York
31. **Date:** 09/29/2008
32. **Was Body Embalmed:** No
33. **Funeral Facility:** Bouton Funeral Home, Inc., 31 W. Church Street, Georgetown, CT 06829
34. **Signature of Funeral Director or Embalmer:** [signed]
35. **License Number of Signee in Box 34:** 1784
36. **Date Pronounced Dead:** 09/26/2008
37. **Time Pronounced:** 6:45 PM
38. **Nurse Pronouncement Name and Degree or Title:** Lynda B. Tucker, RN
39. **Signature:** Linda B. Tucker
40. **Date Signed:** 9/26/08
41. **Was Medical Examiner Contacted:** No
42. **Was an Autopsy Performed:** No
43. **Were the Autopsy Findings Available to Complete the Cause of Death:** N/A

Cause of Death

44. **Part I.**
   (a) Immediate Cause: Acute Lymphoblastic Leukemia — Approximate Interval Onset to Death: 5 mos

45. **Part II. Other Significant Conditions:** Coronary Artery Disease

46. **If Female:** Not pregnant within past year
47. **Did Tobacco Use Contribute to Death:** No

48. **Certifier:** Certifying physician
   Certifier Name: Robert Altbaum
   Title of Certifier: MD
   Date Certified: 9/27/08
49. **Mailing – Certifier:** 162 Kings Highway North, Westport, CT 06880

This Certificate was Received for Record on: September 29, 2008
By Registrar: Colleen Tarpey, Asst.

50. **Decedent's Education:** Bachelor's degree
51. **Decedent of Hispanic Origin:** No, Not Spanish/Hispanic/Latino
52. **Decedent's Race:** White
53. **Decedent's Usual Occupation:** Actor, Director, Producer
54. **Kind of Business/Industry:** Entertainment

I certify that this is a true transcript of the information on the death record as recorded in this office.

Attest: Colleen Tarpey, Asst.
Colleen E. Tarpey, Asst. Registrar of Vital Statistics, Town of Westport, Connecticut

Dated: 10/3/08

CERTIFIED COPY

NOT GOOD WITHOUT SEAL OF CERTIFYING OFFICIAL

MABEL NORMAND

STATE OF CALIFORNIA
CERTIFICATION OF VITAL RECORD

COUNTY OF LOS ANGELES • REGISTRAR-RECORDER/COUNTY CLERK

INFORMATIONAL, NOT A VALID DOCUMENT TO ESTABLISH IDENTITY

STATE OF CALIFORNIA — DEPARTMENT OF PUBLIC HEALTH — VITAL STATISTICS — STANDARD CERTIFICATE OF DEATH

771 / Local Registered No. 31

1. PLACE OF DEATH. Dist. No. 1908
   - County of: Los Angeles
   - City or Town of: Monrovia
   - (No. Pottenger Sanatorium St.; Ward)

2. FULL NAME: Mabel Normand Cody

PERSONAL AND STATISTICAL PARTICULARS

- 3. SEX: Female
- 4. COLOR OR RACE: white
- 5. SINGLE, MARRIED, WIDOWED, OR DIVORCED: married
- 5a. HUSBAND of (or) WIFE of: Lewis Cody
- 6. DATE OF BIRTH: Nov. 10 About 1895
- 7. AGE: About 34 years 3 months 13 days
- 8. OCCUPATION:
  - (a) Actress
  - (b) Motion pictures
- 9. BIRTHPLACE: Staton Island, New York
- 10. NAME OF FATHER: Claude Normand
- 11. BIRTHPLACE OF FATHER: Unknown
- 12. MAIDEN NAME OF MOTHER: Mary Draig
- 13. BIRTHPLACE OF MOTHER: unknown
- 13a. LENGTH OF RESIDENCE: At Place of Death — years 5 months 12 days
  - Beverly Hills, Calif.
  - In California 15 years
- 14. THE ABOVE IS TRUE TO THE BEST OF MY KNOWLEDGE
  - (Informant) Pottenger Sanatorium
  - (Address) Monrovia, Calif.

Filed 2/26/30 J.M. Furstman, M. D. Registrar or Deputy

FILED MAR 10 1930 C. L. LOGAN, COUNTY RECORDER

MEDICAL CERTIFICATE OF DEATH

- 16. DATE OF DEATH: Feb. 23 1930
- 17. I Hereby Certify, That I attended deceased from Sept. 11, 1929, Feb. 23, 1930 that I last saw her alive on Feb. 22, 1930 and that death occurred on the date stated above at 2:25 A. m.
- The CAUSE OF DEATH was as follows: 31
  - Pulmonary Tuberculosis
  - (Duration) 1 years 1 months days
  - Contributory
- 18a. Where was disease contracted If not at place of death? unknown
- Did an operation precede death? no Date of
- Was there an autopsy? no
- What test confirmed diagnosis? sputum examination
- (Signed) Robert V. Pottenger M.D.
- Feb. 23, 1930 (Address) Pottenger San., Monrovia

- 19. PLACE OF BURIAL OR REMOVAL: Los Angeles, Calif.
- DATE OF BURIAL: Feb. 28, 1930
- 20. UNDERTAKER: Renaker Co.
- ADDRESS: Monrovia, Calif.
- EMBALMER'S LICENSE NO. 1965

This is to certify that this document is a true copy of the official record filed with the Registrar-Recorder/County Clerk.

CONNY B. McCORMACK
Registrar-Recorder/County Clerk

JUL 2 0 2005

019554524

This copy not valid unless prepared on engraved border displaying the Seal and Signature of the Registrar-Recorder/County Clerk.

ANY ALTERATION OR ERASURE VOIDS THIS CERTIFICATE

COUNTY OF LOS ANGELES
DEPARTMENT OF HEALTH SERVICES
CERTIFICATE OF DEATH

STATE OF CALIFORNIA

1. Name of Decedent—First (Given)	CHARLES
3. Last (Family)	KRAUSER
4. Date of Birth	02/23/1923
5. Age Yrs.	76
6. Sex	M
7. Date of Death	07/14/1999
8. Hour	0715
9. State of Birth	MD
10. Social Security No.	215-14-0731
11. Military Service	No
12. Marital Status	Never Married
13. Education—Years Completed	12
14. Race	White
15. Hispanic	No
16. Usual Employer	M.S.F.S. Shipping
17. Occupation	Merchant Seaman
18. Kind of Business	Shipping
19. Years in Occupation	35
20. Residence	2210 Main Street
21. City	Santa Monica
22. County	Los Angeles
23. Zip Code	90405
24. Yrs in County	50
25. State	CA
26. Informant Name, Relationship	Joe Gold - DPOA
27. Mailing Address	2210 Main St. Santa Monica, CA 90405
31. Name of Father—First	Unknown
33. Last	Unknown
34. Birth State	Poland
35. Name of Mother—First	Unknown
37. Last (Maiden)	Unknown
38. Birth State	Poland
39. Date	07/28/1999
40. Place of Final Disposition	Res. Joe Gold 2210 Main St. Santa Monica, CA 90405
41. Type of Disposition	CR/RES
42. Signature of Embalmer	Not Embalmed
44. Name of Funeral Director	CREMATION SOCIETY SO. BAY
45. License No.	FD-1491
47. Date	07/26/1999
101. Place of Death	St. John's Medical Center
102.	IP
104. County	Los Angeles
105. Street Address	1328 22nd Street
106. City	Santa Monica

107. Death was caused by:

- (A) IMMEDIATE CAUSE: Cardiopulmonary Arrest — mins
- (B) DUE TO: Metastatic Prostate Cancer — mons

108. Death Reported to Coroner	No
109. Biopsy Performed	Yes
110. Autopsy Performed	No
111. Used in Determining Cause	No
112. Other Significant Conditions	None
113. Was Operation Performed	No
115. Signature and Title of Certifier	[signature] MD
116. License No.	G36051
117. Date	07/23/1999
114. Decedent Attended Since	07/14/1999
Decedent Last Seen Alive	07/14/1999
118. Type Attending Physician's Name	D. Lieber, M.D. 11645 Wilshire Blvd Los Angeles, CA 90025

Census Tract: 090251657
Fax Auth. #: 374-23668

CERTIFICATION OF VITAL RECORD

COUNTY OF LOS ANGELES • REGISTRAR-RECORDER/COUNTY CLERK

CERTIFICATE OF DEATH
STATE OF CALIFORNIA—DEPARTMENT OF PUBLIC HEALTH

State File Number: 7097-035529

DECEDENT PERSONAL DATA

- 1a. Name of Deceased—First Name: DENNIS
- 1b. Middle Name: EDWARD ••• JAMES
- 1c. Last Name: O'KEEFE AKA: FLANAGAN, SR.
- 2a. Date of Death: August 31, 1968
- 2b. Hour: 8:53 P.M.
- 3. Sex: Male
- 4. Color or Race: Caucasian
- 5. Birthplace: Iowa
- 6. Date of Birth: March 29, 1908
- 7. Age: 60 years
- 8. Name and Birthplace of Father: Edward James Flanagan—Unknown USA
- 9. Maiden Name and Birthplace of Mother: Charlotte Ricks—Unknown USA
- 10. Citizen of What Country: USA
- 11. Social Security Number: 565-12-8785
- 12. Married, Never Married, Widowed, Divorced: Married
- 13. Name of Surviving Spouse: Steffi Duna Berinde
- 14. Last Occupation: Actor
- 15. Number of Years in This Occupation: 40
- 16. Name of Last Employing Company or Firm: Thunderbird Hotel
- 17. Kind of Industry or Business: Show Business

PLACE OF DEATH

- 18a. Place of Death: St. John's Hospital
- 18b. Street Address: 1328 22nd Street
- 18c. Inside City Corporate Limits: Yes
- 18d. City or Town: Santa Monica
- 18e. County: Los Angeles
- 18f. Length of Stay in County of Death: 4 mos
- 18g. Length of Stay in California: 60 years

USUAL RESIDENCE

- 19a. Usual Residence—Street Address: 74860 Fairway Drive
- 19b. Inside City Corporate Limits: (blank)
- 19c. City or Town: Palm Desert
- 19d. County: San Bernardino
- 19e. State: California
- 20. Name and Mailing Address of Informant: Mr. James O'Keefe, Son, 1609½ S. Bentley, West Los Angeles, Calif.

PHYSICIAN'S OR CORONER'S CERTIFICATION

- 21b. Physician: 8-20-68 to 8-31-68 and 8-31-68
- 21c. Physician or Coroner Signature: R Th Barton MD
- 21d. Date Signed: 9-3-68
- 21e. Address: 9730 Wilshire Blvd BH
- 21f. Physician's California License Number: C8974

FUNERAL DIRECTOR AND LOCAL REGISTRAR

- 22a. Specify Burial, Entombment or Cremation: Cremation
- 22b. Date: 9-5-68
- 23. Name of Cemetery or Crematory: Abbott and Hast—Burial At Sea, Santa Monica, California
- 24. Embalmer Signature: Michael R. Decker
- License Number: 2899
- 25. Name of Funeral Director: Forest Lawn Memorial Park Assn., Glendale, California
- 26. Was This Death Reported to Coroner: No
- 27. Local Registrar Signature: (signed) MD
- 28. Date Accepted for Registration: SEP 5 1968

CAUSE OF DEATH

- 29. Part I. Death Was Caused By:
  - (A) Immediate Cause: Bilateral pneumonitis — 2 days
  - (B) Due to: Bronchogenic carcinoma — 1 yr
  - (C):
- 30. Part II. Other Significant Conditions: Carcinoma of tonsil
- 31. Was Operation or Biopsy Performed: Thoracotomy 1967
- 32a. Autopsy: No

This is to certify that this document is a true copy of the official record filed with the Registrar-Recorder/County Clerk.

Beatriz Valdez
BEATRIZ VALDEZ
Registrar-Recorder/County Clerk

AUG 10 1995
19-389292

This copy not valid unless prepared on engraved border displaying the Seal and Signature of the Registrar-Recorder/County Clerk.

ANY ALTERATION OR ERASURE VOIDS THIS CERTIFICATE

COUNTY OF LOS ANGELES
DEPARTMENT OF HEALTH SERVICES
CERTIFICATE OF DEATH

DECEDENT PERSONAL DATA
- 1. Name of Decedent—First (Given): RICHARD
- 2. Middle: FRANCES
- 3. Last (Family): O'NEILL
- 4. Date of Birth: 08/29/1928
- 5. Age Yrs: 70
- 6. Sex: M
- 7. Date of Death: 11/17/1998
- 8. Hour: 2006
- 9. State of Birth: New York
- 10. Social Security No.: 087-22-7508
- 11. Military Service: Yes
- 12. Marital Status: Married
- 13. Education—Years Completed: 14
- 14. Race: White
- 15. Hispanic: No
- 16. Usual Employer: Self Employed
- 17. Occupation: Actor
- 18. Kind of Business: Entertainment
- 19. Years in Occupation: 51

USUAL RESIDENCE
- 20. Residence—Street and Number or Location: 443 S. Oakhurst
- 21. City: Beverly Hills
- 22. County: Los Angeles
- 23. Zip Code: 90212
- 24. Yrs in County: 20
- 25. State or Foreign Country: CA

INFORMANT
- 26. Name, Relationship: Susan Jacqueline O'Neill - Wife
- 27. Mailing Address: 443 S. Oakhurst Beverly Hills, Ca 90212

SPOUSE AND PARENT INFORMATION
- 28. Name of Surviving Spouse—First: Susan
- 29. Middle: Jacqueline
- 30. Last (Maiden Name): Shawl
- 31. Name of Father—First: Frances
- 32. Middle: -
- 33. Last: O'Neill
- 34. Birth State: NY
- 35. Name of Mother—First: Mary
- 36. Middle: Catherine
- 37. Last (Maiden): O'Brien
- 38. Birth State: NY

DISPOSITION(S)
- 39. Date: 12/08/1998
- 40. Place of Final Disposition: Res. Susan Jacqueline O'Neill 443 S. Oakhurst Beverly Hills, Ca 90212
- 41. Type of Disposition(s): CR/RES
- 42. Signature of Embalmer: Not Embalmed
- 44. Name of Funeral Director: Cremation Society South Bay
- 45. License No.: FD-1491
- 47. Date: 12/03/1998

PLACE OF DEATH
- 101. Place of Death: St. John Medical Center (IP)
- 104. County: Los Angeles
- 105. Street Address: 1328 22nd Street
- 106. City: Santa Monica

CAUSE OF DEATH
- 107(A) Immediate Cause: Acute Myocardial Infarction — minutes
- 107(B) Due to: Coronary Artery Thrombosis — minutes
- 107(C) Due to: Atherosclerotic Heart Disease — months
- 108. Death Reported to Coroner: No
- 109. Biopsy Performed: No
- 110. Autopsy Performed: Yes
- 111. Used in Determining Cause: Yes
- 112. Other Significant Conditions: Diabetes, Pneumonia, Myelodysplasia
- 113. Was Operation Performed: No

PHYSICIAN'S CERTIFICATION
- 114. Decedent Attended Since: 08/18/1983; Last Seen Alive: 11/17/1998
- 116. License No.: G10128
- 117. Date: 11/23/1998
- 118. Type/Attending Physician's Name, Mailing Address, Zip: Charles Mulry, M.D. 8920 Wilshire Blvd Beverly Hills, CA 90212

CORONER'S USE ONLY
- 30F

Census Tract: 090192934
Fax Auth. #: 374-25430

Date Issued: DEC 10 1998

STATE OF CALIFORNIA
CERTIFICATION OF VITAL RECORD
COUNTY OF LOS ANGELES • REGISTRAR-RECORDER/COUNTY CLERK

CERTIFICATE OF DEATH — STATE OF CALIFORNIA

State File Number: 3200819050554

DECEDENT'S PERSONAL DATA
- 1. Name of Decedent – First (Given): BETTIE
- 2. Middle: MAE
- 3. Last (Family): PAGE
- 4. Date of Birth: 04/22/1923
- 5. Age Yrs: 85
- 6. Sex: F
- 7. Date of Death: 12/11/2008
- 8. Hour (24 Hours): 1841
- 9. Birth State/Foreign Country: TENNESSEE
- 10. Social Security Number: 411-26-2435
- 11. Ever in U.S. Armed Forces?: NO
- 12. Marital Status: DIVORCED
- 13. Education – Highest Level/Degree: BACHELOR
- 14/15. Was Decedent Hispanic/Latino(a)/Spanish?: NO
- 16. Decedent's Race: CAUCASIAN
- 17. Usual Occupation: MODEL
- 18. Kind of Business or Industry: ENTERTAINMENT
- 19. Years in Occupation: 15

USUAL RESIDENCE
- 20. Decedent's Residence: 9229 W. SUNSET BLVD SUITE 820
- 21. City: WEST HOLLYWOOD
- 22. County/Province: LOS ANGELES
- 23. Zip Code: 90069
- 24. Years in County: 15
- 25. State/Foreign Country: CA

INFORMANT
- 26. Informant's Name, Relationship: MARK ROESHER, CONSERVATOR
- 27. Informant's Mailing Address: 9229 W. SUNSET BLVD SUITE 820, WEST HOLLYWOOD, CA 90069

SPOUSE AND PARENT INFORMATION
- 28–30. Name of Surviving Spouse: —
- 31. Name of Father – First: WALTER
- 32. Middle: ROY
- 33. Last: PAGE
- 34. Birth State: TN
- 35. Name of Mother – First: EDNA
- 36. Middle: MAE
- 37. Last (Maiden): PIRTLE
- 38. Birth State: MS

FUNERAL DIRECTOR / LOCAL REGISTRAR
- 39. Disposition Date: 12/16/2008
- 40. Place of Final Disposition: WESTWOOD VILLAGE MEMORIAL PARK, 1218 GLENDON AVE, LOS ANGELES, CA 90024
- 41. Type of Disposition(s): CR/BU
- 42. Signature of Embalmer: NOT EMBALMED
- 44. Name of Funeral Establishment: PIERCE BROTHERS WESTWOOD
- 45. License Number: FD-951
- 46. Signature of Local Registrar: JONATHAN FIELDING, MD
- 47. Date: 12/15/2008

PLACE OF DEATH
- 101. Place of Death: KINDRED HOSPITAL
- 102. If Hospital, Specify One: IP
- 104. County: LOS ANGELES
- 105. Facility Address or Location Where Found: 5525 SLAUSON AVE
- 106. City: CULVER CITY

CAUSE OF DEATH
- 107. Cause of Death:
  - (A) Immediate Cause: CARDIORESPIRATORY ARREST — Time Interval: MINS
  - (B) MYOCARDIAL INFARCTION — 1WK
- 108. Death Reported to Coroner?: NO
- 109. Biopsy Performed?: NO
- 110. Autopsy Performed?: NO
- 111. Used in Determining Cause?: —
- 112. Other Significant Conditions: NONE
- 113. Was Operation Performed: NO
- 113A. If Female, Pregnant in Last Year?: NO

PHYSICIAN'S CERTIFICATION
- 115. Signature and Title of Certifier: MORRIS TOBIAS GRABIE M.D
- 116. License Number: G34196
- 117. Date: 12/14/2008
- Decedent Attended Since: 11/03/2008
- Decedent Last Seen Alive: 12/10/2008
- 118. Type Attending Physician's Name, Mailing Address, Zip Code: MORRIS TOBIAS GRABIE M.D, 1301 20TH STREET NO 200, SANTA MONICA, CA 90404

Barcode: *012008000951929*

This is to certify that this document is a true copy of the official record filed with the Registrar-Recorder/County Clerk.

SEP 2 8 2009

DEAN C. LOGAN
Registrar-Recorder/County Clerk

019581418

INFORMATIONAL, NOT A VALID DOCUMENT TO ESTABLISH IDENTITY

ANY ALTERATION OR ERASURE VOIDS THIS CERTIFICATE

SANTA BARBARA COUNTY
SANTA BARBARA, CALIFORNIA

CERTIFICATE OF DEATH — STATE OF CALIFORNIA — 3200642002390

1. Name of Decedent — First	Walter
2. Middle	Jack
3. Last (Family)	Palance
AKA	Jack Palance
4. Date of Birth	02/18/1920
5. Age	86
6. Sex	M
8. Birth State/Foreign Country	PA
10. Social Security Number	057-12-2514
11. Ever in U.S. Armed Forces?	Yes
12. Marital Status	Divorced
7. Date of Death	11/10/2006
8. Hour	1235
13. Education	Bachelor's
14/15. Hispanic?	No
16. Race	White
17. Usual Occupation	Actor
18. Kind of Business/Industry	Entertainment
19. Years in Occupation	60
20. Decedent's Residence	785 Tucker Road
21. City	Tehachapi
22. County	Kern
23. Zip	93561
24. Years in County	40
25. State	CA
26. Informant's Name, Relationship	Holly Palance, Daughter
27. Informant's Mailing Address	2744 Macadamia Lane, Santa Barbara, CA 93108
31. Name of Father — First	Ivan
33. Last	Palachnuik
34. Birth State	Ukraine
35. Name of Mother — First	Anna
37. Last (Maiden)	Gramiak
38. Birth State	Ukraine
39. Disposition Date	11/15/2006
40. Place of Final Disposition	Elaine Palance Res: 785 Tucker Road, Tehachapi, CA 93561
41. Type of Disposition	CR/RES
42. Signature of Embalmer	Not Embalmed
44. Name of Funeral Establishment	McDermott-Crockett Mortuary
45. License Number	FD 383
47. Date	11/15/2006
101. Place of Death	Daughter's Residence
104. County	Santa Barbara
105. Facility Address	2744 Macadamia Lane
106. City	Santa Barbara
107. Cause of Death (Immediate)	Cardiorespiratory Failure — Hours
(b)	Pancreatic Cancer — Months
108. Death Reported to Coroner?	Yes — CNR-06-1070
109. Biopsy Performed?	No
110. Autopsy Performed?	No
111. Used in Determining Cause?	No
112. Other Significant Conditions	None
113. Was Operation Performed	No
114. Decedent Attended Since	10/15/2006
Decedent Last Been Alive	10/17/2006
116. License Number	G 078514
117. Date	11/14/2006
118. Physician's Name	Babji P. Mesipam M.D. 1478 E. Valley Rd. Santa Barbara, CA 93108

CERTIFIED COPY OF VITAL RECORDS

STATE OF CALIFORNIA
COUNTY OF SANTA BARBARA } SS

DATE ISSUED: DEC 1 2 2006

000098209

JOSEPH E. HOLLAND
COUNTY CLERK, RECORDER and ASSESSOR
SANTA BARBARA, CALIFORNIA

This is a true and exact reproduction of the document officially registered and placed on file in the office of the SANTA BARBARA COUNTY CLERK, RECORDER and ASSESSOR.

This copy not valid unless prepared on engraved border displaying seal and signature of County Clerk, Recorder and Assessor.

INFORMATIONAL, NOT A VALID DOCUMENT TO ESTABLISH IDENTITY

CERTIFICATION OF VITAL RECORD

COUNTY OF LOS ANGELES • REGISTRAR-RECORDER/COUNTY CLERK

CERTIFICATE OF DEATH
STATE OF CALIFORNIA—DEPARTMENT OF HEALTH
OFFICE OF THE STATE REGISTRAR OF VITAL STATISTICS

State File Number: 0190-017100

DECEDENT PERSONAL DATA
- 1a. Name of Deceased—First Name: Lawrence
- 1b. Middle Name: Klusman
- 1c. Last Name: Parks aka Larry Parks
- 2a. Date of Death: April 13 1975
- 2b. Hour: 1 A
- 3. Sex: male
- 4. Color or Race: cauc
- 5. Birthplace: Kansas
- 6. Date of Birth: Dec 13 1914
- 7. Age: 60 years
- 8. Name and Birthplace of Father: Frank Parks — Kansas
- 9. Maiden Name and Birthplace of Mother: Leona Klusman — Kansas
- 10. Citizen of What Country: U.S.A.
- 11. Social Security Number: 056 14 3298
- 12. Married, Never Married, Widowed, Divorced: married
- 13. Name of Surviving Spouse: Betty Garrett
- 14. Last Occupation: Actor / Builder
- 15. Number of Years in This Occupation: 12
- 16. Name of Last Employing Company or Firm: Louis Mendel Prod.
- 17. Kind of Industry or Business: building / Pictures

PLACE OF DEATH
- 18a. Place of Death:
- 18b. Street Address: 3231 Oakdell Rd.
- 18c. Inside City Corporate Limits: yes
- 18d. City or Town: Studio City
- 18e. County: Los Angeles
- 18f. Length of Stay in County: 35 years
- 18g. Length of Stay in California: 35 years

USUAL RESIDENCE
- 19a. Usual Residence—Street Address: 3231 Oakdell Rd.
- 19b. Inside City Corporate Limits: yes
- 19c. City or Town: Studio City
- 19d. County: Los Angeles
- 19e. State: Calif
- 20. Name and Mailing Address of Informant: Betty Parks, same

PHYSICIAN'S OR CORONER'S CERTIFICATION
- 21a. From: 4/1/70 To: 4/8/75 And: 4/8/75
- 21c. Physician or Coroner—Signature: Jack Shankoff
- 21d. Date Signed: 4/14/75
- 21e. Address: 435 No Rexbury Dr.
- 21f. Physician's California License Number: C-8016

FUNERAL DIRECTOR AND LOCAL REGISTRAR
- 22a. Specify Burial, Entombment or Cremation: Cremation
- 22b. Date: 4-16-75
- 23. Name of Cemetery or Crematory: Rosedale Crematory
- 24. Embalmer: not embalmed
- 25. Name of Funeral Director: Pierce Hamrock Mortuary
- 26. If Not Certified by Coroner, Was This Death Reported to Coroner: No
- 27. Local Registrar—Signature: [signature]
- 28. Date Received for Registration: APR 15 1975

CAUSE OF DEATH
- 29. Part I. Death was Caused By:
  - (A) Myocardial Infarction, acute — 6 mins
  - (B) Due to Coronary Artery Disease — 3 yrs
- 31. Was Operation or Biopsy Performed: No
- 32a. Autopsy: No

This is to certify that this document is a true copy of the official record filed with the Registrar-Recorder/County Clerk.

BEATRIZ VALDEZ
Registrar-Recorder/County Clerk

AUG 10 1995
19-389396

This copy not valid unless prepared on engraved border displaying the Seal and Signature of the Registrar-Recorder/County Clerk.

STATE OF CALIFORNIA
CERTIFICATION OF VITAL RECORD

COUNTY OF LOS ANGELES • REGISTRAR-RECORDER/COUNTY CLERK

CERTIFICATE OF DEATH — STATE OF CALIFORNIA

State File Number: 3 2004 19 011272

1. Name of Decedent — First (Given)	Robert
2. Middle	J.
3. Last (Family)	Pastorelli
4. Date of Birth	06/21/1954
5. Age Yrs	49
6. Sex	M
7. Date of Death	03/08/2004
8. Hour (24 Hours)	1449
9. Birth State/Foreign Country	New Jersey
10. Social Security Number	150-50-8120
11. Ever in U.S. Armed Forces?	No
12. Marital Status	Never married
13. Education	Some college
14/15. Hispanic/Latino?	No
16. Decedent's Race	White
17. Usual Occupation	Actor
18. Kind of Business or Industry	Television
19. Years in Occupation	20
20. Decedent's Residence	501 Ocean Ave.
21. City	Sea Girt
22. County/Province	Monmouth
23. Zip Code	08750
24. Years in County	5
25. State/Foreign Country	New Jersey
26. Informant's Name, Relationship	Gwendolyn M. Pastorelli - Sister
27. Informant's Mailing Address	501 Ocean Ave., Sea Girt, New Jersey 08750
31. Name of Father — First	Ledo
33. Last	Pastorelli
34. Birth State	PA
35. Name of Mother — First	Dorothy
37. Last (Maiden)	Pagano
38. Birth State	PA
39. Disposition Date	03/11/2004
40. Place of Final Disposition	St. Catharine's Cemetery, Sea Girt, New Jersey
41. Type of Disposition	TR/BU
43. License Number	5261
44. Name of Funeral Establishment	Crawford Mortuary
45. License Number	FD1228
47. Date	03/11/2004
101. Place of Death	Other
104. County	Los Angeles
105. Facility Address or Location Where Found	2751 Hollyridge Drive
106. City	Hollywood
107. Cause of Death — Immediate Cause (A)	DEFERRED
Death Reported to Coroner	Yes
Coroner Number	2004-01976
110. Autopsy Performed?	Yes
119. Manner of Death	Pending Investigation
127. Date	03/10/2004
128. Type Name, Title of Coroner / Deputy Coroner	REGINA AUGUSTINE, DEPUTY CORONER
Fax Auth. #	179/5048

INFORMATIONAL, NOT A VALID DOCUMENT TO ESTABLISH IDENTITY

This is to certify that this document is a true copy of the official record filed with the Registrar-Recorder/County Clerk.

Conny B. McCormack
CONNY B. McCORMACK
Registrar-Recorder/County Clerk

JAN 26 2005

019025810

STATE OF CALIFORNIA
CERTIFICATION OF VITAL RECORD

COUNTY OF LOS ANGELES • REGISTRAR-RECORDER/COUNTY CLERK

04-002726

AMENDMENT OF MEDICAL AND HEALTH DATA—DEATH 3 2004 19 011272

PART I — INFORMATION TO LOCAL RECORD

1. NAME—FIRST (GIVEN): ROBERT
2. MIDDLE: J.
3. LAST (FAMILY): PASTORELLI
4. SEX: M
5. DATE OF EVENT: 03/08/2004
6. CITY OF OCCURRENCE: HOLLYWOOD
7. COUNTY OF OCCURRENCE: LOS ANGELES

1 OF 2

PART II — INFORMATION AS IT APPEARS ON RECORD

107. DEATH WAS CAUSED BY:
- IMMEDIATE CAUSE (A): DEFERRED

108. DEATH REPORTED TO CORONER: YES — REFERRAL NUMBER 2004-01976
109. BIOPSY PERFORMED: (blank)
110. AUTOPSY PERFORMED: YES
111. USED IN DETERMINING CAUSE: (blank)

119. MANNER OF DEATH: PENDING INVESTIGATION

PART III — INFORMATION AS IT SHOULD APPEAR

107. DEATH WAS CAUSED BY:
- IMMEDIATE CAUSE (A): ACUTE COCAINE-MORPHINE (HEROIN) TOXICITY

TIME INTERVAL BETWEEN ONSET AND DEATH: UNK.

108. DEATH REPORTED TO CORONER: YES — REFERRAL NUMBER 2004-01976
109. BIOPSY PERFORMED: NO
110. AUTOPSY PERFORMED: YES
111. USED IN DETERMINING CAUSE: YES

112. OTHER SIGNIFICANT CONDITIONS CONTRIBUTING TO DEATH BUT NOT RELATED TO CAUSE GIVEN IN 107: NONE
113. WAS OPERATION PERFORMED FOR ANY CONDITION IN ITEM 107 or 112?: NO
119. MANNER OF DEATH: ACCIDENT
120. INJURY AT WORK: NO
121. INJURY DATE: 03/08/2004
122. HOUR: UNK.
123. PLACE OF INJURY: BATHROOM/RESIDENCE
124. DESCRIBE HOW INJURY OCCURRED: INJECTION OF DRUGS
125. LOCATION: 2751 HOLLYRIDGE DRIVE, HOLLYWOOD 90068

DECLARATION OF CERTIFYING PHYSICIAN OR CORONER

8. SIGNATURE OF CERTIFYING PHYSICIAN OR CORONER: Christopher Rogers
9. DATE SIGNED: 03/31/2004
10. TYPED OR PRINTED NAME AND DEGREE/TITLE OF CERTIFIER: CHRISTOPHER ROGERS, M.D. DME
11. ADDRESS: 1104 NORTH MISSION ROAD
12. CITY: LOS ANGELES
13. STATE: CA
14. ZIP CODE: 90033

16. DATE ACCEPTED FOR REGISTRATION: 04/05/2004

INFORMATIONAL, NOT A VALID DOCUMENT TO ESTABLISH IDENTITY

JAN 26 2005

CONNY B. McCORMACK
Registrar-Recorder/County Clerk

019025809

CERTIFICATION OF VITAL RECORD

COUNTY OF LOS ANGELES • REGISTRAR-RECORDER/COUNTY CLERK

CERTIFICATE OF DEATH — STATE OF CALIFORNIA

39219040040

DECEDENT PERSONAL DATA
- 1A. Name (Given): ANTHONY
- 1C. Last (Family): PERKINS
- 2A. Date of Death: SEPT 12, 1992
- 2B. Hour: 1606
- 3. Sex: MALE
- 4. Race: WHITE
- 5. Hispanic: No
- 6. Date of Birth: APRIL 4, 1932
- 7. Age: 60
- 8. State of Birth: N.Y.
- 9. Citizen of: USA
- 10A. Full Name of Father: JAMES OSGOOD RIPLEY PERKINS
- 10B. State of Birth: MASS.
- 11A. Full Maiden Name of Mother: ELIZABETH MARY BAILEY
- 11B. State of Birth: MASS.
- 12. Military Service: 19 To 19 / None
- 13. Social Security No.: 008-20-3325
- 14. Marital Status: MARRIED
- 15. Name of Surviving Spouse: BERINTHIA BERENSON
- 16A. Usual Occupation: ACTOR
- 16B. Kind of Business: MOVIES
- 16C. Usual Employer: SELF-EMPLOYED
- 16D. Years in Occupation: 45
- 17. Education: 16

USUAL RESIDENCE
- 18A. Street: 2840 SEATTLE DRIVE
- 18B. City: LOS ANGELES
- 18C. Zip: 90046
- 18D. County: LOS ANGELES
- 18E. Years in County: 12
- 18F. State: CALIFORNIA
- 20. Informant: BERRY PERKINS-WIFE, 2840 SEATTLE DRIVE, LOS ANGELES, CA. 90046

PLACE OF DEATH
- 19A. Place of Death: RESIDENCE
- 19C. County: LOS ANGELES
- 19D. Street Address: 2840 SEATTLE DRIVE
- 19E. City: LOS ANGELES

CAUSE OF DEATH
- 21. (A) Immediate Cause: GRAM NEGATIVE BACTEREMIA — 2 DAYS
- (B) Due to: BILATERAL PNEUMONITIS — 10 DAYS
- (C) Due to: A.I.D.S. — 14 MOS
- 25. Other Significant Conditions: SEVERE ANEMIA, WASTING SYNDROME
- 22. Was Death Reported to Coroner: No
- 23. Was Biopsy Performed: No
- 24A. Was Autopsy Performed: No
- 26. Operation Performed: NO

PHYSICIAN'S CERTIFICATION
- 27A. Decedent Attended Since: 02 10 83
- Last Seen Alive: 09 12 92
- 27C. License Number: G1-074832
- 27D. Date Signed: 9/14/92
- 27E. Physician: GARY COHAN M.D. 150 N. ROBERTSON BL. #300, BEVERLY HILLS, CA. 90211

FUNERAL DIRECTOR AND LOCAL REGISTRAR
- 34A. Disposition: CR/RES. / RES.
- 34B. Place of Final Disposition: CREMAINS-2840 SEATTLE DR. LA, CA.
- 34C. Date: SEPT 17, 1992
- 35A. Embalmer: NOT EMBALMED
- 36A. Funeral Director: PIERCE BROTHERS CUNNINGHAM O'CONNOR UTTER MCKINLEY
- 36B. License No.: F-168
- 37. Signature of Local Registrar: Robert C. Stats
- 38. Registration Date: SEP 16 1992

BEATRIZ VALDEZ
Registrar-Recorder/County Clerk

AUG 24 1995
19-004243

STATE OF CALIFORNIA
CERTIFICATION OF VITAL RECORD
COUNTY OF SAN DIEGO
CERTIFICATE OF DEATH

State File Number: 3 200037 015958

DECEDENT PERSONAL DATA
- 1. Name of Decedent—First (Given): ELIZABETH
- 2. Middle: JEAN
- 3. Last (Family): PETERS HOUGH
- 4. Date of Birth: 10/15/1926
- 5. Age Yrs: 73
- 6. Sex: F
- 7. Date of Death: 10/13/2000
- 8. Hour: 0245
- 9. State of Birth: OH
- 10. Social Security No: 276-24-5219
- 11. Military Service: No
- 12. Marital Status: WIDOWED
- 13. Education—Years Completed: 14
- 14. Race: CAUCASIAN
- 15. Hispanic: No
- 16. Usual Employer: TWENTIETH CENTURY FOX
- 17. Occupation: ACTRESS
- 18. Kind of Business: MOTION PICTURES
- 19. Years in Occupation: 20

USUAL RESIDENCE
- 20. Residence: 2390 BUENA VISTA CIRCLE
- 21. City: CARLSBAD
- 22. County: SAN DIEGO
- 23. Zip Code: 92008
- 24. Yrs in County: 4
- 25. State or Foreign Country: CA

INFORMANT
- 26. Name, Relationship: SHIRLEY COOK, SISTER
- 27. Mailing Address: 2409 BUENA VISTA CIRCLE CARLSBAD CA 92008

SPOUSE AND PARENT INFORMATION
- 31. Name of Father—First: GERALD
- 32. Middle: MORRIS
- 33. Last: PETERS
- 34. Birth State: OH
- 35. Name of Mother—First: MARY
- 36. Middle: ELIZABETH
- 37. Last (Maiden): THOMAS
- 38. Birth State: PA

DISPOSITION(S)
- 39. Date: 10/17/2000
- 40. Place of Final Disposition: HOLY CROSS CEMETERY 5835 W SLAUSON AVENUE CULVER CITY CA 90230
- 41. Type of Disposition: BU
- 42. Signature of Embalmer: NOT EMBALMED
- 44. Name of Funeral Director: ETERNAL HILLS MORTUARY
- 45. License No: FD-234
- 47. Date: 10/16/2000

PLACE OF DEATH
- 101. Place of Death: SCRIPPS MEMORIAL HOSPITAL
- 102. If Hospital: IP
- 104. County: SAN DIEGO
- 105. Street Address: 9888 GENESEE AVENUE
- 106. City: LA JOLLA

CAUSE OF DEATH
- 107. Death was caused by:
  - (A) Immediate Cause: UNSPECIFIED PNEUMONIA — 3 DAYS
  - (B) Due to: ACUTE MYELOGENOUS LEUKEMIA — 1 YR.
- 108. Death Reported to Coroner: No
- 109. Biopsy Performed: Yes
- 110. Autopsy Performed: No
- 111. Used in Determining Cause: No
- 112. Other Significant Conditions: NONE
- 113. Was Operation Performed: BONE MARROW BIOPSY 09/07/2000, BRONCHOSCOPY 10/05/2000

PHYSICIAN'S CERTIFICATION
- 114. Decedent Attended Since: 09/04/1999; Last Seen Alive: 10/05/2000
- 115. Signature: William E. Miller MD
- 116. License No: G-36197
- 117. Date: 10/14/2000
- 118. Attending Physician: WILLIAM E. MILLER, M.D., 10666 N. TORREY PINES RD., LA JOLLA, CA 92037

Fax Auth #: 2016779

County of San Diego - Department of Health Services – 3851 Rosecrans Street. This is to certify that, if bearing the OFFICIAL SEAL OF THE STATE OF CALIFORNIA, the OFFICIAL SEAL OF SAN DIEGO COUNTY AND THEIR DEPARTMENT OF HEALTH SERVICES EMBOSSED SEAL, this is a true copy of the ORIGINAL DOCUMENT FILED. Required fee paid.

DATE ISSUED: November 10, 2000

GEORGE R. FLORES, M.D.
REGISTRAR OF VITAL RECORDS
County of San Diego

This copy not valid unless prepared on engraved border displaying seal and signature of Registrar

ANY ALTERATION OR ERASURE VOIDS THIS CERTIFICATE

COUNTY OF LOS ANGELES
DEPARTMENT OF HEALTH SERVICES
CERTIFICATE OF DEATH
STATE OF CALIFORNIA

1. Name of Decedent—First (Given)	CHARLES
2. Middle	EDWIN
3. Last (Family)	PIERCE
4. Date of Birth	07/14/1926
5. Age Yrs.	72
6. Sex	M
7. Date of Death	05/31/1999
8. Hour	2045
9. State of Birth	NEW YORK
10. Social Security No.	105-18-8679
11. Military Service	No
12. Marital Status	NEVER MARRIED
13. Education—Years Completed	14
14. Race	WHITE
15. Hispanic	No
16. Usual Employer	SELF EMPLOYED
17. Occupation	ACTOR
18. Kind of Business	ENTERTAINMENT
19. Years in Occupation	32
20. Residence	4445 CARTWRIGHT AVE #309
21. City	NORTH HOLLYWOOD
22. County	LOS ANGELES
23. Zip Code	91602
24. Yrs in County	30
25. State	CA
26. Informant Name, Relationship	DONALD L KOBUS - FRIEND
27. Mailing Address	4445 CARTWRIGHT AVE #309 NORTH HOLLYWOOD CA 91602
31. Name of Father—First	GERALD
32. Middle	SLOAT
33. Last	PIERCE
34. Birth State	NEW YORK
35. Name of Mother—First	JESSIE
37. Last (Maiden)	HICKMAN
38. Birth State	NEW YORK
39. Date	06/07/1999
40. Place of Final Disposition	FOREST LAWN MEMORIAL PARK - 6300 FOREST LAWN DR LOS ANGELES CA 90068
41. Type of Disposition	CR/BU
42. Signature of Embalmer	NOT EMBALMED
44. Name of Funeral Director	FOREST LAWN HOLLYWOOD HILLS
45. License No.	FD 904
47. Date	06/03/1999
101. Place of Death	RESIDENCE
104. County	LOS ANGELES
105. Street Address	4445 CARTWRIGHT AVE #309
106. City	NORTH HOLLYWOOD
107. Death was Caused by: (A) Immediate Cause	Metastatic Prostate Cancer
Time Interval	2 years
108. Death Reported to Coroner	Yes
Referral Number	99-55386
109. Biopsy Performed	Yes
110. Autopsy Performed	No
111. Used in Determining Cause	No
112. Other Significant Conditions	NONE
113. Was Operation Performed	NONE
115. Signature and Title of Certifier	Keith G Kauhanen, M.D.
116. License No.	G35385
117. Date	06/02/1999
114. Physician attended since	09/05/97; last seen alive 04/02/1999
118. Attending Physician	KEITH G KAUHANEN, MD 4323 RIVERSIDE DR, BURBANK, CA 91505
Fax Auth. #	273/7164
Census Tract	090240483

Date Issued: JUN 14 1999

Certificate of Death

State of California

Decedent Personal Data

- **1. Name of Decedent—First (Given):** DON
- **2. Middle:** CECIL
- **3. Last (Family):** PORTER
- **4. Date of Birth:** 09/24/1912
- **5. Age Yrs:** 84
- **6. Sex:** M
- **7. Date of Death:** 02/11/1997
- **8. Hour:** 1830
- **9. State of Birth:** OK
- **10. Social Security No.:** 541-03-9221
- **11. Military Service:** Yes
- **12. Marital Status:** MARRIED
- **13. Education—Years Completed:** 12
- **14. Race:** CAUCASIAN
- **15. Hispanic:** No
- **16. Usual Employer:** FREELANCE
- **17. Occupation:** ACTOR
- **18. Kind of Business:** ENTERTAINMENT
- **19. Years in Occupation:** 50

Usual Residence

- **20. Residence—Street and Number or Location:** 2525 BRIAR CREST ROAD
- **21. City:** BEVERLY HILLS
- **22. County:** LOS ANGELES
- **23. Zip Code:** 90210
- **24. Yrs in County:** 59
- **25. State or Foreign Country:** CA

Informant

- **26. Name, Relationship:** DON C. PORTER JR. - SON
- **27. Mailing Address:** 36 KENSINGTON COURT, KENSINGTON, CA 94707

Spouse and Parent Information

- **28. Name of Surviving Spouse—First:** PEGGY
- **30. Last (Maiden Name):** RANDALL
- **31. Name of Father—First:** JESSE
- **32. Middle:** BRADLEY
- **33. Last:** PORTER
- **34. Birth State:** OK
- **35. Name of Mother—First:** HAZEL
- **36. Middle:** MARGARET
- **37. Last (Maiden):** WILLS
- **38. Birth State:** OK

Disposition(s) / Funeral Director and Local Registrar

- **39. Date:** 02/19/1997
- **40. Place of Final Disposition:** DON C. PORTER JR. FOR RES: 36 KENSINGTON COURT, KENSINGTON, CA 94707
- **41. Type of Disposition(s):** CR/RES
- **42. Signature of Embalmer:** NOT EMBALMED
- **44. Name of Funeral Director:** PIERCE BROS. WESTWOOD VILLAGE
- **45. License No.:** F-951
- **47. Date:** 02/13/1997

Place of Death

- **101. Place of Death:** RESIDENCE
- **104. County:** LOS ANGELES
- **105. Street Address:** 2525 BRIAR CREST ROAD
- **106. City:** BEVERLY HILLS

Cause of Death

- **107. Death was Caused By:**
  - (A) IMMEDIATE CAUSE: PNEUMONIA — 12 HRS
  - (B) DUE TO: CANCER OF GALLBLADDER, METASTATIC TO LIVER — 1 YEAR
- **108. Death Reported to Coroner:** No
- **109. Biopsy Performed:** Yes
- **110. Autopsy Performed:** No
- **112. Other Significant Conditions:** PROBABLE CVA
- **113. Was Operation Performed:** LAPAROSCOPIC CHOLECYSTECTOMY 02/09/1996

Physician's Certification

- **Decedent Attended Since:** 03/17/1986
- **Decedent Last Seen Alive:** 02/11/1997
- **116. License No.:** A 15315
- **117. Date:** 02/13/1997
- **118. Type Attending Physician's Name, Mailing Address, Zip:** PAUL FREEMAN, MD 9730 WILSHIRE BLVD. #101, BEVERLY HILLS, CA 90212

STATE OF CALIFORNIA
CERTIFICATION OF VITAL RECORD
COUNTY OF LOS ANGELES • REGISTRAR-RECORDER/COUNTY CLERK

CERTIFICATE OF DEATH — STATE OF CALIFORNIA

State File Number: 3381503658 9

Decedent Personal Data
- Name of Decedent: ANNE MOBLEY RAMSEY
- Date of Death: AUGUST 11, 1988 — Hour: 1805
- Sex: FEMALE
- Race/Ethnicity: WHITE/AMERICAN
- Date of Birth: MARCH 27, 1929
- Age: 59 YEARS
- Birthplace of Decedent: NEBRASKA
- Name and Birthplace of Father: NATHAN MOBLEY — NORTH CAROLINA
- Birth Name and Birthplace of Mother: ELEANOR SMITH — NEBRASKA
- Citizen of What Country: U.S.A.
- Social Security Number: 043-26-9472
- Marital Status: MARRIED
- Name of Surviving Spouse: LOGAN CARLISLE RAMSEY JR.
- Primary Occupation: ACTRESS
- Number of Years in This Occupation: THIRTY-SEVEN
- Employer: SELF-EMPLOYED
- Kind of Industry or Business: MOTION PICTURE

Usual Residence
- 12923 KILLION STREET
- City or Town: VAN NUYS
- County: LOS ANGELES
- State: CALIFORNIA
- Informant: LOGAN G. RAMSEY JR. — HUSBAND, 12923 KILLION STREET, VAN NUYS, CALIFORNIA 91401

Place of Death
- CEDARS-SINAI MEDICAL CENTER
- County: LOS ANGELES
- Street Address: 3800 BEVERLY BOULEVARD
- City: LOS ANGELES

Cause of Death
- Immediate Cause: (a) Metastatic Tonsilar Carcinoma — 4 months
- Was Death Reported to Coroner? NO
- Was Biopsy Performed? NO
- Was Autopsy Performed? YES

Physician's Certification
- Attended Decedent Since: 5/16/88
- Last Saw Decedent Alive: 8/11/88
- Physician: BARRY ROSENBLOOM M.D., 8635 WEST 3rd ST., LOS ANGELES, CA.
- Date Signed: 8/12/88
- License Number: G-22745

Disposition
- BURIAL — AUGUST 25, 1988
- FOREST LAWN CEMETERY, OMAHA, NEBRASKA
- Embalmer: #6103
- Funeral Director: PRAISWATER FUNERAL HOME — License No. F 78
- Date Accepted by Registrar: AUG 16 1988

This is to certify that this document is a true copy of the official record filed with the Registrar-Recorder/County Clerk.

CONNY B. McCORMACK
Registrar-Recorder/County Clerk

APR 10 2000
19-557847

DAVID RAPPAPORT

CERTIFICATION OF VITAL RECORD

COUNTY OF LOS ANGELES • REGISTRAR-RECORDER/COUNTY CLERK

CERTIFICATE OF DEATH — STATE OF CALIFORNIA

1A. Name of Decedent — First	David
1B. Middle	--
1C. Last (Family)	Rappaport
2A. Date of Death	MAY 2, 1990
2B. Hour	1900
3. Sex	Male
4. Race	Cau
5. Spanish/Hispanic	No
6. Date of Birth	November 23, 1951
7. Age in Years	38
8. State of Birth	England
9. Citizen of What Country	England
10A. Full Name of Father	Mark Rappaport
10B. State of Birth	England
11A. Full Maiden Name of Mother	Diana Schneiderman
11B. State of Birth	England
12. Military Service?	None
13. Social Security No.	123-52-5804
14. Marital Status	Married
15. Name of Surviving Spouse	Jane Unk
16A. Usual Occupation	Actor
16B. Usual Kind of Business or Industry	Show Business
16C. Usual Employer	Various
16D. Years in Occupation	15
17. Education — Years Completed	17+
18A. Residence	6219 Primrose Ave.
18B. City	Los Angeles
18C. Zip Code	90068
18D. County	Los Angeles
18E. Number of Years in This County	5
18F. State or Foreign Country	Calif.
19A. Place of Death	Laurel Canyon Park
19C. County	Los Angeles
18D. Street Address	Mulholland and Laurel Canyon
19E. City	Hollywood
20. Name, Relationship, Mailing Address of Informant	Jane Rappaport (Wife), 21C Cotham Rd. Bristol England BS 6 GDJ
22. Was Death Reported to Coroner?	Yes — Referral Number 90-04388
21. Immediate Cause (A)	Gunshot Wound to Chest
Time Interval	Unk.
23. Was Biopsy Performed?	No
24A. Was Autopsy Performed?	No
24B. Was It Used in Determining Cause of Death?	No
25. Other Significant Conditions	NONE
26. Was Operation Performed	No
28A. Signature and Title of Coroner	Deputy Coroner
28B. Date Signed	5-4-1990
29. Manner of Death	Suicide
30A. Place of Injury	Public Park
30B. Injury at Work	No
30C. Date of Injury	Unknown
31. Hour	Unknown
32. Location	Mulholland and Laurel Canyon, Hollywood
33. Describe How Injury Occurred	With Revolver
34A. Disposition(s)	TR/BU
34B. Place of Final Disposition	Waltham Abbey Cemetery, Essex England
34C. Date	5/7/90
35B. License Number	6873
36A. Name of Funeral Director	Chevra Kadisha Mortuary
36B. License No.	F-1326
38. Registration Date	MAY 4 1990

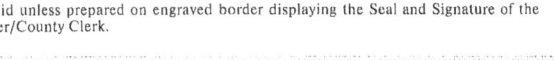

BEATRIZ VALDEZ
Registrar-Recorder/County Clerk

AUG 16 1995
19-397063

This copy not valid unless prepared on engraved border displaying the Seal and Signature of the Registrar-Recorder/County Clerk.

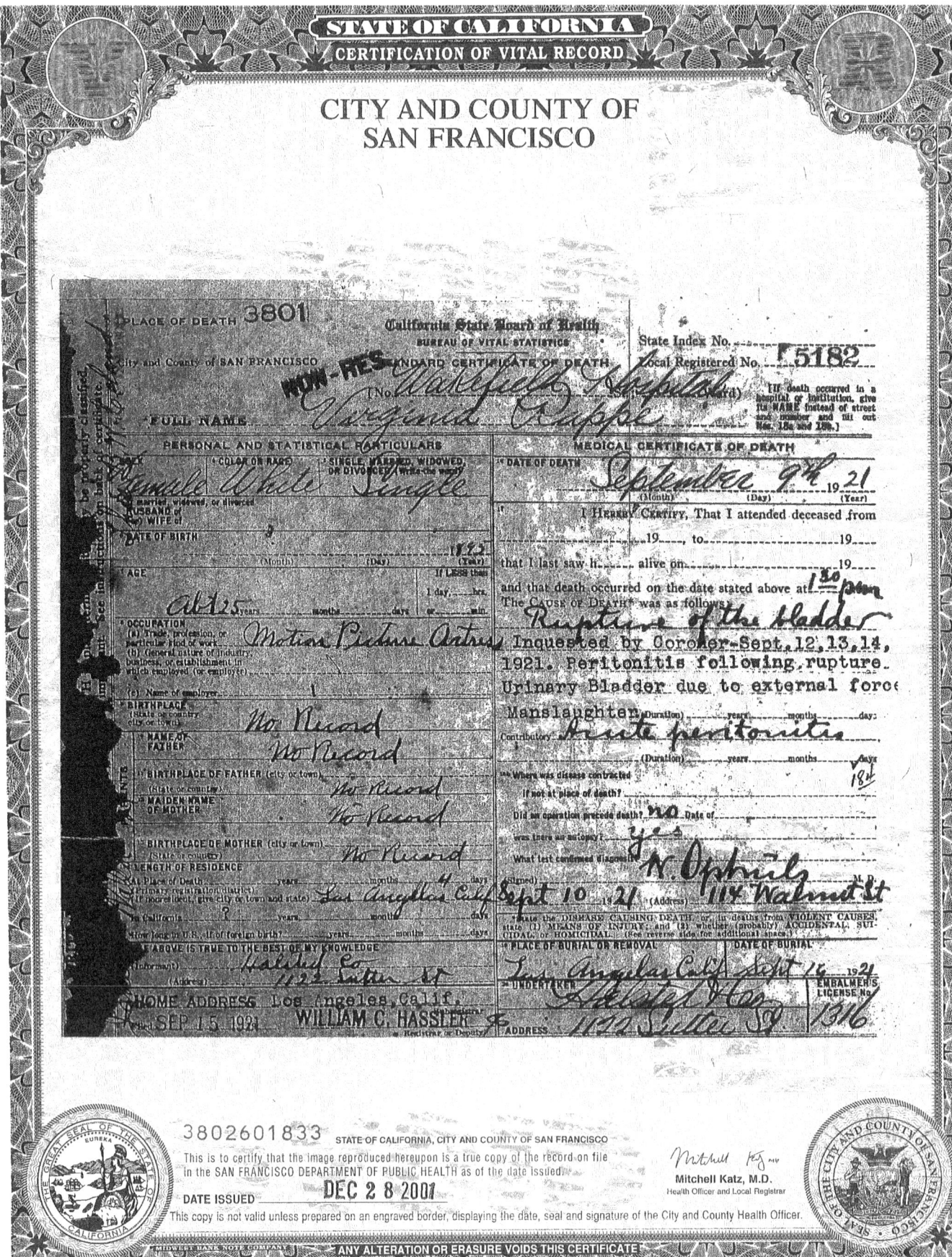

CHARLES NELSON REILLY

STATE OF CALIFORNIA
CERTIFICATION OF VITAL RECORD
COUNTY OF LOS ANGELES • REGISTRAR-RECORDER/COUNTY CLERK

CERTIFICATE OF DEATH

State File Number: 3200719023118

DECEDENT'S PERSONAL DATA
- Name: CHARLES NELSON REILLY
- Date of Birth: 01/13/1931
- Age: 76
- Sex: MALE
- Birth State: NEW YORK
- Social Security Number: 042-24-7586
- Ever in U.S. Armed Forces: NO
- Marital Status: NVR MARRIED
- Date of Death: 05/25/2007
- Hour: 1411
- Education: 12
- Hispanic/Latino: NO
- Race: CAUCASIAN
- Usual Occupation: ACTOR
- Kind of Business/Industry: ENTERTAINMENT
- Years in Occupation: 59

USUAL RESIDENCE
- Address: 2341 GLOAMING WAY
- City: BEVERLY HILLS
- County: LOS ANGELES
- Zip: 90210
- Years in County: 40
- State: CA

INFORMANT
- Name/Relationship: PATRICK W. HUGHES, DPOA
- Mailing Address: 2341 GLOAMING WAY, BEVERLY HILLS, CA 90210

SPOUSE AND PARENT INFORMATION
- Father: CHARLES REILLY — Birth State: UNK
- Mother: SIGNE NELSON — Birth State: UNK

FUNERAL DIRECTOR / LOCAL REGISTRAR
- Disposition Date: 05/29/2007
- Place of Final Disposition: RES OF PATRICK HUGHES, 2341 GLOAMING WAY, BEVERLY HILLS, CA 90210
- Type of Disposition: CR/RES
- Signature of Embalmer: NOT EMBALMED
- Funeral Establishment: HOLLYWOOD FUNERAL HOME
- License Number: FD 1651
- Date: 05/29/2007

PLACE OF DEATH
- Place of Death: UCLA MEDICAL CENTER (IP)
- County: Los Angeles
- Facility Address: 10833 LeConte Avenue
- City: Los Angeles

CAUSE OF DEATH
- Immediate Cause (A): SEPTIC SHOCK — days
- (B): PANCOLITIS — days
- Other Significant Conditions: Chronic Obstructive Pulmonary Disease
- Operation Performed: No
- Biopsy Performed: No
- Autopsy Performed: No
- Death Reported to Coroner: No

PHYSICIAN'S CERTIFICATION
- Decedent Attended Since: 05/22/2007
- Last Seen Alive: 05/25/2007
- Attending Physician: Seth Rivera, M.D., 10833 LeConte Ave, L.A., CA 90095
- License Number: A72432
- Date: 05/25/2007

FAX AUTH. #: 344-8057

INFORMATIONAL, NOT A VALID DOCUMENT TO ESTABLISH IDENTITY

019042562

JAN 2 2 2008

SANTA BARBARA COUNTY
SANTA BARBARA, CALIFORNIA

STATE OF CALIFORNIA — CERTIFICATION OF VITAL RECORD

CERTIFICATE OF DEATH
STATE OF CALIFORNIA

State File Number: 4200
Local Registration District and Certificate Number: 80-1557

Decedent Personal Data
- 1A. Name of Decedent—First: DUNCAN
- 1B. Middle: ---
- 1C. Last: RENALDO
- 2A. Date of Death: September 3, 1980
- 2B. Hour: 0300
- 3. Sex: Male
- 4. Race: White
- 5. Ethnicity: ---
- 6. Date of Birth: April 23, 1904
- 7. Age: 76 years
- 8. Birthplace of Decedent: SPAIN
- 9. Name and Birthplace of Father: Unknown – Unknown
- 10. Birth Name and Birthplace of Mother: Unknown – Unknown
- 11. Citizen of What Country: U.S.A.
- 12. Social Security Number: 568-01-2315
- 13. Marital Status: Married
- 14. Name of Surviving Spouse: Audrey-Leonard
- 15. Primary Occupation: Actor
- 16. Number of Years This Occupation: 30
- 17. Employer: Self
- 18. Kind of Industry or Business: Motion Pictures

Usual Residence
- 19A. Usual Residence—Street Address: 974 Debra Drive
- 19C. City or Town: Santa Barbara
- 19D. County: Santa Barbara
- 19E. State: California
- 20. Name and Address of Informant—Relationship: Audrey Renaldo – Wife, 974 Debra Drive, Santa Barbara, Calif. 93110

Place of Death
- 21A. Place of Death: Goleta Valley Community Hospital
- 21B. County: Santa Barbara
- 21C. Street Address: 351 S. Patterson Ave.
- 21D. City or Town: Santa Barbara

Cause of Death
- 22. Death was caused by:
  - (A) Immediate Cause: Cardiomyopathy — 1 wk
  - (B) Due to: Arteriosclerotic Heart Disease — 10 yr
- 23. Other Conditions: Pneumothorax
- 24. Was Death Reported to Coroner?: No
- 25. Was Biopsy Performed?: No
- 26. Was Autopsy Performed?: No
- 27. Was Operation Performed: No

Physician's Certification
- I Attended Decedent Since: 1968
- I Last Saw Decedent Alive: 9-2-80
- 28C. Date Signed: 9-4-80
- 28D. Physician's License Number: A17564
- 28E. Physician's Name and Address: Robert Parker, M.D., 5333 Hollister Avenue, Santa Barbara, Ca.

Disposition
- 36. Disposition: Burial
- 37. Date: 9-6-80
- 38. Name and Address of Cemetery or Crematory: Calvary Cemetery, Santa Barbara, Ca.
- 39. Embalmer's License Number and Signature: 5993 John A Hauschild
- 40. Name of Funeral Director: Welch-Ryce-Haider Funeral Chapels
- 42. Date Accepted by Local Registrar: Sept. 11, 1980

S324823

CERTIFIED COPY OF VITAL RECORDS

STATE OF CALIFORNIA
COUNTY OF SANTA BARBARA } SS

DATE ISSUED APR 18 2002

KENNETH A. PETTIT
COUNTY CLERK-RECORDER-ASSESSOR
SANTA BARBARA, CALIFORNIA

This copy not valid unless prepared on engraved border displaying seal and signature of County Clerk-Recorder-Assessor.

STATE OF CALIFORNIA — CERTIFICATION OF VITAL RECORD

COUNTY OF LOS ANGELES • REGISTRAR-RECORDER/COUNTY CLERK

CERTIFICATE OF DEATH

STATE FILE NUMBER: (blank) | LOCAL REGISTRATION NUMBER: 3200819002007

1. Name of Decedent — First (Given)	BRAD
2. Middle	BARRON
3. Last (Family)	RENFRO
4. Date of Birth	07/25/1982
5. Age Yrs	25
6. Sex	M
9. Birth State/Foreign Country	TN
10. Social Security Number	411-57-7930
11. Ever in U.S. Armed Forces	NO
12. Marital Status	NEVER MARRIED
7. Date of Death	01/15/2008
8. Hour (24 Hours)	1104
13. Education	HS GRADUATE
14/15. Hispanic/Latino/Spanish	NO
16. Decedent's Race	WHITE
17. Usual Occupation	ACTOR
18. Kind of Business or Industry	ENTERTAINMENT
19. Years in Occupation	14
20. Decedent's Residence	1092 SOUTH OGDEN DR.
21. City	LOS ANGELES
22. County/Province	LOS ANGELES
23. Zip Code	90033
24. Years in County	7
25. State/Foreign Country	CA
26. Informant's Name, Relationship	MARK RENFRO, FATHER
27. Informant's Mailing Address	2715 CAROLINE COURT, LOUISVILLE, TN 37777
31. Name of Father — First	MARK
32. Middle	BARRON
33. Last	RENFRO
34. Birth State	TN
35. Name of Mother — First	ANGELA
36. Middle	DENISE
37. Last (Maiden)	MCCROY
38. Birth State	TN
39. Disposition Date	01/18/2008
40. Place of Final Disposition	RED HOUSE CEMETERY, 3269 RUTLEDGE PIKE, BLAINE, TN 37709
41. Type of Disposition(s)	TR/BU
42. Signature of Embalmer	GREGORY MACIAS
43. License Number	EMB8010
44. Name of Funeral Establishment	THOMAS MILLER MORTUARY
45. License Number	FD 66
46. Signature of Local Registrar	JONATHAN FIELDING, MD
47. Date	01/18/2008
101. Place of Death	RESIDENCE
103. Other than hospital, specify one	Decedent's Home
104. County	LOS ANGELES
105. Facility Address or Location Where Found	1092 SOUTH OGDEN DRIVE
106. City	LOS ANGELES
107. Cause of Death — Immediate Cause (A)	DEFERRED
108. Death Reported to Coroner	YES — Referral Number 2008-00414
109. Biopsy Performed	NO
110. Autopsy Performed	YES
111. Used in Determining Cause	YES
119. Manner of Death	Pending Investigation
126. Signature of Coroner / Deputy Coroner	REGINA M AUGUSTINE
127. Date	01/18/2008
128. Type Name, Title of Coroner / Deputy Coroner	REGINA M AUGUSTINE, DEPUTY CORONER

012008000707921

This is to certify that this document is a true copy of the official record filed with the Registrar-Recorder/County Clerk.

SEP 16 2009

DEAN C. LOGAN
Registrar-Recorder/County Clerk

000004574

INFORMATIONAL, NOT A VALID DOCUMENT TO ESTABLISH IDENTITY

ANY ALTERATION OR ERASURE VOIDS THIS CERTIFICATE

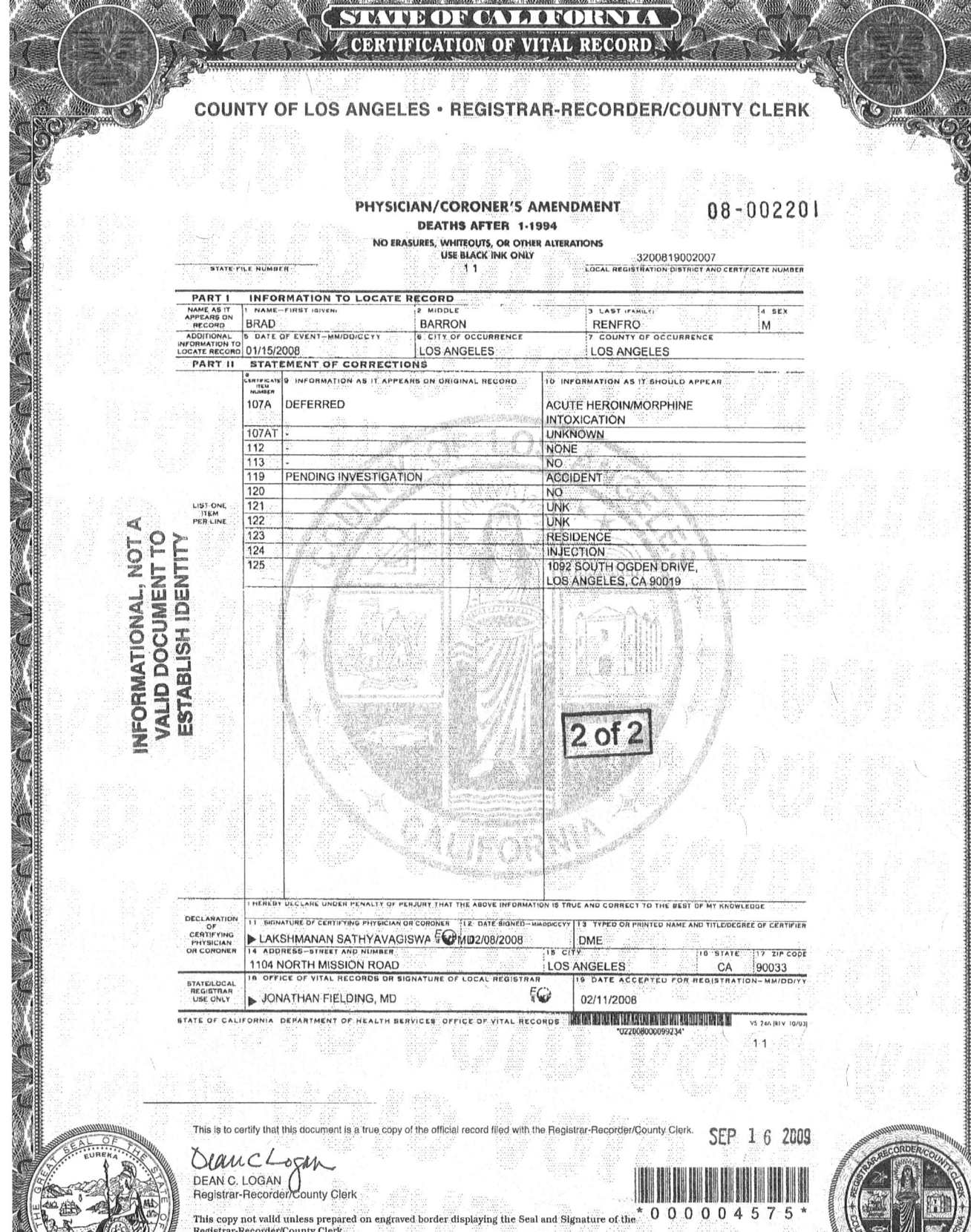

CERTIFICATE OF DEATH
STATE OF CALIFORNIA—DEPARTMENT OF HEALTH
OFFICE OF THE STATE REGISTRAR OF VITAL STATISTICS

Local Registration District and Certificate Number: 0190-050458

DECEDENT PERSONAL DATA

- **1a. Name of Deceased — First Name:** Stafford
- **1b. Middle Name:** Alois
- **1c. Last Name:** Repp
- **2a. Date of Death:** November 6, 1974
- **2b. Hour:** 10:50 P
- **3. Sex:** Male
- **4. Color or Race:** Caucasian
- **5. Birthplace:** California
- **6. Date of Birth:** Apr. 26, 1918
- **7. Age:** 56 years
- **8. Name and Birthplace of Father:** Herbert Repp – Ohio
- **9. Maiden Name and Birthplace of Mother:** Carol Marks – California
- **10. Citizen of What Country:** U.S.A.
- **11. Social Security Number:** 566-07-8138
- **12. Married/Never Married/Widowed/Divorced:** Married
- **13. Name of Surviving Spouse:** Theresa Valenti
- **14. Last Occupation:** Actor
- **15. Number of Years in This Occupation:** 25
- **16. Name of Last Employing Company or Firm:** Self
- **17. Kind of Industry or Business:** Entertainment

PLACE OF DEATH

- **18a. Place of Death:** Centinella Valley Hospital
- **18b. Street Address:** 555 E. Hardy Avenue
- **18c. Inside City Corporate Limits:** Yes
- **18d. City or Town:** Inglewood
- **18e. County:** Los Angeles
- **18f. Length of Stay in County of Death:** EnRoute
- **18g. Length of Stay in California:** Life

USUAL RESIDENCE

- **19a. Usual Residence — Street Address:** 5132 Berkeley Avenue
- **19b. Inside City Corporate Limits:** Yes
- **20. Name and Mailing Address of Informant:** Mrs. Theresa Repp, 5132 Berkeley Avenue, Westminster, California
- **19c. City or Town:** Westminster
- **19d. County:** Orange
- **19e. State:** California

PHYSICIAN'S OR CORONER'S CERTIFICATION

- **21d. Date Signed:** NOV 7 1974
- **21e. License Number:** GC27530
- Address: 1800 Mission Rd., Los Angeles, Calif. 90033

FUNERAL DIRECTOR AND LOCAL REGISTRAR

- **22a. Specify Burial/Entombment or Cremation:** Burial
- **22b. Date:** 11/9/74 / 9Nov74
- **23. Name of Cemetery or Crematory:** Westminster Mem. Park, Westminster, Ca.
- **24. Embalmer Signature:** Raymond L. McKee 4512
- **25. Name of Funeral Director:** Westminster Mortuary
- **28. Date Received for Registration:** NOV 7 1974

CAUSE OF DEATH

- 29. Part I. Death was caused by:
  - (A) Immediate Cause: Acute Cardiac Insufficiency
  - (B) Due to: Arteriosclerotic Cardiovascular Disease

This is to certify that this document is a true copy of the official record filed with the Registrar-Recorder/County Clerk.

CONNY B. McCORMACK
Registrar-Recorder/County Clerk

OCT 04 2001
19-673408

CERTIFICATE OF DEATH
STATE OF CALIFORNIA

DECEDENT PERSONAL DATA
- 1. Name of Decedent—First (Given): MARJORIE
- 2. Middle: -
- 3. Last (Family): REYNOLDS HAFFEN
- 4. Date of Birth: 08/12/1917
- 5. Age Yrs.: 79
- 6. Sex: F
- 7. Date of Death: 02/01/1997
- 8. Hour: 0330
- 9. State of Birth: IDAHO
- 10. Social Security No.: 569-18-8844
- 11. Military Service: No
- 12. Marital Status: Widowed
- 13. Education—Years Completed: 12
- 14. Race: White
- 15. Hispanic: No
- 16. Usual Employer: Self Employed
- 17. Occupation: Actress
- 18. Kind of Business: Entertainment
- 19. Years in Occupation: 12

USUAL RESIDENCE
- 20. Residence—Street and Number or Location: #3 Catalina Court
- 21. City: Manhattan Beach
- 22. County: Los Angeles
- 23. Zip Code: 90266
- 24. Yrs in County: 77
- 25. State or Foreign Country: CA

INFORMANT
- 26. Name, Relationship: Lin Hinshaw - Daughter
- 27. Mailing Address: 8114 Manitoba St., #102 Playa del Rey, CA 90293

SPOUSE AND PARENT INFORMATION
- 28-30. Name of Surviving Spouse: -
- 31. Name of Father—First: Harry
- 32. Middle: W.
- 33. Last: Goodspeed
- 34. Birth State: MAINE
- 35. Name of Mother—First: Grace
- 36. Middle: -
- 37. Last (Maiden): Jennings
- 38. Birth State: "UNK-USA"

DISPOSITION(S)
- 39. Date: 02/06/1997
- 40. Place of Final Disposition: Res. Lin Hinshaw 8114 Manitoba St. #102 Playa del Rey, CA 90293

FUNERAL DIRECTOR AND LOCAL REGISTRAR
- 41. Type of Disposition(s): CR/RES
- 42. Signature of Embalmer: Not Embalmed
- 43. License No.: -
- 44. Name of Funeral Director: White & Day Funeral Chapel
- 45. License No.: FD769
- 47. Date: 02/06/1997

PLACE OF DEATH
- 101. Place of Death: South Bay Medical Center (IP)
- 104. County: Los Angeles
- 105. Street Address: 514 No. Prospect
- 106. City: Redondo Beach

CAUSE OF DEATH
- 107. Death was caused by:
  - (A) Immediate Cause: Arrhythmia — mins
  - (B) Due to: Congestive Heart Failure — hours
  - (C) Due to: Aortic Stenosis — years
  - (D) Due to: Coronary Artery Disease — years
- 108. Death reported to coroner: No
- 109. Biopsy Performed: No
- 110. Autopsy Performed: No
- 111. Used in Determining Cause: No
- 112. Other Significant Conditions: No
- 113. Was Operation Performed: No

PHYSICIAN'S CERTIFICATION
- 114. Decedent Attended Since: 01/31/1997; Decedent Last Seen Alive: 01/31/1997
- 115. Signature and Title of Certifier: K. Black, MD
- 116. License No.: G066433
- 117. Date: 02/04/1997
- 118. Type Attending Physician's Name, Mailing Address, Zip: K. Black, M.D. 3445 Pacific Coast Highway Torrance, CA 90503

CORONER'S USE ONLY
- 119. Manner of Death: Natural

- Fax Auth. #: 374-9249

STATE OF CALIFORNIA — CERTIFICATION OF VITAL RECORD

COUNTY OF LOS ANGELES • REGISTRAR-RECORDER/COUNTY CLERK

CERTIFICATE OF DEATH — STATE OF CALIFORNIA

0190-031370

DECEDENT PERSONAL DATA
- 1A. Name of Decedent—First: Minnie
- 1B. Middle: Riperton
- 1C. Last: Rudolph
- 2A. Date of Death: July 12 1979
- 2B. Hour: 1045
- 3. Sex: female
- 4. Race: Black
- 5. Ethnicity: not stated
- 6. Date of Birth: Nov 8 1947
- 7. Age: 31 years
- 8. Birthplace of Decedent: Ill
- 9. Name and Birthplace of Father: Daniel W Riperton – Ky
- 10. Birth Name and Birthplace of Mother: Thelma Mathews – Miss.
- 11. Citizen of What Country: U.S.A.
- 12. Social Security Number: 354 42 2621
- 13. Marital Status: married
- 14. Name of Surviving Spouse: Richard J. Rudolph
- 15. Primary Occupation: Entertainer
- 16. Number of Years in This Occupation: 15
- 17. Employer: self
- 18. Kind of Industry or Business: Entertainment

USUAL RESIDENCE
- 19A. Street Address: 1008 Hilts Avenue
- 19C. City or Town: Los Angeles
- 19D. County: Los Angeles
- 19E. State: Calif
- 20. Name and Address of Informant—Relationship: Richard J Rudolph (Husband) same address

PLACE OF DEATH
- 21A. Place of Death: Cedars Sinai Hospital
- 21B. County: Los Angeles
- 21C. Street Address: 8700 Beverly Blvd.
- 21D. City or Town: Los Angeles

CAUSE OF DEATH
- 22. Death was caused by:
  - (A) Immediate Cause: Metastatic Adenocarcinoma
  - (B) Due to: Breast
- Approximate Interval Between Onset and Death: mos
- 24. Was Death Reported to Coroner: NO
- 25. Was Biopsy Performed: YES
- 26. Was Autopsy Performed: NO
- 27. Was Operation Performed / Type of Operation: Mastectomy — Date: 1977

PHYSICIAN'S CERTIFICATION
- 28A. Attended Decedent Since: 1977; Last Saw Decedent Alive: 7/12/79
- 28B. Physician's Signature: Robert J Taub MD
- 28C. Date Signed: 7/12/79
- 28D. Physician's License Number: G7294
- 28E. Physician's Name and Address: Robert J Taub M.D. 8733 Beverly Blvd. Los Angeles Calif

DISPOSITION
- 36. Disposition: burial
- 37. Date: 7-15-79
- 38. Name and Address of Cemetery or Crematory: Westwood Memorial Park Los Angeles Calif
- 39. Embalmer's License Number and Signature: 5595 W R Price
- 40. Name of Funeral Director: Westwood Village Mortuary
- 41. Local Registrar — Signature
- 42. Date Accepted by Local Registrar: JUL 13 1979

INFORMATIONAL, NOT A VALID DOCUMENT TO ESTABLISH IDENTITY

Date issued: JAN 04 2010

Dean C. Logan, Registrar-Recorder/County Clerk

000187412

STATE OF CALIFORNIA
CERTIFICATION OF VITAL RECORD
COUNTY OF LOS ANGELES • REGISTRAR-RECORDER/COUNTY CLERK

STATE OF CALIFORNIA
DEPARTMENT OF PUBLIC HEALTH
VITAL STATISTICS
STANDARD CERTIFICATE OF DEATH

Place of Death. Dist. No. 1901
County of Los Angeles
City or Town of Los Angeles
No. 1915 N Vine St.

Local Registered No. 13289

FULL NAME: THEODORE ROBERTS

PERSONAL AND STATISTICAL PARTICULARS

- **Sex:** Male
- **Color or Race:** Cauc
- **Single, Married, Widowed, or Divorced:** Widowed
- **Husband of (or) Wife of:** —
- **Date of Birth:** Oct. 8, 1861
- **Age:** 67 years, 2 months, 6 days
- **Occupation:** Motion picture artist
- **Birthplace:** Calif.
- **Name of Father:** Capt. M. R. Roberts
- **Birthplace of Father:** England
- **Maiden Name of Mother:** Mary Nowlan
- **Birthplace of Mother:** Md.
- **Length of Residence:**
  - At Place of Death: 13 years
  - In California: life years
- **Informant:** Sidney Moore
- **Address:** 1915 N Vine St.
- **Filed:** 12/15/1928

MEDICAL CERTIFICATE OF DEATH

- **Date of Death:** December 14th, 1928
- I Hereby Certify, That I attended deceased from July-10, 1928 to Dec. 14, 1928, that I last saw him alive on Dec. 14, 1928, and that death occurred on the date stated above at 2 P.m.
- **Cause of Death:** Uremia
- (Duration) months 4 days
- **Contributory:** Acute acidosis
- (Duration) months 7 days
- **Did an operation precede death?** Yes Date of Nov. 22-28
- **Was there an autopsy?** No
- **What test confirmed diagnosis?** Lab. tests
- (Signed) Howard W. Seager, M.D.
- 12-15-1928 Address Los Angeles Co.

- **Place of Burial or Removal:** Hollywood Cemetery
- **Date of Burial:** Dec. 18, 1928
- **Undertaker:** Pierce Bros. & Co
- **Address:** Los Angeles, Calif.
- **Embalmer's License No.:** 1846

CONNY B. McCORMACK
Registrar-Recorder/County Clerk

NOV 28 2000
19-118088

CERTIFICATION OF VITAL RECORD

COUNTY OF LOS ANGELES • REGISTRAR-RECORDER/COUNTY CLERK

CERTIFICATE OF DEATH — 0190-008931
STATE OF CALIFORNIA—DEPARTMENT OF PUBLIC HEALTH

Decedent Personal Data

- **1A. Name of Deceased—First Name:** EDDIE
- **1B. Middle Name:** Rochester
- **1C. Last Name:** ANDERSON
- **2A. Date of Death:** 2/28/77
- **2B. Hour:** 11:05 A
- **3. Sex:** M
- **4. Color or Race:** Negro
- **5. Birthplace:** California
- **6. Date of Birth:** 9/18/05
- **7. Age:** 71 Years
- **8. Name and Birthplace of Father:** Edmund L. Anderson — Mich.
- **9. Maiden Name and Birthplace of Mother:** Maude Ella Mae Williams — Ka.
- **10. Citizen of What Country:** USA
- **11. Social Security Number:** 568-07-9361
- **12. Married, Never Married, Widowed, Divorced:** Married
- **13. Name of Surviving Spouse:** Eva Simon
- **14. Last Occupation:** ACTOR
- **15. Number of Years in This Occupation:** 45
- **16. Name of Last Employing Company or Firm:** A.F.T.R.A.
- **17. Kind of Industry or Business:** Union

Place of Death

- **18A. Place of Death:** MOTION PICTURE AND TELEVISION HOSPITAL
- **18B. Street Address:** 23450 CALABASAS ROAD
- **18C. Inside City Corporate Limits:** yes
- **18D. City or Town:** WOODLAND HILLS
- **18E. County:** Los Angeles
- **18F. Length of Stay in County of Death:** Life Years
- **18G. Length of Stay in California:** Life Years

Usual Residence

- **19A. Usual Residence—Street Address:** 1932 W. 37 STREET
- **19B. Inside City Corporate Limits:** yes
- **19C. City or Town:** LOS ANGELES
- **19D. County:** Los Angeles
- **19E. State:** CALIFORNIA
- **20. Name and Mailing Address of Informant:** Mrs. Eva Anderson, 1932 W. 37th Street, Los Angeles, California

Physician's / Coroner's Certification

- **21A. Coroner / Physician dates:** 12/17/76 — 2/28/77 — 2/28/77
- **21C. Physician/Coroner Signature:** M. B. Daitch, M.D.
- **21D. Address:** 23450 Calabasas Road, Woodland Hills, Calif.
- **21E. Date Signed:** 2-28-77
- **21F. Physician's License Number:** C 7197

Funeral Director and Local Registrar

- **22A. Specify Burial, Entombment or Cremation:** Burial
- **22B. Date:** 3/5/77
- **23. Name of Cemetery or Crematory:** Evergreen Cemetery
- **24. Embalmer License Number:** 5677
- **25. Name of Funeral Director:** Angelus Funeral Home
- **26. Was Death Reported to Coroner:** no
- **28. Date Accepted for Registration by Local Registrar:** MAR 3 – 1977

Cause of Death

- **29. Part I. Death Was Caused By:**
  - (A) CONGESTIVE HEART FAILURE
  - (B) ARTERIOSCLEROTIC HEART DISEASE
  - (C)
- **30. Part II. Other Significant Conditions:** METASTATIC CARCINOMA TO LIVER (PRIMARY IN COLON)
- **31. Operation:** —
- **32. Autopsy:** NO

State Registrar

04-3-1-0552

This is to certify that this document is a true copy of the official record filed with the Registrar-Recorder/County Clerk.

OCT 2 6 1995

19-048129

This copy not valid unless prepared on engraved border displaying the Seal of the Registrar-Recorder/County Clerk.

STATE OF CALIFORNIA
CERTIFICATION OF VITAL RECORD

COUNTY OF RIVERSIDE
RIVERSIDE, CALIFORNIA

CERTIFICATE OF DEATH — STATE OF CALIFORNIA

State File Number: 3 1999 33003756
Local Registration Number: (as shown)

DECEDENT PERSONAL DATA
- 1. Name (First): CHARLES
- 2. Middle: BUDDY
- 3. Last: ROGERS
- 4. Date of Birth: 08/13/1904
- 5. Age: 94
- 6. Sex: M
- 7. Date of Death: 04/21/1999
- 8. Hour: 0915
- 9. State of Birth: KANSAS
- 10. Social Security No.: 568-12-0777
- 11. Military Service: YES
- 12. Marital Status: MARRIED
- 13. Education — Years Completed: 17
- 14. Race: WHITE
- 15. Hispanic: No
- 16. Usual Employer: SELF EMPLOYED
- 17. Occupation: ACTOR
- 18. Kind of Business: ENTERTAINMENT
- 19. Years in Occupation: 60

USUAL RESIDENCE
- 20. Residence: 8 CROMWELL COURT
- 21. City: RANCHO MIRAGE
- 22. County: RIVERSIDE
- 23. Zip Code: 92270
- 24. Yrs in County: 45
- 25. State or Foreign Country: CA

INFORMANT
- 26. Name, Relationship: BEVERLY ROGERS – WIFE
- 27. Mailing Address: 8 CROMWELL COURT, RANCHO MIRAGE, CA 92270

SPOUSE AND PARENT INFORMATION
- 28. Name of Surviving Spouse — First: BEVERLY
- 29. Middle: L
- 30. Last (Maiden Name): RICONO
- 31. Name of Father — First: BURT
- 32. Middle: HENRY
- 33. Last: ROGERS
- 34. Birth State: KANSAS
- 35. Name of Mother — First: MAUDE
- 36. Middle: –
- 37. Last (Maiden): MOLL
- 38. Birth State: KANSAS

DISPOSITION(S)
- 39. Date: 04/24/1999
- 40. Place of Final Disposition: PALM SPRINGS MAUSOLEUM, 69901 E RAMON RD, CATHEDRAL CITY, CA 92234
- 41. Type of Disposition: BURIAL
- 42. Signature of Embalmer: Gloria Morris
- 43. License No.: 8367
- 44. Name of Funeral Director: PALM SPRINGS MORT., CATHEDRAL CITY
- 45. License No.: FD 1513
- 46. Signature of Local Registrar: Gary Feldman MD
- 47. Date: 04/28/1999

PLACE OF DEATH
- 101. Place of Death: RESIDENCE
- 104. County: RIVERSIDE
- 105. Street Address: 8 CROMWELL COURT
- 106. City: RANCHO MIRAGE

CAUSE OF DEATH
- 107. Death was caused by:
  - (A) Immediate Cause: CARDIOPULMONARY ARREST — MINUTES
  - (B) Due to: CEREBRAL VASCULAR ACCIDENT — WEEKS
  - (C) Due to: ATRIAL FIBRILLATION — YEARS
  - (D) Due to: ASHD — YEARS
- 108. Death Reported to Coroner: YES — Referral Number 992256
- 109. Biopsy Performed: No
- 110. Autopsy Performed: No
- 112. Other Significant Conditions: DEHYDRATION
- 113. Was Operation Performed: NO

PHYSICIAN'S CERTIFICATION
- 114. Decedent Attended Since: 10/17/1994; Last Seen Alive: 04/21/1999
- 116. License No.: G 40006
- 117. Date: 04/21/1999
- 118. Attending Physician: JOEL HIRSCHBERG MD, 39000 BOB HOPE DR #P102, RANCHO MIRAGE, CA 92270

State Registrar: 889972
Fax Auth. #: 740530

CERTIFIED COPY OF VITAL RECORDS

STATE OF CALIFORNIA
COUNTY OF RIVERSIDE } ss

This is a true and exact reproduction of the document officially registered and placed on file in the office of County of Riverside, Department of Health.

Date Issued: 04/28/1999

Gary Feldman M.D.
Local Registrar
RIVERSIDE COUNTY, CALIFORNIA

This copy not valid unless prepared on engraved border displaying seal and signature of Registrar.

ANY ALTERATION OR ERASURE VOIDS THIS CERTIFICATE

CERTIFICATE OF DEATH
STATE OF CALIFORNIA

State File Number: 3951905 1309

1. Name of Decedent—First (Given)	ROXIE
2. Middle	ALBERTHA ROKER
3. Last (Family)	KRAVITZ
4. Date of Birth	08/29/1929
5. Age Yrs.	66
6. Sex	F
7. Date of Death	12/02/1995
8. Hour	0100
9. State of Birth	FL
10. Social Security No.	116-18-8726
11. Military Service	None
12. Marital Status	DIVORCED
13. Education—Years Completed	17+
14. Race	BLACK
15. Hispanic	No
16. Usual Employer	S.A.G.
17. Occupation	ACTRESS
18. Kind of Business	ENTERTAINMENT
19. Years in Occupation	43
20. Residence—Street and Number or Location	4061 CLOVERDALE AVE
21. City	LOS ANGELES
22. County	LOS ANGELES
23. Zip Code	90008
24. Yrs in County	21
25. State or Foreign Country	CA
26. Name, Relationship	LENNY KRAVITZ — SON
27. Mailing Address	4061 CLOVERDALE AVE - LOS ANGELES, CA 90008
28-30. Name of Surviving Spouse	—
31-33. Name of Father	ALBERT S ROKER
34. Birth State	BAHAMAS
35-37. Name of Mother	BESSIE — MITCHELL
38. Birth State	GA
39. Date of Disposition	12/11/1995
40. Place of Final Disposition	SOUTHERN MEMORIAL PARK 15000 W DIXIE HWY-N. MIAMI BEACH, FL 33181
41. Type of Disposition(s)	TR/BU
43. License No.	8260
44. Name of Funeral Director	INGLEWOOD CEMETERY MORTUARY
45. License No.	FD-1101
47. Date	12/05/1995
101. Place of Death	ST. VINCENT MED CTR — IP
104. County	LOS ANGELES
105. Street Address	2131 W. 3RD ST
106. City	LOS ANGELES

Cause of Death

		Time Interval
Immediate Cause (A)	RESPIRATORY ARREST	10 MINS
Due to (B)	BREAST CANCER WITH LUNG METASTASTS	3½ YRS
Due to (C)		
Due to (D)		

108. Death Reported to Coroner: YES
109. Biopsy Performed: NO
110. Autopsy Performed: NO
111. Used in Determining Cause: NO

112. Other Significant Conditions: NONE

113. Was Operation Performed: LUMPECTOMY 06/02/1992

114. Decedent Attended Since: 08/25/1995
Decedent Last Seen Alive: 12/01/1995
116. License No.: C38037
117. Date: 12/04/1995
118. Attending Physician: PETER KENNEDY 201 S ALVARADO ST LOS ANGELES, CA 90057

Gilbert Roland

CERTIFICATE OF DEATH
STATE OF CALIFORNIA

1. NAME OF DECEDENT—FIRST (GIVEN): GILBERT
2. MIDDLE: —
3. LAST (FAMILY): ROLAND
4. DATE OF BIRTH: 12/11/1905
5. AGE YRS: 88
6. SEX: M
7. DATE OF DEATH: 05/15/1994
8. HOUR: 1505
9. STATE OF BIRTH: MEXICO
10. SOCIAL SECURITY NO.: 565-18-1775
11. MILITARY SERVICE: 1941 to 1944
12. MARITAL STATUS: MARRIED
13. EDUCATION—YEARS COMPLETED: 7
14. RACE: CAUCASIAN
15. HISPANIC—SPECIFY: X YES MEXICAN
16. USUAL EMPLOYER: SELF EMPLOYED
17. OCCUPATION: ACTOR
18. KIND OF BUSINESS: MOTION PICTURES
19. YEARS IN OCCUPATION: 65
20. RESIDENCE: 518 N. ROXBURY DR.
21. CITY: BEVERLY HILLS
22. COUNTY: LOS ANGELES
23. ZIP CODE: 90210
24. YRS IN COUNTY: 70
25. STATE OR FOREIGN COUNTRY: CALIFORNIA
26. NAME, RELATIONSHIP: GUILLERMINA ROLAND-WIFE
27. MAILING ADDRESS: 518 N. ROXBURY DR., BEVERLY HILLS, CA 90210
28. NAME OF SURVIVING SPOUSE—FIRST: GULLERMINA
29. MIDDLE: —
30. LAST (MAIDEN NAME): CANTU
31. NAME OF FATHER—FIRST: FRANCISCO
32. MIDDLE: —
33. LAST: ALONZO
34. BIRTH STATE: SPAIN
35. NAME OF MOTHER—FIRST: CONSUELO
36. MIDDLE: —
37. LAST (MAIDEN): UNKNOWN
38. BIRTH STATE: SPAIN
39. DATE: 05/24/1994
40. PLACE OF FINAL DISPOSITION: PACIFIC OCEAN 3 MILES OFF SAN PEDRO, CA
41. TYPE OF DISPOSITION(S): CR/SEA
42. SIGNATURE OF EMBALMER: NOT EMBALMED
43. LICENSE NO.: —
44. NAME OF FUNERAL DIRECTOR: THE NEPTUNE SOCIETY
45. LICENSE NO.: FD-1289
47. DATE: 05/23/1994
101. PLACE OF DEATH: RESIDENCE
103. FACILITY OTHER THAN HOSPITAL: X RES.
104. COUNTY: LOS ANGELES
105. STREET ADDRESS: 518 N. ROXBURY DR.
106. CITY: BEVERLY HILLS

107. DEATH WAS CAUSED BY:
- (A) PNEUMONIA — 1 WEEK
- (B) METASTATIC SQUAMONS CELL CARCINOMA — YRS

108. DEATH REPORTED TO CORONER: X NO
109. BIOPSY PERFORMED: X NO
110. AUTOPSY PERFORMED: X NO

112. OTHER SIGNIFICANT CONDITIONS: NONE
113. WAS OPERATION PERFORMED: NO
115. SIGNATURE AND TITLE OF CERTIFIER: Cynthia M. Watson M.D.
116. LICENSE NO.: G52886
117. DATE: 05/18/1994
DECEDENT ATTENDED SINCE: 05/10/1994
DECEDENT LAST SEEN ALIVE: 05/10/1994
118. ATTENDING PHYSICIAN'S NAME: C.WATSON,M.D., 530 WILSHIRE BLVD., SANTA MONICA, CA 90401

COUNTY OF ORANGE
HEALTH CARE AGENCY
1200 N. MAIN STREET, SUITE 100-A
SANTA ANA, CA 92701

CERTIFICATE OF DEATH — STATE OF CALIFORNIA

State File Number: 3-199930 011247

DECEDENT PERSONAL DATA
- 1. Name (First): RUTH
- 2. Middle: —
- 3. Last (Family): ROMAN
- 4. Date of Birth: 12/22/1922
- 5. Age: 76
- 6. Sex: F
- 7. Date of Death: 09/09/1999
- 8. Hour: 1201
- 9. State of Birth: MA
- 10. Social Security No.: 017-14-6766
- 11. Military Service: No
- 12. Marital Status: divorced
- 13. Education — Years Completed: 16
- 14. Race: WHITE
- 15. Hispanic: No
- 16. Usual Employer: SELF EMPLOYED
- 17. Occupation: ACTRESS
- 18. Kind of Business: MOTION PICTURE
- 19. Years in Occupation: 40

USUAL RESIDENCE
- 20. Residence: 1225 Cliff Dr
- 21. City: Laguna Beach
- 22. County: ORANGE
- 23. Zip Code: 92651
- 24. Yrs in County: 37
- 25. State: CA

INFORMANT
- 26. Name, Relationship: Richard Hall-son
- 27. Mailing Address: 58975 Kessen Ln Anza, CA 92539

SPOUSE AND PARENT INFORMATION
- 28-30. Name of Surviving Spouse: —
- 31. Name of Father: unknown
- 32. Middle: unknown
- 33. Last: unknown
- 34. Birth State: unknown
- 35. Name of Mother: Suki
- 36. Middle: unknown
- 37. Last (Maiden): unknown
- 38. Birth State: unknown

DISPOSITION(S)
- 39. Date: 09/14/1999
- 40. Place of Final Disposition: sea burial off coastline of Laguna Beach Orange County, CA
- 41. Type of Disposition: cr/sea
- 42. Signature of Embalmer: McCormick
- 43. License No.: 6161
- 44. Name of Funeral Director: McCormick & Son
- 45. License No.: FD1212
- 46. Signature of Local Registrar: Hildy B. Meyers, MD
- 47. Date: 09/10/1999

PLACE OF DEATH
- 101. Place of Death: residence
- 104. County: Orange
- 105. Street Address: 1225 Cliff Dr
- 106. City: Laguna Beach

CAUSE OF DEATH
- 107(A). Immediate Cause: CARDIOPULMONARY ARREST — 10 mins
- 107(B). Due to: HYPERTENSIVE VASCULAR DISEASE — 10 yrs
- 108. Death Reported to Coroner: Yes — Referral Number 9905945LL
- 109. Biopsy Performed: No
- 110. Autopsy Performed: No
- 112. Other Significant Conditions: NONE
- 113. Was Operation Performed: NO

401.9

PHYSICIAN'S CERTIFICATION
- 114. Decedent attended since: 09/28/1998; last seen 07/01/1999
- 115. Signature of Certifier: Nancy Boerner, MD
- 116. License No.: A044509
- 117. Date: 09/09/1999
- 118. Attending Physician: N. Boerner MD, 31862 Coast Hwy, Laguna Beach CA 92651

601184

CERTIFIED COPY OF VITAL RECORDS
Date Issued: 1999
MARK B. HORTON, M.D. — HEALTH OFFICER

Hildy B. Meyers, MD
ACTING HEALTH OFFICER
ORANGE COUNTY, CALIFORNIA

FAX AUTH. # 7435

STATE OF CALIFORNIA
CERTIFICATION OF VITAL RECORD

COUNTY OF LOS ANGELES • REGISTRAR-RECORDER/COUNTY CLERK

CERTIFICATE OF DEATH — 3 2004 19 029340

1. Name of Decedent — First	ISABEL
3. Last (Family)	SANFORD
4. Date of Birth	08/17/1917
5. Age	86
6. Sex	F
7. Date of Death	07/09/2004
8. Hour	1955
9. Birth State	NY
10. Social Security Number	109-10-3372
11. Ever in U.S. Armed Forces?	NO
12. Marital Status	WIDOWED
13. Education	DOCTORATE
14/15. Hispanic/Latino?	NO
16. Race	BLACK
17. Usual Occupation	ACTRESS
18. Kind of Business	ENTERTAINMENT
19. Years in Occupation	60
20. Decedent's Residence	2501 COLORADO AVE #350
21. City	SANTA MONICA
22. County	LOS ANGELES
23. ZIP	90404
24. Years in County	43
25. State	CA
26. Informant's Name	BRAD LEMACK, FRIEND
27. Informant's Mailing Address	221 S GALE DR #403, BEVERLY HILLS, CA 90211
33. Name of Father — Last	PERRY
34. Birth State	UNK
35. Name of Mother — First	JOSEPHINE
37. Last (Maiden)	UNK
39. Birth State	UNK
39. Disposition Date	07/21/2004
40. Place of Final Disposition	FOREST LAWN MEMORIAL PARK, LOS ANGELES, CA 90068
41. Type of Disposition	BURIAL
43. License Number	8861
44. Funeral Establishment	FOREST LAWN HOLLYWOOD HILLS
45. License Number	FD 904
47. Date	07/19/2004
101. Place of Death	CEDARS SINAI MED CTR
104. County	LOS ANGELES
105. Facility Address	8700 BEVERLY BLVD
106. City	LOS ANGELES
107. Cause of Death — Immediate	CARDIOPULMONARY ARREST — 35 MIN
(B)	ARTERIOSCLEROTIC HEART DISEASE — 20 YRS
112. Other Significant Conditions	NONE
113. Was Operation Performed	NO
(A) Decedent Attended Since	--/--/1985
(B) Decedent Last Seen Alive	07/09/2004
118. Attending Physician	DAVID FRISCH, MD 150 N ROBERTSON BLVD #350 BEVERLY HILLS, CA 90211
116. License Number	G2616
117. Date	07/14/2004
FAX AUTH. #	273/137

INFORMATIONAL, NOT A VALID DOCUMENT TO ESTABLISH IDENTITY

This is to certify that this document is a true copy of the official record filed with the Registrar-Recorder/County Clerk.

CONNY B. McCORMACK
Registrar-Recorder/County Clerk

019483120

STATE OF CALIFORNIA

CERTIFICATION OF VITAL RECORD

COUNTY OF LOS ANGELES • REGISTRAR-RECORDER/COUNTY CLERK

CERTIFICATE OF DEATH
STATE OF CALIFORNIA

0190-057187

STATE FILE NUMBER — LOCAL REGISTRATION DISTRICT AND CERTIFICATE NUMBER

DECEDENT PERSONAL DATA

1A. NAME OF DECEDENT—FIRST: Ernest	1B. MIDDLE: Beaumont	1C. LAST: Schoedsack	2A. DATE OF DEATH (MONTH, DAY, YEAR): Dec 23 1979	2B. HOUR: 1610
3. SEX: male	4. RACE: cauc	5. ETHNICITY: not stated	6. DATE OF BIRTH: June 8 1893	7. AGE: 86 YEARS
8. BIRTHPLACE OF DECEDENT (STATE OR FOREIGN COUNTRY): Iowa	9. NAME AND BIRTHPLACE OF FATHER: Gustav Schoedsack- Germany		10. BIRTH NAME AND BIRTHPLACE OF MOTHER: Ruth Beaumont- Ireland	
11. CITIZEN OF WHAT COUNTRY: U.S.A.	12. SOCIAL SECURITY NUMBER: 555 09 3555	13. MARITAL STATUS: married	14. NAME OF SURVIVING SPOUSE (IF WIFE, ENTER BIRTH NAME): Ruth Rose	
15. PRIMARY OCCUPATION: Director	16. NUMBER OF YEARS THIS OCCUPATION: 30	17. EMPLOYER (IF SELF-EMPLOYED, SO STATE): R.K.O	18. KIND OF INDUSTRY OR BUSINESS: Motion Pictures	

1 of 2

USUAL RESIDENCE

19A. USUAL RESIDENCE—STREET ADDRESS (STREET AND NUMBER OR LOCATION): 370 20th St.	19B.	19C. CITY OR TOWN: Santa Monica
19D. COUNTY: Santa Monica	19E. STATE: Calif	20. NAME AND ADDRESS OF INFORMANT—RELATIONSHIP: Peter Schoedsack (Son) same address

PLACE OF DEATH

21A. PLACE OF DEATH: Santa Monica Hospital	21B. COUNTY: Los Angeles
21C. STREET ADDRESS (STREET AND NUMBER OR LOCATION): 1250 16th St.	21D. CITY OR TOWN: Santa Monica

CAUSE OF DEATH

22. DEATH WAS CAUSED BY: (ENTER ONLY ONE CAUSE PER LINE FOR A, B, AND C)

IMMEDIATE CAUSE (A) Ventricular fibrillation	30 min	24. WAS DEATH REPORTED TO CORONER? No
DUE TO, OR AS A CONSEQUENCE OF (B) Broncho pneumonia	3 days	25. WAS BIOPSY PERFORMED? No
DUE TO, OR AS A CONSEQUENCE OF (C)		26. WAS AUTOPSY PERFORMED? No

CONDITIONS, IF ANY, WHICH GAVE RISE TO THE IMMEDIATE CAUSE, STATING THE UNDERLYING CAUSE LAST. APPROXIMATE INTERVAL BETWEEN ONSET AND DEATH.

23. OTHER CONDITIONS CONTRIBUTING BUT NOT RELATED TO THE IMMEDIATE CAUSE OF DEATH: None

27. WAS OPERATION PERFORMED FOR ANY CONDITION IN ITEMS 22 OR 23? TYPE OF OPERATION: No — DATE

PHYSICIAN'S CERTIFICATION

28A. I CERTIFY THAT DEATH OCCURRED AT THE HOUR, DATE AND PLACE STATED FROM THE CAUSES STATED. I ATTENDED DECEDENT SINCE (ENTER MO, DA, YR): Jan. 24, 1974 — I LAST SAW DECEDENT ALIVE (ENTER MO, DA, YR): Dec. 20, 1979

28B. PHYSICIAN—SIGNATURE AND DEGREE OR TITLE: J. Richard Harelik

28C. DATE SIGNED: 12-26-79

28D. PHYSICIAN'S LICENSE NUMBER: G-06391

28E. TYPE PHYSICIAN'S NAME AND ADDRESS: J.R. Harelik, M.D. 910 Via De LA Paz, Pacific Pallisades, Ca. 90272

INJURY INFORMATION

29. SPECIFY ACCIDENT, SUICIDE, ETC. — 30. PLACE OF INJURY — 31. INJURY AT WORK — 32A. DATE OF INJURY—MONTH DAY YEAR — 32B. HOUR

33. LOCATION (STREET AND NUMBER OR LOCATION AND CITY OR TOWN) — 34. DESCRIBE HOW INJURY OCCURRED (EVENTS WHICH RESULTED IN INJURY)

CORONER'S USE ONLY

35A. I CERTIFY THAT DEATH OCCURRED AT THE HOUR, DATE AND PLACE STATED FROM THE CAUSES STATED. AS REQUIRED BY LAW I HAVE HELD AN (INQUEST-INVESTIGATION) — 35B. CORONER—SIGNATURE AND DEGREE OR TITLE — 35C. DATE SIGNED

36. DISPOSITION: Cremation	37. DATE (MONTH DAY YEAR): 12-28-79	38. NAME AND ADDRESS OF CEMETERY OR CREMATORY: Grandview Crematory Glendale Calif	39. EMBALMER'S LICENSE NUMBER AND SIGNATURE: not embalmed
40. NAME OF FUNERAL DIRECTOR (OR PERSON ACTING AS SUCH): Westwood Village Mortuary	41. LOCAL REGISTRAR—SIGNATURE: Robert W. Whitt	jw	42. DATE ACCEPTED BY LOCAL REGISTRAR: DEC 27 1979

STATE REGISTRAR: A. B. C. D. E. F.

VS-11 (10-78)

This is to certify that this document is a true copy of the official record filed with the Registrar-Recorder/County Clerk.

AUG 01 2005

Conny B. McCormack

CONNY B. McCORMACK
Registrar-Recorder/County Clerk

019579679

This copy not valid unless prepared on engraved border displaying the Seal and Signature of the Registrar-Recorder/County Clerk.

THE GREAT SEAL OF THE STATE OF CALIFORNIA — EUREKA

COUNTY OF LOS ANGELES — CALIFORNIA

ANY ALTERATION OR ERASURE VOIDS THIS CERTIFICATE

STATE OF CALIFORNIA
CERTIFICATION OF VITAL RECORD

COUNTY OF RIVERSIDE
RIVERSIDE, CALIFORNIA

CERTIFICATE OF DEATH

STATE FILE NUMBER: 3200733001030

DECEDENT'S PERSONAL DATA

1. Name of Decedent — First (Given)	SIDNEY
2. Middle	KING
3. Last (Family)	SHELDON
4. Date of Birth	02/11/1917
5. Age	89
6. Sex	M
9. Birth State/Foreign Country	IL
10. Social Security Number	259-07-0066
11. Ever in U.S. Armed Forces?	YES
12. Marital Status	MARRIED
7. Date of Death	01/30/2007
8. Hour (24 Hours)	1628
14/15. Education	SOME COLLEGE
16. Hispanic/Latino	NO
16. Decedent's Race	WHITE
17. Usual Occupation	AUTHOR
18. Kind of Business/Industry	ENTERTAINMENT
19. Years in Occupation	70

USUAL RESIDENCE

20. Decedent's Residence	425 VIA LOLA
21. City	PALM SPRINGS
22. County/Province	RIVERSIDE
23. Zip Code	92262
24. Years in County	55
25. State/Foreign Country	CA

INFORMANT

26. Informant's Name, Relationship	ALEXANDRA SHELDON, WIFE
27. Informant's Mailing Address	425 VIA LOLA, PALM SPRINGS, CA 92262

SPOUSE AND PARENT INFORMATION

28. Name of Surviving Spouse — First	ALEXANDRA
29. Middle	JOYCE
30. Last (Maiden Name)	KOSTOFF
31. Name of Father — First	OTTO
33. Last	SHELDON
34. Birth State	IL
35. Name of Mother — First	NATALIE
37. Last (Maiden)	LIEB
38. Birth State	RUSSIA

FUNERAL DIRECTOR / LOCAL REGISTRAR

39. Disposition Date	02/01/2007
40. Place of Final Disposition	RES. ALEXANDRA SHELDON, 425 VIA LOLA, PALM SPRINGS, CA 92262
41. Type of Disposition(s)	CR/RES
42. Signature of Embalmer	NOT EMBALMED
44. Name of Funeral Establishment	FOREST LAWN CATHEDRAL CITY
45. License Number	FD 1847
46. Signature of Local Registrar	GARY M FELDMAN, MD
47. Date	01/31/2007

PLACE OF DEATH

101. Place of Death	EISENHOWER MEMORIAL HOSPITAL
102. If Hospital, Specify One	IP
104. County	RIVERSIDE
105. Facility Address or Location Where Found	39000 BOB HOPE DRIVE
106. City	RANCHO MIRAGE

CAUSE OF DEATH

107. Cause of Death:
- (A) Immediate Cause: CARDIOPULMONARY ARREST — MIN.
- (B) PNEUMONIA — WKS.
- (C) CHRONIC OBSTRUCTIVE PULMONARY DISEASE — YRS.
- (D) MYCOBACTERIUM AVIUM COMPLEX — YRS.

108. Death Reported to Coroner: NO
109. Biopsy Performed? NO
110. Autopsy Performed? NO
111. Used in Determining Cause?

112. Other Significant Conditions: CARCINOMA OF THE LUNG

113. Was Operation Performed: NONE

PHYSICIAN'S CERTIFICATION

Decedent Attended Since	03/09/1993
Decedent Last Seen Alive	01/30/2007
115. Signature and Title of Certifier	JOEL HIRSCHBERG, M.D.
116. License Number	G40006
117. Date	01/31/2007
118. Attending Physician's Name, Mailing Address	JOEL HIRSCHBERG, M.D., 39000 BOB HOPE DRIVE, RANCHO MIRAGE, CA 92270

---

0 3 3 8 5 7 4 5 1

CERTIFIED COPY OF VITAL RECORDS
STATE OF CALIFORNIA, COUNTY OF RIVERSIDE

This is a true and exact reproduction of the document officially registered and placed on file in the office of the County of Riverside, County Clerk-Recorder.

DATE ISSUED: MAY 29 2008

LARRY W. WARD
ASSESSOR-COUNTY CLERK-RECORDER
RIVERSIDE COUNTY, CALIFORNIA

This copy is not valid unless prepared on engraved border displaying date, seal and signature of the County Clerk-Recorder.

INFORMATIONAL, NOT A VALID DOCUMENT TO ESTABLISH IDENTITY

CERTIFICATE OF DEATH
STATE OF CALIFORNIA

0190-001858

1A. NAME OF DECEDENT—FIRST	1B. MIDDLE	1C. LAST	2A. DATE OF DEATH	2B. HOUR
Jack AKA Goro	Soo	Suzuki	January 11, 1979	1330

3. SEX	4. RACE	5. ETHNICITY	6. DATE OF BIRTH	7. AGE
Male	Asian	Japanese	October 28, 1917	61

8. BIRTHPLACE OF DECEDENT	9. NAME AND BIRTHPLACE OF FATHER	10. BIRTH NAME AND BIRTHPLACE OF MOTHER
California	George Kanichiro Suzuki – Japan	Haruko Shiozawa – Japan

11. CITIZEN OF WHAT COUNTRY	12. SOCIAL SECURITY NUMBER	13. MARITAL STATUS	14. NAME OF SURVIVING SPOUSE
USA	571-09-1009	Married	Jean Ann Zdelar

15. PRIMARY OCCUPATION	16. NUMBER OF YEARS THIS OCCUPATION	17. EMPLOYER	18. KIND OF INDUSTRY OR BUSINESS
Actor	13 yrs	ABC Television	Television

19A. USUAL RESIDENCE—STREET ADDRESS	19B.	19C. CITY OR TOWN
118 N Highland Avenue		Los Angeles

19D. COUNTY	19E. STATE	20. NAME AND ADDRESS OF INFORMANT—RELATIONSHIP
Los Angeles	California	Mrs. Jean Ann Soo, wife / 118 N Highland Avenue / Los Angeles, California

21A. PLACE OF DEATH	21B. COUNTY
UCLA Hospital	Los Angeles

21C. STREET ADDRESS	21D. CITY OR TOWN
10833 Le Conte	Los Angeles

CAUSE OF DEATH

(A) metastatic carcinoma — 11 mons
(B) carcinoma of esophagus — 11 mons

23. OTHER CONDITIONS: None

27. TYPE OF OPERATION: esophagogastrectomy   DATE: 2/78

24. WAS DEATH REPORTED TO CORONER? no
25. WAS BIOPSY PERFORMED? no
26. WAS AUTOPSY PERFORMED? no

PHYSICIAN'S CERTIFICATION
I attended decedent since 1/5/79 — I last saw decedent alive 1/11/79
Robert G Burns, MD 1/10/79 G035693
Robert G Burns, MD, 10833 Le Conte, Los Angeles, CA 90024

36. DISPOSITION	37. DATE	38. NAME AND ADDRESS OF CEMETERY OR CREMATORY	39. EMBALMER'S LICENSE
Burial	Jan 15, 1979	ForestLawn Memorial Park, 6300 Forest Lawn Drive, Los Angeles	6061 Paul A. Thomas

40. NAME OF FUNERAL DIRECTOR: Fukui Mortuary, Inc.
42. DATE ACCEPTED BY LOCAL REGISTRAR: JAN 15 1979

This is to certify that this document is a true copy of the official record filed with the Registrar-Recorder/County Clerk.

Conny B. McCormack
CONNY B. McCORMACK
Registrar-Recorder/County Clerk

OCT 3 1996
19-386523

This copy not valid unless prepared on engraved border displaying the Seal and Signature of the Registrar-Recorder/County Clerk.

ANY ALTERATION OR ERASURE VOIDS THIS CERTIFICATE

COUNTY of SAN BERNARDINO
DEPARTMENT OF PUBLIC HEALTH
351 MT. VIEW AVENUE, SAN BERNARDINO, CALIFORNIA 92415-0010

CERTIFICATE OF DEATH — 39636007849

DECEDENT PERSONAL DATA
- 1. Name of Decedent—First (Given): KENNETH
- 2. Middle: KEITH
- 3. Last (Family): STEADMAN
- 4. Date of Birth: 06/26/1969
- 5. Age: 27
- 6. Sex: M
- 7. Date of Death: 09/20/1996
- 8. Hour: 1304
- 9. State of Birth: WASHINGTON
- 10. Social Security No.: 537-88-8537
- 11. Military Service: NONE
- 12. Marital Status: NEVER MARRIED
- 13. Education—Years Completed: 13
- 14. Race: CAUCASIAN
- 15. Hispanic: No
- 16. Usual Employer: UNIVERSAL STUDIOS
- 17. Occupation: ACTOR
- 18. Kind of Business: ENTERTAINMENT
- 19. Years in Occupation: 10

USUAL RESIDENCE
- 20. Residence—Street and Number or Location: 8159 SANTA MONICA BLVD., #202
- 21. City: LOS ANGELES
- 22. County: LOS ANGELES
- 23. Zip Code: 90046
- 24. Yrs in County: 5
- 25. State or Foreign Country: CA

INFORMANT
- 26. Name, Relationship: CARL M. PRINCE, STEP-FATHER
- 27. Mailing Address: 4024 PIPELINE RD., BLAINE, WA 98230

SPOUSE AND PARENT INFORMATION
- 31. Name of Father—First: KENNETH
- 32. Middle: JOHN
- 33. Last: STEADMAN
- 34. Birth State: WA
- 35. Name of Mother—First: LISA
- 36. Middle: ANN
- 37. Last (Maiden): DELANEY
- 38. Birth State: WA

FUNERAL DIRECTOR AND LOCAL REGISTRAR
- 39. Date: 09/30/1996
- 40. Place of Final Disposition: RES: CARL M. PRINCE STEP-FATHER, 4024 PIPELINE RD, BLAINE, WA 98230
- 41. Type of Disposition: CR/TR/RES
- 42. Signature of Embalmer: Elizabeth Derrick
- 43. License No.: 7435
- 44. Name of Funeral Director: FOREST LAWN HOLLYWOOD HILLS
- 45. License No.: F 904
- 47. Date: 09/27/1996

PLACE OF DEATH
- 101. Place of Death: San Bernardino Co Med Ctr
- 102. If Hospital, Specify One: ER/OP
- 104. County: San Bernardino
- 105. Street Address: 780 E. Gilbert St.
- 106. City: San Bernardino

CAUSE OF DEATH
- 107. (A) Immediate Cause: Blunt Head Injury
- 108. Death Reported to Coroner: Yes — Referral Number 96-5366 RY
- 109. Biopsy Performed: No
- 110. Autopsy Performed: Yes
- 111. Used in Determining Cause: Yes
- 112. Other Significant Conditions: None
- 113. Was Operation Performed: No

CORONER'S USE ONLY
- 119. Manner of Death: Accident
- 120. Injury at Work: No
- 121. Injury Date: 09/20/1996
- 122. Hour: 1150
- 123. Place of Injury: Dry Lake Bed
- 124. Describe How Injury Occurred: Single vehicle rollover, driver ejected, not seat-belted
- 125. Location: 1/2 Mi. E/O Old El Mirage Dry Lake Rd & 1 Mi S/O Cedros Rd.
- 126. Signature of Coroner: James R. Sedgwick
- 127. Date: 09/23/1996
- 128. Typed Name, Title of Coroner: James R. Sedgwick, Deputy Coroner
- Fax Auth. #: 1218961

677053

CERTIFIED COPY OF VITAL RECORDS

STATE OF CALIFORNIA } SS
COUNTY OF SAN BERNARDINO

DATE ISSUED: OCT 0 4 1996

This is a true and exact reproduction of the document officially registered and placed on file in the VITAL RECORDS SECTION, SAN BERNARDINO DEPARTMENT OF PUBLIC HEALTH.

THOMAS J. PRENDERGAST, M.D.
COUNTY HEALTH OFFICER
REGISTRAR OF VITAL STATISTICS

This copy not valid unless prepared on engraved border displaying seal and signature of Registrar.

STATE OF CALIFORNIA
CERTIFICATION OF VITAL RECORD

COUNTY OF LOS ANGELES
DEPARTMENT OF HEALTH SERVICES

CERTIFICATE OF DEATH
STATE OF CALIFORNIA

DECEDENT PERSONAL DATA
- 1. Name of Decedent—First (Given): JESS
- 2. Middle: E.
- 3. Last (Family): STEARN
- 4. Date of Birth: 04/16/1914
- 5. Age Yrs.: 87
- 6. Sex: M
- 7. Date of Death: 03/27/2002
- 8. Hour: 0500
- 9. State of Birth: NEW YORK
- 10. Social Security No.: 074-07-1608
- 11. Military Service: No
- 12. Marital Status: DIVORCED
- 13. Education—Years Completed: 16
- 14. Race: CAUCASIAN
- 15. Hispanic: No
- 16. Usual Employer: SELF EMPLOYED
- 17. Occupation: WRITER/AUTHOR
- 18. Kind of Business: LITERATURE
- 19. Years in Occupation: 60

USUAL RESIDENCE
- 20. Residence: 21510 PACIFIC COAST HIGHWAY
- 21. City: MALIBU
- 22. County: LOS ANGELES
- 23. Zip Code: 90265
- 24. Yrs in County: 36
- 25. State: CA

INFORMANT
- 26. Name, Relationship: FRED STEARN – SON
- 27. Mailing Address: 29926 FORT CADY RD., NEWBERRY SPRINGS, CA. 92365

SPOUSE AND PARENT INFORMATION
- 31. Name of Father—First: DAVID
- 33. Last: STEARN
- 34. Birth State: UNK
- 35. Name of Mother—First: JENNY
- 37. Last (Maiden): RAMPEL
- 38. Birth State: RUSSIA

FUNERAL DIRECTOR AND LOCAL REGISTRAR
- 39. Date: 04/04/2002
- 40. Place of Final Disposition: RES: FRED STEARN 29926 FORT CADY RD. NEWBERRY SPRINGS, CA. 92365
- 41. Type of Disposition: CR/RES
- 42. Signature of Embalmer: NOT EMBALMED
- 44. Name of Funeral Director: PIERCE BROS. WESTWOOD
- 45. License No.: FD-951
- 47. Date: 04/01/2002

PLACE OF DEATH
- 101. Place of Death: RESIDENCE
- 105. Street Address: 21510 PACIFIC COAST HIGHWAY
- 104. County: LOS ANGELES
- 106. City: MALIBU

CAUSE OF DEATH
- 107. Death was caused by:
  - Immediate Cause (A): DEMENTIA, PROBABLE ALZHEIMER'S TYPE — 2 years
- 108. Death Reported to Coroner: No
- 109. Biopsy Performed: No
- 110. Autopsy Performed: No
- 112. Other Significant Conditions: NONE
- 113. War Operation Performed: NO

PHYSICIAN'S CERTIFICATION
- 114. Decedent Attended Since: 07/15/2001; Last Seen Alive: 03/27/2002
- 115. Signature: James W. Davis, Jr. MD
- 116. License No.: G032480
- 117. Date: 03/28/2002
- 118. Attending Physician: JAMES W. DAVIS, JR. MD, 200 MEDICAL PLAZA, LOS ANGELES, CA. 90024

State Registrar: G 30.9

Census Tract: 09052 0390

This is a true certified copy of the record filed in the County of Los Angeles Department of Health Services if it bears the Registrar's signature in purple ink.

DATE ISSUED: APR 1 5 2002

Director of Health Services and Registrar

This copy not valid unless prepared on engraved border displaying seal and signature of Registrar.

ANY ALTERATION OR ERASURE VOIDS THIS CERTIFICATE

CERTIFICATE OF DEATH
STATE OF CALIFORNIA
State File Number: 39619012825

Decedent Personal Data
- **1. Name of Decedent—First (Given):** EDGAR
- **2. Middle:** MCLEAN
- **3. Last (Family):** STEVENSON JR.
- **4. Date of Birth:** 11/14/1927
- **5. Age Yrs:** 68
- **6. Sex:** MALE
- **7. Date of Death:** 02/15/1996
- **8. Hour:** 1846
- **9. State of Birth:** ILL
- **10. Social Security No.:** 345-12-6856
- **11. Military Service:** NONE
- **12. Marital Status:** MARRIED
- **13. Education—Years Completed:** 16
- **14. Race:** CAUCASIAN
- **15. Hispanic:** NO
- **16. Usual Employer:** SELF EMPLOYED
- **17. Occupation:** ACTOR/WRITER
- **18. Kind of Business:** MOTION PICTURE & TELEVISION
- **19. Years in Occupation:** 30

Usual Residence
- **20. Residence—Street and Number or Location:** 4911 VAN NUYS BL. #309
- **21. City:** SHERMAN OAKS
- **22. County:** LOS ANGELES
- **23. Zip Code:** 91403
- **24. Yrs in County:** 26
- **25. State or Foreign Country:** CALIFORNIA

Informant
- **26. Name, Relationship:** VIRGINIA F. STEVENSON - WIFE
- **27. Mailing Address:** 4911 VAN NUYS BL. #309, SHERMAN OAKS, CA 91403

Spouse and Parent Information
- **28. Name of Surviving Spouse—First:** VIRGINIA
- **29. Middle:** -
- **30. Last (Maiden Name):** FOSDICK
- **31. Name of Father—First:** EDGAR
- **32. Middle:** MCLEAN
- **33. Last:** STEVENSON SR.
- **34. Birth State:** ILL
- **35. Name of Mother—First:** SARA
- **36. Middle:** -
- **37. Last (Maiden):** MOWRY
- **38. Birth State:** CANADA

Disposition / Funeral Director and Local Registrar
- **39. Date:** 02/26/1996
- **40. Place of Final Disposition:** VIRGINIA F. STEVENSON RES: 4911 VAN NUYS BL. #309, SHERMAN OAKS, CA 91403
- **41. Type of Disposition(s):** CR/RES
- **42. Signature of Embalmer:** NOT EMBALMED
- **43. License No.:** -
- **44. Name of Funeral Director:** NEPTUNE SOCIETY - BURBANK
- **45. License No.:** F-1289
- **47. Date:** 02/26/1996

Place of Death
- **101. Place of Death:** MEDICAL CENTER OF TARZANA
- **102. If Hospital, Specify One:** IP
- **104. County:** LOS ANGELES
- **105. Street Address:** 18321 CLARK ST.
- **106. City:** TARZANA

Cause of Death
- **107. Death was caused by:**
  - (A) Immediate Cause: DEFERRED
- **108. Death Reported to Coroner:** YES
- **Referral Number:** 96-1420
- **110. Autopsy Performed:** YES

Coroner's Use Only
- **119. Manner of Death:** PENDING INVESTIGATION
- **126. Signature of Coroner or Deputy Coroner:** Mary T. Macias
- **127. Date:** 02/21/1996
- **128. Typed Name, Title of Coroner or Deputy Coroner:** MARY T. MACIAS/DEPUTY CORONER

CERTIFICATE OF DEATH
STATE OF CALIFORNIA—DEPARTMENT OF PUBLIC HEALTH

Local Registration District and Certificate Number: 7013 / 12955

1a. Name of Deceased—First Name: Anita (AKA Anita)
1b. Middle Name: Mary (Mary)
1c. Last Name: Converse / Stewart
2a. Date of Death: May 4, 1961
2b. Hour: 6:41 A.M.

3. Sex: Female
4. Color or Race: Caucasian
5. Birthplace: New York
6. Date of Birth: February 17, 1902
7. Age (Last Birthday): 59 years

8. Name and Birthplace of Father: William H. Stewart – Pa.
9. Maiden Name and Birthplace of Mother: Martha Lee – New York
10. Citizen of What Country: U.S.A.
11. Social Security Number: Unknown

12. Last Occupation: Actress
13. Number of Years in This Occupation: 25
14. Name of Last Employing Company or Firm: Metro Goldwyn Mayer
15. Kind of Industry or Business: Motion Pictures

16. If Deceased Was Ever in U.S. Armed Forces: None
17. Specify Married, Never Married, Widowed, Divorced: Divorced
18a. Name of Present Spouse: ---
18b. Present or Last Occupation of Spouse: ---

19a. Place of Death—Name of Hospital: (None)
19b. Street Address: 1029 Hanover Drive
19c. City or Town: Beverly Hills
19d. County: Los Angeles
19e. Length of Stay in County of Death: 41 years
19f. Length of Stay in California: 41 years

20a. Last Usual Residence—Street Address: 1029 Hanover Drive
20c. City or Town: Beverly Hills
20d. County: Los Angeles
20e. State: California

21a. Name of Informant: Lucille L. Stewart
21b. Address of Informant: ---

22a. Physician: (signature)
22b. Coroner: autopsy
22c. Physician or Coroner—Signature: Theo. J. Curphey, M.D., Coroner
22d. Address: Hall of Justice, Los Angeles
22e. Date Signed: 7-21-61

23. Specify Burial, Entombment or Cremation: Entombment
24. Date: 5-9-61
25. Name of Cemetery or Crematory: Forest Lawn Memorial-Park Mausoleum
26. Embalmer—Signature: Wayne A. Bauman, License Number 4365
27. Name of Funeral Director: Forest Lawn Memorial-Park Ass'n., Glendale, California
28. Date Accepted for Registration by Local Registrar: JUL 24 1961

30. Cause of Death:
Part I. Death was caused by:
(a) Immediate Cause: Acute barbiturate intoxication

31. Operation—Check One: No Operation Performed ☒
33. Autopsy: Gross Findings Used in Determining Above Stated Causes of Death ☒

34a. Specify Accident, Suicide or Homicide: probable suicide
34b. Describe How Injury Occurred: INGESTION OF OVERDOSE OF BARBITURATES
35a. Time of Injury: 6:41 A.M. 5-4-61 PRIOR TO
35b. Injury Occurred: Not While At Work ☒
35c. Place of Injury: HOME
35d. City, Town, or Location: BEVERLY HILLS, LA, CALIF.

State File Number: #66084

This is to certify that this document is a true copy of the official record filed with the Registrar-Recorder/County Clerk.

Conny B. McCormack
Registrar-Recorder/County Clerk

NOV 28 2000
19-114025

This copy not valid unless prepared on engraved border displaying the Seal and Signature of the Registrar-Recorder/County Clerk.

STATE OF CALIFORNIA
CERTIFICATION OF VITAL RECORD
COUNTY OF LOS ANGELES • REGISTRAR-RECORDER/COUNTY CLERK

CERTIFICATE OF DEATH
State of California — Department of Public Health

Registrar's Number: 15779

DECEDENT PERSONAL DATA

- 1a. Name of Deceased — First Name: Lewis
- 1b. Middle Name: Shepard
- 1c. Last Name: Stone
- 2a. Date of Death: September 13, 1953
- 2b. Hour: 9:10 P.M.
- 3. Sex: Male
- 4. Color or Race: White
- 5. Married
- 6. Date of Birth: November 15, 1879
- 7. Age: 73 Years
- 8a. Usual Occupation: Actor
- 8b. Kind of Business or Industry: Motion Pictures
- 9. Birthplace: Worcester, Mass.
- 10. Citizen of What Country: United States
- 11. Name and Birthplace of Father: Bertrand Timothy Stone, Mass.
- 12. Maiden Name and Birthplace of Mother: Philena Ball, Mass.
- 13. Name of Present Spouse: Hazel Elizabeth Stone
- 14. Was Deceased Ever in U.S. Armed Forces: Yes — Sp. Amer. & WW I
- 15. Social Security Number: 563-03-1812
- 16. Informant: Mrs. Hazel E. Stone

PLACE OF DEATH

- 17a. County: Los Angeles
- 17b. City or Town: Los Angeles
- 17c. Length of Stay in This City or Town: 47 Years
- 17d. Full Name of Hospital or Institution: —
- 17e. Address: 455 So. Lorraine Boulevard

LAST USUAL RESIDENCE

- 18a. State: California
- 18b. County: Los Angeles
- 18c. City or Town: Los Angeles
- 18d. Street or Rural Address: 455 So. Lorraine Blvd.

PHYSICIAN'S OR CORONER'S CERTIFICATION

- 19a. Coroner: —
- 19b. Physician: Death occurred 9/13/53, last saw deceased 9/9/53
- 19c. Signature: Henry J. L. Beneiter, M.D.
- 19d. Address: 1919 Wilshire Boulevard
- 19e. Date Signed: 9/15/53

FUNERAL DIRECTOR AND REGISTRAR

- 20a. Burial: Cremation
- 20b. Date: 9/16/53
- 20c. Cemetery or Crematory: Rosedale Cemetery
- 21. Signature of Embalmer: Walter F. Kelly
- License Number: 2847
- 22. Funeral Director: Cunningham & O'Connor, L.A.
- 23. Date Received by Local Registrar: SEP 15 1953

CAUSE OF DEATH

- 25. Disease or Condition Directly Leading to Death: Coronary Thrombosis — approximate interval: 5 min
- Antecedent Causes (Due to): Coronary Sclerosis — 8 yrs
- 28. Autopsy: No

Conny B. McCormack
Registrar-Recorder/County Clerk

NOV 28 2000
19-118079

CERTIFICATE OF DEATH
STATE OF CALIFORNIA

State File Number: 39419026639

DECEDENT PERSONAL DATA
- 1. Name (First): PATRICK
- 2. Middle: BARRY
- 3. Last: SULLIVAN
- 4. Date of Birth: 08/29/1912
- 5. Age: 81
- 6. Sex: M
- 7. Date of Death: 06/06/1994
- 8. Hour: 1847
- 9. State of Birth: NY
- 10. Social Security No.: 113-09-2837
- 11. Military Service: None
- 12. Marital Status: DIVORCED
- 13. Education — Years Completed: 15
- 14. Race: CAUCASIAN
- 15. Hispanic: No
- 16. Usual Employer: SELF-EMPLOYED
- 17. Occupation: ACTOR
- 18. Kind of Business: ENTERTAINMENT
- 19. Years in Occupation: 50

USUAL RESIDENCE
- 20. Residence: 14687 ROUND VALLEY DRIVE
- 21. City: SHERMAN OAKS
- 22. County: LOS ANGELES
- 23. Zip Code: 91403
- 24. Yrs in County: 51
- 25. State: CA

INFORMANT
- 26. Name, Relationship: JENNY SULLIVAN, DAUGHTER
- 27. Mailing Address: 14687 ROUND VALLEY DRIVE, SHERMAN OAKS, CA 91403

SPOUSE AND PARENT INFORMATION
- 31. Name of Father: CORNELIUS
- 33. Last: SULLIVAN
- 34. Birth State: UNK
- 35. Name of Mother: HELEN
- 37. Last (Maiden): UNK
- 38. Birth State: UNK

DISPOSITION(S)
- 39. Date: 06/14/1994
- 40. Place of Final Disposition: RES: JENNY SULLIVAN, 14687 ROUND VALLEY DRIVE, SHERMAN OAKS, CA 91403
- 41. Type of Disposition: CR/RES
- 43. License No.: 7917
- 44. Name of Funeral Director: FOREST LAWN HOLLYWOOD HILLS
- 45. License No.: F-904
- 47. Date: 06/13/1994

PLACE OF DEATH
- 101. Place of Death: RESIDENCE
- 103. Facility Other Than Hospital: RES
- 104. County: LOS ANGELES
- 105. Street Address: 14687 ROUND VALLEY DRIVE
- 106. City: SHERMAN OAKS

CAUSE OF DEATH
- 107. Death Was Caused By:
  - (A) Immediate Cause: CARDIAC ARREST — 1 MIN
  - (B) Due To: MYOCARDIAL INFARCTION — 5 MINS
- 108. Death Reported to Coroner: No
- 109. Biopsy Performed: No
- 110. Autopsy Performed: No
- 112. Other Significant Conditions: EMPHYSEMA, MELANOMA
- 113. Operation Performed: NO

PHYSICIAN'S CERTIFICATION
- 116. License No.: G 32106
- 117. Date: 06/07/1994
- Decedent Attended Since: 10/20/1987
- Decedent Last Seen Alive: 06/02/1994
- 118. Attending Physician: STEVEN SIMENS, MD, 435 NO. ROXBURY, BEVERLY HILLS, CA 90210

STATE OF CALIFORNIA — CERTIFICATION OF VITAL RECORD

COUNTY OF LOS ANGELES • REGISTRAR-RECORDER/COUNTY CLERK

CERTIFICATE OF DEATH — State File Number: 3200919037017

Decedent's Personal Data
- **Name:** PATRICK WAYNE SWAYZE
- **Date of Birth:** 08/18/1952
- **Age:** 57
- **Sex:** M
- **Birth State:** TX
- **Social Security Number:** 455-94-4555
- **Ever in U.S. Armed Forces:** No
- **Marital Status:** MARRIED
- **Date of Death:** 09/14/2009
- **Hour:** 1000
- **Education:** HS GRADUATE
- **Hispanic/Latino:** No
- **Race:** CAUCASIAN
- **Usual Occupation:** ACTOR
- **Kind of Business/Industry:** ENTERTAINMENT
- **Years in Occupation:** 37

Usual Residence
- **Address:** 1901 AVENUE OF THE STARS SUITE 1100
- **City:** LOS ANGELES
- **County:** LOS ANGELES
- **Zip Code:** 90067
- **Years in County:** 30
- **State:** CA

Informant
- **Name/Relationship:** LISA SWAYZE, WIFE
- **Mailing Address:** 1901 AVENUE OF THE STARS SUITE 1100, LOS ANGELES, CA 90067

Spouse and Parent Information
- **Surviving Spouse:** LISA HAAPANIEMI
- **Father:** JESSE WAYNE SWAYZE — Birth State: TX
- **Mother:** YVONNE PATSY KARNES — Birth State: UNKNOWN

Funeral Director / Local Registrar
- **Disposition Date:** 09/17/2009
- **Place of Final Disposition:** RESIDENCE OF LISA SWAYZE, 1901 AVENUE OF THE STARS SUITE 1100, LOS ANGELES, CA 90067
- **Type of Disposition:** CR/RES
- **Signature of Embalmer:** NOT EMBALMED
- **Name of Funeral Establishment:** PIERCE BROTHERS WESTWOOD
- **License Number:** FD951
- **Signature of Local Registrar:** JONATHAN FIELDING, MD
- **Date:** 09/16/2009

Place of Death
- **Place of Death:** RESIDENCE (Decedent's Home)
- **County:** LOS ANGELES
- **Facility Address:** 1901 AVENUE OF THE STARS SUITE 1100
- **City:** LOS ANGELES

Cause of Death
- **Immediate Cause (A):** CARDIORESPIRATORY ARREST — MINS
- **(B):** ADVANCED PANCREATIC CANCER — YEARS
- **Other Significant Conditions:** NONE
- **Death Reported to Coroner:** No
- **Biopsy Performed:** No
- **Autopsy Performed:** No
- **Used in Determining Cause:** —

Physician's Certification
- **Certifier:** GLEN ISAMU KOMATSU M.D.
- **License Number:** A35086
- **Date:** 09/16/2009
- **Attending Physician:** GLEN ISAMU KOMATSU M.D., LITTLE COMPANY OF MARY HOSP, 4101 TORRANCE BLVD, TORRANCE, CA
- **Decedent Attended Since:** 09/09/2009
- **Decedent Last Seen Alive:** 09/14/2009

Coroner's Use Only
- **Manner of Death:** Natural

This is to certify that this document is a true copy of the official record filed with the Registrar-Recorder/County Clerk.

DEAN C. LOGAN
Registrar-Recorder/County Clerk

JAN 0 4 2010

INFORMATIONAL, NOT A VALID DOCUMENT TO ESTABLISH IDENTITY

STATE OF CALIFORNIA
CERTIFICATION OF VITAL RECORD
COUNTY OF LOS ANGELES • REGISTRAR-RECORDER/COUNTY CLERK

PHYSICIAN/CORONER'S AMENDMENT
NO ERASURES, WHITEOUTS, PHOTOCOPIES, OR ALTERATIONS

STATE FILE NUMBER: 3052009138039
LOCAL REGISTRATION NUMBER: 3200919037017

☐ BIRTH ☒ DEATH ☐ FETAL DEATH

TYPE OR PRINT CLEARLY IN BLACK INK ONLY – THIS AMENDMENT BECOMES AN ACTUAL PART OF THE OFFICIAL RECORD

PART I — INFORMATION TO LOCATE RECORD

INFORMATION AS IT APPEARS ON ORIGINAL RECORD:

1A NAME—FIRST	1B MIDDLE	1C LAST	2 SEX
PATRICK	WAYNE	SWAYZE	M

3 DATE OF EVENT—MM/DD/CCYY	4 CITY OF EVENT	5 COUNTY OF EVENT
09/14/2009	LOS ANGELES	LOS ANGELES

PART II — STATEMENT OF CORRECTIONS

6 CERTIFICATE ITEM NUMBER	7 INFORMATION AS IT APPEARS ON ORIGINAL RECORD	8 INFORMATION AS IT SHOULD APPEAR
105	1901 AVENUE OF THE STARS SUITE 1100	10440 KURT STREET
106	LOS ANGELES	SYLMAR
118	GLEN ISAMU KOMATSU M.D LITTLE COMPANY OF MARY HOSP 4101 TORRANCE BLVD, TORRANCE, CA	GLEN ISAMU KOMATSU M.D LITTLE COMPANY OF MARY HOSP 4101 TORRANCE BLVD, TORRANCE, CA 90503

DECLARATION OF CERTIFYING PHYSICIAN OR CORONER

I HEREBY DECLARE UNDER PENALTY OF PERJURY THAT THE ABOVE INFORMATION IS TRUE AND CORRECT TO THE BEST OF MY KNOWLEDGE.

9 SIGNATURE OF CERTIFYING PHYSICIAN OR CORONER	10 DATE SIGNED—MM/DD/CCYY	11 TYPED OR PRINTED NAME AND TITLE/DEGREE OF CERTIFIER
Glen Isamu Komatsu M.D	09/30/2009	GLEN ISAMU KOMATSU M.D

12 ADDRESS—STREET AND NUMBER	13 CITY	14 STATE	15 ZIP CODE
4101 TORRANCE BLVD.	TORRANCE	CA	90503

STATE/LOCAL REGISTRAR USE ONLY

16 OFFICE OF VITAL RECORDS OR LOCAL REGISTRAR	17 DATE ACCEPTED FOR REGISTRATION—MM/DD/CCYY
STATE REGISTRAR - OFFICE OF VITAL RECORDS	10/07/2009

STATE OF CALIFORNIA, DEPARTMENT OF PUBLIC HEALTH, OFFICE OF VITAL RECORDS
FORM VS 24A (REV. 1/08)

DC2009000002869

INFORMATIONAL, NOT A VALID DOCUMENT TO ESTABLISH IDENTITY

2 of 2

This is to certify that this document is a true copy of the official record filed with the Registrar-Recorder/County Clerk

JAN 0 4 2010

Dean C. Logan
DEAN C. LOGAN
Registrar-Recorder/County Clerk

This copy not valid unless prepared on engraved border displaying the Seal and Signature of the Registrar-Recorder/County Clerk.

000179256

ANY ALTERATION OR ERASURE VOIDS THIS CERTIFICATE

CERTIFICATE OF DEATH
STATE OF CALIFORNIA—DEPARTMENT OF PUBLIC HEALTH

Local Registration District and Certificate Number: 7053 1597

Decedent Personal Data

- **Name of Deceased:** Carl Dean Switzer
- **Date of Death:** Jan. 21, 1959
- **Hour:** 7:27 P.M.
- **Sex:** Male
- **Color or Race:** Cauc
- **Birthplace:** Illinois
- **Date of Birth:** Aug. 7, 1927
- **Age:** 31 years
- **Name and Birthplace of Father:** George F. Switzer – Illinois
- **Maiden Name and Birthplace of Mother:** Gladys Shanks – Illinois
- **Citizen of what Country:** U.S.A.
- **Social Security Number:** 564-16-6997
- **Last Occupation:** Actor
- **Number of Years in this Occupation:** 26
- **Name of Last Employing Company or Firm:** Stanley-Kramer Productions
- **Kind of Industry or Business:** Motion Pictures
- **If Deceased was ever in U.S. Armed Forces:** No
- **Married, Never Married, Widowed, Divorced:** Divorced

Place of Death

- **Place of Death—Name of Hospital:** Valley Receiving Hospital
- **Street Address:** 14500 Sherman Circle
- **City or Town:** Los Angeles
- **County:** Los Angeles
- **Length of Stay in County of Death:** 26 years
- **Length of Stay in California:** 26 years

Last Usual Residence

- **Street Address:** 5415 Sepulveda Blvd. Apt #2
- **City or Town:** Van Nuys
- **County:** Los Angeles
- **State:** Calif.
- **Name of Informant:** George F. Switzer
- **Address of Informant:** 6122½ Santa Monica Blvd.

Physician's or Coroner's Certification

- **Coroner:** Autopsy & Inquest
- **Address:** Hall of Justice, Los Angeles
- **Date Signed:** 1-26-59

Funeral Director and Local Registrar

- **Burial:** Jan. 27, 1959
- **Name of Cemetery:** Hollywood Memorial Park
- **Embalmer:** Stanley Stratton 4511
- **Name of Funeral Director:** Pierce Bros. Hollywood

Cause of Death

Part I. Death was caused by:
Immediate cause (A): GUNSHOT WOUND OF ABDOMEN WITH MASSIVE INTRA-ABDOMINAL HEMORRHAGE.

Injury Information

- **Specify Accident, Suicide or Homicide:** Justifiable Homicide
- **Describe how injury occurred:** During an altercation
- **Time of Injury:** 7 P.M. 1-21-59
- **Injury Occurred:** Not while at work
- **Place of Injury:** house
- **City, Town, or Location:** Los Angeles, Los Angeles, Calif.

CONNY B. McCORMACK
Registrar-Recorder/County Clerk

JUL 20 2005

019554525

CERTIFICATION OF VITAL RECORD

COUNTY OF LOS ANGELES • REGISTRAR-RECORDER/COUNTY CLERK

PLACE OF DEATH DIST. No. 1901

County of LOS ANGELES
City of LOS ANGELES

California State Board of Health
BUREAU OF VITAL STATISTICS
STANDARD CERTIFICATE OF DEATH

State Index No. 1244
Local Registered No. 967
22-005881

(No. 404 B. So. Alvarado Ward)

FULL NAME William D. Taylor

PERSONAL AND STATISTICAL PARTICULARS

- **SEX:** M
- **COLOR OR RACE:** W
- **SINGLE, MARRIED, WIDOWED, OR DIVORCED:** Divorced
- **DATE OF BIRTH:** March 26, 1872
- **AGE:** 49 years 10 months 5 days
- **OCCUPATION:** Motion Picture Director
- **BIRTHPLACE:** Ireland

CORONER'S CERTIFICATE OF DEATH

DATE OF DEATH: Feb 1st 1922

I HEREBY CERTIFY, as to the person above named and herein described, That on _____ 1922 I held an inquest and the jury rendered a verdict on the death. Or, that I have investigated the death officially on account of

The CAUSE OF DEATH was as follows: Gunshot Wound of the Chest, Homicidal

(Signed) A. F. Wagner
Approved (Signed) Frank A. Nance, Coroner
Feb 3 1922

PLACE OF BURIAL OR REMOVAL: Hollywood Cem. Vault
DATE OF BURIAL: 2/7/22
UNDERTAKER: IVY H OVERHOLTZER

Filed FEB 6 1922
L. M. POWERS, M.D.
Registrar

This is to certify that this document is a true copy of the official record filed with the Registrar-Recorder/County Clerk.

Conny B. McCormack
CONNY B. McCORMACK
Registrar-Recorder/County Clerk

OCT 1 1996
19-382343

This copy not valid unless prepared on engraved border displaying the Seal and Signature of the Registrar-Recorder/County Clerk.

ANY ALTERATION OR ERASURE VOIDS THIS CERTIFICATE

STATE OF CALIFORNIA — CERTIFICATION OF VITAL RECORD

COUNTY OF RIVERSIDE
RIVERSIDE, CALIFORNIA

CERTIFICATE OF DEATH — STATE OF CALIFORNIA
State File Number: 3 2002 33 011949

DECEDENT PERSONAL DATA
- 1. Name (First): JESSE
- 2. Middle: KENNETH
- 3. Last: TOBEY
- 4. Date of Birth: 03/23/1917
- 5. Age: 85
- 6. Sex: M
- 7. Date of Death: 12/22/2002
- 8. Hour: 2109
- 9. State of Birth: CA
- 10. Social Security No.: 572-09-7414
- 11. Military Service: No
- 12. Marital Status: WIDOWED
- 13. Education — Years Completed: 17
- 14. Race: WHITE
- 15. Hispanic: No
- 16. Usual Employer: SELF EMPLOYED
- 17. Occupation: ACTOR
- 18. Kind of Business: T.V., MOTION PICTURES & STAGE
- 19. Years in Occupation: 40

USUAL RESIDENCE
- 20. Residence: 107 SOUTH CALLE MARCUS
- 21. City: PALM SPRINGS
- 22. County: RIVERSIDE
- 23. Zip Code: 92262
- 24. Yrs in County: 2
- 25. State: CA

INFORMANT
- 26. Name, Relationship: TINA R. TOBEY/DAUGHTER
- 27. Mailing Address: P.O. BOX 5233/PALM SPRINGS, CA 92263

SPOUSE AND PARENT INFORMATION
- 31. Name of Father — First: JESSE
- 32. Middle: V.
- 33. Last: TOBEY
- 34. Birth State: CA
- 35. Name of Mother — First: FRANCES
- 37. Last (Maiden): KASAVAN
- 38. Birth State: ARGENTINA

DISPOSITION(S)
- 39. Date: 12/30/2002
- 40. Place of Final Disposition: RES: TINA R. TOBEY, 107 SOUTH CALLE MARCUS/PALM SPRINGS, CA 92262
- 41. Type of Disposition: CR/RES
- 42. Signature of Embalmer: NOT EMBALMED
- 44. Name of Funeral Director: NEPTUNE SOCIETY/RIVERSIDE
- 45. License No.: FD-1307
- 47. Date: 12/26/2002

PLACE OF DEATH
- 101. Place of Death: EISENHOWER MEMORIAL HOSPITAL (IP)
- 104. County: RIVERSIDE
- 105. Street Address: 39000 BOB HOPE DRIVE
- 106. City: RANCHO MIRAGE

CAUSE OF DEATH
- 107. Death was caused by:
  - (A) IMMEDIATE CAUSE: CARDIORESPIRATORY ARREST — IMMED.
  - (B) DUE TO: MULTI-ORGAN SYSTEM FAILURE — DAYS
  - (C) DUE TO: MRSA WITH FUNGAL SEPSIS — DAYS
  - (D) DUE TO: PEMPHIGUS — YEARS
- 108. Death Reported to Coroner: YES — 2002-7552
- 109. Biopsy Performed: No
- 110. Autopsy Performed: No
- 112. Other Significant Conditions: DIABETES MELLITUS, CORONARY ARTERY DISEASE
- 113. Was Operation Performed: NO

PHYSICIAN'S CERTIFICATION
- 116. License No.: A55350
- 117. Date: 12/26/2002
- 118. Attending Physician: RAVINDERPAL S. MANN, M.D., 39000 BOB HOPE DRIVE/RANCHO MIRAGE, CA 92270
- Decedent Attended Since: 12/04/2002
- Decedent Last Seen Alive: 12/22/2002

FAX AUTH. #: 261685

CERTIFIED COPY OF VITAL RECORDS
STATE OF CALIFORNIA, COUNTY OF RIVERSIDE

33372201

DATE ISSUED: JAN 0 8 2003

GARY L. ORSO
COUNTY CLERK-RECORDER
RIVERSIDE COUNTY, CALIFORNIA

CERTIFICATE OF DEATH
STATE OF CALIFORNIA

State File Number: 38956003375

Decedent Personal Data
- **1A. Name (Given):** LEE
- **1B. Middle:** ---
- **1C. Last (Family):** VAN CLEEF
- **2A. Date of Death:** Dec. 16, 1989
- **2B. Hour:** 0004
- **3. Sex:** Male
- **4. Race:** White
- **5. Spanish/Hispanic:** No
- **6. Date of Birth:** January 9, 1925
- **7. Age in Years:** 64
- **8. State of Birth:** NJ
- **9. Citizen of What Country:** U.S.A.
- **10A. Full Name of Father:** Clarence L. Van Cleef
- **10B. State of Birth:** NJ
- **11A. Full Maiden Name of Mother:** Marian L. Van Fleet
- **11B. State of Birth:** NJ
- **12. Military Service:** 1942 to 1945
- **13. Social Security Number:** 006-26-2483
- **14. Marital Status:** Married
- **15. Name of Surviving Spouse:** Barbara Hevelope
- **16A. Usual Occupation:** Actor
- **16B. Usual Kind of Business or Industry:** Entertainment
- **16C. Usual Employer:** Self-employed
- **16D. Years in Usual Occupation:** 40
- **17. Number of Highest Grade Completed:** 12

Usual Residence
- **18A. Street:** 19471 Rosita St.
- **18B. City:** Tarzana
- **18C. Zip:** 91356
- **18D. County:** Los Angeles
- **18E. Number of Years in this County:** 40
- **18F. State:** California
- **20. Name, Relationship, Mailing Address of Informant:** Mrs. Barbara Van Cleef (wife), 19471 Rosita St., Tarzana, CA 91356

Place of Death
- **19A. Place of Death:** St. John's Reg. Med. Ctr.
- **19B. If Hospital:** ER
- **19C. County:** Ventura
- **19D. Street Address:** 333 No. F St.
- **19E. City:** Oxnard
- **22. Was Death Reported to Coroner:** Yes, 1881-89

Cause of Death
- **21.** Death was caused by:
  - (A) Acute Myocardial infarction — 1 hr. — Autopsy: No
  - (B) Carcinoma of epiglottis c̄ neck metastases — 2 wks.
  - (C) Congestive cardiomyopathy — 1-2 yrs.
- **24.** Other significant conditions: Peripheral vascular disease
- **25.** Operation: 12/14/89 — Panendoscopy with biopsy

Physician's Certification
- **27A. Decedent attended since:** 4/28/88
- **Last seen alive:** 12/14/89
- **27C. Physician's License Number:** A35437
- **27D. Date Signed:** 12/18/89
- **27E. Physician's Name and Address:** Stephen Hong, M.D., 921 W. 7th St., Oxnard, CA

Funeral Director and Local Registrar
- **34A. Disposition:** Burial
- **34B. Place of Final Disposition:** Forest Lawn Memorial Park, Los Angeles, CA
- **34C. Date of Disposition:** 12/21/89
- **35B. License Number:** 7653
- **36A. Name of Funeral Director:** Forest Lawn-Hollywood Hills Mty
- **36B. License No.:** F904
- **38. Registration Date:** 12/19/89

This is a true certified copy of the record if it bears the seal, imprinted in purple ink, of the County Recorder.

FEB 26 1990

RICHARD D. DEAN, COUNTY RECORDER
VENTURA COUNTY, CALIFORNIA

Certificate of Death

State of California — County of Los Angeles • Registrar-Recorder/County Clerk

State File Number: 3 2001 19 010765

Decedent Personal Data

- 1. Name (First): KIM
- 2. Middle: ANNE
- 3. Last: WALKER
- 4. Date of Birth: 06/19/1968
- 5. Age: 32
- 6. Sex: F
- 7. Date of Death: 03/06/2001
- 8. Hour: 0630
- 9. State of Birth: NY
- 10. Social Security No.: 085-68-1387
- 11. Military Service: No
- 12. Marital Status: NEVER MARRIED
- 13. Education—Years Completed: 13
- 14. Race: CAUCASIAN
- 15. Hispanic: No
- 16. Usual Employer: SELF-EMPLOYED
- 17. Occupation: ACTRESS
- 18. Kind of Business: ENTERTAINMENT
- 19. Years in Occupation: 17
- 20. Residence: 11930 BRIARVALE LANE
- 21. City: STUDIO CITY
- 22. County: LOS ANGELES
- 23. Zip: 91604
- 24. Yrs in County: 9
- 25. State: CA
- 26. Informant Name/Relationship: RUTH M. WALKER — MOTHER
- 27. Mailing Address: 530 E. 20TH ST., APT. 3B, NEW YORK, NEW YORK 10009

Spouse and Parent Information

- 31. Father First: HERBERT
- 32. Middle: H.
- 33. Last: WALKER
- 34. Birth State: NY
- 35. Mother First: RUTH
- 36. Middle: MARY
- 37. Last (Maiden): WEIGEL
- 38. Birth State: NY

Disposition / Funeral Director

- 39. Date: 03/10/2001
- 40. Place of Final Disposition: PINELAWN MEMORIAL PARK, FARMINGDALE, NEW YORK 11735
- 41. Type of Disposition: TR/BU
- 43. License No.: 6353
- 44. Name of Funeral Director: VALLEY FUNERAL HOME
- 45. License No.: FD 976
- 47. Date: 03/07/2001

Place of Death

- 101. Place of Death: RESIDENCE
- 104. County: LOS ANGELES
- 105. Street Address: 11930 BRIARVALE LANE
- 106. City: STUDIO CITY

Cause of Death

- 107. (A) Immediate Cause: CEREBRAL HERNIATION — Hours
- (B) Due to: MALIGNANT GLIOMA — 2 YEARS
- 108. Death Reported to Coroner: No
- 109. Biopsy Performed: Yes
- 110. Autopsy Performed: No
- 112. Other Significant Conditions: NONE
- 113. Operation Performed: YES, CRANIOTOMY 01/10/1999

Physician's Certification

- 114. Decedent Attended Since: 06/15/2000; Last Seen Alive: 03/04/2001
- 116. License No.: G63435
- 117. Date: 03/07/2001
- 118. Attending Physician: TIMOTHY F. CLOUGHESY, M.D., 710 WESTWOOD PLAZA, LOS ANGELES, CA 90095

Fax Auth. #: 195/4976

Conny B. McCormack, Registrar-Recorder/County Clerk

OCT 04 2001
19-673779

COUNTY OF LOS ANGELES
DEPARTMENT OF HEALTH SERVICES

CERTIFICATE OF DEATH
STATE OF CALIFORNIA

1. NAME OF DECEDENT — FIRST (Given): Michael
2. MIDDLE: Anthony
3. LAST (Family): Wayne
4. DATE OF BIRTH: 11/23/1934
5. AGE Yrs.: 68
6. SEX: Male
9. BIRTH STATE/FOREIGN COUNTRY: California
10. SOCIAL SECURITY NUMBER: 551-42-4154
11. EVER IN U.S. ARMED FORCES?: Yes
12. MARITAL STATUS: Married
7. DATE OF DEATH: 04/02/2003
8. HOUR: 1443
13. EDUCATION: Bachelor's
14/15. WAS DECEDENT SPANISH/HISPANIC/LATINO?: No
16. DECEDENT'S RACE: White
17. USUAL OCCUPATION: Film Producer/Executive
18. KIND OF BUSINESS OR INDUSTRY: Entertainment
19. YEARS IN OCCUPATION: 50
20. DECEDENT'S RESIDENCE: 10425 Kling St.
21. CITY: North Hollywood
22. COUNTY/PROVINCE: Los Angeles
23. ZIP CODE: 91602
24. YEARS IN COUNTY: 68
25. STATE/FOREIGN COUNTRY: CA
26. INFORMANT'S NAME, RELATIONSHIP: Gretchen A. Wayne - Wife
27. INFORMANT'S MAILING ADDRESS: 10425 Kling St., North Hollywood, CA 91602
28. NAME OF SURVIVING SPOUSE — FIRST: Gretchen
29. MIDDLE: Ann
30. LAST (Maiden Name): Deibel
31. NAME OF FATHER — FIRST: John
32. MIDDLE: —
33. LAST: Wayne
34. BIRTH STATE: Iowa
35. NAME OF MOTHER — FIRST: Josephine
36. MIDDLE: Alicia
37. LAST (Maiden): Saenz
38. BIRTH STATE: Texas
39. DISPOSITION DATE: 04/09/2003
40. PLACE OF FINAL DISPOSITION: Forest Lawn Memorial Park, 6300 Forest Lawn Dr., Los Angeles, CA 90068
41. TYPE OF DISPOSITION(S): BU
42. SIGNATURE OF EMBALMER: Jeff Turner
43. LICENSE NUMBER: 7693
44. NAME OF FUNERAL ESTABLISHMENT: O'Connor Laguna Hills Mortuary
45. LICENSE NUMBER: FD1293
46. SIGNATURE OF LOCAL REGISTRAR: Thomas L Garthwaite
47. DATE: 04/04/2003
101. PLACE OF DEATH: Providence St. Joseph Medical Center
102. IF HOSPITAL, SPECIFY ONE: IP
104. COUNTY: Los Angeles
105. FACILITY ADDRESS OR LOCATION WHERE FOUND: 501 South Buena Vista
106. CITY: Burbank

107. CAUSE OF DEATH:
- IMMEDIATE CAUSE (A): Cardiopulmonary Arrest — Mins
- (B): Septic Shock — Days
- (C): Fungemia — Days
- (D): Diverticulitis — Days

108. DEATH REPORTED TO CORONER?: No
109. BIOPSY PERFORMED?: Yes
110. AUTOPSY PERFORMED?: No
111. USED IN DETERMINING CAUSE?: —

112. OTHER SIGNIFICANT CONDITIONS CONTRIBUTING TO DEATH: Lupus Erythematosus; Coronary Artery Disease
113. WAS OPERATION PERFORMED FOR ANY CONDITION IN ITEM 107 OR 112?: Partial Subtotal Colectomy 03/25/2003
115. SIGNATURE AND TITLE OF CERTIFIER: David Sato
116. LICENSE NUMBER: G43700
117. DATE: 04/04/2003
Decedent Attended Since: 03/31/2003
Decedent Last Been Alive: 04/02/2003
118. TYPE ATTENDING PHYSICIAN'S NAME, MAILING ADDRESS, ZIP CODE: David Sato MD 2601 W. Alameda #100, Burbank, CA 91505

This is a true certified copy of the record filed in the County of Los Angeles Department of Health Services if it bears the Registrar's signature in purple ink.

Thomas L Garthwaite
Director of Health Services and Registrar

DATE ISSUED: APR 09 2003

This copy not valid unless prepared on engraved border displaying seal and signature of Registrar.

Certificate of Death — State of California

1A. Name of Decedent (First)	LAWRENCE
1C. Last (Family)	WELK
2A. Date of Death	MAY 17, 1992
3. Sex	M
4. Race	CAUCASIAN
5. Hispanic	No
6. Date of Birth	MARCH 11, 1903
7. Age in Years	89
8. State of Birth	ND
9. Citizen of What Country	USA
10A. Full Name of Father	LUDWIG WELK
10B. State of Birth	GERMANY
11A. Full Maiden Name of Mother	CHRISTINA SCHWAHN
11B. State of Birth	GERMANY
12. Military Service	NONE
13. Social Security No.	508-05-6713
14. Marital Status	MARRIED
15. Name of Surviving Spouse	FERN RENNER
16A. Usual Occupation	MUSICIAN
16B. Usual Kind of Business or Industry	ENTERTAINMENT
16C. Usual Employer	SELF-EMPLOYED
16D. Years in Occupation	63
17. Education — Years Completed	3
18A. Residence — Street and Number or Location	1299 OCEAN AVE. #800
18B. City	SANTA MONICA
18C. Zip Code	90401
18D. County	LOS ANGELES
18E. Number of Years in This County	41
18F. State or Foreign Country	CA
20. Name, Relationship, Mailing Address and Zip Code of Informant	SHIRLEY FREDRICKS - DAUGHTER, 1299 OCEAN AVE. #800, SANTA MONICA, CA. 90401
19A. Place of Death	RESIDENCE
19C. County	LOS ANGELES
19D. Street Address	1299 OCEAN AVE. #800
19E. City	SANTA MONICA
21. Death Was Caused By: Immediate Cause (A)	BRONCHO PNEUMONIA
Time Interval Between Onset and Death	4 DAYS
22. Was Death Reported to Coroner?	NO
23. Was Biopsy Performed?	NO
24A. Was Autopsy Performed?	NO
24B. Was It Used in Determining Cause of Death?	NO
25. Other Significant Conditions Contributing to Death But Not Related to Cause Given in 21	CEREBROVASCULAR INSUFFICENCY
26. Was Operation Performed for Any Condition in Item 21 or 25?	NO
27A. Decedent Attended Since	3/12/81
Decedent Last Seen Alive	5/12/92
27B. Signature and Degree or Title of Certifier	Jaime Paris MD
27C. Certifier's License Number	G7370
27D. Date Signed	5.18.92
27E. Attending Physician's Name and Address	JAIME PARIS, MD. 2021 SANTA MONICA BL. SANTA MONICA, CA. 90404
34A. Disposition	BURIAL
34B. Place of Final Disposition	HOLY CROSS CEMETERY, CULVER CITY, CA.
34C. Date	5/20/92
35A. Signature of Embalmer	Bernard Johnson
35B. License Number	7317
36A. Name of Funeral Director	GATES, KINGSLEY & GATES SM
36B. License No.	FD-451
37. Signature of Local Registrar	Robert C. [illegible]
38. Registration Date	MAY 19 1992

THIS IS A TRUE CERTIFIED COPY OF THE RECORD FILED IN THE COUNTY OF LOS ANGELES DEPARTMENT OF HEALTH SERVICES IF IT BEARS THIS SEAL IN PURPLE INK.

MAY 20 1992

CERTIFICATION OF VITAL RECORD

COUNTY OF LOS ANGELES • REGISTRAR-RECORDER/COUNTY CLERK

CERTIFICATE OF DEATH — STATE OF CALIFORNIA

State File Number: 39019008223

1A. Name of Decedent: CHARLES WEEDON WESTOVER
3A. Date of Death: February 8, 1990 — 2341
3B. Sex: MALE
4. Race: CAU/AMERICAN
5. Spanish/Hispanic: No
6. Date of Birth: DECEMBER 30, 1934
7. Age: 55
8. State of Birth: MI
9. Citizen of What Country: U.S.A.
10A. Full Name of Father: BERT LEON WESTOVER
10B. State of Birth: MI
11A. Full Maiden Name of Mother: LEONE MOSHER
11B. State of Birth: MI
12. Military Service: 1955 to 1957
13. Social Security No.: 365-34-3005
14. Marital Status: MARRIED
15. Name of Surviving Spouse: BONNIE TYSON
16A. Usual Occupation: SINGER-SONGWRITER
16B. Usual Kind of Business or Industry: MUSIC INDUSTRY
16C. Usual Employer: SELF-EMPLOYED
16D. Years in Occupation: 25
17. Education — Years Completed: 12

18A. Residence — Street and Number or Location: 15519 SADDLEBACK ROAD
18B. City: CANYON COUNTRY
18C. Zip Code: 91351
18D. County: LOS ANGELES
18E. Number of Years in This County: 25
18F. State or Foreign Country: CALIFORNIA

20. Name, Relationship, Mailing Address and Zip Code of Informant: BONNIE WESTOVER — WIFE, 15519 SADDLEBACK ROAD, CANYON COUNTRY, CA 91351

19A. Place of Death: Residence
19B. Hospital: —
19C. County: Los Angeles
19D. Street Address: 15519 Saddleback Rd.
19E. City: Canyon Country

Was Death Reported to Coroner? Yes — 90-01453

21. Death was Caused By:
(A) IMMEDIATE CAUSE: GUNSHOT WOUND OF HEAD — Time Interval: UNK.

22. Was Biopsy Performed? No
24A. Was Autopsy Performed? Yes
24B. Was It Used in Determining Cause of Death? Yes

23. Other Significant Conditions Contributing to Death: NONE
25. Was Operation Performed for Any Condition: NO

26A. Signature and Title of Coroner: Deputy Coroner — [signature]
26B. Date Signed: 2-12-1990

29. Manner of Death: Suicide
30A. Place of Injury: Office
30B. Injury at Work: No
30C. Date of Injury: 2-8-1990
31. Hour: Unk.
32. Location: 15519 Saddleback Rd., Canyon Country
33. Describe How Injury Occurred: Self inflicted Shot

34A. Disposition: CR/RES
34B. Place of Final Disposition: RES: 15519 SADDLEBACK RD., CANYON COUNTRY, CA
34C. Date: 2/2/90
35A. Signature of Embalmer: NOT EMBALMED
35B. License Number: N/A
36A. Name of Funeral Director: NEPTUNE SOCIETY
36B. License No.: F1289

Registration Date: FEB 26 1990

This is to certify that this document is a true copy of the official record filed with the Registrar-Recorder/County Clerk.

Beatriz Valdez
BEATRIZ VALDEZ
Registrar-Recorder/County Clerk

NOV 22 1990

This copy not valid unless prepared on engraved border displaying the Seal and Signature of the Registrar-Recorder/County Clerk.

CERTIFICATE OF DEATH

STATE OF CONNECTICUT — DEPARTMENT OF PUBLIC HEALTH
VS-4 REV. 1/04

1. **Decedent's Legal Name:** RICHARD WIDMARK
2. **Sex:** Male
3. **Actual or Presumed Date of Death:** MARCH 24, 2008
4. **Actual or Presumed Time of Death:** 3:44 PM
5. **Age Last Birthday:** 93
7. **Date of Birth:** DECEMBER 26, 1914
8. **Birthplace:** SUNRISE, MN
9. **Residence (State):** CONN
10. **Residence (County):** LITCHFIELD
11. **Residence (City or Town):** ROXBURY
12. **Residence (Street and No.):** 76 DAVENPORT ROAD
14. **Zip Code:** 06783
15. **Ever in US Armed Forces?** No
16. **Marital Status at Time of Death:** Married
17. **Surviving Spouse's Name:** SUSAN JACOBSON
18. **Father's Name:** CARL WIDMARK
19. **Mother's Name Prior to First Marriage:** MAE BARR
20. **Informant's Name:** SUSAN BLANCHARD
21. **Informant's Relationship to Decedent:** SPOUSE
22. **Mailing Address:** 76 DAVENPORT RD, ROXBURY, CT 06783
23. **If Death Occurred in a Hospital:** (none checked)
24. **If Death Occurred Somewhere Other Than a Hospital:** Decedent's Home
25. **Facility Name:** 76 DAVENPORT ROAD
26. **City or Town of Death:** ROXBURY
    Zip Code: 06783
27. **County of Death:** LITCHFIELD
28. **Method of Disposition:** Cremation
29. **Disposition (Name of cemetery, crematory, other place):** MOUNTAIN GROVE
30. **Location (city/town, state):** BRIDGEPORT, CT 06776
31. **Date:** 03/27/0
32. **Was Body Embalmed?** No
33. **Funeral Facility:** Lillis F.H. 58 Bridge St. New Milford, CT
34. **Signature of Funeral Director or Embalmer:** Lawrence Lillis
35. **License Number:** 1953
36. **Date Pronounced Dead:** 03/24/08
37. **Time Pronounced:** 3:44 PM
38. **Nurse Pronouncement Name:** Sharilynne Buchanan RN
40. **Date Signed:** 3/24/0
41. **Was Medical Examiner Contacted?** No / CASE 08-04114
42. **Was an Autopsy Performed?** No

Cause of Death

PART I.
(a) **Immediate Cause:** Aspiration Pneumonia
(b) **Due to:** Renal Failure

46. **If Female:** —
47. **Did Tobacco Use Contribute to Death?** No
48. **Certifier:** Certifying Practitioner
    Certifier Name: Alphonse D. Altorelli, MD
    Date Certified: 03/27/08
49. **Mailing - Certifier:** 115 New Milford Tpke, New Preston, CT 06777

This Certificate Was Received for Record on: Mar. 28, 2008

50. **Decedent's Education:** Bachelor's degree
51. **Decedent of Hispanic Origin?** No, Not Spanish/Hispanic/Latino
52. **Decedent's Race:** White
53. **Decedent's Usual Occupation:** ACTOR
54. **Kind of Business/Industry:** THEATRE & FILM

Dick Wilson

STATE OF CALIFORNIA — CERTIFICATION OF VITAL RECORD

COUNTY OF LOS ANGELES • REGISTRAR-RECORDER/COUNTY CLERK

CERTIFICATE OF DEATH — State File Number: 3200719047337

- **Name of Decedent:** DICK WILSON
- **Date of Birth:** 07/30/1916
- **Age:** 91
- **Sex:** M
- **Birth State/Foreign Country:** ENGLAND
- **Social Security Number:** 112-22-9885
- **Ever in U.S. Armed Forces:** No
- **Marital Status:** MARRIED
- **Date of Death:** 11/18/2007
- **Hour:** 0252
- **Education:** BACHELOR
- **Hispanic/Latino:** No
- **Race:** WHITE
- **Usual Occupation:** ACTOR
- **Kind of Business/Industry:** ENTERTAINMENT
- **Years in Occupation:** 65
- **Decedent's Residence:** 4323 BAKMAN AVE, STUDIO CITY, LOS ANGELES, 91602, CA
- **Years in County:** 65
- **Informant's Name, Relationship:** MARGARET WILSON, WIFE
- **Informant's Mailing Address:** 4323 BAKMAN AVE., STUDIO CITY, CA 91602
- **Name of Surviving Spouse:** EMILY MARGARET BROWN
- **Name of Father:** RANDOLPH WILSON — Birth State: ENGLAND
- **Name of Mother:** VERONICA BROWN — Birth State: ENGLAND
- **Disposition Date:** 11/26/2007
- **Place of Final Disposition:** FOREST LAWN MEMORIAL PARK, 6300 FOREST LAWN DR., LOS ANGELES, CA 90068
- **Type of Disposition:** CR/BU
- **Signature of Embalmer:** NOT EMBALMED
- **Name of Funeral Establishment:** FOREST LAWN MEMR PRKS & MTYS
- **License Number:** FD-904
- **Signature of Local Registrar:** JONATHAN FIELDING, MD — 11/21/2007
- **Place of Death:** MOTION PICTURE HOSPITAL (Hospital: Inpatient)
- **County:** LOS ANGELES
- **Facility Address:** 23388 MULHOLLAND DR
- **City:** WOODLAND HILLS
- **Cause of Death (Immediate):** DEMENTIA OF ALZHEIMER'S TYPE — YRS
- **Death Reported to Coroner:** No
- **Biopsy Performed:** No
- **Autopsy Performed:** No
- **Other Significant Conditions:** NONE
- **Operation Performed:** No
- **Certifier:** SAEED HUMAYUN M.D., License A39209, 11/21/2007
- **Attending Physician:** SAEED HUMAYUN M.D., 23388 MULHOLLAND DR, WOODLAND HILLS, CA 91364
- **Decedent Attended Since:** 08/21/2002
- **Decedent Last Seen Alive:** 11/16/2007

Date issued: SEP 16 2009

Dean C. Logan, Registrar-Recorder/County Clerk

Arthur Wilson

CERTIFICATE OF DEATH
STATE OF CALIFORNIA—DEPARTMENT OF PUBLIC HEALTH

Registration District No: 1901
Registrar's Number: 9672

Name of Deceased: ARTHUR DOOLEY WILSON
Date of Death: May 30, 1953, 5:10 PM
Sex: Male
Color or Race: Negro
Marital Status: Married
Date of Birth: April 3, 1886
Age: 67 years
Usual Occupation: Actor (Retired)
Kind of Business or Industry: Stage and Screen
Birthplace: Tyler, Texas
Citizen of: USA
Father: Unknown Wilson — Unknown
Mother: Amanda Lampkin — Unknown
Present Spouse: Estelle Wilson
Was deceased ever in U.S. Armed Forces: No
Social Security Number: 124-01-8377
Informant: Estelle Wilson

Place of Death:
- County: Los Angeles
- City or Town: Los Angeles
- Length of stay in this city or town: 12 yrs
- Address: 2800 So. Sycamore

Last Usual Residence:
- State: California
- County: Los Angeles
- City or Town: Los Angeles
- Street: 2800 So. Sycamore

Physician's Certification: M. A. Rosenfeld, M.D., 6317 Wilshire Blvd
- Attended deceased from 3-23-44 to 5-30-53
- Last saw deceased alive 5-30-53
- Date Signed: 6-1-53

Funeral Director and Registrar:
- Burial: 6-6-1953
- Cemetery: Rosedale Cemetery
- Embalmer: Ralph L. Turner, License 3316
- Funeral Director: Angelus Funeral Home, 1030 E. Jefferson Blvd
- Date Received by Local Registrar: JUN 2 1953

Cause of Death:
(a) Cerebral Thrombosis — 1 mo.
Antecedent causes:
(b) Coronary Thrombosis —
Essential Hypertension
Cardiac Hypertrophy — 6 yrs+

This is to certify that this document is a true copy of the official record filed with the Registrar-Recorder/County Clerk.

Conny B. McCormack
Registrar-Recorder/County Clerk

JAN 2 2002
19-796834

STATE OF CALIFORNIA
CERTIFICATION OF VITAL RECORD

COUNTY OF LOS ANGELES • REGISTRAR-RECORDER/COUNTY CLERK

CERTIFICATE OF DEATH — STATE OF CALIFORNIA
State File Number: 3 2006 19 048460

DECEDENT'S PERSONAL DATA

- **1. Name of Decedent – First (Given):** JOY
- **2. Middle:** WINDSOR
- **3. Last (Family):** ELLIS
- **4. Date of Birth:** 02/04/1935
- **6. Age:** 71
- **8. Sex:** F
- **9. Birth State/Foreign Country:** MISSOURI
- **10. Social Security Number:** 555-10-1510
- **11. Ever in U.S. Armed Forces?:** NO
- **12. Marital Status at Time of Death:** DIVORCED
- **7. Date of Death:** 11/05/2006
- **8. Hour (24 Hours):** 0934
- **13. Education – Highest Level/Degree:** BACHELOR'S
- **14/15. Was Decedent Hispanic/Latino(a)/Spanish?:** NO
- **16. Decedent's Race:** CAUCASIAN
- **17. Usual Occupation:** ACTRESS
- **18. Kind of Business or Industry:** MOTION PICTURES
- **19. Years in Occupation:** 26

USUAL RESIDENCE

- **20. Decedent's Residence:** 1437 14TH STREET #36
- **21. City:** SANTA MONICA
- **22. County/Province:** LOS ANGELES
- **23. Zip Code:** 90404
- **24. Years in County:** 67
- **25. State/Foreign Country:** CA

INFORMANT

- **26. Informant's Name, Relationship:** PAULA STEIGER – DAUGHTER
- **27. Informant's Mailing Address:** 6740 WILDLIFE ROAD MALIBU, CA 90265

SPOUSE/SRDP AND PARENT INFORMATION

- **28. Name of Surviving Spouse/SRDP – First:** —
- **29. Middle:** —
- **30. Last (Birth Name):** —
- **31. Name of Father/Parent – First:** WILLIAM
- **32. Middle:** E
- **33. Last:** SMITH
- **34. Birth State:** MISSOURI
- **35. Name of Mother/Parent – First:** EMILY
- **36. Middle:** —
- **37. Last (Birth Name):** RICHARDS
- **38. Birth State:** MISSOURI

FUNERAL DIRECTOR/LOCAL REGISTRAR

- **39. Disposition Date:** 11/17/2006
- **40. Place of Final Disposition:** OFF THE COAST OF MARINA DEL REY, LOS ANGELES COUNTY
- **41. Type of Disposition(s):** CR/SEA
- **42. Signature of Embalmer:** NOT EMBALMED
- **44. Name of Funeral Establishment:** HOLY CROSS MORTUARY
- **45. License Number:** FD-1711
- **46. Signature of Local Registrar:** Jonathan E Fielding MD MPH
- **47. Date:** 11/15/2006

PLACE OF DEATH

- **101. Place of Death:** CRESENT BAY CONVALESCENT
- **102:** Nursing Home
- **104. County:** LOS ANGELES
- **105. Facility Address or Location:** 1437 14TH STREET
- **106. City:** SANTA MONICA

CAUSE OF DEATH

- **107. Cause of Death:**
  - (A) Immediate Cause: RESPIRATORY ARREST — MINS
  - (B) END STAGE RESPIRATORY FAILURE — MOS
  - (C) CHRONIC OBSTRUCTIVE LUNG DISEASE — YRS
  - (D) TOBACCO USE — YRS
- **108. Death Reported to Coroner?:** NO
- **109. Biopsy Performed?:** NO
- **110. Autopsy Performed?:** NO
- **111. Used in Determining Cause?:** NO
- **112. Other Significant Conditions:** NONE
- **113. Was Operation Performed:** NO
- **113A. If Female, Pregnant in Last Year?:** NO

PHYSICIAN'S CERTIFICATION

- **114.** I certify that to my knowledge death occurred at the hour, date, and place stated from the causes stated.
- **115. Signature and Title of Certifier:** [signed]
- **116. License Number:** G30557
- **117. Date:** 11/08/2006
- **(A) Decedent Attended Since:** 04/18/1994
- **(B) Decedent Last Seen Alive:** 11/02/2006
- **118. Type Attending Physician's Name, Mailing Address, Zip Code:** SCOTT BATEMAN, MD 23410 CIVIC CENTER WAY MALIBU, CA 90265

Fax Auth #: 162-4426

This is to certify that this document is a true copy of the official record filed with the Registrar-Recorder/County Clerk.

SEP 16 2009

Dean C. Logan
DEAN C. LOGAN
Registrar-Recorder/County Clerk

000004573

STANLEY WINSTON

COUNTY OF LOS ANGELES
DEPARTMENT OF HEALTH SERVICES

CERTIFICATE OF DEATH — 3 2005 19 000 618

1. Name of Decedent — First	THELMA
3. Last (Family)	MILLARD
AKA	THELMA WHITE
4. Date of Birth	12/04/1910
5. Age	94
6. Sex	F
9. Birth State/Foreign Country	NEBRASKA
10. Social Security Number	553-12-7006
11. Ever in U.S. Armed Forces?	NO
12. Marital Status	WIDOWED
7. Date of Death	01/04/2005
8. Hour	2355
13. Education	8
14/15. Hispanic?	NO
16. Race	CAUCASIAN
17. Usual Occupation	ACTRESS
18. Kind of Business/Industry	MOTION PICTURES
19. Years in Occupation	67
20. Decedent's Residence	23388 MULHOLLAND DR.
21. City	WOODLAND HILLS
22. County	LOS ANGELES
23. Zip Code	91302
24. Years in County	60
25. State	CALIFORNIA
26. Informant's Name, Relationship	MICHAEL HOMEIER — GOD-SON
27. Informant's Mailing Address	1134 EUCLID ST. SANTA MONICA, CA 90403
31. Name of Father — First	HARRY
32. Middle	DAVID
33. Last	WOLPA
34. Birth State	NB
35. Name of Mother — First	MYRTLE
36. Middle	NINA
37. Last (Maiden)	JOHNSON
38. Birth State	IOWA
39. Disposition Date	01/28/2005
40. Place of Final Disposition	VALHALLA MEMORIAL PARK — NORTH HOLLYWOOD, CA
41. Type of Disposition	CR/BU
42. Signature of Embalmer	NOT EMBALMED
44. Name of Funeral Establishment	BASTIAN & PERROTT MORTUARY
45. License Number	FD-1198
47. Date	01/26/2005
101. Place of Death	MOTION PICTURE & T.V. HOSPITAL
104. County	LOS ANGELES
105. Facility Address	23388 MULHOLLAND DR.
106. City	WOODLAND HILLS

107. Cause of Death:
- (A) IMMEDIATE CAUSE: ACUTE RESPIRATORY FAILURE — 6 HRS
- (B) PNEUMONIA — 12 HRS
- (C) CHRONIC OBSTRUCTIVE PULMONARY DISEASE — 10 YRS

112. Other Significant Conditions: GENERALIZED ATHEROSCLEROSIS

113. Was Operation Performed: NO

114. Decedent Attended Since	08/31/1999
Decedent Last Seen Alive	01/04/2005
116. License Number	A39209
117. Date	01/05/2005
118. Attending Physician	SAEED HUMAYUN, MD. 23388 MULHOLLAND DR. WOODLAND HILLS, CA 91364
Fax Auth. #	197/3673

DATE ISSUED: MAY 0 3 2005

Director of Health Services and Registrar

CERTIFICATE OF DEATH
STATE OF CALIFORNIA—DEPARTMENT OF PUBLIC HEALTH

Local Registration District and Certificate Number: 7097-026585

DECEDENT PERSONAL DATA

- 1a. Name of Deceased—First Name: ED
- 1b. Middle Name: (blank)
- 1c. Last Name: WYNN
- 2a. Date of Death: JUNE 19, 1966
- 2b. Hour: 7:33 A.M.
- 3. Sex: male
- 4. Color or Race: caucasian
- 5. Birthplace: Pennsylvania
- 6. Date of Birth: November 9, 1886
- 7. Age: 79 years
- 8. Name and Birthplace of Father: Joseph Leopold–Austria
- 9. Maiden Name and Birthplace of Mother: Emily Unknown–Turkey
- 10. Citizen of What Country: U.S.A.
- 11. Social Security Number: 125-03-7803
- 12. Last Occupation: Actor
- 13. Number of Years in This Occupation: 65
- 14. Name of Last Employing Company or Firm: Self Employed
- 15. Kind of Industry or Business: Entertainment
- 16. If Deceased was Ever in U.S. Armed Forces: No
- 17. Specify Married, Never Married, Widowed, Divorced: Divorced
- 18a. Name of Present Spouse: —

PLACE OF DEATH

- 19a. Place of Death—Name of Hospital: None
- 19b. Street Address: 10401 Wilshire Blvd.
- 19c. City or Town: Los Angeles
- 19d. County: Los Angeles
- 19e. Length of Stay in County of Death: 20 years
- 19f. Length of Stay in California: 20 years

LAST USUAL RESIDENCE

- 20a. Street Address: 10401 Wilshire Blvd.
- 20c. City or Town: Los Angeles
- 20d. County: Los Angeles (2651)
- 20e. State: California
- 21a. Name of Informant: Frank Keenan Wynn
- 21b. Address of Informant: 12760 Hanover St., Los Angeles, Calif.

PHYSICIAN'S OR CORONER'S CERTIFICATION

- 22a. Physician: present; From 1951 to present; Last saw deceased alive on 6-18-66
- 22c. Physician or Coroner—Signature: John B. McDonald M.D.
- 22d. Address: 133 S. Lasky Drive, Beverly Hills, California
- 22e. Date Signed: 6-20-66

FUNERAL DIRECTOR AND LOCAL REGISTRAR

- 23. Specify Burial, Entombment or Cremation: Cremation
- 24. Date: 6-23-66
- 25. Name of Cemetery or Crematory: Forest Lawn Memorial-Park
- 26. Embalmer—Signature: Frederick B. MacDonald 3657
- 27. Name of Funeral Director: Forest Lawn Memorial-Park, Glendale, California
- 28. Date Accepted for Registration by Local Registrar: JUN 23 1966
- 29. Local Registrar—Signature: (signed)

CAUSE OF DEATH

- 30. Part I. Death was caused by:
  - (a) Immediate Cause: Undifferentiated Malignant neoplasm with widespread metastasis — Approximate Interval Between Onset and Death: 1 yr.

OPERATION AND AUTOPSY

- 31. Operation: Operation Performed—Findings Not Used in Determining Causes of Death (X)
- 32. Date of Operation: 6-8-65
- 33. Autopsy: Gross Findings Not Used in Determining Causes of Death (X)

Filed JUL 15 1966 — RAY E. LEE, COUNTY RECORDER

Signed: Beatriz Valdez, Registrar-Recorder/County Clerk

AUG 10 1995
19-389289

BIOGRAPHICAL NOTES

Edie Adams (Professional Name and Name on the Death Certificate); Elizabeth Edith Eke (Birth Name); **p. 4**—She started her career on Broadway in *Blithe Spirit*. She appeared in three of Ernie Kovacs' early television programs, *Ernie in Kovacsland, Kovacs on the Korner*, and the *Ernie Kovacs Show*. She was the spokesperson for Muriel Cigars for many years.

Stella Adler (Professional Name, Birth Name and Name on Death Certificate); Stella Ardler (Professional Name for her short movie career); **p. 5**—Known more for her teaching methods than her acting, she appeared on the silver screen in *My Girl Tisa* and the *Shadow of the Thin Man*. Her stage career began at age four in the play *Broken Hearts*.

Renée Adorée (Professional Name); Renee Gill AKA Renee Adore (Names on the Death certificate); Jeanne de la Font (reported Birth Name but name does not appear on Death Certificate); Father's name is listed as Unknown on the Death Certificate so verification is difficult); **p. 6**—Several of her film credits include *The Big Parade, Man and Maid* and *Mr. Wu*.

Eddie Albert (Professional Name and Name on the Death Certificate); Edward Albert Heimberger (Birth Name); **p. 7**—In June 1936 on the first television broadcast (experimental), he wrote his own script and was his own makeup artist. His TV series were *Green Acres* and *Switch*. *Brother Rat, On Your Toes* and *Four Wives* were his first three films.

Edward Albert (Professional Name); Edward Lawrence Albert (Birth Name and Name on the Death Certificate); **p. 8**—Some of his more memorable film roles were *Butterflies Are Free, Midway* and *The Greek Tycoon*. On the small screen he appeared on the daytime soap *Port Charles* for three seasons, *Power Rangers Time Force* and *Beauty and the Beast*.

Peter Allen (Professional Name); Peter Richard Woolnough (Name on the Death Certificate); there is an affidavit to amend a record, which is not shown, which adds the name Peter Allen to the official record; **p. 9**—Received an Academy Award for the theme song for the movie *Arthur*. His music is also heard in such films as *The Fabulous Baker Boys, Muriel's Wedding* and *The Wedding Planner*.

Steve Allen (Professional Name); Stephen Valentine Allen (Birth Name and Name on the Death Certificate); also shown is a medical amendment listing the official cause of death; **p. 10-11**—Prolific is the word that comes to mind when one thinks of Steve Allen, whether it be writing of books and songs or appearances on the small screen. He made numerous appearances on the game shows, including *The New Hollywood Squares* and *Match Game*. *This Could Be the Start of Something Big* was probably his biggest hit song.

Robert Altman (Professional Name); Robert Bernard Altman (Birth Name and Name on the Death Certificate); biographers list his cause of death as complications from leukemia, but the Death Certificate lists cancer of the kidney with the heart transplant as a contributing cause; **p. 12**—He directed such movies as *A Prairie Home Companion, The Player* and *Shortcuts*. On television, he directed multiple episodes of *Tanner '88, Combat*, and *The Roaring 20's*.

Dana Andrews (Professional Name); Carver Dana Andrews (Birth Name and Name on the Death Certificate); **p. 13**—A star in the mid 1940s. A few of his films include *Laura, The Best Years of Our Lives*, and *The Westerner*. On the small screen he appeared in a number of episodic series including *Ironside* and *Night Gallery*.

Pier Angeli (Professional Name); Anna Maria Pierangeli (Birth Name and Name on the Death Certificate); biographers list her cause of death as barbiturate overdose, but an amendment of medical and health section lists it as an inflammation of the heart muscle; **p. 14-15**—*The Silver Chalice, Flame and Flesh* and *The Light Touch* were three of her films before she moved to Italy to makes movies.

Robert Armstrong (Professional Name); Robert William Armstrong (Birth Name and Name on the Death Certificate); **p. 16**—Armstrong learned his craft on the Broadway stage. *Is Zat So* was probably his first prime role. The Cooper/Schoedsack team brought him prominence with *King Kong, The Son of Kong*, and *Mighty*

BIOGRAPHICAL NOTES

Joe Young. His television appearances included *Perry Mason*, *Lassie*, and *Rawhide*, to name just a few.

Edward Arnold (Professional Name and Name on the Death Certificate); Gunther Schneider (Birth Name); **p. 17**—*Mr. Smith Goes to Washington*, *The Devil and Daniel Webster*, and *Meet Nero Wolf* were three of his films. *Ethel Barrymore Theater*, *Celebrity Playhouse* and The *Eddie Cantor Comedy Theater* were three of the small screen appearances in his 50-year acting career.

Bea Arthur (Professional Name); Bernice Frankel (Birth Name); Bernice Saks (Name on the Death Certificate); **p. 18**—She had a stage career appearing in *The Threepenny Opera*, *Mame*, and *Fiddler on the Roof*. Probably best know for her TV series, *All in the Family*, *Maude*, and *The Golden Girls*.

Agnes Ayres (Professional Name and Name on the Death Certificate); Agnes Ayres Hinkel (Birth Name); **p. 19**—One of the myriad actors who could not transition from silent films to talkies. *The Sheik*, *The Son of the Sheik*, and *The Ten Commandments* (1923) were three of her films.

Raymond Bailey (Professional Name); Raymond Thomas Bailey (Name on the Death Certificate); **p. 20**—In his career he progressed from an unknown into his own as a character actor. Many of his film appearances were uncredited. The small screen is where he is remembered. Probably best known as Milburn Drysdale on the *Beverly Hillbillies*. He also made multiple appearances on *Bonanza* and *The Many Loves of Dobie Gillis*, among other shows.

Suzan Ball (Professional Name and Birth Name); Susan Ball Long (Name on Death Certificate referring to her marriage to Richard Long); **p. 21**—Her career was cut short when she developed bone cancer in her right leg at age 19. Thee of her films were *Chief Crazy Horse*, *War Arrow* and *City Beneath the Sea*.

Gene Barry (Professional Name and Name on the Death Certificate); Eugene Klass (Birth Name); **p. 22**—*New Moon* and *Catherine Was Great* were two of his early films. On the small screen his series were *Bat Masterson*, *Burke's Law*, and *The Name of the Game*.

Judith Barsi (Professional Name); Judith Eva Barsi (Birth Name and Name on the Death Certificate); an affidavit to amend a record, which is not shown, changes her birthplace from Burbank to California; **p. 23**—She appeared in *Jaws the Revenge* and did voices in *All Dogs Go to Heaven* and *The Land Before Time*. Small screen appearances were on *St. Elsewhere*, *Growing Pains* and *The New Gidget*. She made numerous commercials in her nearly five-year career.

Warner Baxter (Professional Name); Warner Leroy Baxter (Birth Name and Name on the Death Certificate); **p. 24**—From vaudeville to Broadway to Hollywood was the progression of Baxter's career. He found his niche in Hollywood. *In Old Arizona*, *Penthouse* and *The Prisoner of Shark Island* were three of his films. At one time he was the highest paid actor in Tinseltown.

Wallace Beery (Professional Name and Name on the Death Certificate); Wallace Fitzgerald Beery (Birth Name according to biographers); **p. 25**—His professional career began at 16, when he joined the Ringling Bros. Barnum and Bailey Circus. Received an Academy Award for *The Champ* in 1931 and a nomination for *The Big House* in 1930.

Ralf Belmont (Professional Name and Name on the Death Certificate); (Birth Name could not be verified); **p. 26**—A Broadway actor and writer of the teens and twenties. *A Divine Drudge*, *Rust*, and *Declassee* were three of his plays. He and Percy Kilbride were walking together when they were struck by a car in Hollywood. Both died from their injuries.

Bea Benaderet (Professional Name); Beatrice Benaderet (Birth Name); Beatrice Twombly (Name on the Death Certificate); **p. 27**—She began her career in radio and smoothly transitioned into television. *The George Burns and Gracie Allen Show*, *The Flintstones* and *Petticoat Junction* were three of the long running series in which she starred.

Joey Bishop (Professional Name and Name on the Death Certificate; There is an also-known-as listed which is also his Birth Name, Joseph Abraham Gottlieb); there is an affidavit to amend a record which is not shown that changes the disposition of his cremains from all going to sea to ½ going to sea and the other ½ going to his informant at her residence; **p. 28**—He got his start in vaudeville doing a comedy act with his brother. *Ocean's Eleven* and *Sergeants 3* were two of his films. Better known for the small screen here he was dependable on game shows, talk shows, and sitcoms. He was a frequent guest host on *The Tonight Show Starring Johnny Carson*.

Erma Bombeck (Professional Name); Erma L. Bombeck (Name on the Death Certificate); Erma Louise Fiste (Birth Name); **p. 29**—A humorist with midwestern roots and values. She was a newspaper columnist and author. She was also a correspondent for *Good Morning America*.

Frank Brill (Professional Name and Name on the Death Certificate); Frank Feinman (Birth Name could not be verified); There are also two affidavits to amend a record which are not shown: the first changes the location for his cremains from his residence to that of his DPOA, the second changes the AKA from Frank Finestein to Frank Feinman; also changed his dad's surname from Feinstein to Feinman; **p. 30**—The Death Certificate indicates that he was a producer for 60 years. His professional credits are listed only as producer for *Without Her Consent*, *Family Secrets*, and *The John Davidson Show*.

Sorrell Brooke (Professional Name); Sorrell L. Brooke (Name on the Death Certificate); (Birth Name could not be verified); **p. 31**—Made appearances in many TV series of the 60's and 70's. Several are *All in the Family* and *Love Boat*. He is best remembered for his role as Boss Hogg on *The Dukes of Hazzard*.

Roscoe Lee Browne (Professional Name, Birth Name and Name on the Death Certificate); There is an affidavit which is not shown, showing final dispositions: ½ going to the informant and the other ½ going to him too); **p. 32**—Browne was a college professor before taking to the New York stage in *Julius Caesar*. On the big screen, he had roles in *The Comedians*, *Up Tight* and *Topaz*. *Maude*, *Sanford and Son* and *All in the Family* were some of his small screen appearances.

Kathie Browne (Professional Name); Jacqueline Katherine Browne (Birth Name as listed by biographers), Katherine Jacqueline Browne-McGavin (Name on the Death Certificate); **p. 33**—Mostly remembered for her television appearances. She has multiple roles on *Sea Hunt*, *Rawhide*, *Wagon Train* and *Laramie*.

Lenny Bruce (Professional Name); Leonard Alfred Schenider AKA Lenny Bruce (Birth Name AKA and Name on the Death Certificate); **p. 34**—Bruce was a stand-up comedian who continued to push the envelope with profanity until law enforcement pushed back. He did make a few small screen appearances including the *Arthur Godfrey Talent Scouts* and *The Steve Allen Show*.

Smiley Burnette (Professional Name); Lester Alvin Burnette (Birth Name); Lester Alvin Burnette AKA Smiley Alvin Burnette (Names on the Death Certificate); **p. 35**—His niche in the movies was as the sidekick to the star in westerns, particularly Gene Autry. *Kind of the Cowboys* and *Pride of the Plains* were two of these films.

Judy Canova (Professional Name); Juliette Canova (Birth Name); Juliette AKA Judy Canova (Names on the Death Certificate); **p. 36**—She played the country bumpkin to perfection. *Honeychile*, *Hit the Hay* and *Joan of the Ozark* are three of her films. On the small screen she appeared in *The Love Boat*, *Police Woman* and *Li'l Abner*.

Kathryn Card (Professional Name and Birth Name); Kathryn Card Sullivan/Kathryn Card (Names listed on the Death Certificate); **p. 37**—The majority of her film appearances were uncredited. The small screen was her bigger success. Best remembered as Mrs. McGillicuddy, Lucy's mother on *I Love Lucy*. She also made multiple appearances on the *Red Skelton Show* and *Perry Mason*.

Ron Carey (Professional Name); Ronald L. Cicenia (Birth Name and Name on the Death Certificate with AKA Ron Carey); **p. 38**—His movie credits include *The Out of Towners*, *Who Killed Mary What's 'Er Name* and *Made for Each Other*. On television, he made the rounds of the talk show circuit including *The Tonight Show Starring Johnny Carson* and *The Merv Griffin Show*. Best remembered for his role on *Barney Miller* as officer Carl Levitt.

George Carlin (Professional Name); George Denis Patrick Carlin (Birth Name as listed by biographers); George Denis Carlin (Name on the Death Certificate): **p. 39**—Considered by many to be the most influential stand-up comedian of all time, after Lenny Bruce. He was the narrator for *Thomas the Tank Engine and Friends* on the small screen. His television series *The George Carlin Show* lasted for 13 episodes.

Karen Carpenter (Professional Name); Karen Anne Carpenter (Birth Name and Name on the Death Certificate); There is a medical Amendment showing the cause of death as anorexia nervosa; **p. 40–41**—A musician-singer with her brother Richard, she made appearances on *The Tonight Show Starring Johnny Carson*, *American Bandstand* and *This Is Your Life*.

Allan Carr (Professional Name and Name on the Death Certificate); Allan Solomon (Birth Name); **p. 42**—He was the manager for Ann-Margret, Peter Sellers, and Herb Alpert to name just a few. He produced such films as *La Cage aux Folles*, *Can't Stop the Music*, and *Grease 2*.

Charles Chaplin, Jr. (Professional Name); Charles Spencer Chaplin, Jr. (Birth Name and Name on the Death Certificate); **p. 43**—He appeared with his famous father in his first film, *Limelight*. *The Beat Generation* and *High School Confidential* were other films in which he made appearances.

Virginia Christine (Professional Name); Virginia Field (Name on the Death Certificate); Virginia Christine Kraft (Listed Birth Name, but father's surname on the Death Certificate is Ricketts); **p. 44**—Despite her long career, she will always be "Mrs. Olson," the maven for Folgers coffee. She also appeared in *Judgment in Nuremberg*, *The Prize*, and *High Noon*.

Andy Clyde (Professional Name); Andrew Allen Clyde (Name on the Death Certificate and presumed Birth Name); **p. 45**—Got his start in movies in the Mack Sennett reels and found his niche as the grizzled sidekick in cowboy movies, often times with William Boyd in the *Hopalong Cassidy* series. On television, he had reoccurring roles on *Lassie*, *The Real McCoys*, and *The Tall Man*.

Lee J. Cobb (Professional Name and Name on he Death Certificate); Lee Jacoby (Birth Name, but his father's surname on the Death Certificate is spelled Jaboc); **p. 46**—His portrayal of Willy Loman in *Death of a Salesman* on both Broadway and the small screen brought him accolades. *The Virginian* and *The Young Lawyers* were two of his other TV series.

Nicholas Colasanto (Professional Name, Name on the Death a Certificate and Birth Name); **p. 47**—He made only a few films including *Fat City* and *Raging Bull*. On the small screen he directed many of the episodic series segments. Best remembered as Coach Ernie Pantusso on *Cheers*.

Chester Conklin (Professional Name); Chester Cooper Conklin (Birth Name and Name on the Death Certificate); **p. 48**—Came up through the ranks, beginning in vaudeville, then became a circus performer and finally got roles in movies. Worked steadily from his first film, *Cupid in a Dental Parlor*, in 1913 until *A Big Hand for the Little Lady* in 1966.

Darlene Conley (Professional Name); Darlene Ann Conley (Birth Name and Name on the Death Certificate); **p. 49**—She began her career in *The Birds*. She had roles on *Days of Our Lives*, *Capitol*, *General Hospital* and finally *The Bold and the Beautiful*, playing Sally Spectra.

Chuck Connors (Professional Name); Kevin Joseph Aloysius Connors (Birth Name); (Aloysius does not appear on the Death Certificate); Kevin Joseph Connors (Name on the Death Certificate); There is also an affidavit to amend a record which is not shown, that adds the name Chuck Connors to the Certificate); **p. 50**—Connors was a professional athlete before being "discovered." *Pat and Mike* was his first film. Best remembered as Lucas McCain on *The Rifleman*, his series on the small screen.

Richard Conte also Nicholas Conte (Professional Names); Richard Nicholas Peter Conte (Birth Name and Name on the Death Certificate); There is also an affidavit to amend a record, which is not shown, correcting the social security number; **p. 51**—*Heaven with a Barbed Wire Fence* was his first film. He made several war movies during World War II, including *A Walk in the Sun* and *A Bell for Adano*. His last American made film was *The Godfather*.

Bert Convy (Professional Name); Bernard Whalen Convy (Birth Name and Name on the Death Certificate); **p. 52**—*Gunman's Walk* and *A Bucket of Blood* were his first two films. On the small screen he appeared in many of the series and game shows of the 60's and 70's, including *77 Sunset Strip*, *Tattletales*, *The Love Boat* and *Fantasy Island*.

Merian C. Cooper (Professional Name); Merian Coldwell Cooper (Name on the Death Certificate); there seems to be a discrepancy as to his middle name: some biographers list it as Caldwell, while the Death Certificate used Coldwell); **p. 53**—He was the producer or executive producer for such films as *King Kong*, *The Quiet Man* and *Little Women*.

Wendell Corey (Professional Name); Wendell Reid Corey (Birth Name and Name on the Death Certificate); **p. 54**—He made his career in films playing strong supporting roles. Several of his movies are *Desert Fury*, *I Walk Alone* and *Holiday Affair*. On the small screen, he made multiple appearances on *Harbor Command*, *Studio One*, and *Branded*. His one series was *Peck's Bad Girl*.

Aneta Corsault (Professional Name); Aneta Louise Corsault (Name on the Death Certificate); **p. 55**—She had a limited movie career. On the small screen, she had reoccurring roles on *Matlock* and *Emergency*. Best remembered for her role as Helen Crump on *The Andy Griffith Show* and *Return to Mayberry*.

Joseph Cotten (Professional Name); Joseph C. Cotten (Name on the Death Certificate); Joseph Cheshire Cotten (Birth Name as listed by biographers); **p. 56**—Three of this films were *Shadow of a Doubt*, *Citizen Kane*, and *The Third Man*. On the small screen, he made multiple appearances on *Ironside* and *It Takes a Thief*.

Mary Jane Croft (Professional Name and Birth Name); Mary Jane Lewis (Name on the Death Certificate); **p. 57**—While she made appearances on other small screen series, her name is tied to Lucille Ball. She had continuing roles in *I Love Lucy*, *The Lucy Show* and *Here's Lucy*.

Pauline Curley (Professional Name); Rose Pauline Curley (Birth Name); Rose Pauline Peach (Name on the Death Certificate); **p. 58**—Her films were all during the silent era. Three of them were *A Case in Law*, *Bound in Morocco*, *Turn in the Road*.

Esther Dale (Professional Name and Birth Name); Esther Dale Beckhard (Name on the Death Certificate); **p. 59**—Many of her movie roles went uncredited. She appeared in *Ma and Pa Kettle at the Fair*, *A Child Is Born*, and *Unfinished Business*. On TV, she had roles in *Wagon Train*, *Four Star Playhouse* and *Mr. and Mrs. North*.

Royal Dano (Professional Name); Royal Edward Dano, Sr. (Name on the Death Certificate); Royal Edward Dano (Birth Name); **p. 60**—Some of his films included are *Moby Dick*, *Red Badge of Courage*, and *Undercover Girl*. On television, he had multiple appearances on *Bonanza*, *The Rifleman*, and *The Virginian*.

Richard Deacon (Professional Name, Birth Name and Name on the Death Certificate); **p. 61**—His motion picture career was quite limited. He had roles in *Invaders from Mars* and *Lay That Rifle Down*. On the small screen was where he shined. Made multiple appearances on *Mr. Ed* and *The Red Skelton Show*. Best remembered for his role as Mel Cooley on *The Dick Van Dyke Show*.

Yvonne DeCarlo (Professional Name and Name on the Death Certificate); Peggy or Margaret Yvonne DeCarlo (Biographers cannot agree); **p. 62**—She had roles in *Where She Danced*, *Song of Scheherazade* and *Brute Force*. On TV she appeared in *Bonanza* and *The Virginian*. Probably best remembered as Lilly Munster on *The Musters*.

Sandra Dee (Professional Name and Name on the Death Certificate); Alexandra Cymboliak Zuck (Birth Name); there are questions as to her middle name which is also her mother's maiden name: is it spelled Cymboliak or Cimboliak?); **p. 63**—Her films included *A Summer Place*, *Tammy Tell Me True*, *Gidget* and *If a Man Answers*. On television, she had roles on *Fantasy Island*, *Police Woman* and *Night Gallery*.

Don DeFore (Professional Name); Donald J. De Fore (Name on the Death Certificate); Donald John DeFore (Birth Name according to biographers); **p. 64**—Appeared on Broadway in *The Male Animal* and reprised his role when it was brought to the big screen. Two long running series where he was a regular were *The Adventures of Ozzie and Harriet* and *Hazel*.

Dom DeLuise (Professional Name and Name on the Death Certificate); Dominic DeLuise (Birth Name); **p. 65**—Had roles in the Burt Reynolds films *Smokey and the Bandit*, *The Cannonball Run* and *The Best Little Whorehouse in Texas*. Also skilled in voiceovers, he is heard in *All Dogs Go to Heaven*, *The Secret of NIMH* and *The American Tail*.

John Derek (Professional Name and Name on the Death Certificate); Derek Delevan Harris (Birth Name according to biographers); **p. 66**—*Ghosts Can't Do It* and *Bolero* were films where he was both cinematographer and writer. On television, *Zane Grey Theater*, *Frontier Justice*, and *Frontier Circus* were series where he had multiple appearances.

Joe Derita (Professional Name and Name on the Death Certificate); Joseph Wardell (Birth Name); **p. 67**—On both the large and small screen, his fame with tied to his appearances as one of The Three Stooges. *The Three Stooges Meet Hercules*, *The Three Stooges Go Around the World*, and *Snow White and the Three Stooges* were three of his films.

Jenny Dolly or Yancsi Dolly (Professional Name); Jenny Dolly Vinisski (Name on the Death Certificate); Janszieka Deutsch (Birth Name according to biographers; surname for her father on the Death Certificate is Dolly, probably anglicized when entering the United States from Hungary; **p. 68**—One of the Ziegfeld Girls in the 1911 Follies. Made two silent films, *Call of the Dance* and *The Million Dollar Dollies*.

Ann Doran (Professional Name); Anna Lee Doran (Birth Name and Name on the Death Certificate); **p. 69**—She made literally hundreds and hundreds of films and small screen appearances from *Robin Hood* in 1922 through the TV series *Hunter* in 1988.

Mignon G. Eberhart (Professional Name and Name on the Death Certificate); Mignon Good (Birth Name); **p. 70**—Prolific mystery writer who had nine of her books or stories turned into films. *The White Cockatoo*, *While the Patient Slept* and the *Patient in Room 18* were three of them.

Herb or Herbert Edelman (Professional Names); Herbert Edelman (Birth Name and Name on the Death Certificate); **p. 71**—*I Love You, Alice B. Toklas*, *Barefoot in the Park* and *In Like Flint* were three of his limited big screen appearances. On television, he had reoccurring roles on *St. Elsewhere*, *Murder She Wrote* and *The Golden Girls*.

Ross Elliott (Professional Name and Name on the Death Certificate); Elliott Blum (Birth Name); there is an affidavit to amend a record which is not shown that adds the name Elliott Blum to the official record; **p. 73**—His professional career began in radio. *This Is the Army, The Burning Cross* and *Angel on the Amazon* were his first three films. His character was Lee Baldwin #1 on *General Hospital* from 1963 to 1965. *The Jack Benny Program* and *The Virginian* were TV series where he had a continuing role.

Muriel Evans (Professional Name); Muriel Adele Evans (Birth Name); Muriel E. Worchester (Name on the Death Certificate); **p. 74**—Because of her roles in the westerns of 1930s and '40's, her niche was referred as "prairie flower" roles. *King of the Pecos, Call of the Prairie, The New Frontier* and *Silver Spurs* are four of her films.

Farrah Fawcett (Professional Name and Name on the Death Certificate); Farrah Leni Fawcett (Birth Name); **p. 75**—She got her big break in *Charlie's Angels*. Most of her movies were for the small screen. They include *The Burning Bed, Poor Little Rich Girl: The Barbara Hutton Story*, and *Children of the Dust*.

Peter Finch (Professional Name and Name on the Death Certificate); Frederick George Peter Ingle-Finch (Birth Name according to biographers); his father's surname on the Death Certificate is Finch; **p. 76**—His Oscar for Best Actor in *Network* was awarded posthumously. *Sunday Bloody Sunday, Trial of Oscar Wilde*, and *Far From the Madding Crowd* are three others of his films which garnered various award nominations.

Larry Fine (Professional Name and Name on the Death Certificate); Louis Feinderg (Birth Name); **p. 77**—He was the middle Stooge of The Three Stooges. *Snow White and the Three Stooges, The Three Stooges Meet Hercules*, and *Three Stooges Fun-O-Rama* are three of their films.

George Fitzmaurice (Professional Name, Birth Name and Name on the Death Certificate); **p. 78**—A prolific director whose credits include *To Have and to Hold, The Witness for the Defense* and *The Mark of Cain*.

Paul Fix (Professional Name); Paul Peter Fix (Birth Name and Name on the Death Certificate); **p. 79**—A prolific character actor, after 20 years, the majority of his roles were uncredited. *Fighting Man of the Plains, Angel and the Badman*, and *Bullfighter and the Lady* were three of them. On the small screen, he is probably best remembered as Marshall Micha Torrance on *The Rifleman*.

Wayland Flowers (Professional Name); Wayland Parrott Flowers (Birth Name and Name on the Death Certificate); **p. 80**—He was a puppeteer, not a ventriloquist. *Madame's Place* was his TV series. He (and Madame) also replaced Paul Lynde in the center square of Hollywood Squares.

Nina Foch (Professional Name); Nina Consuelo Maud Fock (Birth Name according to biographers, but father's surname on the Death Certificate is spelled Foch); Niona Consuelo Maude Foch (Name on the Death Certificate); **p. 81**—*An American in Paris, The Ten Commandments* (1956) and *Spartacus* (1960) are three of her films. Following her acting career, she became a respected acting teacher.

Glenn Ford (Professional Name); Gwyllyn Samuel Newton Ford (Birth Name according to biographers); Glenn Samuel Newton Ford (Name on the Death Certificate); **p. 82**—Three of his films were *The Big Heat, 3:10 to Yuma*, and *Blackboard Jungle*. On the small screen, he had roles on *My Town, Beggerman Thief* and *The Sackettts*.

Michael Fox (Professional Name, Birth Name and Name on the Death Certificate); **p. xxx**—*Whatever Happened to Baby Jane, Young Frankenstein* and *The Longest Yard* are a few of his films. On the small screen, he had a recurring role as the coroner on *Perry Mason* and portrayed Saul Feinberg, the garment cutter on *The Bold and Beautiful*.

Mary Frann (Professional Name and Name on the Death Certificate); Mary Frances Lucke (Birth Name); there is a medical amendment shown which includes the actual cause of death; **p. 83-84**—On the small screen, she appeared in numerous series. Joanna Loudon was her character on the long running show *Newhart*.

Friz Freleng (Professional Name); Isadore Frehleng (Birth Name and Name on the Death Certificate); **p. 85**—A prolific producer, he won his Oscar for *The Pink Blueprint*. He also received nominations for *The Pink Phink* and *The Pied Piper of Guadalupe*.

Bobby Fuller (Professional Name); Robert Gaston Fuller (Birth Name); Robert Gaston Fuller AKA Bobby Gaston Fuller (Names on the Death Certificate); **p. 86**—*The Ghost in the Invisible Bikini* was his only film. On TV his appearances were in *Hullabaloo, Where the Acton Is* and *Shivaree*.

Marvin Gaye (Professional Name); Marvin Penz Gay (Birth Name); Marvin Penz Gaye, Jr. (Name on the Death Certificate); **p. 87**—songwriter and musician; His work is still being heard on television programs. In 2008, his music was heard on *Ugly Betty, Eli Stone* and *Dancing with the Stars*.

Will Geer (Professional Name); Will Augue Geer (Name on the Death Certificate); William Auge Ghere (Birth Name reported by biographers); On the Death Certificate, his father's surname is listed as Geer; **p. 88**—Made his first film in 1932, *Misleading Lady*. He worked steadily until 1972. His role as Grandpa Walton on *The Waltons* made him memorable to generations.

George Gershwin (Professional Name and Name on the Death Certificate); Jacob Gershowitz (Birth Name according to biographers); On the Death Certificate his father's surname is listed as Gershwin; **p. 89**—Prolific composer nominated for an Academy Award along with his brother, Ira, for the song *Shall We Dance*. *Our Love Is Here to Stay*, *Someone to Watch Over Me*, and the music for the American opera *Porgy and Bess* are some of his credits.

Estelle Getty (Professional Name); Estelle Scher (Birth Name); Estelle Gettleman (Name on the Death Certificate): **p. 90**—She had a long career in the theater when she began her career on the small screen. *The Golden Girls*, *The Golden Palace* and *Empty Nest* were three of her series.

Alice Ghostley (Professional Name); Alice Margaret Ghostley (Birth Name and Name on the Death Certificate); **p. 91**—Started on Broadway. On the small screen, she had recurring roles on *Bewitched*, *Evening Shade*, and *Designing Women*.

Jerry Giesley (Professional Name); Harold Lee Giesley (Birth Name and Name on the Death Certificate with an AKA adding Jerry to the official record); **p. 92**—An attorney whose client list looked like the Who's Who of Hollywood. Errol Flynn, Bugsy Siegel and Marilyn Monroe to name just a few.

Samuel Goldwyn (Professional Name and Name on the Death Certificate); Shmuel or Schmuel Gelbfisz (Birth Name/s according to biographers); surname for his father is Goldfish on the Death Certificate); **p. 93**—Hollywood producer of such films as *Porgy and Bess*, *Guys and Dolls*, and *The Secret Life of Walter Mitty*.

Thomas Gomez (Professional Name and Name on the Death Certificate); Sabino Tomas Gomez (Birth Name according to biographers); Death Certificate lists his father as Sabino Thomas); **p. 94**—*Sherlock Holmes and the Voice of Terror*, *Ride the Pink Horse* and *A Night in Paradise* were three of his films. Made appearances on *The Rifleman*, *Shirley Temple's Storybook*, and *Playhouse 90*.

Gerald Gordon (Professional Name, Birth Name and Name on the Death Certificate); **p. 95**—He spent his working career on the small screen. He had recurring roles on *Valerie*, *Dallas*, and spent over 10 years on *The Doctors* playing Dr. Nick Bellini.

Leo Gordon (Professional Name); Leo Vincent Gordon, Jr. (Birth Name and Name on the Death Certificate); **p. 96**—Some of his films include *Black Patch*, *The Intruder* and *Riot in Cell Block 11*. On TV he had roles on many of the Westerns of the 1950's and 60's, such as *The Rifleman*, *Bat Masterson*, and *Have Gun Will Travel*.

Sandra Gould (Professional Name); Sandra Gould Morse (Name on the Death Certificate); presumably Sandra Gould was her Birth Name, but it cannot be confirmed; **p. 97**—Started in radio on such programs as *My Friend Irma*, *The Jack Benny Show* and *Duffy's Tavern*. Her films included *The Ghost and Mr. Chicken*, *Teacher's Pet* and *Honeymoon Hotel*. On the small screen, she appeared on *I Love Lucy*, *Our Miss Brooks* and five seasons on *Bewitched* as Gladys Kravitz.

Robert Goulet (Professional Name); Robert Gerard Goulet (Birth Name and Name on the Death Certificate); **p. 98**—Achieved Broadway success with *Camelot* and *Happy Time*. He appeared in *Beetle Juice* and *Naked Gun 2½ The Smell of Fear* on the big screen. *In the Heat of the Night*, *Berke's Law* and *Matt Houston* were three television series in which he appeared.

Sid Grauman (Professional Name); Sydney P. Grauman (Birth Name and Name on the Death Certificate); **p. 99**—Best known as the builder of Grauman's Chinese Theater. Had a few uncredited roles in films. *Star Dust*, *The Gold Rush* and *Ben-Hur; A Tale of the Christ*, were three of them.

Sydney Greenstreet (Professional Name); Sydney Hughes Greenstreet (Birth Name and Name on the Death Certificate); **p. 100**—*Casablanca*, *The Verdict*, and *The Woman in White* are three of his films. He came to films from the stage late in life for an actor.

Jane Greer (Professional Name); Bettejane Greer (Birth Name); Jane Greer Laser (Name on the Death Certificate); **p. 101**—She was known for her facial expressions to convey human emotions. *The Company She Keeps*, *The Big Steal*, and *Sunset Pass* are three of her films. She had recurring roles on *Twin Peaks* and *Falcon Crest*.

Merv Griffin (Professional Name); Mervin Edward Griffin (Birth Name and Name on the Death Certificate); **p. 102**—He was the creator of such game shows as Jeopardy and *Wheel of Fortune*, as well as being a successful talk-show host.

David Groh (Professional Name); David Lawrence Groh (Birth Name); David L. Groh (Name on the Death Certificate) **p. 103**—Spent most of his career on the small screen. He had multiple appearances on *Police Story* and *Another Day*. Probably best knows for his role as Joe Gerard on *Rhoda*.

William Haines (Professional Name); Charles William Haines (Birth Name and Name on the Death Certificate); **p. 104**—An actor who went from silents to talkies. He was regularly listed as the #1 box-office draw at the end of the silent era. His films include *A Man's Man*, *Brown of Harvard* and *A Slave of Fashion*. He was probably the first actor fired because he would not give up his long-time homosexual lover in order to marry a woman to please the studio head (Louis B. Mayer) happy.

Conrad L. Hall (Professional Name); Conrad Lafcadio Hall (Birth Name and Name on the Death Certificate); **p. 105**—He was nominated for 10 Academy Awards for Cinematography. He received them for *Road to Perdition*, *American Beauty*, and *Butch Cassidy and the Sundance Kid*.

Carrie Hamilton (Professional Name); Carrie Louise Hamilton (Birth Name and Name on the Death Certificate); there is an affidavit of correction showing a division of her cremated remains and where they were to go; **p. 106**—A short career due to her premature death. She made multiple appearances on *Walker, Texas Ranger*, *Fame* and *Hollywood Squares*.

Neil Hamilton (Professional Name); James Neil Hamilton (Birth Name and Name on the Death Certificate); **p. 107**—Three of his films are *The Modern Age*, *The Great Lover* and *The Cat Creeps*. On the small screen, he had multiple appearances on *Perry Mason* and *Kraft Suspense Theater*. Probably best known as Commissioner Gordon on *Batman*.

Oliver Hardy (Professional Name); Oliver Norvell Hardy (Birth Name and Name on the Death Certificate); **p. 108**—He was the rotund partner in the Oliver and Hardy series of movies. Three of them are *Babes in Toyland*, *A Chump at Oxford* and *A-Haunting We Will Go*.

Vinton Hayworth (Professional Name and Birth Name according to biographers); Vinton Jackson Hayworth (Name on the Death Certificate); **p. 109**—Almost all of this silver screen appearances went uncredited. On the small screen, he made multiple appearances on *Dragnet 1967*, *Green Acres*, and *I dream of Jeannie*.

Ted Healy (Professional Name); Ernest Lee Nash (Birth Name); Ernest Lee Nash AKA Ted Healy (Names on the Death Certificate); biographers list his cause of death as a result of a bar fight, but the coroner's office makes no reference to that; **p. 110**—His career was tied to his success with the Three Stooges, The *Casino Murder*, *Death on the Diamond* and *Hollywood Party* are three of his films.

Van Heflin (Professional Name); Emmett Evan Heflin, Jr. (Birth Name); Emmett Evan Heflin (Name on the Death Certificate); **p. 111**—Three of his films are *Possessed*, *Santa Fe Trail* and *Green Dolphin Street*. Certain Honorable Mention, *A Case of Libel* and *The Last Child* are three of the movies made for television in which he appeared.

Leona Helmsley (Professional Name and Name on the Death Certificate); Leona Mindy Rosenthal (Birth Name); **p. 112**—Her professional career on television was limited to her commercials for the family hotel chain.

Margaux Hemingway (Professional Name): Margot Louise Hemingway (Birth Name and Name on the Death Certificate); there is a medical amendment shown that lists her cause of death as drug overdose; **p. 113–114**—*Lipstick*, *Inner Sanctum* and *Double Obsession* were three of her silver screen appearances.

Shirley Hemphill (Professional Name); Shirley Ann Hemphill (Birth Name and Name on the Death Certificate); there is a medical amendment showing the cause of death included since it varies from the cause listed by biographers; **p. 115–116**—*What's Happening Now*, *One in a Million* and *What's Happening* were three of her TV series.

Charlton Heston (Professional Name and Name on the Death Certificate); John Charles Carter or Charles Carter (Birth Name depending on the biographer); **p. 117**—*The Ten Commandments*, *The Big Country* and *Ben-Hur* are three of his films. On the small screen, he had recurring roles on *The Bold and the Beautiful*, *The Colbys* and *Dynasty*.

Dana Hill (Professional Name); Dana Lynne Goetz (Birth Name and Name on the Death Certificate); **p. 118**—*Fallen Angel* and *Shoot the Moon* were two of her films. She did voiceovers for *Jetsons: The Movie*, *Goof Troop* and *Duckman: Private Dick/Family Man*.

Jonathan Hole (Professional Name); Jonathan F. Hole (Birth Name and Name on the Death Certificate); **p. 119**—He found a niche in television, frequently playing insignificant or nervous men. He made multiple appearances on *Green Acres*, *Perry Mason* and *Petticoat Junction*.

Fred Holliday (Professional Name and Name on the Death Certificate); biographers list no birth name, but father's surname was Grossing; **p. 120**—He made appearances on many of the television series from the 1960's through the 1980's. *The Big Valley*, *Ben Casey* and *Dr. Kildare* are but three of them.

John Holmes (Professional Name); John Curtis Estes (Birth Name according to biographers; his death certificate lists his father's surname as Holmes); John Curtis Homes (Name on the Death Certificate); **p. 121**—He is credited with over 2,000 adult features, stag films and loops. *Strangers When We Met*, *Cabin Fever*, and *The Tropic of Passion* are but three of them.

Edward Everett Horton (Professional Name, Birth Name and Name on the Death Certificate); **p. 122**—One of the actors who went from silent films to talkies. *Arsenic and Old Lace*, *Ziegfeld Girl* and *Lady on a Train* were thee of his films. He made multiple appearances on *F Troop*, *Burke's Law*, and *Batman* for the small screen.

Betty Hutton (Professional Name and Name on the Death Certificate); Elizabeth June Thornburg (Birth Name according to biographers); **p. 123**—*Dream Girl*, *The Greatest Show on Earth*, and *The Perils of Pauline* are thee other films. *The Betty Hutton Show* was her only television series.

Michael Jackson (Professional Name): Michael Joseph Jackson (Birth Name and Name on the Death Certificate); there is a medical amendment shown which lists the cause of death; **p. 124-125**—Nominated for two Emmy Awards, *Sammy Davis Jr. 60 Anniversary Celebration* and *Motown 25: Yesterday, Today, Forever*. Won a Grammy Award for *Thriller*, nominated for *Moonwalker*.

Brion James (Professional Name); Biron Howard James (Birth Name and Name on the Death Certificate); **p. 126**—*The Blade Runner*, *Cabin Boy* and *Tango and Cash* were some of his films. He made appearances on *Walker, Texas Ranger*, *Superman* and *Batman*.

Dennis James (Professional Name and Name on the Death Certificate); Demie James Sposa (Birth Name according to biographers); **p. 127**—An early host of game shows on television. The *Dennis James Show*, *Two for the Money* and *The Name's the Same* were three of his programs.

Michael Jeter (Professional Name, Birth Name and Name on the Death Certificate); Biographers list his cause of death as epileptic seizure/asphyxiation but there is a medical amendment from the Los Angeles County Coroner's office which lists the cause of death as multiple drug intoxication; **p. 128-129**—Received Emmy nominations for his roles on *Chicago Hope*, *Picket Fences*, and *Evening Shade* (twice; he won the award only once, in 1992).

Henry Jones (Professional Name); Henry Burk Jones (Birth Name and Name on the Death Certificate); **p. 130**—He had roles in *3:10 to Yuma*, *The Bad Seed*, and *Vertigo*. On television, he appeared in *Studio One*, *Murder, She Wrote*, and *Burke's Law*.

Spike Jones (Professional Name); Lindley Armstrong Jones (Birth Name); Lindley Armstrong Jones AKA Spike Jones (Names on the Death Certificate); **p. 131**—*Idaho*, *Meet the People* and *Bring on the Girls* were three of his early films. *The Spike Jones Show* was his TV program.

Janis Joplin (Professional Name); Janis Lyn Joplin (Birth Name and Name on the Death Certificate); there is a medical amendment for the Death Certificate showing cause of death to be acute heroin-morphine intoxication, injection of overdose, and it was considered an accidental overdose); **p. 132-133**—She was the lead singer for rock bands. In 1995 she was inducted to the Rock and Roll Hall of Fame. She performed her music in *Woodstock Diary*, *Household Saints* and *The Indian Runner*, among others.

Stanley Kamel (Professional Name); Stanley M. Kamel (Birth Name and Name on the Death Certificate); biographers list cause of death as heart attack, but the Death Certificate lists the cause as hyperosmolar state, HIV, heart disease and diabetes); **p. 134**—He had recurring roles on television series *Cagney and Lacy*, *Melrose Place*, *General Hospital* and finally *Monk*.

Andy Kaufman (Professional Name); Andrew Geoffrey Kaufman (Birth Name); Andrew G. Kaufman (Name on the Death Certificate); **p. 135**—He was a regular on *Saturday Night Live*, and had a continuing role on *Taxi* for five seasons.

Buster Keaton (Professional Name); Joseph Frank Keaton VI (Birth Name according to biographers); Joseph F. (Buster) Keaton AKA Buster Keaton (Names on the Death Certificate); **p. 136**—He transitioned from the Silent era to talkies. *The Saphead*, *The General* and *The Cameraman* were three of his films.

Biographical Notes

DeForest Kelley (Professional Name); Jackson De Forest Kelley (Birth Name and Name on the Death Certificate); **p. 137**—His career worked backward from the careers of most actors. He went from the small screen to the silver screen. He starred in *Ironside* and *Owen Marshall: Counselor at Law*, then moved on to *Star Trek*.

Edgar Kennedy (Professional Name); Edgar Livingston Kennedy (Birth Name); Edgar L. Kennedy (Name on the Death Certificate); biographers list his cause of death as throat cancer, while the Death Certificate lists it as lung cancer; **p. 138**—*Tillie's Punctured Romance* was one of his acting efforts. He directed such films as *You're Darn Tootin'* and *From Soup to Nuts*.

Eartha Kitt (Professional Name and Name on the Death Certificate); Eartha Mae Kitt (Birth Name according to biographers); **p. 139**—Received two Daytime Emmy Awards for her voiceover in *The Emperor's New School* and an Emmy for an appearance on *I Spy*. She also was Catwoman in four episodes of *Batman* on the small screen.

Ted Knight (Professional Name); Tadeus Wladyslaw Konapka (Birth Name according to biographers); Theodore Charles Konopka AKA Theodore Charles Knight (Names on the Death Certificate); **p. 140**—Spent most of his career on the small screen. *Too Close for Comfort* and *The Ted Night Show* were two of them. Probably best remembered for his role as Ted Baxter on *Mary Tyler Moore*.

Harvey Korman (Professional Name); Harvey Herschel Krorman (Birth Name and Name on the Death Certificate); **p. 141**—He was nominated seven times for Emmy Awards for *The Carol Burnett Show*. He received the award four times. He also received one Golden Globe award from four nominations, also for *The Carol Burnett Show*.

Elsa Lanchester (Professional Name); Elizabeth Lanchester Sullivan (Birth Name according to biographers); Elsa Lanchester AKA Elsa Laughton (Names on the Death Certificate); **p. 142**—*Bride of Frankenstein*, *The Bishop's Wife*, and *Come to the Stable* were three of her films. On the small screen, she had multiple appearances on *Mannix*, *Nanny and the Professor* and *The Bill Cosby Show*.

Carole Landis (Professional Name); Carol Landis Schmidlapp (Name on the Death Certificate); Frances Lillian Mary Ridste (Birth name according to biographers); **p. 143**—*One Million B.C.*, *A Gentleman at Heart*, *Topper Returns* and *Having Wonderful Crime* were four of her films.

Charles Lane (Professional Name); Charles Gerstle Levison (Birth Name); Charles G. Lane (Name on the Death Certificate); **p. 144**—He is credited with over 350 roles on both the big and small screen. On the TV he had multiple appearances on *I Love Lucy*, *Dear Phoebe*, and *Dennis the Menace*.

Harry Langdon (Professional Name); Harry Philmore Langdon (Birth Name and Name on the Death Certificate); **p. 145**—He was a comedian during the silent era. *Saturday Afternoon*, *The Strong Man* and *Long Pants* were three of his films.

Charles Laughton (Professional Name, Birth Name and Name on the Death Certificate); **p. 146**—*The Hunchback of Notre Dame*, *I, Claudius*, and *Mutiny on the Bounty* were three of his films.

Stan Laurel (Professional Name and Name on the Death Certificate); Arthur Stanley Jefferson (Birth Name); **p. 147**—*From Soup to Nuts*, *The Bullfighters* and *Sugar Daddies* were three of the Laurel and Hardy movies.

Anthony Lee (Professional Name); Anthony Dwain Lee (Birth name and name on the Death Certificate); **p. 148–149**—He made appearances on *ER*, *Chicago Hope*, and *Brooklyn South*. He was shot by a police officer by mistake at a Halloween party at a private residence.

Phil Leeds (Professional Name); Philip Leeds (Birth Name and Name on the Death Certificate); **p. 150**—He was character actor who made multiple appearances on *Maude*, *The Jackie Gleason Show* and *Barney Miller*.

Queenie Leonard (Professional Name and Name on the Death Certificate); Pearl Walker (Birth Name); **p. 151**—She was an actress with many of her roles going uncredited. She made appearances in *D-Day in the South Pacific*, *All the Fine Young Cannibals*, and *The Notorious Landlady*. On the small screen, *I Dream of Jeannie*, *Bewitched* and *Hazel* are three of the series in which she worked.

Terry Lester (Professional Name); Terry Leroy Lester (Birth Name and Name on the Death Certificate); **p. 152**—He spent most of his career on the soaps. *Art II*, *Santa Barbara*, and *As the World Turns* were three of them.

Oscar Levant (Professional Name, Birth Name and Name on the Death Certificate); **p. 153**—Composer for the music such as *Made for Each Other*, *Nothing Sacred* and *Romance on the High Seas*.

Peter Lorre (Professional Name and Name on the Death Certificate); Laszlo Lowenstein (Birth Name according to biographers, but the Death Certificate lists his father's surname as Lorant); **p. 154**—*You'll Find Out, Mr. Moto Takes a Vacation*, and *Crime and Punishment* are three of his films.

Allen Ludden (Professional Name and Name on the Death Certificate); Allen Ellsworth (Birth Name); **p. 155**—He spent most of his working career on game shows. *What's My Line, Password, Password Plus* were three of them.

James Luisi (Professional Name); James Anthony Luisi (Birth Name and Name on the Death Certificate; **p. 156**—He made his name on television. *Valerie, Knots Landing*, and *Vega$* are three of them. Perhaps best remembered as Police Captain Doug Chapman on *The Rockford Files*.

Charles Macaulay (Professional Name, Birth Name and Name on the Death Certificate); **p. 157**—He spent most of his career on the small screen. *Ironside, The F.B.I.*, and *Barnaby Jones* were a few of them. Best remembered as District Attorney Markham on the *Perry Mason* television movies. He was a longtime friend of Raymond Burr.

Karl Malden (Professional Name and Name on the Death Certificate); Mladen George Sekulovich (Birth Name according to biographers); **p. 158**—He was nominated for an Academy Award for *On the Waterfront*. He received an Oscar for *A Street Car Named Desire*. He received four Emmy Award nominations for his series *The Streets of San Francisco*.

Louis Malle (Professional Name); Louis Marie Malle (Birth Name and Name on the Death Certificate); **p. 159**—He directed such films as *Pretty Baby, My Dinner with Andre*, and *Black Moon*.

Frederic March (Professional Name); Ernest Frederick McIntyre Bickel (Birth Name); Frederic McIntyre March (Name on the Death Certificate); **p. 160**—He received Oscars for *The Best Years of Our Lives* and *Dr. Jekyll and Mr. Hyde*. Also nominated for an Academy Award for *Death of a Salesman, A Star Is Born*, and *The Royal Family of Broadway*.

Hal March (Professional Name and Name on the Death Certificate); Harold Mendelson (Birth Name); **p. 161**—He made appearances on many of the TV series of the '50s and '60's, *I Love Lucy, Burke's Law*, and *Studio One* to name a few.

Herbert Marshall (Professional Name); Herbert Brough Falcon Marshall (Birth Name according to biographers); Herbert B. Marshall (Name on the Death Certificate); **p. 162**—He appeared in such films as *The Letter, Zaza*, and *Breakfast for Two*. On the small screen, he had roles on *Zane Grey Theater, Alfred Hitchcock Presents*, and five appearances on *77 Sunset Strip*.

Dick Martin (Professional Name); Thomas Richard Martin (Birth Name); Dick Martin AKA Thomas Richard Martin (Names on the Death Certificate); **p. 163**—Co-host of *Rowan & Martin's Laugh-In. Newhart, Brothers* and *The Bob Newhart Show* were three series he directed.

Roddy McDowall (Professional Name); Roderick Andrew Anthony Jude McDowall (Birth name according to biographers); Roderick Andrew McDowall (Name on the Death Certificate); **p. 164**—He appeared in *How Green Was My Valley, My Friend Flicka, Lassie Come Home*, and *Planet of the Apes*, where his character was Galen.

Cameron Mitchell (Professional Name); Cameron McDowell Mitchell (Birth Name and Name on the Death Certificate, however, on the Death Certificate, his father's surname is listed as Mitzell); **p. 165**—His TV series were *The Beachcomber* and *The High Chaparral*.

Vic Mizzy (Professional Name); Victor Mizzy (Birth Name and Name on the Death Certificate); **p. 166**—A composer whose music is heard on such TV programs as *The Adams Family, Green Acres*, and *Captain Nice*.

Ricardo Montalban (Professional Name and Name on the Death Certificate); Ricardo Gonzalo Pedro Montalban y Merino (Birth Name according to biographers); **p. 167**—*Border Incident, Mystery Street* and *Battleground* were three of his films. On the small screen, probably best remembered for *Fantasy Island* and his car commercials where he was the pitchman.

Elizabeth Montgomery (Professional Name); Elizabeth Victoria Montgomery (Birth Name according to biographers); Elizabeth A. Montgomery (Name on the Death Certificate); **p. 168**—She received Emmy nominations for *Bewitched, The Untouchables, A Case of Rape, The Legend of Lizzie Borden*, and *The Awakening Land*.

Harry Monty (Professional Name); Harry Hymie Lichenstein (Birth Name and Name on the Death Certificate); **p. 169**—Many movie roles went uncredited including *The Wizard of Oz*. On the small screen, he played various characters on *H.R. Pufnstuf* and *Lost in Space*.

BIOGRAPHICAL NOTES

Frank Morgan (Professional Name and Name on the Death Certificate); Francis Wupperman (Birth name according to biographers); **p. 170**—He was nominated for Academy Awards for *Tortilla Flat* and *The Affairs of Cellini*.

Gary Morton (Professional Name and Name on the Death Certificate); Morton Goldaper (Birth Name); **p. 171**—Probably best know as Lucille Ball's second husband. Much of his work in television was on her projects. He produced *Here's Lucy*, *The Lucy Show* and *CBS Salutes Lucy: The First 25 Years*.

Richard Mulligan (Professional Name); Richard Dana Michael Mulligan (Name on the Death Certificate); probably Birth Name, but could not be verified); **p. 172**—He won Emmys for *Empty Nest* and *Soap*. Was nominated twice more for *Empty Nest* and once more for *Soap*.

Gene Nelson (Professional Name and Name on the Death Certificate); Leander Eugene Berg (Birth Name); **p. 173**—A director for such TV series as *Burke's Law*, *The Farmer's Daughter* and *The Rifleman*.

Evelyn Nesbit or Evelyn Nesbit-Thaw (Professional Names); Evelyn Florence Nesbit (Birth Name and Name on the Death Certificate); **p. 174**—*A Lucky Leap*, *A Fallen Idol* and *Woman, Woman* are three of her films. She was at the central figure in the Crime of the Century, when her husband murdered her ex-lover.

Paul Newman (Professional Name); Paul Leonard Newman (Birth Name); Paul L. Newman (Name on the Death Certificate); **p. 175**—Nominated for 9 Academy Awards, he only won the Oscar for *The Color of Money*. *Butch Cassidy and the Sundance Kid* and *Hud* were among his other films.

Mabel Normand (Professional Name); Mabel Ethelreid Normand (Birth name according to biographers); Mabel Normand Cody (Name on the Death Certificate); **p. 176**—A silent era actress, she made such films as *Tillie's Punctured Romance*, *Over the Garden Wall* and *Mabel's Busy Day*.

Paul Novak (Preferred Name); Chester Ribonsky (Birth Name); Charles Krauser (name on the Death Certificate); **p. 177**—A professional wrestler, he also appeared in Mae West's chorus line of muscle men. He was her companion for 26 years.

Merle Oberon (Professional Name); Estelle Merle O'Brien Thompson (Birth Name according to biographers); Merle Oberon Wolders (Name on the Death Certificate); note that biographers list her ethnicity as Welsh-Indian, while the Death Certificate lists Irish-English; **p. 178**—*Over the Moon*, *Wuthering Heights* and *Berlin Express* are three of her film.

Dennis O'Keefe (Professional Name); Edward James Flanagan (Birth Name); Dennis O'Keefe AKA Edward James Flanagan, Sr. (Names on the Death Certificate); there is also an affidavit to correct a record which is not shown that changes the county of usual residence from San Bernardino to Riverside; **p. 179**—A career from 1930 through the mid '60s, he has credits for 250 appearances, mostly as an extra. He did have his own TV series for a brief time, *The Dennis O'Keefe Show*.

Dick O'Neil (Professional Name); Richard Frances O'Neil (Birth Name and Name on the Death Certificate); **p. 180**—His niche was playing middle-aged working class men. His two TV series were *Cagney & Lacy* and *Dark Justice*.

Bette Page (Professional Name); Betty Mae Page (Birth Name); Bette Mae Page (Name on the Death Certificate); **p. 181**—Her career was primarily as a pinup girl. She was known as "the Girl with the Perfect Figure."

Jack Palance (Professional Name); Volodymyr Palahniuk (Birth Name) Walter Jack Palance AKA Jack Palance (Names on the Death Certificate); **p. 182**—He received his Oscar and Golden Globe for *City Slicker*. He was also nominated for an Academy Award for his work in *Shane* and *Sudden Fear*.

Larry Parks (Professional Name); Samuel Klusman Lawrence Parks (Birth Name according to biographers); Lawrence Klusman Parks AKA Larry Parks (Name on the Death Certificate); **p. 183**—*Tiger by the Tail* and *Jolson Sings Again* are two of his films. He received an Academy Award nomination for *The Jolson Story*.

Robert Pastorelli (Professional Name); Robert Joseph Pasorelli (Birth Name); Robert J. Pastorelli (Name on the Death Certificate); there is a medical amendment shown listing the cause of death as a drug overdose; **p. 184-185**—Some of his films are *Outrageous Fortune*, *Beverly Hills Cop II*, and *Dances with Wolves*. On the small screen, he is probably best remembered as the house painter on *Murphy Brown*, Eldin Bernecky.

Anthony Perkins (Professional Name, Birth Name and Name on the Death Certificate); **p. 186**—Starred in *Psycho*, *Psycho II* and *Psycho III*. Received his Academy Award nomination for *Friendly Persuasion*.

Jean Peters (Professional Name); Elizabeth Jean Peters (Birth Name); Elizabeth Jean Peters Hough (Name on the Death Certificate); **p. 187**—Three of her movies are *Three Coins in the Fountain*, *A Man Called Peter*, and *A Blueprint for Murder*.

Charles Pierce (Professional Name); Charles Edwin Pierce (Birth Name and Name on the Death Certificate); **p. 188**—He was a female impersonator who specialized in Hollywood legends. *The Butcher's Wife*, *Nerds of a Feather* and *Torch Song Trilogy* were some of his films. He made appearances on *Chico and the Man*, *Laverne & Shirley*, and *Designing Women*.

Suzanne Pleshette (Professional Name and Birth Name); Suzanne Pleshette-Poston (Name on the Death Certificate); **p. 189**—She was nominated for four Emmy Awards for her roles in *Leona Helmsley: The Queen of Mean*, *The Bob Newhart Show* (twice) and *Dr. Kildare* (once). She never received the award.

Don Porter (Professional Name); Don Cecil Porter (Birth Name and name on the Death Certificate); **p. 190**—His three television series were *Private Secretary*, *The Ann Southern Show* and *Gidget*.

Tom Poston (Professional Name); Thomas Gordon Poston (Birth Name and Name on the Death Certificate); **p. 191**—Received Emmy nominations for Best Supporting Actor in a Comedy Series for *The Steve Allen Show* and three times for *Newhart*. He received his Emmy for a guest appearance on *Coach*.

Dick Powell (Professional Name); Richard Ewing Powell (Birth Name and Name on the Death Certificate); **p. 192**—*Murder My Sweet* and *Climax* were two films starring his character Philip Marlowe. On the small screen, his two series were *Four Star Playhouse* and *Zane Grey Theater*.

Richard Pryor (Professional Name); Richard Franklin Lennox Thomas Pryor III (Birth Name according to biographers); Richard Franklin Lennox Thomas Pryor (Name on the Death Certificate); **p. 193**—Received Emmy nominations for *Chicago Hope* and *Motown 25: Yesterday, Today, Forever*. He received his Emmy for *Lily*.

Anne Ramsey (Professional Name); Anne Mobley (Birth Name); Anne Mobley Ramsey (Name on the Death Certificate); **p. 194**—She appeared with her husband, Logan Ramsey, in *The Sporting Club*, *The Law and Ambition*. Received an Oscar nomination for her work on *Throw Mamma from the Train*.

David Rappaport (Birth Name and Name on the Death Certificate); David Stephen Rappaport (Birth Name according to biographers); **p. 195**—He made multiple appearances on the small screen in *The Wizard*, *L.A. Law*, and *Captain Planet and the Planeteers*.

Virginia Rappe (Professional Name and Name on the Death Certificate); Virginia Caroline Rapp (Birth Name according to biographers); **p. 196**—She only made a handful of films before her untimely death in San Francisco at the St. Francis Hotel. *Paradise Garden*, *An Adventuress*, and *A Game Lady* are three of the films in which she made an appearance.

Gene Raymond (Professional Name and Name on the Death Certificate); Raymond Guion (Birth Name); **p. 197**—Some of his films are *Red Dust* and *Ex-Lady*. *Smilin' Through* was his only film with his wife, Jeannette MacDonald.

Steve Reeves (Professional Name); Stephen Lester Reeves (Birth Name and Name on the Death Certificate); **p. 198**—*Athena* and *Trooper* were two of his films before his move to Italy where his had greater success. *La querra di Troia* and *La leggenda di Enea* were two of his films there.

Charles Nelson Reilly (Professional Name, Birth Name and Name on the Death Certificate); **p. 199**—Nominated for an Emmy for his performance on *The Drew Carey Show*, *Millennium* and *The Ghost & Mrs. Muir*. He received Tony Awards for *The Gin Game*, *Hello Dollly*, and *How to Succeed in Business Without Really Trying*.

Duncan Renaldo (Professional Name and Name on the Death Certificate); Renault Renaldo Duncan (Birth Name according to biographers); **p. 200**—*Pals of the Plains*, *The Painted Stallion* and *The Lone Ranger Rides Again* are three of his films. To many, however, he will always be the *Cisco Kid* from the series of the same name.

Brad Renfro (Professional Name); Brad Barron Renfro (Birth Name and Name on the Death Certificate); there is a medical amendment to the Death Certificate showing the cause of death as acute heroin/morphine intoxication via accidental overdose by injection; **p. 201–202**—His first three films were *The Client*, *The Cure* and *Tom and Huck*.

Stafford Repp (Professional Name); Stafford Alois Repp (Birth Name and Name on the Death Certificate); **p. 203**—Had multiple appearances on *Petty Mason* and *The New Phil Silvers Show*. Probably best remembered for his role as Chief O'Hara on *Batman*.

Marjorie Reynolds (Professional Name); Marjorie Goodspeed (Birth Name); Marjorie Reynolds Haffen (Name on the Death Certificate); **p. 204**—Her movie career included *Murder in Greenwich Village*, *Up in Mabel's Room*, *Meet Me on Broadway*, and *Holiday Inn*. On the small screen, she was co-star in *The Life of Riley*.

Minnie Riperton (Professional Name); Minnie Julia Riperton (Birth Name according to biographers); Minnie Riperton Rudolph (Name on the Death Certificate); **p. 205**—A singer-songwriter whose music was heard in *First Sunday*, *Vegas Vacation* and *The Nutty Professor* among other films.

Theodore Roberts (Professional Name and Name on the Death Certificate); Theodore Roberts (probably Birth Name, but it could not be verified); **p. 206**—Some of his appearances on the silver screen were in *The Ten Commandments*, *Something to Think About*, and *Forbidden Fruit*.

Rochester (Professional Name); Edmund L. Anderson (Birth Name according to biographers); Eddie Rochester Anderson (Name on the Death Certificate); **p. 207**—Played the foil for Jack Benny for 23 years on radio, in movies and on television. *Love Thy Neighbor*, *Buck Benny Rides Again*, and *Mad About Town* were three of their films. *The Jack Benny Program* was their TV series.

Charles Buddy Rogers (Professional Name and Name on the Death Certificate); Charles Rogers (Probably Birth Name, but it could not be verified): **p. 208**—*Along Came Youth*, *Halfway to Heaven* and *Abie's Irish Rose* are three of his films.

Roxie Roker (Professional Name); Roxie Albertha Roker (Birth Name); Roxie Albertha Roker Kravitz (Name on the Death Certificate); there is also a physicians amendment, which is not shown, correcting the spelling of the word metastasis; **p. 209**—She had a few appearances on television before being cast as Helen Willis on *The Jeffersons*.

Gilbert Roland (Birth Name and Name on the Death Certificate); Luis Antonio Damaso de Alonso (Birth Name according to biographers); **p. 210**—*She Done Him Wrong*, *After Tonight* and *Eleanor Norton* are three of his films. On the small screen, he had appearances on *Kung Fu*, *Barnaby Jones* and *Medical Center*.

Ruth Roman (Professional Name, Birth Name and Name on the Death Certificate); **p. 211**—Most of her roles in films in the 1940's were uncredited. *Tomorrow is Another Day*, *Three Secrets* and *Colt. 45* were three for which she did receive credit. *Murder, She Wrote* and *Knots Landing* were two television series where she had a continuing role.

Ruth Rose (Professional Name and Birth Name); Ruth Schoedsack (Name on the Death Certificate); **p. 212**—She wrote screenplays, *King Kong* the most memorable. She also wrote the early versions for *The Son of Kong* and *Mighty Joe Young*.

Isabel Sanford (Professional Name and Name on the Death Certificate); Eloise Gwendolyn Sanford (Birth Name according to biographers); father's surname is listed as Perry on the Death Certificate; **p. 213**—*Guess Who's Coming to Dinner*, *The Young Runaways* and *Pendulum* were her first three movies. For her role as Louise Jefferson on *The Jeffersons* she received seven Emmy nominations.

Ernest Schoedsack (Professional Name); Ernest Beaumont Schoedsack (Birth Name and Name on the Death Certificate); there is an affidavit to amend a record which is not shown that changes him from being married to Ruth Rose to being a widower; **p. 214**—The director of *King Kong*, *The Son of Kong* and *Dr. Cyclops*, among others.

Sidney Sheldon (Professional Name); Sidney Schechtel (Birth Name according to biographers, but his Father's surname on the Death Certificate is listed as Sheldon); Sidney King Sheldon (Name on the Death Certificate): **p. 215**—Received an Academy Award for *The Batchelor and the Bobby-Soxer*. He was nominated for an Emmy for *I Dream of Jeannie*. He was nominated for a Writers Guild of America Award for *Billy Rose's Jumbo* and received one for *Annie Get Your Gun*.

Jack Soo (Professional Name); Goro Suzuki (Birth Name); Goro Suzuki AKA Jack Soo (Names on the Death Certificate); there is a medical amendment which is not shown that changes the date the doctor signed the Death Certificate from January 10 to January 11, 1979; **p. 216**—Reprised his role on Broadway for the movie *Flower Drum Song*. TV series on which he had continuing roles were *Valentine's Day* and *Ironsides*. Probably best remembered as Det. Sgt. Nick Yemana on *Barney Miller*.

Ken Steadman (Professional Name); Kenneth Keith Steadman (Birth Name and Name on the Death Certificate); **p. 217**—His career was cut short when he died in a car accident during the filming of an episode of *Sliders*. He also had appearances on *Moloney*, *Baywatch Nights* and *NYPD Blue*.

Jess Stearn (Professional Name); Jess E. Stearn (Probably Birth Name, but it could not be verified); Jess E. Stearn (Name on the Death Certificate); **p. 218**—A best-selling author who specialized on the occult, particularly in his later years. *The Sleeping Prophet: The Life and Word of Edgar Cayce*, *A Prophet in His Own Country: The Story of the Young Edgar Cayce*, and *The Search for a Soul* were three of his many books.

McLean Stevenson (Professional Name); Edgar McLean Stevenson, Jr. (Birth Name and Name on the Death Certificate); there is a medical amendment which is not shown that indicates death was caused by a heart attack with coronary arthrosclerosis and effects of operation for cancer as additional causes; **p. 219**—Spent his career on the small screen. He had recurring roles on *Hello, Larry*, *Condo*, and *The Doris Day Show*. Probably best remembered as Lt. Commander Henry Black on *M*A*S*H*.

Anita Mary Stewart, Anna M. Stewart, Anna Stewart and Anne Stuart (Professional Names); Anita Mary Stewart (Birth Name); Anita Mary Converse AKA Anita Mary Stewart (Name on the Death Certificate); **p. 220**—Spanned the silent era into talkies on the silver screen. In *The Virtuous*, she is credited as a co-producer with Louis B. Mayer. *Wild Geese* and *Her Mad Bargain* are two of her other films.

Lewis Stone (Professional Name); Lewis Shepard Stone (Birth Name and Name on the Death Certificate); **p. 221**—He received an Academy Award nomination for *The Patriot*. *Judge Hardy and Son*, *Andy Hardy's Dilemma: A Lesson in Mathematics and Other Things*, *Andy Hardy Meets Debutante* were three of his Andy Hardy films.

Barry Sullivan (Professional Name); Patrick Barry Sullivan (Birth Name and Name on the Death Certificate); **p. 222**—He was never a leading man; his niche was in supporting roles. *Grounds for Marriage*, *A Life of Her Own* and *Three Guys Named Mike* are three of his films. He received an Emmy nomination for his role in *The Caine Mutiny Court-Martial* for *Ford Star Jubilee*.

Patrick Swayze (Professional Name); Patrick Wayne Swayze (Birth Name and Name on the Death Certificate); there is a physician/coroner's amendment to change the address where death occurred from an office building in Century City to the home in Sylmar and changes the address to include the zip code); **p. 223-224**—Received Golden Globe nominations for *To Wong Foo, Thanks for Everything, Julie Newmar!*, *Ghost*, and *Dirty Dancing*. Even as his cancer progressed, he starred in the TV series *The Beast*.

Carl Switzer (Professional Name); Carl Dean Switzer (Birth Name and Name on the Death Certificate); **p. 225**—"Alfalfa" in the Our Gang series of films. *Roamin' Holiday*, *Two Too Young*, and *General Spanky* were three of them.

William Desmond Taylor (Professional Name); William Cunningham Deane-Tanner (Birth Name according to some biographers, however no name for his father appears on the Death Certificate); William D. Taylor (Name on the Death Certificate); **p. 226**—Considering that his career was cut short by his murder, he still managed to direct a number of films. *Tom Sawyer*, *Huck and Tom*, *Anne of Green Gables*, and *Huckleberry Finn* were four of his silver screen directorial projects.

Kenneth Tobey (Professional Name); (Birth Name could not be verified); Jesse Kenneth Toby (Name on the Death Certificate); **p. 227**—*The Thing from Another World*, *The Beast from 20,000 Fathoms*, *It Came From Beneath the Sea* were three of his science-fiction movies. His TV series was *Whirlybirds*.

William Tuttle (Professional Name); William Julian Tuttle (Birth Name and Name on the Death Certificate); **p. 228**—Received four awards from the Academy of Science Fiction, Fantasy & Horror Film, USA, for *Love at First Bite*, *The Fury*, *Logan's Run* and *Young Frankenstein*.

Lee Van Cleef (Professional Name and Name on the Death Certificate); Clarence Leroy Van Cleef, Jr. (Birth Name according to biographers, but it could not be verified); **p. 229**—*High Noon*, *The Vanishing American*, and *The Naked Street* are three of his films. He had multiple appearances on the small screen in *Gunsmoke*, *Branded*, and *The Master*.

Harry von Zell (Professional Name); Harry Rudolph von Zell (Name on the Death Certificate; may be Birth Name, but it could not be verified); **p. 230**—His deep voice made him a natural for radio announcing. He moved from radio to the silver screen in *Radio Rhapsody*. He went on to make *Dear Wife* and *Radio Riot* among others. On the small screen he had multiple appearances on *The George Burns and Grace Allen Show*, *The George Burns Show* and *Bachelor Father*.

Kim Walker (Professional Name); Kimberly Anne Walker (Birth Name); Kim Anne Walker (Name on the Death Certificate); **p. 231**—Some of her big screen appearances included *Say Anything* and *Nervous Tickets*, but she is probably best remembered as Heather in *Heathers*. One the small screen she had roles in *Picket Fences*, *Matlock* and her series *The Outsiders*.

Michael Wayne (Professional Name); Michael Anthony Morrison (Birth Name according to biographers); Michael Anthony Wayne (Name on the Death Certificate); **p. 232**—He made several films for which he received no credit. The movies he did receive credit were *The Lost Platoon* and *Rapid Fire*. *The Green Berets* and *The Train Robbers* were two films he produced.

Lawrence Welk (Professional Name, Birth Name and Name on the Death Certificate); **p. 233**—His music is heard on *Good Morning, Vietnam*, *Heaven Help Us*, and *Swingers*. His television series was *The Lawrence Welk Show*.

Del Shannon (Professional Name); Charles Weedon Westover (Birth Name and Name on the Death Certificate); **p. 234**—A singer-songwriter whose work is heard in the films *Just a Kiss*, *Dragon: The Bruce Lee Story*, and *Catch Me If You Can*.

Richard Widmark (Professional Name and Name on the Death Certificate); Richard Weedt Widmark (Birth Name according to biographers); **p. 235**—Received an Oscar nomination and a Golden Globe for *Kiss of Death*. *Coma* and *Judgment at Nuremberg* were two of this films. On the small screen, his short lived series was *Madigan*.

Dick Wilson (Professional Name and Name on the Death Certificate); Riccardo DiGugliemo (Birth name according to biographers, but the Death Certificate lists his father as Randolph Wilson); **p. 236**—Found his niche on the small screen. He had appearances on *Ben Casey*, *The Virginian* and *Checkmate*, among others. Probably best remembered as Mr. Whipple in the Charmin toilet tissue commercials.

Dooley Wilson (Professional Name); Arthur Wilson (Birth Name); Arthur Dooley Wilson (Name on the Death Certificate); **p. 237**—*Passage West*, *Free For All* and *Racing Luck* are three of his films. Best remembered for his role as piano-playing Sam in *Casablanca*.

Joy Windsor (Professional Name); (Birth Name could not be verified); Joy Windsor Ellis (Name on the Death Certificate); **p. 238**—Biographers have her listed as being in three films before she was born. She had small roles in *Come on Seven*, *Rainbow 'Round My Shoulder* and *The First Time*.

Stan Winston (Professional Name); Stanley Winston (Birth Name and Name on the Death Certificate); there is an affidavit to amend a record which is not shown that changes his place of birth from Virginia to Washington, D.C.; **p. 239**—Nominated for Best Makeup Oscar for *Edward Scissorhands*, won the Best Effects, Visual Effects Oscar for *Terminator 2: Judgment Day* and *Jurassic Park*, and was nominated for the Best Effects, Visual Effects Oscar for *The Lost World: Jurassic Park*.

Thelma White (Professional Name); Thelma Wolpa (Birth Name); Thelma Millard AKA Thelma White (Names on the Death Certificate); **p. 240**—Her films included *In the Family* and *One Way Out*. In 1936 she starred in *Tell Your Children*. This was rediscovered in 1972 and renamed *Reefer Madness*. It became a cult classic.

Jane Wyatt (Professional Name); Jane Waddington Wyatt (Birth Name); Jane Wyatt Ward AKA Jane Wyatt (Names on the Death Certificate); **p. 241**—*Lost Horizon*, *My Blue Heaven*, and *No Minor Vices* were three of her films. She received her three Emmy Awards for her role as Margaret Anderson in *Father Knows Best*.

Ed Wynn (Professional Name and Name on the Death Certificate); Isaiah Edwin Leopold (Birth Name according to biographers); **p. 242**—Received an Emmy for Most Outstanding Live Personality. He received Emmy nominations for *Westinghouse Desilu Playhouse*, *Hallmark Hall of Fame* and *Playhouse 90*.